Communications
in Computer and Information Science   2299

Series Editors

Gang Li ⓘ, *School of Information Technology, Deakin University, Burwood, VIC,
Australia*
Joaquim Filipe ⓘ, *Polytechnic Institute of Setúbal, Setúbal, Portugal*
Zhiwei Xu, *Chinese Academy of Sciences, Beijing, China*

Rationale

The CCIS series is devoted to the publication of proceedings of computer science conferences. Its aim is to efficiently disseminate original research results in informatics in printed and electronic form. While the focus is on publication of peer-reviewed full papers presenting mature work, inclusion of reviewed short papers reporting on work in progress is welcome, too. Besides globally relevant meetings with internationally representative program committees guaranteeing a strict peer-reviewing and paper selection process, conferences run by societies or of high regional or national relevance are also considered for publication.

Topics

The topical scope of CCIS spans the entire spectrum of informatics ranging from foundational topics in the theory of computing to information and communications science and technology and a broad variety of interdisciplinary application fields.

Information for Volume Editors and Authors

Publication in CCIS is free of charge. No royalties are paid, however, we offer registered conference participants temporary free access to the online version of the conference proceedings on SpringerLink (http://link.springer.com) by means of an http referrer from the conference website and/or a number of complimentary printed copies, as specified in the official acceptance email of the event.

CCIS proceedings can be published in time for distribution at conferences or as post-proceedings, and delivered in the form of printed books and/or electronically as USBs and/or e-content licenses for accessing proceedings at SpringerLink. Furthermore, CCIS proceedings are included in the CCIS electronic book series hosted in the SpringerLink digital library at http://link.springer.com/bookseries/7899. Conferences publishing in CCIS are allowed to use Online Conference Service (OCS) for managing the whole proceedings lifecycle (from submission and reviewing to preparing for publication) free of charge.

Publication process

The language of publication is exclusively English. Authors publishing in CCIS have to sign the Springer CCIS copyright transfer form, however, they are free to use their material published in CCIS for substantially changed, more elaborate subsequent publications elsewhere. For the preparation of the camera-ready papers/files, authors have to strictly adhere to the Springer CCIS Authors' Instructions and are strongly encouraged to use the CCIS LaTeX style files or templates.

Abstracting/Indexing

CCIS is abstracted/indexed in DBLP, Google Scholar, EI-Compendex, Mathematical Reviews, SCImago, Scopus. CCIS volumes are also submitted for the inclusion in ISI Proceedings.

How to start

To start the evaluation of your proposal for inclusion in the CCIS series, please send an e-mail to ccis@springer.com.

Khalid S. Soliman

Editor

Artificial Intelligence and Machine Learning

43rd IBIMA Conference, IBIMA-AI 2024
Madrid, Spain, June 26–27, 2024
Revised Selected Papers, Part I

 Springer

Editor
Khalid S. Soliman
International Business Information Management
Association
Norristown, PA, USA

ISSN 1865-0929   ISSN 1865-0937 (electronic)
Communications in Computer and Information Science
ISBN 978-3-031-77492-8   ISBN 978-3-031-77493-5 (eBook)
https://doi.org/10.1007/978-3-031-77493-5

Preface

This volume of CCIS presents the revised papers (post-proceedings) of IBIMA-AI 2024, the 43rd IBIMA International Conference on Artificial Intelligence and Machine Learning, held on June 26–27, 2024, in Madrid, Spain. This compilation features an extensive range of research within the fields of Artificial Intelligence, Machine Learning, Information Systems, and Communications Technologies. Out of 119 papers submitted, we have a total of 44 full papers and 18 short papers published, split into two parts. Each paper was sent to 3 reviewers in a triple-blind review process and was revised according to review comments, ensuring the quality and relevance of the contributions.

The section on Artificial Intelligence (AI) and Machine Learning highlights a broad spectrum of innovative approaches at the intersection of technology, engineering, and management. The featured papers emphasize the use of advanced methods, such as AI, data analytics, and automation, to enhance decision-making processes and operational efficiency across various sectors. These papers demonstrate the significant impact of technological advancements in addressing practical challenges and optimizing processes in areas such as disaster management, healthcare, finance, and industrial production.

The section on Information Systems and Communications Technologies brings together research addressing critical challenges and innovations in networking, enterprise systems, and digital communication. Highlights include papers on optimizing network performance, such as the impact of prioritized multicast connections on traffic effectiveness and the use of genetic algorithms for bandwidth optimization in wireless networks. The section also delves into advanced communication techniques, including the development of two-way free-space laser communication systems. In addition, papers explore the evolution of enterprise systems like SAP S/4HANA. These papers underscore the evolving landscape of Information Systems and Communications Technologies and their role in enhancing connectivity, security, and enterprise efficiency.

We hope that this collection will inspire ongoing research, collaboration, and innovation in the fields of Artificial Intelligence, Machine Learning, Information Systems, and Communications Technologies. The insights and findings presented in these papers are designed to drive future advancements, expand our collective understanding, and contribute to the development of a more technologically advanced and empowered world.

September 2024   Khalid S. Soliman

Organization

General Chair of the Conference

Khalid S. Soliman
International Business Information Management Association, USA

Program Committee

Khalid S. Soliman	International Business Information Management Association, USA
Liana-Elena Anica-Popa	Bucharest University of Economic Studies, Romania
Arkadiusz Banasik	Silesian University of Technology, Poland
Mariusz Bednarczyk	Military University of Technology, Poland
Constanta-Nicoleta Bodea	Bucharest University of Economic Studies, Romania
Bassem Bsir	ISITCOM, Tunisia
Emna Chikhaoui	Prince Sultan University, KSA
Andrey S. Dorofeev	Irkutsk National Research Technical University, Russia
Mohammad Ekhlaque Ahmed	Institute of Business Management, Pakistan
Tiago Eny Relim	University of Brasília, Brazil
Bahjat Fakieh	King Abdulaziz University, KSA
Irina Alexandra Georgescu	Bucharest University of Economics, Romania
Constantin Ilie	Ovidius University of Constanţa, Romania
Grażyna Kowalewska	University of Warmia and Mazury, Poland
Jaroslaw Michalak	Military University of Technology, Poland
Błażej Nowak	Poznań University of Technology, Poland
Cristina Popescu	Petroleum-Gas University of Ploiesti, Romania
Laura Florentina Stoica	Lucian Blaga University of Sibiu, Romania
Aurelia-Mihaela Voican	Politehnica University of Bucharest, Romania

Organization

General Chair of the Conference

Program Committee

Contents – Part I

Information Systems and Communications Technologies

Contents – Part II

Computer Security and Privacy

Artificial Intelligence and Machine Learning

A Perspective Approach: Developing a Unified Management System for Disaster Prevention and Emergency Relief

Mohammad Ali A. Hammoudeh[✉]

Department of Information Technology, College of Computer, Qassim University, Buraydah 51941, Saudi Arabia
maah37@qu.edu.sa

Abstract. Disasters are preventable and mitigable through timely measures such as disaster management, public education among other preventive methods. The complexity and frequency with which disasters have increased during the past years make it necessary to have an advanced management system that provides efficiency and coordination. Existing research may not fully address the integration of AI in disaster management for improved decision-making and security. This article proposes a system architecture that supports the effectiveness and interoperability in disaster risk and emergency management response, as well as improving efficiency in emergency response management for increased disaster resilience. This is about how to exploit new and promising techniques of artificial intelligence aimed at guaranteeing the defense of several fields under critical contingencies and circumstances. The paper also recommends a roadmap and strategies for a new era focused on the "Digital Economy" in the context of disaster management on how information resources can be updated as well as the reengineering of problem management processes and the way governing organizations work at various levels. It also effectively enhances region/country security against natural disasters and human made hazards by applying artificial intelligence decision making.

Keywords: Artificial Intelligence · Supply Chain Resources · Big Data · Information Management · Information Processing · Decision Making · Risk

1 Introduction

The global coronavirus situation has exposed significant issues in national administration and a lack of preparedness for dealing with uncertainty [13]. Factors that contribute to the rise in the number and scale of emergency situations (ES) as shown in Fig. 1. Encompass not only climate change, aging technological facilities, and increased energy intensity of production but also a managerial crisis tied to the overproduction of non-formalized information, a decline in competence levels, and elongated decision-making chains.

In contrast to managing a global pandemic, authorities have amassed significant experience in preventing and mitigating natural and man-made emergencies. Numerous

K. S. Soliman (Ed.): IBIMA-AI 2024, CCIS 2299, pp. 3–14, 2025.
https://doi.org/10.1007/978-3-031-77493-5_1

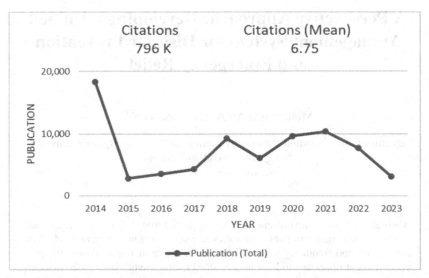

Fig. 1. # of Publications in Disaster Prevention and Emergency Relief from 2014 to 2023 (June). *(Own Creation).*

hazardous events occur on a near-daily basis, necessitating the deployment of emergency services and the establishment of a unified state system for emergency prevention and response [6]. This system enables the effective acquisition and application of such experience.

Despite each situation being unique in terms of types, scales, causes, and development patterns, actions to eliminate hazardous factors and implement safety measures can be formalized through algorithms, business processes, and other structured frameworks [7].

Emergency prevention measures, such as comprehensive situation monitoring, addressing forecasting issues, early warning, and emergency risk assessment, are of great importance. Enhancing predictive methods necessitates the use of vast amounts of data and real-time mining technologies. Employing machine learning in devising solutions for resource and personnel management enables a detailed consideration of the current situation, increased responsiveness, the minimization of management errors, and the preservation and dissemination of effective event experiences.

The remarkable progress of technology and the impressive potential of artificial intelligence (AI) systems have attracted considerable attention [5]. Large corporations, both abroad and domestically, use self-learning systems that can process petabytes of data in real-time to form solutions superior to those created by humans. For example, Alibaba Cloud has been implementing City Brain in cities across China and Southeast Asia since 2016, monitoring traffic and people flows. When an accident is detected, the system swiftly directs calls to operational services and coordinates their rapid response to the scene, managing traffic light operations. Concurrently, the expansion of the spectrum of tasks to be addressed and the "absorption" of new data arrays proceed in parallel [3].

A primary challenge in applying contemporary technologies for managing natural and man-made safety lies in preparing data for processing by intelligent systems and services. This involves formalizing a vast volume of accumulated multi-format documents that describe management processes during hazardous situations as well as the characteristics of objects and the dynamics of their changes. The paper delineates strategies for revolutionizing information resources, enhancing the processes for addressing management issues, and justifying the need to modify the business models of governing bodies at various levels.

2 Concepts and Definitions for the Proposed Unified Emergency System

Information flows supporting management across various cities, sectors, and regions within the country can be approximately represented using a diagram, as illustrated in Fig. 2.

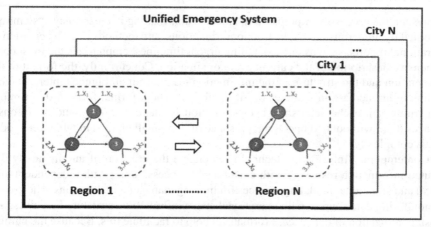

Fig. 2. A Conceptual Diagram of Information Processes in Decision-Making. *(Own Creation).*

The diagram depicts three key elements—data collection (1), data processing (2), and decision-making (3)—which are categorized based on the characteristics of the subject area. Information resources are formed by consolidating instrumental monitoring data, including ground and aerospace observation networks, as well as information from reports and other documents from different regions/cities within the country. In the case of accumulating "big data," the process is well-developed, employing technologies such as the Internet of Things, cloud storage, and fog computing in the construction of "Smart City" and "Safe City" systems [4]. However, formalizing data exchange in office formats, prevalent in national administration bodies, presents a challenging task [1]. Management process automation has only affected a small portion of the information resources. Directly translating a document into an electronic format without considering the specifics of management tasks and features of intellectual data processing results in duplicate information representations [9].

The data processing process encompasses analytical modeling and data visualization methods, with contemporary smart technologies incorporating both functions. The balance of their use and the degree of human involvement depend on the nature of the problem being addressed, data completeness, decision-maker preferences, and the conditions of a specific situation.

Automated systems employed for operational security management typically do not generate multiple solutions for a single problem. This is attributed to the limited time available to comprehend machine-generated results and execute orders and instructions. In strategic management, which involves planning preventive measures to reduce risks, it is recommended to issue two decisions: one comprising a list of measures without resource constraints and another that considers the actual situation. Comparing the anticipated results enables the evaluation of resource expenditure efficiency and various long-term management implementation options.

2.1 Renewing Information Resources in Emergency Management Tasks

At present, the processes of preparation and decision-making in emergency systems are governed by numerous orders, instructions, directions, and methods [2]. The creation of operational reports, such as those detailing urgent timelines, emphasizes the most comprehensive description of the current event or situation. Concurrently, the format of the presentation and the structure of the information may permit ambiguous interpretation, leading to an increase in volumes of informal data. The informal form of descriptions concerning object characteristics, events, previously made decisions, and their consequences (e.g., without text encoding, presence of non-small entities in tables, etc.) adds to this complexity.

Contemporary information technologies enable the creation of automatically distributed information resources with customizable access, along with independent analytical and situational modeling services for making management decisions. The growth of monitoring data sources with operational status information, structured archives, and the standardization of data access formats all help to facilitate this. Because the number of information resources is growing quickly and access and processing technologies are getting better, it is becoming more and more important to structure information in a systematic way by making models that represent information resources. These models should encompass data organization, relationships, and principles that dictate the design, configuration, and updating of information resources. The development of an information resource representation model involves the following steps:

1. Describe the unified automated information management system.
2. Develop the system architecture.
3. Design the information source ontology.
4. Describe distributed data storage informationally.
5. Design data structures physically and lexically.

Steps 1 through 3 involve fewer entities but offer more flexibility when transitioning to implementing specific data structures. These steps are utilized in conceptual design, and any changes require significant reformulation of the functions within information and analytical systems. Step 4 encompasses the description of management tasks and types of data sources for different information sources. As new data sources emerge and management tasks and requirements for data processing technologies change, the approved and physical models of information sources can be altered within certain limits. Therefore, during the operation of information and analysis systems, it is advisable to periodically repeat the design process to expand data structures. Below is a brief description of the resource model development steps. The representation of information resources R with two subgroups, D and, I where D, I ∈ R: is based on the need to bring together the needs of the subject area and the information technologies used in a single system.

D: Types of information resources used in building information and supporting analytical management systems (data); I: Types of information resources used to support information management of the natural and technological integrity of the region, reflecting the conceptual tools of decision-makers (information). A set, D, made up of five distinct elements, represents the data:

$D = \{d_1, d_2, ..., d_5\}$, where:

d_1: Represents the backbone elements, such as reference books, workbooks, and records;

d_2: Describes objects or things;

d_3: Outline's operations;

d_4: Displays data on maps, and.

d_5: Is used to control the overall process.

It is permissible for elements of Group D to intersect. For instance, some subgroups, like d_1, d_2, and d_3, may have a spatial component, which is utilized together with d_5 to form control decisions. We will now provide a more detailed explanation of the d_1 processes. The results gleaned from monitoring the state of the natural environment and the Technosphere can be presented as a linear table with a limited number of fields. When controlled parameters exceed normative values, the event is registered as requiring an extended form of information description [11].

Information is presented in several ways:

$$I = P_1 U P_2 U P_3,$$

where P_1 represents potentially hazardous operations; P_2 – protected objects; and P_3 – control objects (elements of the regional subsystem of the Unified Emergency System of Prevention and Elimination).

For P_1 hazardous processes, hazardous events can be represented as $E = P_1 (\Delta t)$ – a description of a hazardous process over a time period Δt, and mode $IT = P_1 (t)$ – the values of one or more parameters of potentially hazardous processes at a given time. The intersection of group S elements is allowed. For example, the properties of health care facilities are described as P_2 elements, and in the case of a need for medical care, P_3 is described. When assessing the safety of objects and Regions, a similar division of state standards into "risk", "vulnerability", "security" is used [12].

In response to an event, the actions taken can be thoroughly represented using a hierarchical structure consisting of multiple tables and directories that display a range of logical relationships. Complex descriptions are commonly associated with large-scale, long-term emergencies involving numerous measures, such as population protection, life support, resource allocation logistics, and interaction descriptions [10]. The ontology of information resources describes the characteristics and logical relationships of elements S and D, as well as the management tasks and types of situations as categorized by the Ministry of Emergency Situations in different countries [8]. This also covers data source types (S) and data access types (A). At the same time, we define the set of data sources S and types of data access A as follows:

$S = \{s_1, ..., s_5\}$, where:
s_1: Useful controllers;
s_2: Reporting systems;
s_3: Monitoring of information systems, including companies, facilities, and data integrity monitoring;
s_4: Methods of organizing the storage of monitoring data (portals, sites, information portals);
s_5: Selections from databases and other information resources uploaded using "manual" batch processing.

Types of data access used in analytical processing tasks:

$A = \{a_1, a_2, a_3\}$, where:
a_1: One central data repository;
a_2: Distributed (cloud) storage services;
a_3: Access to limited data samples from distributed resources and use of links.

Considering the composition of information sources, the primary source is P_3 (control objects). These include the characteristics of the formations of ministries and emergency bodies of the country, other departments within the unified system of prevention and elimination of emergency situations, and additional forces and means, such as transport and fuel companies. District administrations and supervisory authorities are included as separate elements in the notification and subscriber notification lists.

P_2 protected objects consist of buildings and their groups in the form of institutions and organizations, as well as the people associated with them—individuals, labor groups, and small gatherings. Natural and technological safety management processes do not require work with personal data, except for call centers, dispatching unified tasks for municipalities, and other operational services. The compilation of victim lists is entrusted to social protection services, and the proportion of citizens with limited mobility for evacuation and medical care must be calculated using statistical data with a large margin.

The properties of P_2 protected objects are considered "big data" (several million records for a single subject) and must be imported almost entirely from external information systems. For instance, spatial data (d_4) comes from specific resources, while characteristics of healthcare and education institutions are sourced from relevant departmental databases. Various supervisory agencies (such as the environmental and technological supervision service, tax service, consumer rights supervision service of protection and welfare) maintain information on the location, contacts, working hours, number of employees, and visitors to institutions. Features of protection systems, including alarms, warnings, and autonomous operation, are available from the Ministry of Internal Affairs and State Fire Oversight.

Comprehensive operational monitoring also generates big data. Examples of meteorology, radiological conditions, control of technological processes, and the state of engineering structures, as well as archives of hydrological and seismic observations. Examples of E include all types of fires, traffic accidents, housing and communal service accidents, and emergency service calls. Most of the listed resources are hosted on external resources with a_2 and a_3 access.

3 Proposed Automated Information Processes for Unified System Architecture

Structured data and high-quality data generation contribute to the efficiency of algorithms. Contemporary control and decision support systems can process vast amounts of real-time data, enabling timely responses and self-learning. The extensive collection and storage of information provide sufficient historical depth for detecting patterns and extracting essential knowledge. Informed decision-making under uncertainty can be represented as information processes integrated into the system architecture.

We suggest a unified system architecture for information support in managing the natural and man-made safety of regions. This architecture enables the creation of multitask, problem-oriented software complexes for regional management. Using parts of the system model, the architecture lets you define how the synthesized information and analytical system work for different operational modes and levels of managing the safety of the region. It also helps justify the selection of software components and rational approaches to solving complex management problems. The process of constructing a system architecture can be represented through functional diagrams, illustrating the transformation of information resources and the nuances of solving management problems in information and analytical systems. The unified system architecture outlines data sources and the sequence of information processes, as depicted in Fig. 3.

Data sources and standardization processes are defined in ontologies and structural models of information resources. Subsystems and data processing services handle analytical and situational modeling, as well as dynamic visualization of decision-making outcomes. Data visualization through human-machine interfaces accommodates all information access types for decision-makers, including desktop software systems, websites, and mobile applications.

Specialized automated workstations cater to different user groups. Shift operators and experts use the automated workplace for rapid situation modeling, alert text creation, information coordination, hazard mitigation, and protective measure implementation.

The expert robotic workstation focuses on situational scenario development using modeling and mapping, as well as creating analytical models for reporting, forecasting, and event planning. The Administrator Automated Workstation manages data and data sources in the repository and directory maintenance system. The decision-maker's automated workplace provides an overview of regional security situations with detailed information on specific incidents and timeframes.

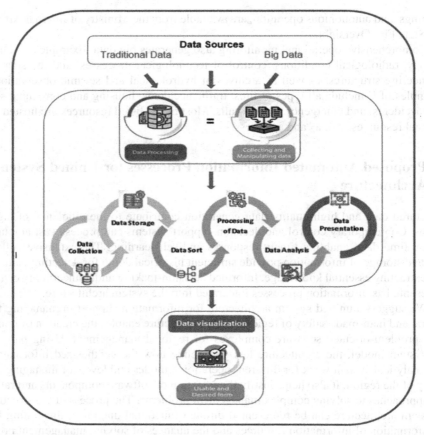

Fig. 3. Automated Information Processes for Unified System Architecture. *(Own Creation).*

Based on the generalized architecture, problem-oriented architectures are developed. For instance, a decision support system for land flooding focuses on coordinating the unified emergency prevention and response system's resources to protect the population and infrastructure. The natural fire information and control system encompasses monitoring data acquisition, processing, control, and measures to address threats to protected organisms. In these cases, specialized data sources, software modules, or situational and analytical modeling services are utilized.

The approach's originality lies in the expandable system architecture, which accommodates necessary information resources, technologies, and programs. This adaptability allows for the customization of information and analytical systems for different levels and administrative tasks. Required information resources and software units that implement analytical and situational modeling techniques for specific control tasks, as well as visualization tools needed at each decision-making level. Defining a system architecture for a specific type of hazardous situation enables the identification of these units.

4 Transforming Strategies in Government Business Models at Various Levels

Many international companies have excelled in the competitive field of smart technologies by transforming their entire business management models and devising strategies to address challenges and capitalize on opportunities in automation. The shift towards employing artificial intelligence (AI) technologies for local and regional security management necessitates significant and difficult personal decisions. This includes not only reducing the number of management personnel with limited data skills but also recruiting IT professionals such as big data analysts, deep learning experts, knowledge engineers, and information security specialists well-versed in cloud services. Within a relatively short time frame, it is crucial to revamp the curricula of educational institutions associated with emergency response ministries and other agencies. This necessitates broadening the focus of specialist training to include the utilization of digital platforms and solutions for addressing regional and local security management issues.

A unified automated information management system (UAIMS) should be developed for the prevention and mitigation of emergency situations, necessitating a shift in priorities. The focus should be on providing information support at the facility and municipal levels rather than generating, storing, and transmitting documents to higher management levels. By analyzing the statistical distribution of hazardous events by size, a systematic reallocation of authority and responsibilities can be implemented, leading to more efficient control processes.

With the National Crisis Management Center (NCMC) providing overall coordination, constituent entities within a country should work together to develop the UAIMS as an integral component of a unified emergency prevention and response system. This should include data storage capabilities. By employing cloud technologies and container computing, a modular and automated system can be built, offering maximum flexibility to accommodate regional differences and achieve the objectives of ensuring both natural and technological safety.

By refraining from outsourcing software development to external organizations, the proposed approach fosters the growth of in-house specialists while engaging external experts to share their knowledge. As competitiveness does not determine management effectiveness in government structures, this strategy offers several benefits, including enhanced information quality, faster access to data, and a more balanced use of data in decision-making processes as Key Transforming Strategies in Unified National Security Management System.

The purpose of Key Transforming Strategies in Unified National Security Management System actions is to enhance effectiveness and interoperability in disaster risk management as well as emergency management response as the following:

Current Action 1: Facilitating interdepartmental information exchange.

Suppose to be: Using different access types for automatic updating of data.

The first measure recommended here is to promote cross departmental flow of information. This implies that various departments engaged in disaster prevention and response ought to have a simple process of exchanging data. This can be achieved through use of various types of access for automatic updating of data. This will make sure that each department has current data which is essential in decision making.

Current Action 2: Internal information resources.

Suppose to be: Structuring data into supervisor-oriented formats and building exchange gateways.

Secondly, they recommended that organizations should work on developing information services internally. In other words, data must be organized into a format oriented towards supervision and exchange gateways need to be designed. This will promote orderly arrangement of data, thus making it easy to comprehend and retrieve.

Current Action 3: Developing a plethora of reports in several formats.

Suppose to be: Formalizing every event or response, building knowledge bases and learning sets for artificial intelligence software.

As the final action, the institution would generate several reports using multiple formats. In essence, this implies that each event or response should be institutionalized and creation of knowledge bases as well as learning sets for AI software. This will provide assurance that data is analyzed for purposes of improving preparedness as well as mitigation practices, and ensuring appropriate disaster response measures and management.

Current Action 4: From a management perspective at national and regional levels.

Suppose to be: Giving increased independence of local and municipal authorities to decision making capabilities.

The fourth proposed action, the move from control to management the national and regional levels should be undertaken. Such implies that there should be more independence allowed for local and municipal authorities when it comes to making decisions. This will help to make prompt and prudent decisions on the grass root level.

Current Action 5: Creating a "roadmap", ideas, and strategies of a new era named, "Digital Economy"

Suppose to be: Developing domestic software whilst safeguarding data confidentiality and individual freedom.

The last measure that has been suggested is about creating a "roadmap" for ideas and approaches for another epoch termed as the "digital economy". In so doing, it implies that domestic software should be built whilst guarding data privacy and personal liberty. Doing so will also facilitate the protection of data while improving disaster response and emergency assistance.

Several actions mentioned are developed at both conceptual and technical levels such as creating a unified emergency prevention and response system and utilizing artificial intelligence (AI), necessitates systematic organizational actions. These include conducting exploratory research, fostering collaboration among specialists of various disciplines, and supplementing daily activities with developmental tasks. The success of these actions depends on recognizing the benefits of transforming management methods, resources, and information processing technologies. In recent decades, the management system's transformation has been a natural part of technological security.

However, the dramatic change in external conditions calls for choosing new directions for the unified emergency prevention and response system's development. The "broad" approach involves preserving the trend of increasing local and regional administrative levels, but a decrease in efficiency will impact the safety of the population, regions, and resource allocation.

An alternative management approach using smart technologies presents significant opportunities for systematically reducing risks in emergency situations and achieving a global level of population safety. AI's ability to learn from past situations and quickly enumerate solution sets will soon surpass that of human professionals in most management areas. For instance, call centers have increasingly and accurately handled a large number of calls, with financial organizations nearing 100% accuracy. Soon, the approved system can become the default "big data" provider.

However, like any new technology, AI is not always used optimally or for good. Care must be taken to ensure AI benefits people and society rather than working against them or at their expense. Transitioning to a digital security platform requires further research on the consequences of replacing humans with AI and potential threats to individuals and society.

Implementing the proposed methods requires joint efforts from different departments to change management models, improve employee training systems, and improve regulatory frameworks. Reducing losses from emergencies will help the economy recover from a deep crisis. The ability to construct future development scenarios will allow for rational resource allocation and guide society on a path of progress.

5 Conclusion

Enhancing resilience against natural and man-made hazards: the need for Unified Management System (UMS) for disaster risk management and emergency response leveraging artificial intelligence-based decision support systems. On the other hand, it is possible to use contemporary technologies for preparing data for intelligent systems in managing safety, but formalizing accumulated multi-format documents creates challenges. This paper proposed strategies of updating information resources, improving management processes and changing business models of governing bodies. The development of monitoring data sources and unification of formats to access data could help in the formation of automatically distributed information resources with personalized access. The paper also points at the format and structure of information presentation that might result in an ambiguous interpretation of data and be another source for increase in volumes in response to informal data.

References

1. Burrough, P.A., McDonnell, R.A., Lloyd, C.D.: Principles of Geographical Information Systems, 4th edn. Oxford University Press, Oxford (2015)

14   M. A. A. Hammoudeh

2. Daellenbach, H., McNickle, D., Dye, S.: Management Science: Decision-Making Through Systems Thinking, 2nd edn. Bloomsbury Publishing (2017). https://www.perlego.com/book/2995885/management-science-decisionmaking-through-systems-thinking-pdf
3. Hasija, S., Shen, Z.M., Teo, C.: Smart city operations: modeling challenges and opportunities. Manuf. Serv. Operat. Manage. **22**(1), 203–213 (2020). https://doi.org/10.1287/msom.2019.0823
4. Hazra, A., et al.: Fog computing for next-generation Internet of Things: Fundamental, state-of-the-art and research challenges. Comput. Sci. Rev. **48**, 100549 (2023). https://doi.org/10.1016/j.cosrev.2023.100549
5. Janiesch, C., Zschech, P., Heinrich, K.: Machine learning and deep learning. Electron. **31**(3), 685–695 (2021). https://doi.org/10.1007/s12525-021-00475-2
6. Jiang, Y., Zhang, R., Wang, B.: Scenario-based approach for emergency operational response: Implications for reservoir management decisions. Int. J. Disaster Risk Reduct. **80**, 103192 (2022). https://doi.org/10.1016/j.ijdrr.2022.103192
7. Merz, B., et al.: Impact forecasting to support emergency management of natural hazards. Rev. Geophys. (2020). https://doi.org/10.1029/2020RG000704
8. Petrenko, S.: Big Data Technologies for Monitoring of Computer Security: A Case Study of the Russian Federation. Springer International Publishing, Cham (2018). https://doi.org/10.1007/978-3-319-79036-7
9. Phadtare, S.P., Magdum, S.B.: World wide web metasearch using TF-IDF method. Int. J. Sci. Res. **5**(1), 710–712 (2016). https://doi.org/10.21275/v5i1.nov152833
10. Shahrah, A.Y., Al-Mashari, M.A.: Developing a case-based emergency response system with adaptive case management. J. Homeland Secur. Emerg. Manag. **18**(1), 23–47 (2020). https://doi.org/10.1515/jhsem-2017-0073
11. Shi, P.: Disaster Risk Science. Springer Singapore, Singapore (2019)
12. Sun, X., Richard Yu, F., Zhang, P.: A survey on cyber-security of connected and autonomous vehicles (CAVs). IEEE Trans. Intell. Transport. Syst. **23**(7), 6240–6259 (2022). https://doi.org/10.1109/TITS.2021.3085297
13. Zhang, J., Hayashi, Y., Frank, L.D.: COVID-19 and transport: findings from a world-wide expert survey. Transport Policy **103**, 68–85 (2021). https://doi.org/10.1016/j.tranpol.2021.01.011

Addressing Challenges in AI-Based Systems Development: A Proposal of Adapted Requirements Engineering Process

Kamil Jabłoński and Aleksander Jarzębowicz[(✉)] [iD]

Gdańsk University of Technology, Gdańsk, Poland
s165165@student.pg.edu.pl, olek@eti.pg.edu.pl

Abstract. [Context] Present-day IT systems are more and more dependent on artificial intelligence (AI) solutions. Developing AI-based systems means facing new challenges, not known for more conventional systems. Such challenges need to be identified and addressed by properly adapting the existing development and management processes. [Objective] In this paper, we focus on the requirements engineering (RE) area of IT projects and aim to propose the RE process that would be able to address at least some of the reported challenges. No proposal of such process could be found in the existing literature. [Method] We conducted a literature review using a snowballing technique to identify RE-related challenges for AI-based systems. Then, we compared several RE industry guides, selected a well-established RE process and adapted it by introducing additional practices. The additional practices were proposed as result of brainstorming and ideation process. [Results] The contributions of this paper include: a list of identified challenges, a set of additional practices to mitigate challenges and a model of the adapted RE process which integrates such practices. [Conclusions] The proposed process is available for validation activities and can be used by researchers and practitioners as a base for further adaptations of RE approaches to AI solutions.

Keywords: Requirements engineering · Artificial intelligence · RE4AI · challenges

1 Introduction

In recent years significant advances in the field of Artificial Intelligence (AI) could be observed, as more effective technologies, in particular machine learning and deep learning, enable more effective predictions and decision-making [13]. As a result, there is a growing demand from the business side for AI-based systems that would provide advantage in a competitive market and a large number of industrial projects dedicated to such a purpose is initiated [4].

Such projects are still IT projects that need to follow software engineering processes. However, the specifics of developing AI-based systems result in a need to adapt the existing processes, practices and techniques used. In this paper, we focus on requirements engineering (RE), which is one of the core activities of every IT project, as it is

K. S. Soliman (Ed.): IBIMA-AI 2024, CCIS 2299, pp. 15–31, 2025.
https://doi.org/10.1007/978-3-031-77493-5_2

necessary to capture customers' requirements in order to provide them with a system that matches their needs [18, 19, 23]. A substantial body of RE knowledge is available, however it is unrealistic to expect that RE could be conducted exactly the same way as for a more conventional system. For example, conventional systems are in most cases requirements-driven i.e. particular requirements like expected software features are expressed by human stakeholders, while AI-based system is often driven by outcome of AI model i.e. developers are asked to experiment with different solutions to achieve a given metric e.g. prediction rate [3]. Another example concerns new key categories of non-functional requirements like transparency or retrainability which were previously either unknown or their significance was negligible [7]. Such and other issues resulted in the emergence of a new research trend (called "RE for AI" or "RE4AI") aimed at developing or adapting RE processes for AI-related projects [2].

In our work, we intended to learn about the additional challenges encountered in RE for AI-based systems. Next, we made an attempt to select a base RE process among existing ones and adapt it by introducing additional practices addressing the identified challenges. This paper provides answers to the following research questions:

- **RQ1**: What additional RE-related challenges are reported for AI-based systems, compared to more conventional systems?
- **RQ2**: Which of existing proposals of RE process can be adapted for development of AI-based systems?
- **RQ3**: What practices can be introduced to address the reported challenges?

The paper is organized as follows. First, we outline the background and related work. Next, we describe the literature search on RE-related challenges for AI-based systems and its results. In the subsequent section we present our main proposal – the adapted RE process and the practices introduced to it. The paper ends with conclusions.

2   Background and Related Work

It is recognized that development of AI-based systems is to some extent different in comparison to more conventional systems and, as such, requires more dedicated methods and processes [3, 23]. This includes, among others, a need for adapted RE processes, adjusted to AI specifics [4].

RE is a widely recognized discipline, with a documented body of knowledge e.g. [9, 24], yet still considered as difficult and prone to challenges [14]. A number of recent works on general RE challenges applicable to virtually all IT projects [11, 14, 18] or a specific sub-class of them e.g. Agile projects [19, 22] is available. While it may be interesting to investigate whether all such known general challenges are applicable to AI-related projects, our work focused solely on RE challenges encountered during AI-based systems development and caused by the specific aspects of AI. Such specific challenges are reported by several sources, but they are rather a result of a single study e.g. series of interviews, than a summary of known RE-related challenges for AI-based systems we aimed at. We omit listing and describing such sources here, as the entire next section is dedicated to this purpose.

Several ideas on adapting RE practices for AI-based systems were proposed. A general SE process (not focused on RE) was designed by [6]. [15] introduced the

RE framework, utilizing Goal-Oriented Requirements Engineering models to specify requirements for machine learning systems. [2] provided a mapping between the challenges concerning AI-related entities and high-level RE activities that should address them. [21] proposed additional practices to 4 key RE activities, as a response to challenges communicated by data scientists. There is however, at least to our knowledge, no proposal of a complete RE process for AI-based systems available.

3   Literature Review on Challenges

To learn about challenges reported about RE for AI-based system we performed a literature search and review using a snowballing approach [25]. Snowballing means starting with an initial set of previously identified papers and investigating the papers related to them through a citation network. The process is iteratively repeated for all papers qualified as relevant to the study's topic. We conducted the search using a number of previously identified papers as a start set and Google Scholar as a means to navigate through the citation network.

The qualification of the candidate sources was based on the following inclusion/exclusion criteria: IC1 – Peer-reviewed sources; IC2 – Sources in English; IC3 – Sources reporting RE-related challenges; EC1 – Non peer-reviewed sources (blogs, white papers etc.); EC2 – Sources in languages other than English; EC3 – Sources not available online; EC4 – Sources that do not contribute to knowledge about RE-related challenges (though instead they could e.g. present other aspects of RE in the context of AI-based systems or challenges that are completely not related to RE).

Data extraction was limited to identifying challenges described in the papers, together with all accompanying information, in order to fully understand a nature of each challenge and its contributing factors. We intentionally tried to be more inclusive i.e. consider the challenges that somehow relate to RE or can be addressed by RE (e.g. a challenge mainly related to testing can partially be mitigated by establishing acceptance criteria during RE). Only the completely unrelated challenges (e.g. the need for more computational power) were excluded. We omitted the explicit quality assessment of the sources found – it would be more appropriate if we e.g. tried to identify some RE/SE methods, tools or controlled experiments, but in case of challenges we did not filter them on the basis of the assessed sources' quality scores. The results of data extraction were further processed to find the same or very similar challenges and group them. The final results of the literature review are presented in Table 1.

Table 1. Challenges related to requirements engineering activities for AI-based systems

ID	Challenge	Description	Sources
Ch1	Difficult decision-making with stakeholders	It is much more difficult to establish stakeholders' expectations, as it requires determining unambiguous criteria regarding AI-based system's operation. Moreover, making key project decisions together with customers is problematic, due to their lack of knowledge and misunderstandings of AI mechanisms and their abilities (what is a realistic expectation, what is possible at all)	[10, 21]
Ch2	Effective quality evaluation	It is difficult to evaluate the quality of the proposed solution and select the appropriate metrics. In particular, it may be problematic to determine the performance measures of the solution, as the scope of testing is hardly obvious	[1, 10, 21]
Ch3	Effective configuration and change management	Development of AI-based system requires experimenting with alternative solutions and optimizing the finally selected solution. After some changes/updates are introduced or an alternative is proposed, such new version is evaluated through experimenting on datasets. The management of such experiments is time-consuming, moreover one should expect difficulty in comparing experiment results	[1, 10]
Ch4	Critical importance of data	Data – especially training data – has a much greater significance for AI-based systems than for conventional ones and to a large extent determines system's future operations. Thus, the data should be prepared and tested as carefully as code for a more conventional system. Both, data quantity and quality should be carefully considered, which may not be possible at the same time, as there is often a choice between small sets of reliable, verified data and large sets of questionable quality, originating from uncertain sources	[2, 10, 21]
Ch5	The need for unique competencies	Development of an AI-based system and associated experiments/evaluations often require unique competencies, in particular from the mathematical domain (especially statistics)	[10]
Ch6	Complex and diversified testing process	AI-based systems require more extensive testing, including several "objects of interest": the system as a whole, AI training model, other (non-AI) system components and finally the datasets used in training. The testing approaches to each of such objects differ significantly	[1]
Ch7	Communication impaired by cultural differences	To succeed, all project team members have to cooperate and communicate, but such communication can be impaired by various differences related to e.g. geographical location, but also to their professional background and related mindsets	[1]

(*continued*)

Table 1. (*continued*)

ID	Challenge	Description	Sources
Ch8	Restrictions imposed by legal and ethical aspects	Application of the generic legal requirements can result in unexpected consequences. For example, the General Data Protection Regulation states that personal data can only be used in ways specified by an explicit consent of the person involved. It implies that the developers must know what data will be required by their AI model before they start its development. Also, domain regulations (e.g. finances) and ethical guidelines, e.g. by [5] may need to be addressed	[21]
Ch9	Negative side-effects of profiling	Many AI-based systems use profiling to determine user's characteristics and consequently provide him/her with the more fitting information. However, it results in filtering information, as such solutions omit everything that does not adhere to a given level of computed similarity. Therefore, a user potentially loses a lot of valuable content. An appropriate balance should be found for profiling mechanisms and the corresponding requirements should be agreed between stakeholders	[12]
Ch10	Lack of oracle	It is difficult or even impossible to clearly define the correctness criteria for AI-based system outputs as well as the right outputs for each individual input	[10]
Ch11	Imperfection	It is intrinsically impossible to make adequate outputs for any of various possible inputs (i.e., 100% accuracy). It is unlikely that the same accuracy can be achieved for any input, for example neural networks are known to be prone to so called "adversarial examples", where a small modification of input (e.g. a few pixels of an image) results in completely different response of a network	[10]
Ch12	Explainability	AI-based systems are not necessarily transparent in their operation. It can be very difficult to explain the model (what has been learned) and even harder to explain particular decisions/predictions of the model	[10, 21] [1]
Ch13	Interdependencies between system components	The components responsible for AI models and algorithms are just a part of a larger system. The data flow and dependencies between components are not easy to track (thus so called "unintended feedback loops" can be introduced). It can also be hard to determine which component or particular code fragment is responsible for implementing a given requirement. Moreover, a significant effort is required to update components, adjust interfaces etc. without introducing CACE (Changing Anything Changes Everything) effect	[1, 2]
Ch14	Effort estimation	The estimation of time and resources required is problematic due to the specifics of AI components' training and operation. A goal of the system can be well defined, but it does not directly translate into e.g. the number of iterations and experiments necessary before the acceptable results can be achieved	[1]

(*continued*)

Table 1. (*continued*)

ID	Challenge	Description	Sources
Ch15	Ensuring data privacy	Ensuring the adequate level of users' privacy is not easy, especially regarding users' data included in training datasets and the data used during system's operation. External regulations may restrict the way the data can be used e.g. request that only aggregated and/or anonymized data is used as input. Another issue is to prevent users' data retrieval – although the information in an AI model is obscured and not easy to transform back to humanly readable form, it is not impossible to do so. Finally, there is also a need to efficiently perform data exploration, develop models, and troubleshoot problems, thus a proper balance between that and privacy has to be found	[1]
Ch16	Freedom from discrimination	AI-based systems are designed to "discover" patterns in the training data and apply them to make decisions/predictions during their operation. However, some possible patterns would be clearly unacceptable according to law regulations and/or social standards e.g. filtering job candidates according to race or gender. In case of AI-based systems, the discrimination is not easy to determine because it is not reflected in explicit encoded rules, but can e.g. be a result of an unbalanced training set, where some groups are underrepresented	[21]

4 A Proposal of the Requirements Engineering Process for AI-based Systems

4.1 Selection of the Base Process

We planned to address the identified challenges by introducing dedicated mitigating practices to the RE process. This brought us to RQ2 and the decision which RE process should be used as a base. As we wanted it to be a process used in practice, we reviewed the available industrial standards and guidelines dedicated to RE and to business analysis (BA). BA is a more general domain that focuses on identifying the needs of an organization and introducing changes that will deliver value to stakeholders. Such change can have nothing to do with developing or modifying IT system(s), but in case it does, sources on BA provide a good guidance on RE activities, thus they were considered as well.

We selected four well-established sources: Certified Professional for Requirements Engineering syllabus by International Requirements Engineering Board [9], Business Analysis Body of Knowledge (BABOK v3) by International Institute of Business Analysis [8], and two sources published by Project Management Institute: Business Analysis for Practitioners: A Practice Guide [16] and Requirements Management: A Practice Guide [17]. All the documents were reviewed and compared with respect to scope and detailed contents (the results of scope comparison are shown in Fig. 1, where corresponding areas described in particular sources are juxtaposed). The results were thoroughly discussed by both authors and finally a decision to select [17] was reached, because this source covers a wide spectrum of areas/processes (see Fig. 1) and thus enables RE activities to have impact on other areas of development and management in an IT project. Moreover, the source is dedicated to RE, without dealing with some issues covered by BA sources, but not applicable to IT projects.

BABOK	IREB	PMI BA Guide	PMI RM Guide
Strategy analysis		Needs assessment	Needs assessment
Business analysis planning and monitoring		Business analysis planning	Requirements management planning
Elicitation and collaboration	Requirements elicitation		Requirements elicitation
Requirements analysis and design definition	Requirements documentation	Requirements elicitation and analysis	Requirements analysis
	Requirements negotiation and validation		
Requirements life cycle management	Requirements management	Traceability and monitoring	Requirements monitoring and controlling
Solution evaluation		Solution evaluation	Solution evaluation
			Project or phase closure

Fig. 1. The scope of RE and BA industrial guides – a comparison

4.2 Adaptation of the Process to Address Challenges

The next step was to adapt the selected process, so it would mitigate the challenges described in the previous section). We planned to achieve it by introducing additional practices, rather than by significantly modifying the base process. The reason was that the base process covers the RE activities to be done for probably any IT project – it is hard to expect that in case of an AI-based system e.g. requirements elicitation or solution evaluation could be omitted. During our work, we thoroughly reviewed the guide and identified (sub)activities where remedies to particular challenges could be added. We also relied on brainstorming and exchange of ideas to establish the challenge-mitigating practices. The existing literature was used as one of the inputs to brainstorming e.g. some of the papers found in our literature review mentioned potential remedies. We built upon such proposals, however due to a very dynamic and adaptive nature of our ideation process, it is impossible to document full traceability of each idea's origins. Our work took several iterations as both authors exchanged and discussed ideas, before deciding about the final adapted RE process.

4.3 The Description of the Resulting Process

The RE process according to [17] is shown in Fig. 2. The figure depicts the activities and their main sub-activities (except **Needs assessment**, which is not decomposed). The arrows indicate the ordering the activities take place in the RE process. The loop between **Requirements elicitation**, **Requirements analysis** and **Solution evaluation** indicates that several iterations including these activities can take place. **Requirements monitoring and controlling** is not connected using arrows, because it is conducted continuously "in the background", like most of management activities in IT projects. The red circles with identifiers like P1 symbolize additional practices we propose to include. In the remainder of this section we briefly outline the activities of the RE process, based on [17]. Due to space limitations and possible copyright violations we are not able to provide all the details and the interested reader is referred to the source document. Our descriptions will focus on the additional practices that can be included in the process to address the challenges identified for AI-based systems. The key areas and activities of the RE process as well as challenges and practices discussed are distinguished using bold fonts.

The RE process starts with **Needs assessment**, which often precedes the project itself. It is supposed to identify and analyze a business problem or strategic organizational need in order to determine high-level needs definition that will ultimately be used to determine viable solution options. As the business problem is usually quite abstract, our analysis did not identify any additional practices for this activity. For this reason we also omitted visualizing its sub-activities in Fig. 2.

The **Requirements management planning** activity includes the sub-activities that take place at the beginning of the project. One of them is **Stakeholder analysis and engagement**, which should result in creating a stakeholder register, analyzing stakeholders' characteristics and initiating contact with them to foster their engagement. The RE process for AI-based system should involve specific additional stakeholders. The critical importance of data (**Ch4**) and the expectations to ensure freedom from discrimination (**Ch16**) suggest a need for adequate competencies in preparing and processing data i.e. involvement of a data scientist (**P1**). The impact of legal and ethical requirements (**Ch8**) translates into a need for a legal expert as an additional stakeholder (**P2**). The adequate data privacy (**Ch15**) would probably require competencies in both legal regulations and AI mechanisms, thus both stakeholders (**P1&P2**) should cooperate on that throughout the project. The need for unique competencies in mathematics and statistics (**Ch5**) has also to be considered and, in case project team lacks them, additional people should be hired or at least some consultancy provided (**P3**). The analysis of stakeholders' characteristics should consider the potential cultural differences (**Ch7**) and ensure that the overall group of stakeholders covers all the relevant viewpoints with respect to nationalities, mindsets etc. (**P4**).

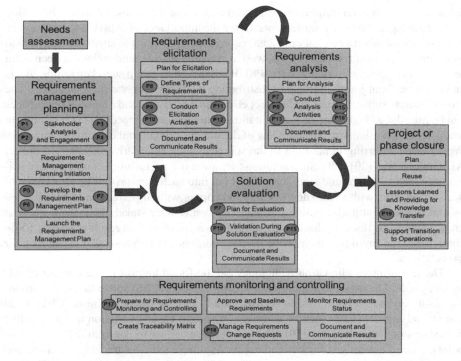

Fig. 2. Adapted requirements engineering process model with additional practices

Another sub-activity (**Development of requirements management plan**) is supposed to define how requirement activities of the project will be planned and managed. The plan should foresee the need to consider the issue of profiling (**Ch9**) – such task has to be conducted jointly by all relevant stakeholders in order to reach a consensus about the degree to which profiling will be used by the system (**P5**). The anticipated communication problems with customer representatives (**Ch1**) should result in planning additional resources and time dedicated for educating stakeholders and for eliciting, analyzing and validating their requirements (**P6**). Another issue is the difficulty to evaluate the quality of the proposed solution (**Ch2**). Handling this challenge requires allocating necessary time and resources to think over and define the metrics and acceptance criteria as well as to ensure that all interested parties understand and accept such metrics/criteria (**P7**).

Requirements elicitation activity covers the discovery process by gathering information from stakeholders and other sources. Effective elicitation is warranted by active involvement of stakeholders and communication with them. One of its initial sub-activities is to **Define types of requirements**, which should result in designing the classification of requirements to be elicited with respect to the level of abstraction/detail (e.g. business goals, user requirements, system requirements) and addressed aspect (e.g. functional, non-functional, constraints). Different classifications can be found in renown sources – e.g. [24] vs. [8] – in each project it is possible to develop a classification most suitable for it. However, requirements related to data are rarely distinguished, but rather included in e.g. functional requirements. Given the importance of data (**Ch4**), we propose to explicitly establish a category of "data requirements", define the attributes that have to be specified for such requirements as well as possible interdependencies between them and other categories of requirements (**P8**). It will allow to group such key requirements and consider them jointly, instead of distributing them between various categories. The most elaborate sub-activity is to **Conduct elicitation activities** and a number of practices can be introduced here. One of the elicitation techniques mentioned in [17] is document analysis, which usually means a review of documents related to the client organization. We advocate referring in addition to the sources which summarize the state-of-the-art AI solutions, e.g. [20] (**P9**). Such solutions are quite often a result of cooperation of scientific/industrial teams and significant effort put into such enterprise. The challenges of decision-making with stakeholders (**Ch1**) and coping with imperfection (**Ch11**) caused by stakeholders' attitude, can be mitigated by confronting stakeholders with the best known solutions. If such solutions are not able to achieve a given result or ensure 100% correctness for any input, then probably stakeholders can be persuaded to adjust their expectations.

The use of other elicitation techniques can be found helpful in the context of AI-based system. The needs to acquire unique competencies (**Ch5**) and to facilitate consensus about key issues (like: data to be used (**Ch4**), quality metrics/criteria (**Ch2**), legal and ethical aspects (**Ch8**)) can be addressed by group-based elicitation techniques like workshops or focus groups (**P10**). These techniques allow to confront different viewpoints, share knowledge, discuss and reconcile differences. As tracking dataflow and dependencies between the components of an AI-based system is challenging (**Ch13**), a special attention should be paid to the technique called interface analysis. It can help to establish interdependencies and boundaries by determining the input and output needs of each interfacing component. This technique can be supported by document analysis focused on technical documentation of components and external cooperating systems (**P11**).

Prototyping is a RE technique often used to learn more about expectations about user interface and human-computer interaction. It is also however possible to design technical prototypes aimed at developing a working solution to test whether a given idea or requirement is technically feasible. Given difficulty in effort estimation (**Ch14**) and large costs (AI model training can take weeks), it seems worthy to build a technical prototype with a reduced training dataset (in cases it is possible) and demonstrate it to stakeholders in order to obtain their feedback (**P12**).

In case of **Requirements analysis** activity, its main sub-activity **Conduct analysis activities** is of primary interest. This sub-activity has a substantial scope and includes: developing requirements' attributes, selecting requirement models, deriving additional requirements, assigning priorities and conducting verification and validation. The significance of data to be used in AI solution's training and operation (**Ch4**) implies that a particularly careful analysis is necessary for all items from "data requirements" category. It is a follow-up of the work done in **Define types of requirements**. Data requirements must ensure that the training dataset is representative to the target operating environment. Both the quantity and quality of training data have to be considered and a decision balancing them has to be made (larger datasets with more examples vs. completeness, consistency, quality of annotations etc.) (**P8**).

In addition, data requirements should tend to be assigned with higher priorities, as their importance to the final project's outcome cannot be overstated (**P13**). In case of more iterative/adaptive development process, the higher priorities will also cause such requirements to be implemented sooner and thus allow to minimize the related risk. Similarly, the requirements about the explainability of the system's operation (**Ch12**) should be assigned with higher priorities and carefully analyzed, verified and validated with stakeholders (**P14**).

Requirements analysis should also focus on metrics and acceptance criteria for quality evaluation (**Ch2**). Similarly to requirements elicitation, additional resources should be allocated to ensure that such metrics and criteria are commonly understood and acceptable to all interested stakeholders (**P7**). Another issue is the selection of a testing dataset that will be used to check if the developed system fulfills its requirements, as testing is always limited and cannot demonstrate 100% correctness (**Ch11**) is A question arises: who should be responsible for such selection? The developers may not be the best choice, as they could focus on optimizations for this dataset only, while system's effectiveness in target environment will turn out to be worse. The customer and non-technical stakeholders may in turn lack sufficient competencies. A possible solution is to involve an independent third party assigned with such responsibility (**P15**).

Considering the challenges of tracking relationships between system components (**Ch13**) and problematic configuration and change management (**Ch3**), the selection of requirement models should take such issues into account. It can be beneficial to rely on modeling techniques that allow to capture the interfaces between components or systems and the interaction between them expressed as events, dataflows etc. (**P16**). A number of techniques is potentially useful here, including scope models (context diagram, ecosystem map), data models (data flow diagram, data dictionary) and interface models (system interface table, N2 diagram).

The activity of **Solution evaluation** is performed to validate the solution (system), to determine how well it meets the expressed needs. No new practices were proposed here, but some of those described earlier have impact on **Solution evaluation** as well. In case additional effort was made to explain the metrics and acceptance criteria to the stakeholders (**Ch2**), all agreements made then (metrics, evaluation techniques) should be incorporated in **Plan for evaluation** sub-activity (**P7**). The group-based techniques (**P10**), already suggested for requirements elicitation, will also be suitable for **Validation during solution evaluation** sub-activity, as they enable knowledge sharing and discussions. This sub-activity may also involve an independent third party (**P15**), if a decision was previously made to make them responsible for conducting validation.

The continuous process of **Requirements monitoring and controlling** covers issues like configuration management, change management, maintaining traceability and monitoring the current state of requirements. Such tasks are performed according to procedures defined during **Prepare for requirements monitoring and controlling** sub-activity. One should expect difficulties in configuration and change management caused by specifics of AI-related projects – introducing changes in datasets and/or AI models, tracking such "versions", comparing them etc. differs from the established practices of software engineering (**Ch3**). For this purpose, a dedicated change management procedure that incorporates specifics of AI context should be explicitly defined (**P17**). The already introduced challenges about change management (**Ch3**) and establishing training data (**Ch4**) suggest that **Manage requirements change requests** can benefit from more advanced techniques of dependency analysis and impact analysis, as well as traceability matrices and change control boards (**P18**).

   Project or phase closure is the last activity with the purpose of finalizing all works to formally complete the project or phase. It includes **Lessons learned and providing for knowledge transfer** sub-activity. In the context of AI-related projects, the knowledge about comparing different AI models and managing changes introduced to them (**Ch3**), as well as effort estimations and their accuracy known on hindsight (**Ch14**) are especially valuable. Thus, project closure needs to ensure that essential information (especially about datasets, AI models and metrics used in the project) is properly documented and can be transferred to other projects (**P19**).

   In addition to Fig. 2 and the descriptions provided in this section, Table 2 shows the mapping between challenges and practices that address them.

Table 2. Requirements engineering additional practices introduced to address challenges

Challenge	Practice	Practice description
Ch1: Difficult decision-making with stakeholders	P6	Plan additional resources and time dedicated for eliciting, analyzing and validating stakeholders' requirements
	P9	Conduct document analysis and review of sources summarizing state-of-the-art solutions and trends in the AI domain
	P14	Assign higher priorities to requirements on explainability
Ch2: Effective quality evaluation	P6	Plan additional resources and time dedicated for eliciting, analyzing and validating stakeholders' requirements
	P7	Plan additional resources and time for defining adequate metrics/acceptance criteria and for educating customer representatives and other stakeholders in this matter
	P10	Use group-based techniques like workshop or focus group for the purpose of requirements elicitation and solution evaluation

(continued)

Table 2. (*continued*)

Challenge	Practice	Practice description
Ch3: Effective configuration and change management	P16	During requirements analysis, use modeling techniques that enable capturing interdependencies and interactions between components/systems (e.g. context diagram, ecosystem map, data flow diagram, data dictionary, state diagram, system interface table, N2 diagram)
	P17	Define (and follow) a dedicated change management procedure that incorporates specifics of AI context
	P18	Conduct dedicated dependency analysis and impact analysis for each change to requirements from Data Requirements category
	P19	Document lessons learned including all datasets, AI models and metrics used in the project in a suitable form that enables easy reuse and information retrieval
Ch4: Critical importance of data	P1	Include data scientists as stakeholders (or, if already present, extend their responsibilities in the project)
	P8	Define a new category of requirements: Data Requirements and pay special attention to eliciting, analyzing and verifying such requirements
	P10	Use group-based techniques like workshop or focus group for the purpose of requirements elicitation and solution evaluation
	P13	Assign higher priorities to requirements from Data Requirements category
	P18	Conduct dedicated dependency analysis and impact analysis for each change to requirements from Data Requirements category
Ch5: The need for unique competencies	P3	Involve experts from mathematics and statistics domains as stakeholders

(*continued*)

Table 2. (*continued*)

Challenge	Practice	Practice description
	P10	Use group-based techniques like workshop or focus group for the purpose of requirements elicitation and solution evaluation
Ch6: Complex and diversified testing process	P8	Define a new category of requirements: Data Requirements and pay special attention to eliciting, analyzing and verifying such requirements
Ch7: Communication impaired by cultural differences	P4	Ensure that the overall group of stakeholders includes the representatives who cover all the relevant viewpoints with respect to different cultures and mindsets
Ch8: Restrictions imposed by legal and ethical aspects	P2	Include legal experts as stakeholders (or, if already present, extend their responsibilities in the project)
	P10	Use group-based techniques like workshop or focus group for the purpose of requirements elicitation and solution evaluation
Ch9: Negative side-effects of profiling	P5	Guide the stakeholders to reach a consensus and explicitly state the degree to which user profiling is desirable and how the information gathered this way is to be processed
Ch10: Lack of oracle	P7	Plan additional resources and time for defining adequate metrics/acceptance criteria and for educating customer representatives and other stakeholders in this matter
Ch11: Imperfection	P9	Conduct document analysis and review of sources summarizing state-of-the-art solutions and trends in AI domain
	P15	Involve an independent third party responsible for preparing testing dataset and for solution evaluation
Ch12: Explainability	P14	Assign higher priorities to requirements on explainability

(*continued*)

Table 2. (*continued*)

Challenge	Practice	Practice description
Ch13: Interdependencies between system components	P11	Use interface analysis and document analysis in requirements elicitation
	P16	During requirements analysis, use modeling techniques that enable capturing interdependencies and interactions between components/systems (e.g. context diagram, ecosystem map, data flow diagram, data dictionary, state diagram, system interface table, N2 diagram)
Ch14: Effort estimation	P12	Use technical prototypes in requirements elicitation
	P19	Document lessons learned including all datasets, AI models and metrics used in the project in a suitable form that enables easy reuse and information retrieval
Ch15: Ensuring data privacy	P1	Include data scientists as stakeholders (or, if already present, extend their responsibilities in the project)
	P2	Include legal experts as stakeholders (or, if already present, extend their responsibilities in the project)
Ch16: Ensuring freedom from discrimination	P1	Include data scientists as stakeholders (or, if already present, extend their responsibilities in the project)

5 Conclusions

In this paper we reported a research study aimed at identifying RE-related challenges for AI-based systems and addressing them with a tailored RE process which includes additional dedicated practices. The answers to the research questions posed were obtained through literature search (RQ1), analysis and comparison of industrial RE and BA guides (RQ2) and ideation process (RQ3). We were able to identify 16 unique challenges specific for RE activities applied to AI-based systems (RQ1). We reviewed 4 well-established industry guides with respect to their scope, structure and detailed contents and decided to use one of them – "Requirements management: A practice guide" published by Project Management Institute [17] as a base for designing a dedicated RE4AI process (RQ2). We identified 19 additional RE practices addressing the challenges and positioned them within the specific activities of the base RE process (RQ3). We also started validating such results through interviews with industry experts and the feedback obtained up to now is encouraging (validation activities are not described here due to paper size restrictions).

Our study has several limitations which could affect its validity. The literature search is prone to omitting some relevant sources due to a non-representative start set or wrong decisions about papers' qualification. We tried to minimize these threats by following the guidelines on snowballing, but they could not be entirely eliminated. The ideation process could fail to produce the most optimal result as it is dependent on its contributors and their creativity.

As (according to our knowledge) no complete RE process for AI-based systems was published, our proposal's implications for research include the possibility for other researchers to modify the described process by adding/changing practices or to design a completely alternative one (e.g. using other standard/guide as a basis). A comparison and validation of such RE processes is also a way our contributions can be built upon. As for implications for practice, our work can be used by practitioners, especially business and system analysts, working on AI-based systems to improve their RE processes.

The promising directions of future research include further validation and improvements of the process model according to feedback obtained from the industry. It is also possible (and desirable) to keep track of new reports on challenges and, accordingly, adjust the RE process to address them as well.

References

1. Arpteg, A., Brinne, B., Crnkovic-Friis, L., Bosch, J.: Software engineering challenges of deep learning In: Proceedings of 44th Euromicro Conference on Software Engineering and Advanced Applications (SEAA), pp. 50–59 (2018)
2. Belani, H., Vukovic M., Car, Z.: Requirements engineering challenges in building AI-based complex systems. In: Proceedings of the 27th International Requirements Engineering Conference Workshops, pp. 252–255 (2019)
3. Bosch, J., Olsson, H., Crnkovic, I.: It takes three to tango: requirement, outcome/data, and AI driven development. In: Proceedings of the International Workshop on Software-intensive Business: Start-ups, Ecosystems and Platforms (SiBW 2018), Espoo, Finland, 3 December 2018, pp. 177–192 (2018)
4. Dalpiaz, F., Niu, N.: Requirements engineering in the days of artificial intelligence. IEEE Softw. 37(4), 7–10 (2020)
5. European Commission's Independent High-level Expert Group on Artificial Intelligence: 'Ethics Guidelines for Trustworthy AI,' (2019). https://ec.europa.eu/newsroom/dae/doc ument.cfm?doc_id=60419. Accessed: 29 Sep 2023
6. Hesenius, M., Schwenzfeier, N., Meyer, O., Koop, W., Gruhn, V.: Towards a software engineering process for developing data-driven applications. In: Proceedings of 7th International Workshop on Realizing Artificial Intelligence Synergies in Software Engineering, pp. 35–41 (2019)
7. Horkoff, J.: Non-functional requirements for machine learning: Challenges and new directions. In: Proceedings of 27th International Requirements Engineering Conference (RE), pp. 386–391 (2019)
8. IIBA International Institute of Business Analysis, A guide to the business analysis body of knowledge (BABOK Guide), ver. 3. (2015)
9. IREB International Requirements Engineering Board: IREB Certified Professional for Requirements Engineering, ver. 2.2 (2017)

10. Ishikawa, F., Yoshioka, N.: How Do Engineers perceive difficulties in engineering of machine-learning systems? – questionnaire survey. In: Proceedings of the IEEE/ACM Joint 7th International Workshop on Conducting Empirical Studies in Industry (CESI) and 6th International Workshop on Software Engineering Research and Industrial Practice (SER&IP), pp. 2–9 (2019)
11. Jarzębowicz, A., Ślesiński, W.: What is troubling IT analysts? A survey report from Poland on requirements-related problems. In: Proceedings of the 20th KKIO Software Engineering Conference, pp. 3–19 (2019)
12. Kostova, B., Gürses, S., Wegmann, A.: On the Interplay between Requirements, Engineering, and Artificial Intelligence. In: Proceedings of the 26th International Conference on Requirements Engineering: Foundation for Software Quality (REFSQ) Workshops (2020)
13. Lukac, D., Milic, M., Nikolic, J.: From artificial intelligence to augmented age an overview. In: Proceedings of the 2018 Zooming Innovation in Consumer Technologies Conference, pp. 100–103 (2018)
14. Fernández, D.M., et al.: Naming the pain in requirements engineering. Empir. Softw. Eng. **22**(5), 2298–2338 (2016). https://doi.org/10.1007/s10664-016-9451-7
15. Nalchigar, S., Yu, E., Keshavjee, K.: Modeling machine learning requirements from three perspectives: a case report from the healthcare domain. Requirements Eng. **26**, 237–254 (2021)
16. PMI Project Management Institute, Business analysis for practitioners. A practice guide (2015)
17. PMI Project Management Institute, Requirements management: A practice guide (2016)
18. Przybyłek, A.: A Business-Oriented Approach to Requirements Elicitation, In Proc. of 9th International Conference on Evaluation of Novel Approaches to Software Engineering (ENASE), pp. 152–163 (2014)
19. Przybyłek, A., Zakrzewski, M.: Adopting collaborative games into agile requirements engineering. In: Proceedings of 13th International Conference on Evaluation of Novel Approaches to Software Engineering (ENASE), pp. 54–64 (2018)
20. Stateofheart AI, Stateofheart AI community website. https://www.stateofheart.ai (2023). Accessed 2 October 2023
21. Vogelsang, A., Borg, M.: Requirements engineering for machine learning: perspectives from data scientists. In: Proceedings of the 27th International Requirements Engineering Conference Workshops, pp. 245–251 (2019)
22. Wagner, S., Méndez Fernández, D., Kalinowski, M., Felderer, M.: Agile requirements engineering in practice: Status quo and critical problems. CLEI Electron. J. **21**(1), 6:1–6:15 (2018)
23. Wan, Z., Xia, X., Lo, D., Murphy, G.: How does machine learning change software development practices? IEEE Trans. Software Eng. **47**(9), 1857–1871 (2019)
24. Wiegers, K., Beatty, J.: Software Requirements, 3rd edn. Microsoft Press (2013)
25. Wohlin, C.: Guidelines for snowballing in systematic literature studies and a replication in software engineering. In: Proceedings of 18th Conference on Evaluation and Assessment in Software Engineering (EASE), pp. 1–10 (2014)

Comprehensive Analysis of Football Player Performance with WorldfootballR: Data Insights and Key Variables

Irina Cristina Cojocariu[✉] and Marin Fotache

Alexandru Ioan Cuza University of Iasi, Iasi, Romania
cojocariu.irina96@yahoo.com, fotache@mail.uaic.ro

Abstract. This study is based on the performance analysis of football players from five significant countries: United Kingdom, France, Germany, Italy and Spain. It uses a carefully chosen set of key variables that have relevance in the field of football. Data extraction and cleaning were performed using the WorldfootballR package in the R programming environment. This study sheds light on potential research avenues, such as expanding the analysis to encompass a wider range of countries and deepening the intricate relationship between player performance and socio-economic factors. With this comprehensive overview, the analysis provides an initial look at the performance of football players and the disparities that exist on an international scale; therefore, a solid foundation can be established for future research in this area.

Keywords: football player performance · worldfootballr · key variables

1 Introduction

Football is one of the most revered and cherished sports across the globe. In an age dominated by digital advancements, football-related data has gained unprecedented importance, serving as the basis for sports analytics, predictive modeling and informed decision-making. As millions of fans eagerly await match results, examine player stats and debate team rankings, the need for complete, accurate and accessible data has never been more pronounced.

In response to this growing demand for reliable football categorical or numeric data [14], the WorldfootballR package [6] has emerged as a powerful and indispensable tool in the field of sports analysis. Developed to seamlessly integrate with the R language, this package helps researchers, coaches, and fans extract and clean football data. By leveraging the capabilities of WorldfootballR, users can effortlessly access a wide range of football-related information pulled from various sources, including official competition websites, data provider APIs and publicly accessible databases. This wealth of data encompasses a wide spectrum of elements, ranging from match results and league standings to detailed individual player statistics and full team profiles.

Amidst this abundance of football data a critical challenge that cannot be overlooked – data cleaning [1, 12]. In the context of football data analysis, data cleaning

© The Author(s), under exclusive license to Springer Nature Switzerland AG 2025
K. S. Soliman (Ed.): IBIMA-AI 2024, CCIS 2299, pp. 32–41, 2025.
https://doi.org/10.1007/978-3-031-77493-5_3

is an indispensable facet of the analytical process, requiring meticulous error correction, intelligent handling of missing values, and solving other data quality issues. This crucial step is essential in guaranteeing the veracity and credibility of the extracted information, ultimately supporting the accuracy and reliability of all subsequent analytical efforts. Fortunately, the WorldfootballR package provides users with a number of tools specifically designed to accelerate and optimize this essential stage of the analytical journey.

As we embark on this exploration of football data analysis facilitated by the WorldfootballR package, we deep in a realm where the passion for the sport converges with the rigor of data science, opening up a world of possibilities for research, developing strategy and appreciating the game at a higher level. In the following sections, the capabilities of WorldfootballR are discussed, highlighting its essential role in data mining and cleaning, while delving into the broader context of football data analysis as a foundation for reliable information and informed decision-making.

2   Types of Analyzed Data

The WorldfootballR package is a versatile tool capable of analyzing a wide range of football-related data types, making it an invaluable resource for researchers, coaches, and sports fans.

The key data types that can be analyzed using this package include:

a) Match Results: With WorldfootballR, users can effortlessly extract and analyze football match results. This includes information such as final scores, goal scorers, and other relevant match details. This data is essential for understanding team performance and match dynamics [2, 3].

b) League Standings: The package provides access to and analysis of football league standings. Users can explore team positions, points earned, goal differences, and other associated statistics. League standings offer insights into the overall performance and competitiveness of teams [7].

c) Individual Player Statistics: For a deeper dive into player performance, WorldfootballR allows the extraction and analysis of individual player statistics. This includes data on the number of goals scored, assists, yellow cards received, and more. Individual player statistics are crucial for evaluating player contributions to their teams [8].

d) Team Information: WorldfootballR offers comprehensive details about football teams. Users can access information such as club names, countries of origin, head coaches, and other relevant factors [11]. Understanding team characteristics is essential for team management and strategy development.

e) Competition Information: The package provides insights into various football competitions, including competition names, respective seasons, and other competition-related details. This data is vital for tracking the progress of tournaments and understanding the context of match results and standings.

If we managed to establish the type of information needed for sports analyses, the next challenge is to determine the source of the data from which we can get access to the resources. The power of WorldfootballR is the ability to significantly reduce time research, therefore providing access to complete and updated information.

This package extracts data from the following sources:

a) Official Competition Websites: WorldfootballR can access and extract data from the official websites of football competitions. This includes national leagues, cups, and international tournaments. These sources typically offer detailed information about matches, standings, individual player statistics, and more.
b) Data Provider APIs: Leveraging APIs provided by platforms and specialized data providers in football, WorldfootballR offers programmatic access to structured and current data. This data includes match results, standings, player statistics, and more. APIs are a valuable source for real-time data updates.
c) Public Databases: The package can extract data from public databases that contain a wealth of football-related information. These databases may be managed by organizations, institutions, or communities dedicated to collecting and sharing data about matches, players, and competitions.

The WorldfootballR package empowers users to analyze a diverse range of football data types from multiple sources. This comprehensive approach to data analysis opens doors to deeper insights into football performance, strategy, and trends, making it an indispensable tool for those involved in the world of football.

3   Selection of Key Variables

In the field of sports analysis, variables serve as fundamental components, playing an essential role in understanding and evaluating various aspects of sports performance.

These variables can generally be classified into two main types [5]:

3.1   Independent Variables

Independent variables are an integral part of the research or analysis process because they are the aspects under the researcher's control or manipulation. These variables represent the causes or factors that have the potential to influence the outcome being studied. In the context of sports analysis, independent variables could encompass a wide range of factors, such as training methods, environmental conditions, or specific strategies used by players or at the team level. Researchers often manipulate these variables to examine their effects on sports performance or outcomes.

3.2   Dependent Variables

On the other side of the analytical spectrum, we have dependent variables. These variables are observed and measured to assess the consequences, impact or outcomes of the study. In the context of sports analysis, dependent variables serve as indicators or metrics that reflect the outcome or response to changes in the independent variables [10]. Examples of dependent variables in sport analysis include measures of sport performance such as scoring statistics or physiological responses. By analyzing these dependent variables, researchers can gain valuable insight into how changes in the independent variables affect different aspects of sports performance.

Understanding the interplay between these two types of variables is critical to conducting rigorous and insightful sports analysis. Researchers in sport science and analysis often carefully select and manipulate independent variables to investigate their influence on dependent variables, ultimately contributing to the broader understanding of sport.

In the context of football data, we have identified a series of important variables that can influence a player's market value. These variables include (Table 1):

Table 1. Key variables

Variable Name	Meaning	Description
Player_foot	Dominant foot	In football, the dominant foot refers to the foot that a player typically uses to take shots and control the ball during the game. It is the foot with which the player feels the most comfortable and has the highest precision and power
Mins_per_90_playing	Minutes per match	Players who record a low value spend more time on the field, which may indicate an important role in the team or a good ability to maintain a high level of performance throughout the entire match
Gls	Goals	A point is scored when the ball completely crosses the goal line, between the goalposts, under the goalkeeper's chin, and above the ground during a match. When a team scores a goal, a point is awarded in its favor
Ast	Assists	To be credited with an assist, the pass or supply must be direct and decisive in creating a goal-scoring opportunity for the teammate who finishes it
G_minus_PK	Goals minus Penalties	If the difference is positive, it can indicate strong goal-scoring abilities. On the other hand, if the difference is negative, it suggests that scoring opportunities are not being capitalized upon, indicating a lack of precision and confidence

(continued)

Table 1. (*continued*)

Variable Name	Meaning	Description
PK	Penalty Kicks	This kick is awarded in the case of serious rule violations
Pkatt	Penalty Kicks Attempted	Taking a penalty kick is a unique opportunity for the team that has been awarded the penalty to score a goal
CrdY	Yellow Cards	A yellow card is a warning notification in football, given by the referee to a player as a sanction for a violation of the rules of the game. When a player receives a yellow card, they are cautioned for committing an offense that can be considered unsporting, against the rules, or violating fair play. The reasons for issuing a yellow card can vary
CrdR	Red Cards	A red card is a more severe sanction than a yellow card in football. It is awarded by the referee to a player as a result of a serious violation of the rules of the game or extremely unsporting behavior. When a player receives a red card, they are ejected from the field, and their team must continue the game with one player less for the remainder of the match
Gls_Per	Goal Percentage	The ratio between the number of goals scored and the total number of goal attempts by a player or a team, expressed as a percentage. It is a measure of efficiency in converting goal-scoring opportunities into actual goals scored
Ast_Per	Assist Percentage	The ratio between the number of assists made and the total number of goal-scoring opportunities created by a player or a team, expressed as a percentage. It measures the efficiency of the player or team in providing decisive passes to other players for scoring goals

(*continued*)

Table 1. (*continued*)

Variable Name	Meaning	Description
G_minus_PK_Per	Goals minus Penalties Percentage	The percentage ratio between the difference between the number of goals scored and the number of penalties and the total number of goals scored, expressed as a percentage. It provides insight into the contribution of goals scored in open play compared to those resulting from penalty kicks
xG_Expected	Expected goals	A metric used in football to estimate the likelihood of scoring a goal based on various variables and statistics. It is a measure of the expected value of a goal-scoring opportunity, based on data and statistical algorithms
npxG_Expected	Non-Penalty Expected Goals	A measure of the expected value of goals outside of penalty kicks in football. It is a statistic that evaluates the chances of scoring a goal from open play situations, excluding penalty kicks
xAG_Expected	Expected assisted goals	A metric in football that estimates the number of goals that could be scored from chances created by a player, taking into account the expected value of these goal-scoring opportunities
xAG_Per	Assisted Goals Percentage	The percentage ratio between the number of goals that have been assisted and the total number of goals scored by a player or team, expressed as a percentage. This measures the efficiency of the player or team in providing decisive passes that lead to scoring goals
npxG_Per	Non-Penalty Expected Goals Percentage	The percentage ratio between non-penalty expected goals and the total number of goals scored, excluding goals scored from penalty kicks. This provides insight into the efficiency of converting goal-scoring opportunities created during open play into actual goals

In order to have an overview in the following table, the selected variables are divided according to the type of each one (dependent or independent variable). In creating the table, it was taken into account that the dependent variables measure the results or the performance of the players, and the independent variables represent factors or characteristics that can influence the results [9] (Table 2).

Table 2. Representation of key variables according to type

	Dependent Variables	Independent Variables
1	Mins_per_90_playing	Player_foot
2	Gls	PK
3	Ast	Pkatt
4	G_minus_PK	CrdY
5	Gls_Per	CrdR
6	Ast_Per	
7	G_minus_PK_Per	
8	xG_Expected	
9	npxG_Expected	
10	xAG_Expected	
11	xAG_Per	
12	npxG_Per	

In this data analysis, a subset of variables was carefully selected that were also researched by experts in the field. In addition, we focused on five key countries: the United Kingdom, France, Germany, Italy and Spain [6]. This selection can allow us to gain valuable information about the performance of football players from these countries.

The last column in Table 3 displays the p-value resulting from the non-parametric Kruskall-Wallis test. This test assesses the statistical significance of differences in each variable among the countries. It is important to note that a p-value less than 0.05 indicates significant differences in the distribution of variables among countries.

From the table above, we can observe that, for the majority of the variables included in this analysis, the p-value is less than 0.05. This suggests significant differences among the countries in terms of the analyzed variables. These findings underscore the importance of considering national differences when evaluating player statistics.

These variations could be attributed to a range of factors, including differences in training methodologies, coaching strategies, and even cultural influences on playing styles. Understanding these disparities is crucial for clubs, coaches, and sports analysts seeking to optimize player performance and develop effective strategies in various countries [13].

Table 3. Player Statistics Grouped by Countries

Variable	Country					p-value[2]
	England, N = 2,775[1]	France, N = 2,914[1]	Germany, N = 2,575[1]	Italy, N = 3,232[1]	Spain, N = 2,917[1]	
player_age	26.0 (23.0, 29.0)	24.0 (22.0, 28.0)	25.0 (22.0, 28.0)	26.0 (23.0, 29.0)	26.0 (23.0, 30.0)	<0.001
Unknown	0	0	1	0	1	
player_height_mtrs	1.83 (1.78, 1.88)	1.82 (1.77, 1.86)	1.84 (1.80, 1.88)	1.84 (1.80, 1.88)	1.81 (1.76, 1.85)	<0.001
Unknown	14	30	8	22	17	
player_foot						<0.001
both	68 (2.5%)	85 (3.0%)	110 (4.3%)	163 (5.1%)	77 (2.7%)	
left	670 (24%)	771 (27%)	585 (23%)	836 (26%)	818 (29%)	
right	2,019 (73%)	2,011 (70%)	1,867 (73%)	2,224 (69%)	1,971 (69%)	
Unknown	18	47	13	9	51	
Mins_Per_90_Playing	11 (4, 23)	10 (3, 20)	10 (3, 19)	9 (3, 20)	10 (3, 21)	<0.001
Gls	0.00 (0.00, 2.00)	0.00 (0.00, 2.00)	0.00 (0.00, 2.00)	0.00 (0.00, 2.00)	0.00 (0.00, 2.00)	<0.001
Ast	0.00 (0.00, 2.00)	0.00 (0.00, 1.00)	0.00 (0.00, 2.00)	0.00 (0.00, 1.00)	0.00 (0.00, 1.00)	<0.001
G_minus_PK	0.00 (0.00, 2.00)	0.00 (0.00, 2.00)	0.00 (0.00, 2.00)	0.00 (0.00, 2.00)	0.00 (0.00, 2.00)	<0.001
PK	0.00 (0.00, 0.00)	0.00 (0.00, 0.00)	0.00 (0.00, 0.00)	0.00 (0.00, 0.00)	0.00 (0.00, 0.00)	0.3
PKatt	0.00 (0.00, 0.00)	0.00 (0.00, 0.00)	0.00 (0.00, 0.00)	0.00 (0.00, 0.00)	0.00 (0.00, 0.00)	0.14
CrdY	1.00 (0.00, 3.00)	1.00 (0.00, 3.00)	1.00 (0.00, 3.00)	2.00 (0.00, 4.00)	2.00 (0.00, 4.00)	<0.001
CrdR						
0	2,574 (93%)	2,522 (87%)	2,396 (93%)	2,856 (88%)	2,571 (88%)	
1	192 (6.9%)	348 (12%)	169 (6.6%)	353 (11%)	310 (11%)	
2	9 (0.3%)	39 (1.3%)	9 (0.3%)	23 (0.7%)	36 (1.2%)	
3	0 (0%)	5 (0.2%)	1 (<0.1%)	0 (0%)	0 (0%)	
Gls_Per	0.00 (0.00, 0.14)	0.00 (0.00, 0.15)	0.00 (0.00, 0.17)	0.00 (0.00, 0.14)	0.00 (0.00, 0.14)	0.001
Ast_Per	0.00 (0.00, 0.11)	0.00 (0.00, 0.11)	0.00 (0.00, 0.13)	0.00 (0.00, 0.11)	0.00 (0.00, 0.10)	<0.001
G_minus_PK_Per	0.00 (0.00, 0.13)	0.00 (0.00, 0.13)	0.00 (0.00, 0.16)	0.00 (0.00, 0.13)	0.00 (0.00, 0.13)	<0.001
xG_Expected	0.70 (0.10, 2.10)	0.50 (0.10, 1.70)	0.60 (0.10, 2.00)	0.50 (0.10, 1.70)	0.60 (0.10, 1.80)	<0.001
Unknown	1	4	0	6	3	
npxG_Expected	0.80 (0.10, 1.90)	0.50 (0.10, 1.60)	0.60 (0.10, 1.90)	0.50 (0.10, 1.70)	0.60 (0.10, 1.70)	<0.001
Unknown	1	4	0	6	3	
xAG_Expected	0.60 (0.10, 1.70)	0.40 (0.00, 1.40)	0.50 (0.10, 1.60)	0.40 (0.00, 1.50)	0.40 (0.10, 1.50)	<0.001
Unknown	1	4	0	6	3	
xAG_Per	0.06 (0.01, 0.13)	0.05 (0.01, 0.13)	0.06 (0.01, 0.14)	0.06 (0.01, 0.13)	0.05 (0.01, 0.12)	0.005
Unknown	1	4	0	6	3	
npxG_Per	0.06 (0.02, 0.17)	0.06 (0.01, 0.16)	0.07 (0.02, 0.19)	0.06 (0.02, 0.16)	0.06 (0.02, 0.16)	0.038
Unknown	1	4	0	6	3	
player_market_value_mills_euro	10 (4, 22)	4 (2, 8)	4 (2, 11)	4 (2, 10)	4 (2, 10)	<0.001
Unknown	41	49	11	32	29	

[1]Median (IQR); n (%)

[2]Kruskal-Wallis rank sum test; Pearson's Chi-squared test

This analysis serves as a valuable foundation for future research, allowing to delve deeper into the factors contributing to these performance disparities and exploring potential strategies for improving player performance and development on an international scale.

This section highlights the significance of findings and the implications they hold for the field of football analysis, emphasizing the importance of considering both variables and the unique characteristics of different countries in assessing player performance.

4 Conclusions and Future Directions

While this analysis provides valuable insights into football player performance and international differences, there are several potential directions for future research in this field. These avenues of investigation can further enhance understanding of football and contribute to the development of evidence-based strategies for player development, team management, and talent scouting:

a) Expanding the Dataset: This study focused on five major football nations, but there are numerous other countries with vibrant football scenes. Expanding the dataset to include additional countries and leagues would provide a more comprehensive view of global football performance.

b) Longitudinal Analysis: Conducting a longitudinal analysis that spans multiple seasons or years would enable researchers to assess player development and performance trends over time. This could help identify players with consistent performance and those with potential for improvement.

c) Socio-Economic Factors: Investigating the impact of socio-economic factors on player performance and market value is essential. Factors such as a player's background, access to resources, and the development infrastructure in their home country can significantly influence their journey in professional football.

d) Machine Learning Models: The utilization of machine learning models for predictive analysis could enhance the accuracy of player market value predictions. These models could take into account a broader range of variables and provide more nuanced insights [4].

e) Injury Analysis: Exploring the relationship between injuries and player performance is crucial. Conducting a detailed analysis of how injuries affect a player's market value and career trajectory would be valuable for teams and medical staff.

f) Global Transfer Market Trends: Analyzing trends in the global transfer market, including the impact of transfer fees, agent involvement, and other financial factors, would provide a broader perspective on player valuation.

g) Fan Engagement and Marketing: Studying how player performance and market value correlate with fan engagement and marketing potential could help clubs make strategic decisions.

h) Data Privacy and Ethics: With the increasing reliance on player data, it is crucial to explore the ethical implications and privacy concerns related to data collection and analysis in professional football.

In conclusion, the combination of data analysis tools like the WorldfootballR package and rigorous statistical methods opens up numerous opportunities for in-depth research in the field of football. By addressing these future directions, researchers can contribute to the ongoing evolution of football analytics and decision-making in the sport.

5 Limitations

Although this study has yielded several significant conclusions, it is important to be aware of its limitations:

Data Limitations: The quality of the data used in the study depends on the available sources and their accuracy. Some data may be incomplete or contain errors.

Variable Limitations: The selection of variables for analysis was based on the study's objectives. Other relevant variables may not have been included.

Statistical Limitations: While we conducted statistical tests to assess the significance of differences, we could not establish causality. Other factors may influence the observed results.

In conclusion, this study provides an initial insight into the performance of football players and the factors that may influence it. There are many future research directions, and we must be aware of the current limitations of the analysis. Further research and consideration of more complex factors could lead to a more detailed understanding of this fascinating world of football.

Acknowledgment. This paper is partially supported by the Competitiveness Operational Programme Romania under project number SMIS 124759 – RaaS-IS (Research as a Service Iasi).

References

1. Agresti, A.: Categorical Data Analysis, vol. 792. John Wiley & Sons (2012)
2. Baumer, B.S., Matthews, G.J., Nguyen, Q.: Big ideas in sports analytics and statistical tools for their investigation. WIREs Comput. Stat. **15**, e1612 (2023). https://doi.org/10.1002/wics.1612
3. Cavus, M., Biecek, P.: Explainable expected goal models for performance analysis in football analytics. In: 2022 IEEE 9th International Conference on Data Science and Advanced Analytics (DSAA), pp. 1–9. IEEE (2022)
4. Cran Task View: Machine Learning & Statistical Learning. https://cloud.r-project.org/web/views/MachineLearning.html (2023)
5. Dobson, S., Goddard, J.A., Dobson, S.: The Economics of Football, vol. 10. Cambridge University Press, Cambridge (2001)
6. Cran, : EUfootball: Football Match Data of European Leagues. https://cloud.r-project.org/web/packages/EUfootball/index.html. (2022)
7. Gruber, J.: Football Penalty Kick Success Factors. Doctoral dissertation, University of Innsbruck (2023)
8. Kamel, D., Woo-Mora, L.G.: Skin Tone Penalties: Bottom-up Discrimination in Football (2023). SSRN 4537612
9. Kulikova, L.I., Goshunova, A.V.: Measuring efficiency of professional football club in contemporary researches. World Appl. Sci. J. **25**(2), 247–257 (2013)
10. Miller, T.A., White, E.D., Kinley, K.A., Congleton, J.J., Clark, M.J.: The effects of training history, player position, and body composition on exercise performance in collegiate football players. J. Strength Conditioning Res. **16**(1), 44–49 (2002)
11. Peček, U.: Mera pričakovanih zadetkov v nogometu in njena uporaba (Doctoral dissertation, Univerza v Ljubljani, Fakulteta za elektrotehniko) (2022)
12. Putatunda, S., Ubrangala, D., Rama, K., Kondapalli, R.: SmartEDA: An R package for automated exploratory data analysis. J. Open Sour. Softw. **4**(41), 1509 (2019). https://doi.org/10.21105/joss.01509
13. Sarmento, H., Clemente, F.M., Araújo, D., Davids, K., McRobert, A., Figueiredo, A.: What performance analysts need to know about research trends in association football (2012–2016): a systematic review. Sports Med. **48**, 799–836 (2018)
14. Tukey, J.W.: Exploratory Data Analysis. Addison-Wesley, Reading, MA (1977)
15. worldfootballR: Extract and Clean World Football (Soccer) Data. https://cran.r-project.org/web/packages/worldfootballR/index.html (2022)

Decision Making Process for a Sustainable Horticulture Using AI

Costin Lianu[1], Cezar Braicu[2], and Radu Bucea-Manea-Tonis[2(✉)]

[1] Spiru Haret University, Bucharest, Romania
[2] Hyperion University, Bucharest, Romania
radub_m@yahoo.com

Abstract. This study examines the benefits and uses of Industry 4.0 technologies in horticulture for real-time monitoring of fruit and vegetable conditions for growth and disease estimation. The study also addresses the challenges faced in horticulture and provides recommendations for the widespread adoption of AI-based IoT systems and blockchain supply chain integration. The methodology used in the study combines computer vision with distributed deep learning techniques in order to identify fruits and vegetables by their shape. Finally, the study identifies limitations and provides recommendations for future work.

Keywords: IoT (Internet of Things) · blockchain · object detection · region convolutional neural network (R-CNN)

1 Introduction

In order to produce effectively and sustainably, traditional horticultural methods frequently neglect to properly monitor pest control, water management, soil management, light control, and temperature control. Cybersecurity, blockchain, robotics, digital twins, Internet of Things, and big data integration are examples of Industry 4.0 technology that has shown its worth in a variety of situations. Studying the value of horticultural Industry 4.0 technologies for sustainability is crucial. These technologies can improve conventional methods for identifying maturity, managing irrigation, managing fertilizer, detecting diseases, marketing, supply chain, soil fertility, and weather patterns at the pre-, harvest, and post-harvest stages. Industrial agriculture could advance into a new era with the use of Industry 4.0 technology in horticulture, which would allow for automated and more ecologically friendly processes.

Farmers face a variety of obstacles such as issues with seeds, controlling pests, the fluctuating prices of commodities, and product marketing. However, with the help of the internet and mobile cloud, farmers can access valuable information and participate in interactive vegetable production processes. It is essential to collect ecological statistical data on vegetable-growing regions and identify the key factors that promote pest spread. By utilizing this data, a nutrition-based system for the production and distribution of vegetables could be developed, providing predictions and recommendations for nutritious foods. The IoT (Internet of Things) can be utilized to monitor diseases and pests,

K. S. Soliman (Ed.): IBIMA-AI 2024, CCIS 2299, pp. 42–48, 2025.
https://doi.org/10.1007/978-3-031-77493-5_4

minimizing the use of pesticides and fungicides, and forecasting pest appearance by identifying damaged fruits and vegetables based on their color, shape, and texture.

2 Literature Review

Two billion children have delayed development as a result of malnutrition, according to reports from the Food and Agriculture Organization and the World Health Organization, which claims 45 million under-five deaths annually. Addressing food insecurity and malnutrition resulting from extreme weather conditions and economic disruptions is imperative in order to counteract this. One way to obtain healthy micronutrients is through horticulture, which is the sustainable farming of fruits and vegetables. India is the second-largest producer of fruits and vegetables in the world. It is fostering the growth of holistic horticulture by employing techniques like marketing, post-harvest management, research, and advertising, mentioned Keatings et al. (2018). But it's difficult to meet demand using sustainable methods and the least amount of resources possible. Fruits and vegetables' short shelf-life following plucking is the primary challenge, according to [7].

Significant obstacles that the horticultural industry must overcome include diminishing fertile soil, rising land prices, water scarcity, and a lack of cheap labor. Significant challenges are also presented by abiotic stressors such as drought, salinity, pH, temperature extremes, and flooding. Using sustainable pest-management techniques is essential to warding off infections and pest resistance. [3] observed the absence of markets, intermediaries, marketing organizations, faulty pricing, and a lack of transparency in market-information systems, especially in export markets, are examples of marketing issues.

Romanian company Inter-Bio (https://inter-bio.ro) promotes agri-ecology and organic agri-food goods. Improved research, innovation, and development potential; integration of organic farming into other bio-economy branches; support for value chain manufacturers, processors, and traders; economic competitiveness; exports and internationalization; professional training; participation in national and European networks; and increased public and consumer awareness of the advantages of organic farming are just a few of the outcomes it fosters. [1] mentioned organic farming offers a number of noteworthy benefits, including: fields farmed organically have approximately 30% more biodiversity; animals raised organically have better welfare and use fewer antibiotics; organic farmers become more resilient and profitable; and consumers know exactly what they are getting.

In horticulture settings, robotics, drones with vision technology and AI for the detection of pests, weeds, plant diseases, and malnutrition, edge-computing portable devices developed with IoT and AI for predicting and estimating crop disease are all vital recommendations made by [18].

[19] observed the next principles of sustainable agriculture:

1. Farm productivity is enhanced over the long term;
2. Adverse impacts on the natural resource base and associated ecosystems are ameliorated, minimized or avoided;
3. Residues resulting from the use of chemicals in agriculture are minimized;

4. Net social benefit (in both monetary and non-monetary terms) from agriculture is maximized;
5. Farming systems are sufficiently flexible to manage risks associated with the vagaries of climate and markets.

[9] noticed water scarcity, among other factors like limited access to land, climate change, poorly developed markets for small community sectors, funding constraints, crime (including theft of farm equipment and produce), and low literacy rates, increase the necessity for a sustainable agriculture, food security, and income generation.

Decisions made by farmers today are based on data. Every farm gathers an increasing amount of data points over the course of the year. It can be intimidating to go over all of that information, and if the data starts to prevent you from making decisions that are clear, it can cause decision paralysis. Users can access their maps and data from any device, anywhere using cloud-based platforms such as AgFiniti (https://portal.agleader.com).

3   Blockchain in Horticulture

[10] noticed disease detection, crop grading, and quality assessment are made possible in horticulture by AI. Features are selected and extracted using methods such as gray-level co-occurrence matrix, competitive adaptive weighted sampling, random forest, and linear discriminant analysis. Over the past two decades, research on hyperspectral imaging as advanced, and it is imperative that the world's population continues to grow by means of fresh, healthy food. Applications for artificial intelligence (AI) in horticulture include yield prediction, fruit identification, disease, pest, and weed detection as well as the identification of plant stress.

AI has drawn attention for producing better-dried fruits and vegetables during the drying process. If a climacteric fruit has been artificially ripened, it can be detected by an Internet of Things device. AI-driven Internet of Things systems have the ability to modify indoor environmental parameters in response to external weather and travel duration, thereby preventing fruit and vegetable deterioration. Computer vision techniques can recognize fruits that have been impacted by pests or diseases and provide information for prompt diagnosis and treatment. Monitoring soil organic carbon (SOC) is essential to the sustainable management of soil nutrients mentioned [5]. SOC prediction can be enhanced by random forests, multiple linear regression, cubist regression, support vector machines, and artificial neural networks.

Reducing supply chain losses and increasing yields are two ways that blockchain can enhance pre- and post-harvest management observed [2]. For horticulture to overcome obstacles and boost overall efficiency, big data and AI are essential. The allocation of resources in the fresh fruit supply chain could be tackled by distributed-ledger technology, such as blockchain. Blockchain technology represents one potential means of achieving supply-chain traceability in the pineapple sector. Similar to assuming an honest majority of computer power, the fruit-chain protocol introduced by blockchain is fairly likely and has consistency and liveliness, mentioned [14].

To gain more knowledge about blockchain technology and its possible uses in the retail sector was the aim of this study. When it comes to fruit and the relationships between these factors, blockchain technology is essential. Blockchain makes it possible for various supply chain participants to monitor and track activities in real time from any location in the horticultural industry through a distributed network. Through the use of smart contracts between entities, it facilitates safe and digital trade, observed [13]. According to [8], Blockchain also makes it possible to conduct safe export transactions for produce on the global market.

The increasing number of food disasters around the world that are leading to health insecurity is causing consumers to drive a change in the way that food is purchased. Customers have demanded accountability, traceability, and openness throughout the whole fruit supply chain. Because the products in this industry are perishable and have a short shelf life, the supply chain is even more crucial. Yields are impacted by inconsistent delivery and a lack of fertilizers and insecticides due to dependence on middlemen, market instability, and other factors, observed [16].

The fruit supply chain can streamline post-harvest and inventory management through blockchain integration, which improves operational efficiency and reduces losses. End-to-end traceability using QR codes on fruits gives the final consumer an accurate and trustworthy story. By uniting and working together on a single platform, all parties involved can guarantee a fair price for producers while also promoting transparency and confidence. [4] mentioned simple tracking and tracing are made possible by real-time data collection, and this aids in recall management. Blockchain is also utilized for digital records that are unchangeable and accurately display information to comply with legal requirements, post-harvest management to minimize losses and increase output, and pre-harvest monitoring to ensure yield and quality according to [12].

4   Methodology

The integration of computer-vision methods with an autonomous robotic system that employs deep learning principles can decrease food waste, predict the frequency of food degradation, and evaluate the freshness of food. Robots with vision-based hardware are capable of intelligent spraying, price forecasting, crop yield prediction, predictive insights, and disease diagnosis. A computer vision technique for locating and categorizing objects in an image or video stream is called object detection. There are numerous TensorFlow (TF) models available for image classification and object detection. These models, which are based on computer vision, are used to identify and categorize objects in preexisting photos or videos. Object recognition in images and live videos is a fundamental feature and the foundation of AR, VR, XR, and related platforms.

It is possible to use the C# programming language to develop applications for identifying fresh and safe-to-eat vegetables based on object detection. The pre-trained model we have used is the Faster R-CNN with Inception ResNet V2 architecture trained on COCO, a large-scale object detection, segmentation, and captioning dataset. Outperforming its predecessors in terms of performance speed, the Faster R-CNN model is among the best in the R-CNN family. Faster R-CNN is an object detection model that improves on Fast R-CNN by using a region proposal network (RPN) that shares the convolutional features of the full-image with the detection network, observed [15]. The RPN predicts object bounds and scores simultaneously at each position and generates high-quality region proposals. These proposals are employed by Fast R-CNN for detecting the objects, and the RPN and Fast R-CNN unite into a single network, according to the same author.

In order to use.Net libraries, we decided to convert the TF model to ONNX format, following the Open Neural Network Exchange documentation, using the ***python -m tf2onnx.convert --saved-model C:\\models\\ --output model.onnx*** command and referencing the project from [6]. The result of converting the image might just been seen in Fig. 1:

Fig. 1. Before and after image conversion result

The oranges and grapes achieved the highest predicted values, with scores of 0.9467 and 0.9347, respectively. The final entry assigns the lowest score to 'apple' in the bottom-right corner of the image, with a confidence of 0.5487, which is nearly half that of the initial matches. This is understandable as it resembles a tomato to the trained human eye. For further details, please see Table 1.

Table 1. Detected objects imported from JSON file

Name	Value	Name	Value	Name	Value	Name	Value
Id	0	Id	1	Id	2	Id	3
Label	orange	Label	grape	Label	apple	Label	apple
XStart	417	XStart	590	XStart	192	XStart	978
YStart	2	YStart	13	YStart	58	YStart	543
XEnd	719	XEnd	1275	XEnd	511	XEnd	1193
YEnd	208	YEnd	815	YEnd	365	YEnd	657
Score	0.94672763	Score	0.934712	Score	0.627886	Score	0.548787

Distributed deep learning proves to be particularly beneficial when handling large-scale datasets or models that require intensive computation, according to [20]. This source also suggests that distributed training can provide additional benefits such as enhanced training speed and better scalability. [17] notes that the limitations of Faster R-CNN include significant delays in object proposal, challenges in achieving real-time performance due to its complexity, and the necessity for powerful hardware resources, particularly during the training phase. It is crucial to consider that the implementation specifics of object detection applications can differ based on the scanning device used, the framework selected, and the unique requirements of the application.

5 Discussion

In summary, the outcome demonstrates how to utilize a pre-trained model with TF to detect objects in an image. Developing an efficient object detection system requires a methodical approach. To begin, the dataset should comprise a diverse range of fruits or vegetables captured in various lighting conditions, backgrounds, and orientations. A suitable object detection model, such as Faster R-CNN, YOLO, SSD, or RetinaNet, which are frequently pre-trained on large datasets like COCO or ImageNet, can facilitate transfer learning. It is essential to evaluate the trained model's performance on a separate validation dataset to assess accuracy, precision, recall, and other relevant metrics. Fine-tuning the model and adjusting the hyperparameters can also enhance its effectiveness. Additionally, post-processing techniques, such as non-maximum suppression (NMS), can eliminate redundant or overlapping bounding boxes and improve the final detection results. By following these steps, a highly efficient object detection system can be developed with confidence.

References

1. Adamchak, R.: 'Organic farming', Encyclopedia Britannica, https://www.britannica.com/topic/organic-farming (2024). Retrieved on 27 Mar 2024
2. Beck, J., Birkel, H., Spieske, A., Gebhardt, M.: Will the blockchain solve the supply chain resilience challenges? Insights from a systematic literature review. Comput. Ind. Eng. **185**, 109623 (2023). https://doi.org/10.1016/j.cie.2023.109623
3. Bergemann, D., Ottaviani, M.: Information Markets and Nonmarkets. In: Handbook of Industrial Organization, vol. 4, pp. 593–672. Elsevier (2021). https://doi.org/10.1016/bs.hesind.2021.11.008
4. Chan, K.K.: Chapter 10 – Supply chain traceability systems—robust approaches for the digital age. In: MacCarthy, B.L., Ivanov, D. (eds.) The Digital Supply Chain, pp. 163–179. Elsevier (2022). https://doi.org/10.1016/B978-0-323-91614-1.00010-1
5. Das, S., Ghimire, D.: Soil organic carbon: measurement and monitoring using remote sensing data. In: Dharumarajan, S., Kaliraj, S., Adhikari, K., Lalitha, M., Kumar, N. (eds.) Remote Sensing of Soils, pp. 395–409. Elsevier (2024). https://doi.org/10.1016/B978-0-443-18773-5.00024-7
6. Dirt, L.: Example of how to consume a TensorFlow ONNX model and use it in ML .NET. GitHub (2022). https://github.com/lanedirt/ml.net-onnx-inference-rsa
7. El-Ramady, H.R., Domokos-Szabolcsy, É., Abdalla, N.A., Taha, H.S., Fári, M.: Postharvest management of fruits and vegetables storage. In: Lichtfouse, E. (ed.) Sustainable Agriculture Reviews: Volume 15, pp. 65–152. Springer International Publishing, Cham (2015). https://doi.org/10.1007/978-3-319-09132-7_2
8. Ganne, E.: Blockchain's practical and legal implications for global trade and global trade law. In: Burri, M. (ed.) Big Data and Global Trade Law, Cambridge University Press, pp. 128–159 (2021)

9. Ingrao, C., Strippoli, R., Lagioia, G., Huisingh, D.: Water scarcity in agriculture: an overview of causes, impacts and approaches for reducing the risks. Heliyon **9**(8), e18507 (2023). https://doi.org/10.1016/j.heliyon.2023.e18507

10. Manowarul Islam, M., et al.: DeepCrop: deep learning-based crop disease prediction with web application. J. Agric. Food Res. **14**, 100764 (2023). https://doi.org/10.1016/j.jafr.2023.100764

11. Keatinge, J.D.H., Virchow, D., Schreinemachers, P.: Horticulture for sustainable development: evidence for impact of international vegetable research and development. Acta Horticult. (2018). https://doi.org/10.17660/ActaHortic.2018.1205.20

12. Kumar, K.P., Murthy, H., Pillai, V.J., Prathap, B.R.: Blockchain-enabled model for minimizing post harvest losses. ECS Trans. **107**(1), 17475–17482 (2022). https://doi.org/10.1149/10701.17475ecst

13. Ante, L.: Smart contracts on the blockchain – A bibliometric analysis and review. Telematics Inform. **57**, 101519 (2021). https://doi.org/10.1016/j.tele.2020.101519

14. Pass, R., Shi, E.: FruitChains: a fair blockchain. In: The ACM Symposium, pp. 315–324 (2017). https://doi.org/10.1145/3087801.3087809

15. Ren, S., He, K., Girshick, R., Sun, J.: 'Faster R-CNN: towards real-time object detection with region proposal networks. In: Computer Visual Pattern Recognition – Cornell Univ. (2016). https://doi.org/10.48550/arXiv.1506.01497. Retrieved on 12 May 2024

16. Saliu, F., Luqman, M., AlKhaza'leh, H.: A review on the impact of sustainable agriculture practices on crop yields and soil health. Int. J. Inf. Technol. **2**, 1–13 (2023)

17. Santos, L.A.: Artificial Inteligence. GitBook. https://leonardoaraujosantos.gitbook.io/artificial-inteligence/machine_learning/deep_learning/object_localization_and_detection#faster-rcnn (2020). Retrieved on 10 Apr 2024

18. Singh, R., Singh, R., Gehlot, A., Akram, S.V., Priyadarshi, N., Twala, B.: Horticulture 4.0: adoption of industry 4.0 technologies in horticulture for meeting sustainable farming. Appl. Sci. **12**(24), 12557 (2022). https://doi.org/10.3390/app12241255

19. Trigo, A., Marta-Costa, A., Fragoso, R.: Principles of sustainable agriculture: defining standardized reference points. Sustainability **13**(8), 4086 (2021). https://doi.org/10.3390/su13084086

20. W3.: Deep Learning in C#: Using TensorFlow.NET for Neural Networks. Programming languages (2024). https://www.w3computing.com/articles/deep-learning-csharp-tensorflow-neural-networks/. Retrieved at 14 May 2024

Drug Delivery System – The Construction and Use of the Graphical Interface in Modeling the Controlled Release of Drugs in the Human Body

Olga Malolepsza[1](✉) and Katarzyna Kazimierska-Drobny[2]

[1] Faculty of Computer Science, Kazimierz Wielki University, 85-064 Bydgoszcz, Poland
olga.malolepsza@ukw.edu.pl
[2] Faculty of Mechatronics, Kazimierz Wielki University, 85-064 Bydgoszcz, Poland
kkd@ukw.edu.pl

Abstract. Drug delivery becomes more specific from systemic to organ and cellular targeting. Traditional delivery systems are characterized by immediate and uncontrolled drug release kinetic. Concurrent controlled release systems allow for drug concentration in the blood or target tissues maintained at the desired value as long as possible. The main purpose of the work is (i) a review of the available mathematical models of controlled drug release and then (ii) their implementation in the form of a simple and user-friendly interface. Novelty and contribution lies in combining different models into one coherent system and switching them in a way that makes it easier to compare and choose the best one. The construction of a graphical interface solving the subject of this work, to-gether with the use of models of controlled drug release in the body, helped to understand the mathematical modeling of controlled drug release in the body. This allowed analyzing the drug release process in more detail.

Keywords: computer science · mechatronics · automation · eHealth · drug release · computational model

1 Introduction

In the last 100 years, drug delivery systems have enormously increased their performances, moving from simple pills to sustained/controlled release and sophisticated programmable delivery systems. Meanwhile, drug delivery has also become more specific from systemic to organ and cellular targeting. The method by which a drug is delivered can have a significant effect on its efficacy. Some drugs have an optimum benefit is derived, and a concentration range within which maximum benefit is derived, and concentration above or below this range can be toxic or produce no therapeutic benefit at all. Traditional delivery systems (TDS) are characterized by immediate and uncontrolled drug release kinetic. As a consequence, it may happen that drug concentration dangerously approaches the toxic threshold to subsequently fall below the effective therapeutic

K. S. Soliman (Ed.): IBIMA-AI 2024, CCIS 2299, pp. 49–62, 2025.
https://doi.org/10.1007/978-3-031-77493-5_5

level. Administration of drugs from therapeutic systems with controlled release brings many benefits to the patient. Adjusting the therapy that allows to stay within the therapeutic window all the time and reducing the dosage of the drug translates into the relief of the patient's difficulties associated with taking drugs in the form of injections. Very often it is possible to introduce the drug in such carriers that reach the site of the disease and release the drug locally. In a controlled release system (CRS), also referred to in the literature as a drug delivery system (DDS) the drug concentration in the blood or target tissues is maintained at the desired value as long as possible. In CRS it is possible to control the drug release and duration. For this purpose, the use of mathematical modeling turns out to be very useful as this approach enables, in the best case, the prediction of CRS release kinetics before the release systems are realized. More often, it allows the measurement of some important physical parameters, such as the drug diffusion coefficient, resorting to model fitting on experimental release data. Thus, mathematical modeling, whose development required the comprehension of all the phenomena affecting drug release kinetics, has a very important value in CRS/DDS optimization. There are very different kinds of CRS and drug release kinetics may be affected by many factors such as polymer swelling, polymer erosion, drug dissolution/diffusion characteristics, drug distribution inside the matrix, drug/polymer ratio, and system geometry (cylinder, sphere and so on). Various mathematical theories have been reported in the literature, quantifying the occurring mass transport phenomena in different types of controlled drug delivery systems. These theories can be classified according to the physicochemical phenomena. Roughly, models considered diffusion, swelling, and/or dissolution/erosion can be distinguished. However, in many cases two different mechanisms have to be considered simultaneously. The crucial point for the predictive power of these theories is the adequate consideration of all physicochemical phenomena. Due to the complexity of the phenomena, numerous coupled effects, and often the lack of precise physicochemical data characterizing a specific drug release system, a comprehensive analysis of all factors affecting the dynamics of the drug release process is often impossible. Nevertheless, even simplified mathematical models make it possible to estimate temporal changes in the concentration of the drug released in the material, and in the case of more complex models, also spatial changes in concentration. This makes it possible to trace drug transport, identify mechanisms limiting the rate of release, and then postulate changes necessary to optimize this process. To wish to present new and promising techniques for the production of drug and protein delivery formulation that has been developed in laboratories but also with cooperation with engineers and programmers in computing centers.

The main purpose of the work is (i) a review of the available mathematical models of controlled drug release and then (ii) the implementation of these models in the Matlab computing environment in the form of a simple and user-friendly interface. It creates a graphical form of desktop view presentation, with menus and icons that illustrate objects and commands that can be executed by the recipient. The undoubted benefits of therapy based on controlled drug release systems and significant progress in the field of information technology have prompted researchers to reach for the possibilities of designing and optimizing materials used in such systems using computer methods (in silico). Based on the performed simulations, using an interface with built-in solutions of mathematical models of controlled drug release, it is possible to control the release rate and profile by changing the parameters in the model. In addition, the interface allows you to perform parametric analysis, also known as sensitivity analysis. Parametric analysis of the material in terms of geometry, initial drug concentration, as well as transport coefficients in specific tissues, allows for the optimization of the material for a specific application. Predicting the release rate of the active substance from drug delivery systems saves costs and time for experiments. Novelty and contribution lies in combining different models into one coherent system and switching them in a way that makes it easier to compare and choose the best one.

2   Materials and Methods

Mathematical and computational modeling can provide a better understanding of the influence of different design parameters, which may then either be used to reduce the number of experiments or more ambitiously, as a predictive screening tool for drug carriers. Generally, diffusion in tables, taking into consideration axial and radial transport, can be described as:

$$\frac{\partial c_k}{\partial t} = \frac{1}{r}\left\{\frac{\partial}{\partial r}\left(rD_k\frac{\partial c_k}{\partial r}\right) + \frac{\partial}{\partial \theta}\left(\frac{D_k}{r}\frac{\partial c_k}{\partial \theta}\right) + \frac{\partial}{\partial z}\left(rD_k\frac{\partial c_k}{\partial z}\right)\right\} \tag{1}$$

where c_k and D_k are the concentration and diffusion coefficient of the diffusing species ($k = 1$ for water, $k = 2$ for the drug), respectively, r denotes the radial coordinates, z is the axial coordinate, θ the angular coordinate, and t represents time.

The partial differential Eq. (1) can be solved under various conditions, e.g. constant or non-constant diffusivities, and using stationary or moving boundary conditions. For the investigated controlled drug delivery systems, two cases are relevant: (i) constant diffusion coefficient and stationary boundary conditions; and (ii) non-constant diffusion coefficients and moving boundary conditions. The solutions are briefly presented.

In the alternative approach, the mathematical models are typically empirical or semi-empirical. Such models are also described as 0-dimensional-spatial models, as opposed to models described by partial differential equations (space-time models) called mechanistic models. The former usually results in relatively simple equations that facilitate use for experimental scientists. Since the pioneering work of Higuchi, many empirical and semi-empirical models have been developed through the decades. Empirical and semi-empirical models are the simplest and fastest approach to describe drug release. In most cases, they will not take into account the chemical and physical phenomena that take place during drug release. Empirical models are most often used when comparing release profiles for a single parameter, e.g. release rate constant. They can help determine the mechanism of release, but the ability to estimate the rate of release is relatively low. This chapter presents an overview of the most important zero-dimensional models, including empirical and semi-empirical ones, based on which the graphical interface for modeling the controlled release of drugs was built.

Zero-order release kinetics

In the simplest case, the drug release process can be described by zero-order kinetics. The mass released from the material M_t after time t, the zero-order k_t velocity constant, is given by the equation:

$$M_t = k_t \tag{2}$$

Application of the model: This model is used to describe the drugs dissolution of several types of modified pharmaceutical dosage forms, as in the case of some transdermal systems, as well as matrix tablets with low soluble drugs in coated forms, osmotic systems, etc. Moreover, zero-order oral drug release can be achieved by coating the tablet core. When the coating is permeable to both the active ingredient and water, upon ingestion the core becomes hydrated and the active ingredient dissolves until a saturation concentration or solubility is reached. The active substance is contained in a saturated reservoir and is released by partitioning from the reservoir into the membrane, diffusing through the membrane, and reaching the gastrointestinal fluid. The release rate constant is from core saturation, resulting in a stationary concentration gradient across the membrane. Membrane. When this concentration falls below the saturation level, the rate of drug release decreases to zero. Transdermal patches can be designed to release the active ingredient with zero-order kinetics. The drug reservoir can be constructed of a variety of materials ranging from mineral oil to complex formulations such as aqueous/alcohol gels. The reservoir system should provide zero-order drug release throughout the administration period, which requires the reservoir material to remain saturated with the drug throughout the life of the product. This can usually be achieved by formulating the drug as a suspension.

2.1 First-Order Release Kinetics

The release of a drug that followed first-order kinetics can be expressed by the equation:

$$\frac{dc}{dt} = -k \cdot c \tag{3}$$

where c is the drug concentration, the proportionality constant is the first-order velocity constant k

The modified equation of the first-order kinetics representing the fraction of the released mass is expressed by:

$$\frac{M_t}{M_\infty} = 1 - exp(-kt) \tag{4}$$

where M_t is the total mass of substance present in the material, M_∞ means the amount of drug at equilibrium.

Applicability of the model: The first-order kinetics equation can be used to describe the dissolution of drugs in pharmaceutical dosage forms, such as containing watersoluble drugs in porous matrices. This model is used to describe the absorption and/or elimination of various therapeutic agents. However, it is difficult to define first-order kinetics with basic theory. In this sense, first-order release kinetics states that the change in concentration concerning the change in time depends only on the substance.

2.2 Higuchi Model

The first example of a mathematical model aimed to describe drug release from a matrix system was proposed by Higuchi in 1963. This model applies to studying the release of water-soluble and low-soluble drugs incorporated in semisolid and solid matrices. Higuchi derived his equation for pseudo-steady-state conditions, which is true for systems containing a large excess of the drug. Later changes by Higuchi made it possible to calculate the released mass from other systems with different geometries. The drug mass released M_t at time t from the flat plate is given by the formula:

$$\frac{M_t}{A_t} = \sqrt{D(C_0 - C_s)C_s t} \tag{5}$$

where M_t is the cumulative mass of the released drug, A_t defines the contact surface of the material with the skin, C_0 is the initial drug concentration, C_s – is saturation concentration, and D means diffusion coefficient.

Applicability of the model: The Higuche model can be used to describe drug dissolution from several types of modified-release pharmaceutical forms, as in the case of some transdermal patches and matrix tablets with watersoluble drugs. A mathematical model to describe drug dissolution from matrix systems was developed only in the 1960s. From 1961 to 1963, there was tremendous progress in developing mathematical models to understand drug release. In 1961, Higuchi published probably the most famous and most widely used mathematical equation describing the rate of release of drugs from matrix systems. The subject of the study was the rate of drug release from ointment vehicles (planar systems) containing drugs in suspension. In 1962, the data on the release of the drug from the ointment was analyzed. Moreover, in 1963, a "long-acting drug mechanism" was proposed. Various model expressions can be found, among others, in works.

2.3 Peppas Model

In the literature, the Peppas model is known as the Ritger-Peppas model and the Korsmeyer-Pepppas model, or as the Power Law model. The model proposed by Peppas is the most commonly used. It presents the substance release equation, which is expressed by the formula:

$$\frac{M_t}{M_\infty} = kt^n \tag{6}$$

where M_t is the amount of drug released at time t, M_∞ means the amount of drug at equilibrium (sometimes very close to the amount of drug contained in the dose form at the beginning of the release process), and t is time. The values of the exponent n may vary depending on the geometry of the carrier as well as the release mechanism. Moreover, the parameter k is a constant relating to the structure of the drug-containing carrier. The values of the exponent n are shown in.

Applicability of the model: The Peppas model is typically used to analyze the dissolution of pharmaceutical polymer dosage forms where the release mechanism is not well known or where more than one type of release phenomenon may be involved. This model was developed specifically for the release of drug molecules from a polymer matrix such as a hydrogel. Over the past few decades, many scientists have modified the form of this equation. For HPMC-based systems, it should be noted that the use of exponentiation can only give limited insight into the exact mechanism of drug release. Even if exponent n values were found that would indicate a diffusion-controlled drug release mechanism, this is not automatically valid for HPMC. As with the Higuchi equation, the information obtained should be treated with caution. However, the power law is already more comprehensive than the Higuchi equation. A modification of the Peppas model is the Peppas-Sahlin model described in the papers.

2.4 Hopfenberg Model

Many modifications were made based on the above-mentioned models, including the Hopfenberg model. Hopfenberg developed a mathematical model to correlate drug release from polymers that erode on the surface of the polymers as long as the surface remains solid during the degradation process. This can be described with an equation:

$$\frac{M_t}{M_\infty} = 1 - \left[1 - \frac{k_0 t}{C_L}a\right]^n \tag{7}$$

where M_t is the amount of drug released in time t, M_∞ is the amount of drug released in infinite time, $\frac{M_t}{M_\infty}$ defines the fraction of dissolved drug, k_0 means zero order rate constant describing the polymer degradation process, C_L is initial drug charge in the system, a – half-thickness of the system, n – carrier geometry and t means the time during which the drug is released.

Applicability of the model: The Hopfenberg model is used to identify the release mechanism from optimized oleo spheres based on data obtained from a composite profile that generally exhibits site-specific biphasic release kinetics. This is a model used to explain drug release from erodible polymers with different geometrical forms. Hopfenberg proposed a series of equations to describe drug release from planar, spherical, or cylindrical films with heterogeneous erosion.

2.5 Gompertz Model

The in vitro dissolution profile is often described by a simpler exponential model known as the Gompertz model, expressed by equation:

$$X(t) = X_{max}exp\left[-\alpha e^{\beta logt}\right] \tag{8}$$

where X(t) is the percentage of dissolved solution in time t divided by 100, X_{max} – maximum dissolution, α defines the undissolved part at time $t = 1$, described as a location or scale parameter, β is dissolution rate per unit time, defined as the shape parameter.

Applicability of the model: The Gompertz model is useful for comparing the dissolution profiles of drugs having good solubility and an average release rate.

2.6   Baker-Lonsdale Model

Baker and Lonsdale, inspired by the Higuchi model, created a drug release model, which is described by the following formula:

$$\frac{3}{2}\left[1 - (1 - \frac{M_t}{M_\infty})^{2/3}\right]\frac{M_t}{M_\infty} = k_t \tag{9}$$

where the release rate constant k_t, corresponds to the slope. M_t and M_∞ is the amount of drug released in time t and in infinite time respectively.

Applicability of the model: This equation has been used to linearize the dissolution data from several microcapsules or microsphere formulations.

2.7   Hixson-Crowell Model

Hixson and Crowell noticed that the surface area of a regular molecule is proportional to the cube root of its volume. They derived equation:

$$\sqrt[3]{W_0} - \sqrt[3]{W_t} = \kappa t \tag{10}$$

where W_0 is the initial amount of the drug in the matrix; W_t defines the amount of drug released at time t; k is constant, which considers the relationship between surface and volume.

Applicability of the model: The Hixson-Crowell model is applied to pharmaceutical forms such as tablets where dissolution occurs in planes parallel to the drug surface if the dimensions of the tablet decrease proportionally such that the initial geometric form remains constant throughout.

2.8   Weibull Model

This model uses the Weibull distribution, which is described as an equation for various dissolution processes:

$$M = M_0\left[1 - e^{-\frac{(t-T)^b}{a}}\right] \tag{11}$$

where M is the amount of drug dissolved at time t and M_0 is the total amount of drug released, T defines the delay measured as a result of the dissolution process, a is a scale parameter describing the time dependence, and b describes the shape of the dissolution curve.

Applicability of the model: The Weibull model is more useful for comparing drug release profiles from the matrix.

Other models that can be found in the literature are Gallagher corrigan model, Conney model and Sequential layer model. Comparison of the results of experimental research with the presented mathematical models can be found, among others, in works.

2.9   Construction and Application of the User Interface for Mathematical Modeling of Controlled Release of Drugs

GUIDE (Graphical User Interface Development Environment) is an environment for creating user interfaces (UI) using the "drag and drop" method implemented in Matlab program. The interactive functions of the application are coded separately, in the Matlab editor. Applications created using GUIDE can display any type of Matlab chart. GUIDE also provides various interactive components, including menus, toolbars, and tables. It is run from Matlab by using the guide command. The GUIDE provides several templates that you can modify to create your user interfaces. Templates are fullfeatured applications. This tab contains a list of available templates. Codes for individual models were developed in Matlab based on formulas from the literature (see Sect. 2). The graphical interface contains the most important windows and functions for solving individual models of controlled drug release. Figure 1 presents a project of a graphical interface for modeling controlled drug release in the human body.

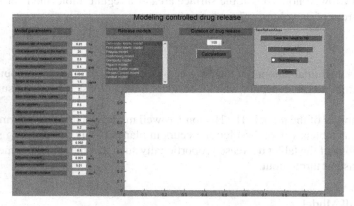

Fig. 1. Graphical interface for modeling controlled drug release in the human body.

The following controls were used to build the interface: StaticText (displaying text), Edit Text (editing text), ListBox (displaying a list of elements and allowing you to select a given element), Panel (arrangement of basic functions in one place), Push Button and Radio Button (buttons generating an action), Axes (axes for displaying charts). The graphical interface includes buttons such as Calculations (causes that a given release model, based on selected parameters, is presented in the form of a graph), Saving the result to the file (the button saves the result to the file, it is possible to select the extension), Refreshing (the button refreshes the chart so that the user does not have to restart the program), Overdraw (overdraws the charts), Close (the button closes the program). Below are examples of model solutions using the interface. Figure 2 shows the operation of the overdraw function and the simultaneous solution of three models, i.e. the zero-order kinetics model (solid line), the first-order kinetics model (dotted line) and the Peppas model (dashed line). The parameters of the model were set as follows: release rate constant k = 0.01 1/s, carrier geometry n = 0.5. The drug release duration was set to 100 s.

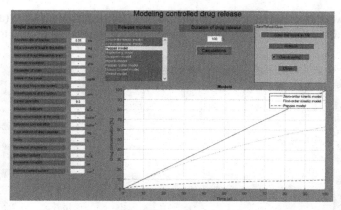

Fig. 2. Zero-order kinetics model, first-order kinetics model and Peppas model.

3 Results

In Fig. 3 the simulation of parametric analysis of the first-order kinetics model is presented in relation to first-order velocity constant k. The values of the k coefficient were assumed equal to 0.05, 0.01 and 0.002 1/s. The duration of the process is 300 s.

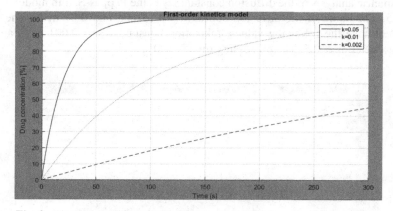

Fig. 3. Simulation of the effect of the constant k on the rate of drug release.

For the first-order kinetics equation, k called the reaction rate constant is the proportionality factor in the kinetic equation. This constant does not depend on the concentration of the released substance. It depends only on the reaction (it is a characteristic of the reaction) and on the temperature. Figure 3 shows that, as predicted by the model, as the kinetics constant k increases, the drug is released faster.

Parametric analysis of the Peppas model (Power low) is presented in Fig. 4. The simulation was carried out for a constant value of the coefficient k = 0.01 1/s. The influence of different geometry of the carrier was investigated. The following values of parameter n were assumed in the simulation: n = 0.5 (Fick diffusion), n = 0.8 (anomalous diffusion) and n = 1 (polymer swelling). The simulation time was assumed to be 300 s.

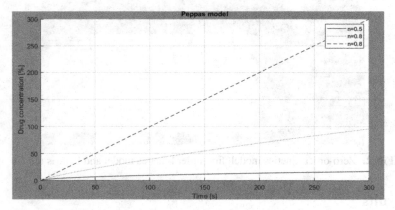

Fig. 4. Simulation of the influence of carrier geometry in the Peppas model.

The simulations presented in the Fig. 4, show that the smaller the carrier geometry, the longer the release of the substance takes place.

Parametric analysis of the diffusion constant K_1 in the Peppas-Sahlin model is show in Fig. 5. The value of the diffusion constant is 0.1, 0.05 and 0.01 m^2/s. The other parameters have the following values: relaxation constant $K_2 = 0.001$ m^2/s and the scale parameter m = 0.5. The processing time is 100 s.

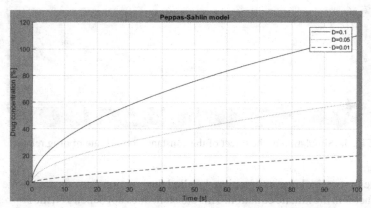

Fig. 5. Simulation of the effect of the diffusion constant K_1 on the rate of drug release in the Peppas-Sahlin model.

The simulations shows that the higher the diffusion constant, the faster the drug is released.

4 Discussion

The discussion of the results and their interpretation from the perspective of previous research and working hypotheses shows that they should be discussed in the broad context of further research and applications.

Controlled drug release in target tissues of the body can be improved through nanomedicine. The identified barriers to the development of the aforementioned group of models and technologies are disease- and therapy-related. The main challenge limiting the efficacy of the proposed approaches is affecting diseased/damaged cells while not damaging the healthy tissue surrounding the diseased site (so-called enhanced specific targeting). With the best design and modelling, drug uptake efficiency is up to 100% in diseased cells with up to 46% in healthy human cells. It is noteworthy that the effect on diseased cells is not immediate (it may be, for example, 52–77% 24 h after administration) and may show some selectivity towards diseased cells. Hence, the need to build whole biodegradable drug delivery systems to overcome a number of challenges and increase their efficacy and safety. It is also important to remember that functional, noncytotoxic, biocompatible and safe drugs for use in cells or small animals still need to be tested for future clinical applications in humans. Precise prolonged controlled release of drugs into tissue parts still remains a great challenge – this applies, for example, to ocular tissues and dedicated biodegradable intraocular implants. The use of, for example, an anterior epithelial polyurethane implant as a drug delivery system in uveitis is being used for this purpose. In it, a rapid initial release is followed by a prolonged controlled release with therapeutic effects, with the by-products of the release not being toxic to human cells.This approach may soon be leading the way in treatment of intraocular inflammation. Multichamber drug delivery systems are often based on the encapsulation of microspheres, e.g. starch microspheres with thermosensitive properties (with a lower critical solution temperature of about 36 degrees Celsius), capable of electrostatically binding drugs. A sharp phase transition around the temperature of the human body is realized while avoiding swelling and diffusion of the above-mentioned substances. Microspheres to an aqueous continuous phase due to the fact that the temperature of the aqueous phase is higher than the volumetric phase transition temperature of the microspheres. Such an implantable drug delivery system may be relevant to, for example, people in dangerous cold areas (travellers, pipeline builders, mountaineers) or working in cold stores. It starts to work when the employee's body temperature drops below the set threshold temperature (there is a health or life threat if there is no reaction). The microspheres then swell when in contact with bodily fluids and burst, releasing the drug and keeping vital organs active. The problem remains that most such microspheres used in controlled drug delivery (eg biocompatible and pH and/or temperature sensitive) are not biodegradable. However, there is more and more research on biodegradable natural polymers. With their phase transition temperature close to human body temperature, appropriate loading and release profiles within the molecular model become crucial.

4.1 Limitations of Current Research

The analysis so far has shown that the problem is the simultaneous fulfillment of many requirements and limitations, and at the same time the development of solutions dedicated to specific, very precise applications (e.g. application of drugs to the eyes). For this purpose, it is necessary to develop, check and select many computational models that reduce the costs of such research. The initial rejection of solutions that do not fit for some reason allows you to focus on the most valuable and promising concepts.

4.2 Directions for Further Studies

The development and first applications of nanocarriers for drug delivery and formulation set the following new directions for further research:

- modeling the delivery of diagnostic or therapeutic agents,
- new designs and routes of administration,
- stimuli-sensitive and/or temperature-sensitive nano-delivery systems,
- particle analysis and effect fluorograms,
- desirable features: high in vivo delivery capacity, good synergy with therapeutic agents,
- milder short- and long-term toxicological effects,
- development of preclinical and clinical trials,
- analysis of risks related to nano-delivery systems,
- avoidance of therapeutic side effects before clinical use.

The key task is to accelerate research procedures without compromising their quality and, consequently, to introduce proven solutions to clinical applications as soon as possible. The requirements are high: a coating process for fine particles, 100–500 μm and smaller in diameter, avoiding the use of liquid plasticisers, solvents, binders and heat treatment, amenable to controlled release, indeed with highly controlled processing intensity and time, amenable to computational modelling, including the effect of coating thickness. It is important to combine the analysis of dissolution-based systems with those based on diffusion, without necessarily being concerned with fixed values for dissolution rate and diffusion coefficient. This will allow a better estimate of the relative effects of dissolution and diffusion on the time it takes for drugs to reach therapeutic levels in the blood. Further development of the aforementioned group of models are individual, patient)tailored therapy models.

5 Conclusions

Medicine is an integral part of many people's lives. Therefore, it is important to know how drugs are released in the body and how to control drug release. Mathematical modeling allows visualization of the distribution of drug concentrations released in a controlled manner in the human body and supports the optimization of existing pharmaceutical products. The construction of a graphical interface solving the subject of this work, together with the use of models of controlled drug release in the body, helped to understand the mathematical modeling of controlled drug release in the body. This allowed analyzing the drug release process in more detail. The proposed model solutions are only successive stages in the entire drug release process. Working in this direction will bring another benefit. Mathematical models used during the simulation can facilitate the optimization of medicinal products. Based on the performed mathematical simulations of modeling the controlled release of the drug, it was found possible to control the release rate and profile by changing the parameters in the model. Choosing the right model for your application depends on various aspects. The most important consideration when developing new pharmaceutical products or elucidating drug release mechanisms is the desired predictive ability.

References

1. Ballet, T., Boulange, I., Brechet, Y., Bruckert, F., Weidenhaupt, M.W.: Protein conformational changes induced by adsorption onto material surfaces: an important issue for biomedical applications of material science. Bull. Polish Acad. Sci.: Tech. Sci. **58**(2), 303–315 (2010)
2. Barbosa Saliba, J., et al.: Anti-inflammatory effect of dex-amethasone controlled released from anterior suprachoroidal polyurethane implants on endotoxin-induced uveitis in rats. Invest. Ophthalmol. Vis. Sci. **57**(4), 1671–1679 (2016)
3. Bhagwat, R.R., Vaidhya, I.S.: Novel drug delivery systems: an overview. Int. J. Pharmaceut. Sci. Res. **4**(3), 970–982 (2013)
4. Bruschi: Strategies to Modify the Drug Release from Pharmaceutical Systems (2015)
5. Dash, S., Murthy, P.N., Nath, L., Chowdhury, P.: Kinetic modeling on drug release from controlled drug delivery systems. Acta Poloniae Pharmaceut. – Drug Res. **67**(3), 217 223 (2010)
6. Freire, M.C., et al.: Understanding drug release data through thermodynamic analysis. Materials **10**(6), 651 (2017)
7. Fundueanu, G.; Constantin, M.; Ascenzi, P.; Simionescu, B.C.: An Intelligent Multicompartmental System Based on Thermosensitive Starch Microspheres for Temperature-controlled Release of Drugs. *Biomed. Microdevices* 12, 4, 693-704 (2010)
8. Grassi, M., Grassi, G.: Mathematical modeling and controlled drug delivery: matrix systems. Curr. Drug Deliv. **2**, 97–116 (2005)
9. Guryev, E.L., et al.: Preclinical study of biofunctional polymer-coated upconversion nanoparticles. Toxicol. Sci. **170**(1), 123–132 (2019)
10. Higuchi, T.: Rate of release of medicaments from ointments bases containing drugs in suspension. J. Pharmaceut. Sci. **50**(874), 875 (1961)
11. Higuchi, T.: Mechanism of Sustained-actionmedication. J. Pharmaceut. Sci. (1963)
12. Higuchi, W.I.: Analysis of data on the medicament release from ointments. J. Pharmaceut. Sci. **51**(8), 802–804 (1962). https://doi.org/10.1002/jps.2600510825
13. Ishii, T., Sakurai, Y.: Challenges and new directions for next-generation drug delivery system (DDS) research based on nano-technology. Yakugaku Zasshi **132**(12), 1345–1346 (2012)
14. Jafari, M., Kaffashi, B.: Mathematical kinetic modeling on isoniazid release from Dex-HEMA-PNIPAAm nanogels. Nanomed. Res. J. **1**(2), 90–96 (2016)
15. Katzhendler, I., Hoffman, A., Goldberger, A., Friedman, M.: Modeling of drug release from erodible tablets. J. Pharmaceut. Sci. **86**(1), 110–115 (1997). https://doi.org/10.1021/js9600538
16. Lao, L.L., Peppas, N.A., Boey, F.Y.C., Venkatraman, S.S.: Modeling of drug release from bulk-degrading polymers. Int. J. Pharmaceut. **418**(1), 28–41 (2011)
17. Lou, X., Munro, S., Wang, S.: Drug Release characterictic of chase separation pHEMA sponge materials. Biomaterials **25**, 5071–5080 (2004)

18. Michalczuk, U., Przekop, R., Moskal, Ar.: The effect of selected nanoparticles on rheological properties of human blood. Bull. Polish Acad. Sci. Tech. Sci. **70**(1), e140437 (2022)
19. Muhammad Shoaib, M.H., et al.: Development and evaluation of hydrophilic collodi matrix of famotidine tablets. Pharm. Sci. Tech. **11**(2), 708–718 (2020)
20. Muresan, C.I., Birs, I.R., Folea, S., Ionescu, C.: Fractional order based velocity control system for a nanorobot in non-newtonian fluids. Bull. Polish Acad. Sci. Tech. Sci. **66**, 991–997 (2018)
21. Nakielski, P.: Systemy uwalniania leków oparte na nanowłóknach, Insytut Podstawowych Problemów Techniki, Polska Akademia Nauk (2015). (in polish)
22. Paarakh, M.P., Jose, P.A., Setty, C.M., Chrostoper, G.V.P.: Release kinetics – concept and application. Int. J. Pharmacy Res. Technol. **8**, 1–20 (2018)
23. Peppas, N.A., Bures, P., Leobandung, W., Ichikawa, H.: Hydrogels in pharmaceutical formulation. Eur. J. Pharm. Biopharm. **50**(1), 27–46 (2000)
24. Peppas, N.A., Narasimhan, B.: Mathematical models in drug delivery: how modeling has shaped the way we design new drug delivery systems. J. Control. Release **190**, 75–81 (2014)
25. Pontrelli, G., Toniolo, G., McGinty, S., Peri, D., Succi, S., Chatgilialoglu, C.: Mathematical modelling of drug delivery from ph-responsive nanocontainers. Comput. Biol. Med. **131**, 104238 (2021)
26. Ramteke, K.H., Dighe, P.A., Kharat, A.R., Patil, S.V.: Mathematical models of drug dissolution: a review. Scholars Acad. J. Pharm. **3**(5), 388–396 (2014)
27. Shamul, J.G., et al.: Verteporfin-loaded anisotropic poly(beta-amino ester)-based micelles demonstrate brain cancer-selective cyto-toxicity and enhanced pharmacokinetics. Int. J. Nanomed. **14**, 10047–10060 (2019)
28. Shubh Biyani, S.R., Moon, R.S., Gattani, S.G., Kothawade, S.A.: Formulation and evaluation of Cevimeline hydrochloride orally dissolving for Sjogrens syndrome by optimal design. World J. Pharmaceut. Med. Res. **5**(8), 166–178 (2019)
29. Siepmann, J., Peppas, N.A.: Modeling of drug release from delivery systems based on hydroxypropyl methylcellulose (HPMC). Adv. Drug Deliv. Rev. **64**, 163–174 (2012)
30. Siepmann, J., Streubel, A., Peppas, N.A.: Understanding and predicting drug delivery from hydrophilic matrix tablets using the "sequential layer" model. Pharm. Res. **19**(3), 306–314 (2002)
31. Walters, K.A., Brain, K.R.: Dermatological formulation and transdermal systems (2009)

Enabling German SMEs and Crafts Through Data-Driven Innovation: Developing a Scoring Model and Chronological Framework for Enhanced Decision-Makin

Alexander Eickelmann$^{(\boxtimes)}$, Thi Cam Van Tran, and Giuseppe Strina

University of Siegen, Siegen, Germany
alexander.eickelmann@uni-siegen.de,
cam.tranthi@student.uni-siegen.de, strina@wiwi.uni-siegen.de

Abstract. This research examines the adoption of data-driven strategies within German Small and Medium-sized Enterprises (SMEs) and crafts, a sector that remains underexplored despite its substantial economic presence. While large corporations have capitalized on the benefits of Artificial Intelligence, Machine Learning, and Big Data, this study addresses the critical question of whether similar data-driven approaches can be effectively implemented in smaller organizations. Our research aims to bridge the existing gap in literature by focusing on the specific challenges and opportunities that German SMEs face in transitioning towards data-driven decision-making. The methodology employs a systematic literature review combined with the Design Science Research (DSR) approach, which facilitates the development of a practical scoring model and a chronological framework for assessing and enhancing data utilization and decision-making processes. Expected results include the identification of key data-driven artifacts and the establishment of a scoring system that quantifies various data-driven criteria relevant to SMEs. This research will not only contribute to academic knowledge by detailing a tailored approach for SMEs but also provide actionable insights that enhance their strategic and operational decisions, ultimately fostering a culture of innovation and competitive advantage within the German SME sector.

Keywords: data-driven decision-making · scoring model · chronological framework · German SMEs

1 Introduction

Artificial Intelligence, Machine Learning, and Big Data technologies have been increasingly adopted by entrepreneurs, becoming key drivers in driving innovation, enhancing business competitiveness, and productivity [1, 11]. These cutting-edge technologies empower organizations to optimize operations and business processes, predict customer needs, run personalized and targeted campaigns, and make informed decisions [3, 15]. Industry giants such as Google, Amazon, and Netflix, for example, have successfully

K. S. Soliman (Ed.): IBIMA-AI 2024, CCIS 2299, pp. 63–67, 2025.
https://doi.org/10.1007/978-3-031-77493-5_6

harnessed these technologies to develop data-centric strategies aimed at enhancing service delivery, operational efficiency, elevating customer satisfaction, and securing market leadership [9]. However, a crucial question remains – is this data-driven approach solely a game for large enterprises, or can it also be effectively adopted by Small and Medium-sized Enterprises (SMEs) and craft businesses, especially in the context of Germany? [8]. If yes, to what extent can data-driven strategies be implemented in SMEs and crafts in Germany? Which aspects of data-driven strategies are most relevant, applicable, and beneficial for those organizations? Many studies have shown that companies that are data-driven make smarter decisions in strategy management, continuously improve, and have output and productivity that is 5–6% higher than those that don't adopt data-driven decision-making [4, 10, 20]. This research focuses on the opportunities and challenges that the transformation of an SME to a data-driven company or data-driven SME could bring, emphasizing the importance of adopting a culture that embraces analytics and evidence-based decision-making as pivotal elements for achieving competitive advantage and operational excellence [14, 16]. To achieve this proposed goal, it is crucial to implement a chronological structure within the data activities of a company so that analysis can take place to find out in which context data-driven decision-making occurs exactly and to get specific measurements at the correct points within the defined structure. This approach could provide the possibility to uncover the most efficient data artifacts so that the identification of those artifacts and how to process them unfolds insights that are not available in the research of data-driven companies yet. The research also investigates challenges and barriers to adopting data-driven decision-making within specified contexts in German SMEs and crafts. This involves understanding what prevents or hinders these organizations from effectively using data to guide their decisions and business. The objectives include identifying barriers to effective data utilization, defining and evaluating the characteristics and levels of data-drivenness, and proposing customized solutions to enhance data utilization and data-drivenness in German SMEs and crafts. The initial phase involves a comprehensive assessment of the current data utilization in German SMEs and crafts, examining how they employ data in decision-making processes. By comparing SMEs with large enterprises, we can establish a baseline for contrasting data practices across different company sizes and uncover nuanced differences in data-drivenness across the business spectrum. The key objective is to develop a flexible scoring model to evaluate the levels of data-drivenness within organizations, which is designed to adapt to varying company sizes by considering the specificities of SMEs and larger entities. This model is crucial for assessing and enhancing the integration and effectiveness of data-driven practices within businesses, offering insights into improving strategic and operational decisions through better data use [2]. Furthermore, we propose a dual-strategy approach. This includes developing a chronological data activity framework and identifying key data artifacts. The framework will empower SMEs with a systematic methodology for data utilization, ensuring optimal applications of data insights for maximum impact. Identifying and incorporating crucial data artifacts into this framework will unlock new potentials for strategic and operational excellence. Through a comprehensive examination of current data practices, a practical scoring model, and a structured data utilization framework, this research aims to equip businesses, particularly German SMEs and crafts, with the knowledge and tools to enhance their data utilization and data-driven capabilities, fostering a culture of operational excellence and strategic foresight across the business landscape.

2 Methodology

To address our objectives, our methodology will be twofold. Firstly, we will employ a literature review as outlined by [17] to systematically gather, analyze, and synthesize existing knowledge pertinent to data-driven strategies in SMEs. This comprehensive review will serve as the foundation for understanding the current landscape of data utilization and data activities within SMEs, identifying gaps in the literature, and highlighting best practices and challenges faced by these enterprises in adopting data-driven approaches. Secondly, for the development of our chronological data utilization framework and scoring model, we will adopt the initial phases of the Design Science Research (DSR) methodology. This approach will enable us to iteratively design, develop, and refine the framework and model based on principles derived from both the literature review and empirical observations. Specifically, we will focus on the first two to three steps of DSR, which include problem identification and motivation, objectives of a solution, and design and development. These steps will guide us in creating a practical and theoretically grounded scoring model and framework tailored for assessing and enhancing the data-drivenness of SMEs. By integrating insights from a structured literature review with the systematic design and development process of DSR, we aim to produce robust tools that SMEs can leverage to navigate the complexities of becoming data-driven organizations [6]. This methodological approach will ensure that our contributions are both research-based and practically applicable, addressing the real-world needs of SMEs in the context of data-driven decision-making.

2.1 Expected Results

The feasibility and efficacy of data-driven strategies, as well as the potential for German SMEs and Crafts to derive valuable benefits from the adoption of these approaches, form the main subject of our exploration. Particularly in the context of Germany, a nation known for its robust SMEs and Crafts sector (which accounts for 99.6% of the total share of all enterprises, according to statistics from the European Commission, 2023), understanding the extent to which SMEs and Crafts can effectively implement data-driven strategies and identifying their most relevant, beneficial aspects within the German context is of paramount importance. Prior research suggests that data-driven approaches can improve the innovation competency of SMEs [5, 7, 18] and can positively impact business performance for SMEs [12, 19]. However, the specific challenges and opportunities faced by German SMEs and crafts still require deeper investigation. Furthermore, this research proposes the development of a scoring model and a chronological framework of data activities. The scoring model will evaluate and quantify the significance and relevance of various data-driven criteria and artifacts from the unique perspective of SMEs and crafts. By assigning scores, the model will inform the current data-driven state of organizations and illuminate which aspects of data-driven strategies hold the most value for these businesses, allowing them to prioritize and implement strategies that yield the most impactful results. The chronological framework, on the other hand, can help to identify the key data artifacts of an organization's data-driven activities. Through this comprehensive analysis, the research aspires to bridge the knowledge gap regarding the applicability of data-driven strategies for German SMEs and crafts, empowering them to leverage the power of data for competitive advantage.

References

1. Alghamdi, O.A., Agag, G.: Boosting innovation performance through big data analytics powered by artificial intelligence use: an empirical exploration of the role of strategic agility and market turbulence. Sustainability **15**(19), 14296 (2023)
2. Ali, S., Khan, D.: 'Data-Driven Decision Support: Leveraging Analytics for Business Success (2023)
3. Bharadiya, J.P.: Machine learning and AI in business intelligence: trends and opportunities. Int. J. Comput. **48**(1), 123–134 (2023)
4. Brynjolfsson, E, Hitt, L.M., Kim, H.H. : 'Strength in numbers: How does data-driven decisionmaking affect firm performance? (2011). Available at SSRN 1819486
5. Chatterjee, S., Chaudhuri, R., Shah, M., Maheshwari, P.: Big data driven innovation for sustaining SME supply chain operation in post COVID-19 scenario: moderating role of SME technology leadership. Comput. Ind. Eng. **168**, 108058 (2022)
6. Deng, Q., Ji, S.: A review of design science research in information systems: concept, process, outcome, and evaluation. Pac. Asia J. Assoc. Inf. Syst. **10**, 2 (2018)
7. Gehrmann, L.C.: 'Data-driven decision-making in the innovation process of SMEs.' Master's Thesis, University of Twente (2020)
8. Goar, V.K., Yadav, N.S.: Business decision making by big data analytics. Int. J. Recent Innov. Trends in Comput. Commun. **10**(5), 22–35 (2022)
9. Kane, F.: 'Building Recommender Systems with Machine Learning and AI: Help people discover new products and content with deep learning, neural networks, and machine learning recommendations.' Independently published (2018)
10. Kopanakis, I., Vassakis, K., Mastorakis, G.: Big data in data-driven innovation: the impact in enterprises' performance, In: Proceedings of 11th Annual MIBES International Conference, pp. 257–263 (2016)
11. Manyika, J., et al.: Big data: The next frontier for innovation, competition, and productivity (2011)
12. Nasrollahi, M., Ramezani, J., Sadraei, M.: The impact of big data adoption on SMEs' performance. Big Data Cognitive Comput. **5**(4), 68 (2021)
13. (N.d.), Europa.Eu. https://ec.europa.eu/docsroom/documents/54967/attachments/1/translations/en/renditions/native. Retrieved 27 Mar 2024
14. Popovič, A., Hackney, R., Coelho, P.S., Jaklič, J.: Towards business intelligence systems success: effects of maturity and culture on analytical decision making. Decis. Support Syst. **54**, 729–739 (2012)
15. Power, D.: Understanding data-driven decision support systems. IS Manage. **25**, 149–154 (2008)
16. Sutriana, R.A.W.: Big data and big data analytics in value creation and innovation. J. Manag. Digit. Bus. Entrepreneurship **187**, 109804 (2023)
17. Tranfield, D., Denyer, D., Smart, P.: Towards a methodology for developing evidence-informed management knowledge by means of systematic review. Br. J. Manag. **14**, 207–222 (2003)

18. Verma, S., Singh, V., Bhattacharyya, S.S.: Do big data-driven HR practices improve HR service quality and innovation competency of SMEs. Int. J. Organ. Anal. **29**(4), 950–973 (2021)
19. Wamba, S.F., Gunasekaran, A., Akter, S., Ren, S.J.F., Dubey, R., Childe, S.J.: Big data analytics and firm performance: effects of dynamic capabilities. J. Bus. Res. **70**, 356–365 (2017)
20. Zeynalli, A.: Data-Driven Decision Making in Strategy Management of Enterprises, Paper presented at the International Academic Conference on Management & Economics, Oxford, UK (2019)

Exploring the Impact of AI-Driven Gamification on Visitor Engagement in Museums: A Critical Review

Lili Zheng[1], Michel Plaisent[2(✉)], Tsun-Hung Tsai[3], Daniel Tomiuk[4], Jean-Marie Lafortune[5], and Shih-Hui Li[6]

[1] Marketing Department, Excelia Business School, La Rochelle, France
[2] Department of Management, University of Quebec in Montreal, Montreal, Canada
plaisent.michel@uqam.ca
[3] Graduate Institute of Art and Technology, National Tsing Hua University, Hsinchu City, Taiwan
[4] Department of Analytics, Operations, and Information Technologies, University of Quebec in Montreal, Montreal, Canada
tomiuk.daniel@uqam.ca
[5] Department of Social and Public Communication, University of Quebec in Montreal, Montreal, Canada
lafortune.jean-marie@uqam.ca
[6] The Graduate School of Museum Studies, Fu Jen Catholic University, Taipei, Taiwan

Abstract. This study investigates the changing dynamics in museum participation, highlighting the growing impact of AI-driven gamification in transforming museum experiences into more interactive and socially enriching encounters. It raises important questions about how AIDG can enhance social interactions among museum visitors while balancing evolving social norms with traditional museum activities. The study emphasizes the ongoing need for exploration and research at the intersection of human sciences and technology to fully comprehend the potential of AIDG within museums. It supports a comprehensive approach that goes beyond technological integration, emphasizing the significance of creating meaningful connections among museum visitors and promoting deeper engagement with cultural artifacts and displays. Furthermore, the present study discusses the complex obstacles that museums encounter in expanding visitor engagement beyond their physical spaces. It underscores the significance of engaging visitors before and after their museum visits to build customer loyalty and promote repeat attendance. The study also raises awareness about the intricate ethical issues and societal effects linked to the widespread use of AI in cultural organizations, advising stakeholders to prioritize ethical development and implementation methods.

Keywords: AI-driven gamification · museums · visitor experiences · social interaction

K. S. Soliman (Ed.): IBIMA-AI 2024, CCIS 2299, pp. 68–72, 2025.
https://doi.org/10.1007/978-3-031-77493-5_7

1 Introduction

In the digital age, museums are undergoing a transformation shaped by Information and Communication Technology (ICT) and gamification [2]. A survey of 200 museums by the Museum Barometer reveals that a vast majority attribute their success to new technologies to attract new visitors and provide more relevant content (Tykhonova and Widmann, 2021). Leveraging intelligent technology, particularly effective among millennials [15], gamification enhances learning, cognitive performance, and memory improvement. Traditionally viewed as repositories for art, artifacts, and cultural collections, museums are undergoing a transformation, aimed at offering to visitors a feeling of participation and an interactive experience [11]. Gamification emerges as a powerful tool, expanding the museum experience beyond the mere observation of art or artifacts to evoke feelings of enjoyment through interactive games and activities.

Artificial Intelligence (AI) revolutionizes museums, addressing challenges in sustaining interest. AIDG, featuring interactive exhibits and virtual reality, signifies museums' commitment to contemporary demands, effectively engaging visitors and enhancing learning outcomes [5]. This shift aligns with changes in visitor behavior towards active and socially engaged participation [14]. AIDG transforms how visitors interact with museums, making art more engaging and immersive. Examples like "Inside Opera" and "The House Museums of Milan" showcase AIDG's power in creating personalized, dynamic experiences. Regardless of museum type, gamification introduces an element of fun, connecting audiences and deepening understanding. In the realm of digital museums, AIDG streamlines work and enriches user experiences, necessitating innovative methodologies to ensure museums remain dynamic and relevant. This evolution calls for new modes of thinking, working, and engaging with the audience in a world shaped by digital experiences.

2 Transforming Museum Experiences: The Rise of AI-Driven Gamification and the Shift Towards Visitor-Centric Engagement

The museum engagement landscape is shifting, turning visitors into participants and explorers of the values of the exhibition, aiming to discover alternate interpretations [1, 7]): "active interpreters and performers of meaning-making practices within complex cultural sites" [6]. This evolution, emphasized by the International Council of Museums (ICOM) in 2019, places visitors at the center of the museum experience, transcending a passive journey to an engaging interaction with space, collections, exhibitions, and fellow attendees [15].

Museum studies highlight emotions [4], and affective pedagogy adding to the traditional mission of object preservation the objective of addressing diverse visitor needs [8]. Visitors, influenced by self-identity, companions, and leisure motivations [10], seek meaning beyond traditional experiences, requiring museums to address introspective and social needs, since visitor favorable reactions are associated positively with the social orientation of the museum experience [1, 9]. From a learning perspective, Blud emphasizes that "interaction between visitors may be as important as interaction between the visitor and the exhibit" ([3], 43). While museums are widely considered social experiences, the prioritization of affective, introspective (or playful) experiences over instructive or informative ones is still debated in some museum circles 13.

Experiments conducted by museums and historic monuments over the past fifteen years align with the objective of adapting to visitors' styles and social needs. Digital technologies introduce dynamism into visitors' actions and behavior, influencing interactions with devices, spatial surroundings, sounds, and fellow patrons, including staff [12]. Interactive AIDG, when incorporated into a museum context, opens new possibilities, allowing the development of characters with feelings and personalities tailored to different visitor interests and age groups. AI enhances the social aspect of gamification by analyzing user data to create more meaningful interactions between players, fostering a collaborative and supportive gaming experience that builds a sense of community.

Games foster connection in cultural institutions, exemplified by the Smithsonian, MoMA, and Google's Arts & Culture app. AI's integration, particularly through natural language processing (NLP), enhances interactive experiences. Museums' experiments with interactive AIDG align with the goal of adapting to visitors' styles and social needs, fostering meaningful interactions [13]. The social aspect of gamification is enhanced by AI, creating collaborative and supportive gaming experiences [15]. Museumgoers seeking social experiences can find inspiration in various gamification examples. Friendly staff enhances positive social interactions throughout the visitor experience. Museums aspiring to create experiences resembling amusement parks prioritize narrative and sensational aspects as cornerstones of the visitor experience. Furthermore, AI adds personalization to gamification, enhancing engagement and motivation. AI algorithms analyze user data, enabling personalized experiences with recommendations, challenges, rewards, and predictive analytics [15]. A clear understanding of the design process, including goals, objectives, and ethical considerations, is therefore crucial for successful AI-driven gamification.

3   Exploring the Uncharted Territory: Harnessing AI-Driven Gamification for Enhanced Social Dynamics and Visitor Engagement in Museums

Gamification plays a crucial role in shaping museum experiences, yet there's still unexplored potential within this domain. Despite advancements in human-computer interaction (HCI) and human social sciences (HSS) supporting social interactions in museums, the exploration of social dynamics during museum visits remains incomplete. This raises important questions: How can AIDG enhance social interactions among museum visitors? What personal and social experiences extend beyond the art, contributing to a more enriching museum visit? How can museums balance traditional activities with evolving social expectations, especially among younger audiences? Moreover, what are the social and legal boundaries of the museum when implementing AIDG, considering the necessity of relinquishing some control over visitors?

This calls for further research at the intersection of human sciences and technology to gain a comprehensive understanding, not only within collections but also in fostering connections among museum visitors. Balancing traditional activities with evolving social expectations, requires exploration into personal and social dimensions beyond art, focusing on elements such as fun and empathy. This prompts investigation into how AIDG impacts the social interactions of museum visitors, providing valuable insights for the future. Moreover, it raises important questions about the social and legal boundaries of museums, recognizing that facilitating play involves ceding some control over visitors.

Furthermore, effective AIDG implementation requires careful design considerations to ensure elements are easy to use for museum audiences. Simple yet effective AIDG elements are essential, with measurability playing a key role in fostering deeper user engagement by allowing users to compare results with others. Moreover, AIDG goals should be achievable to prevent user frustration and potential task abandonment. Moreover, implementing a successful AIDG experience presents a significant challenge, with museums navigating with the complexities of creating engaging encounters when integrating AIDG. The real challenge lies in extending the visitor experience beyond museum walls. Engagement should begin before visitors enter a museum and continue long after they leave. Post-visit experiences are crucial for fostering visitor loyalty and encouraging return visits.

Finally, in the era of widespread AI adoption, its significant impact on the human condition unfolds in ways not fully understood. Unintended negative consequences, such as societal inequalities and divisions, ethical responsibility, inclusivity, and privacy, take center stage in this transformative space. Continually addressing fundamental questions – Why are we building this? What are the benefits, and what are the risks? – is imperative. Recognizing the ethical implications and societal impact is crucial for the responsible development and deployment of AIDG in museums and beyond.

References

1. Addis, M., Copat, V., Martorana, C.: Museum experience and its impact on visitor reactions. J. Philanthropy Market. **29**(1), e1826 (2023)
2. Botte, B., Marinensi, G., Malakuczi, V., Vitaletti, W.: Innovative technologies Iin museums: A review of gamified augmented reality experiences. In: INTED2024 Proceedings, pp. 4338–4345 (2024)
3. Blud, L.: Social interaction and learning among family groups visiting a museum. Museum Manag. Curatorship **9**(1), 43–51 (1990). https://doi.org/10.1016/0260-4779(90)90024-8
4. Cotter, K.N., Rodriguez-Boerwinkle, R.M., Silver, S., Hardy, M., Putney, H., Pawelski, J.O.: Emotional experiences, well-being, and ILL-being during art museum visits: a latent class analysis. J. Happiness Stud. **25**(1), 1–17 (2024)
5. Hettmann, W., Wölfel, M., Butz, M., Torner, K., Finken, J.: Engaging Museum Visitors with AI-Generated Narration and Gameplay. In: Brooks, A.L. (ed.) ArtsIT, Interactivity and Game Creation: 11th EAI International Conference, ArtsIT 2022, Faro, Portugal, 21–22 Nov 2022, Proceedings, pp. 201–214. Springer Nature Switzerland, Cham (2023). https://doi.org/10.1007/978-3-031-28993-4_15
6. Hooper-Greenhill, E.: Museums and Education, Purpose, Pedagogy, Performance, 1st edn. Routledge, London (2007). https://doi.org/10.4324/9780203937525, ISBN9780203937525
7. Kłeczek, R., Hajdas, M.: Transforming practices of co-creating values in a contemporary art exhibition. Qual. Market Res.: An Int. J. **27**, 254–279 (2024)
8. Liu, S., Guo, J.: Original research article smart museum and visitor satisfaction. J. Auton. Intell. **7**(3) (2024)

9. Petrelli, D., Not, E.: User-centred design of flexible hypermedia for a mobile guide: reflections on the hyperaudio experience. User Model. User-Adapted Inter. **15**(3–4), 303–338 (2005). https://doi.org/10.1007/s11257-005-8816-1

10. Ryding, K.: The silent conversation: Designing for introspection and social play in art museums. CHI'20, 25–30 April 2020, Honolulu, HI, USA (2020). https://doi.org/10.1145/331 3831.3376357

11. Saghezchi, F.B., Amorim, M., Rosa, M.J.: Dealing with visitors participation and interaction in museum experiences: a perspective from service quality. Econ. Soc. Dev.: Book of Proc., 375–383. (2023)

12. Smirnova, T., Vinck, D.: The social and sociotechnical interactions of visitors at a digital museum exhibition. The Montreux Digital Heritage Lab, dans Les Cahiers du numérique **15**(1–2), 43–66 (2019)

13. Smith, L., Wetherell, M., Campbell, G. (eds.): Emotion, Affective Practices, and the Past in the Present. Routledge (2018). https://doi.org/10.4324/9781351250962

14. Styx, L.: 'How can games in museums enhance visitor experience?' MuseumNext (2022). https://www.museumnext.com/article/how-can-games-in-museums-enhance-visitor-experience/

15. Vaissière, S.: Le musée de demain doit-il être amusant? Nectart **1**(10), 70–79 (2020)

Framework for Automating Bank Transactions and Invoice Mapping Using Multi-criteria Optimization and Neural Networks

Tomasz Protasowicki[✉]

Institute of Computer and Information Systems, Faculty of Cybernetics, Military University of Technology, Warsaw, Poland
tomasz.protasowicki@wat.edu.pl

Abstract. This study aims to address the labor-intensive process of bank transaction and invoice reconciliation by presenting a comprehensive framework that leverages multi-criteria optimization and neural networks. The literature reveals a significant gap in automating this process with high accuracy and efficiency. The method presented in this paper integrates optimization techniques and neural networks to minimize manual intervention and enhance the precision of the reconciliation process. Utilizing utility functions for multi-criteria decision-making can effectively combine optimization techniques to balance accuracy, processing time, and error rates. Findings indicate that the proposed framework significantly improves processing time and accuracy, providing a scalable and efficient solution for financial operations. The presented framework demonstrates its potential by achieving a high level of F1-score, reducing processing times, and minimizing error rates, thereby advancing the automation of financial reconciliations.

Keywords: multi-criteria optimization · neural networks · transaction-invoice mapping

1 Introduction

In the realm of financial management and accounting, modern enterprises increasingly rely on IT systems to streamline processes and reduce errors. A critical aspect of these systems is the automation of mapping bank transactions to corresponding invoices, a task that traditionally involves substantial manual effort. Effective automation of this task not only enhances efficiency but also minimizes errors ([13, 17]).

This paper introduces a framework for developing an optimal configuration of artificial intelligence methods and its software implementation that automates the processing of bank transactions and their mapping to invoices. The aim is to minimize manual intervention and optimize the assignment process by integrating multi-criteria optimization with neural networks. The framework is designed to address the needs of financial institutions, enhancing the accuracy and efficiency of transaction-invoice reconciliation..

K. S. Soliman (Ed.): IBIMA-AI 2024, CCIS 2299, pp. 73–81, 2025.
https://doi.org/10.1007/978-3-031-77493-5_8

2 Literature Review

Optimization in financial systems involves complex decision-making processes, balancing multiple objectives such as accuracy, efficiency, and error minimization ([5, 8]). Traditional techniques like linear programming, integer programming, and dynamic programming have been extensively used but often struggle with high-dimensional and dynamic financial data [10]. Recent advancements have introduced multi-criteria optimization methods such as the weighted sum method, ε-constraint method, and Pareto optimization ([1]; Chudy, 1983). These methods provide a flexible framework for addressing multiple objectives in financial decision-making, particularly useful in automating transaction-invoice mapping [7]. The incorporation of utility functions in multi-criteria optimization allows for the aggregation of various objectives into a single function, simplifying the optimization process and enabling clear trade-offs between different objectives (Burlaga & Kacprzyk, 2013).

Neural networks have revolutionized data processing in various domains, including finance. Their ability to learn complex patterns from data makes them ideal for tasks such as transaction classification and invoice matching ([14, 15]). Specifically, Convolutional Neural Networks (CNNs) and Recurrent Neural Networks (RNNs) have shown effectiveness in handling sequential financial data [9]. In this study, neural networks enhance the accuracy of transaction-invoice mapping by learning from historical data and improving decision-making processes [3]. This reduces reliance on manual mapping and increases the system's ability to handle diverse transactions and invoices. Combining neural networks with optimization techniques allows the system to adapt dynamically to changes in data patterns and improve its decision-making capabilities over time [12].

3 Research methodology and research objective

The research methodology is based on generalized systems analysis, providing a systematic approach to problem-solving in complex systems [4]. The methodology encompasses:

1. Identification of Objectives: Define research goals and specific problems.
2. Exploration of Options: Investigate alternative solutions and evaluate their potential.
3. Assessment of Effects: Analyze the impact of each option, considering uncertainty and risk.
4. Comparative Analysis: Compare options based on selected criteria.
5. Decision Making: Present results to facilitate decision-making.

Based on this general methodology, a detailed research procedure was developed for the implementation. The aim was to refer to specific research goals and cognitive processes that are specific to the R&D work carried out. In short, the research activity was as follows:

1. general literature studies focused mainly on identifying the state of knowledge in the problem area of the task;
2. identification, analysis, and indication of optimization methods and techniques applicable in the problem area of the task;

3. determining the characteristics of the optimization process in the process of mapping invoices with bank transactions supported by machine learning systems;
4. developing several variants of the mathematical model of the optimization task and recommending the best one, i.e. the one that will achieve the best possible configuration of the artificial intelligence models implemented in software;
5. developing a method for solving the optimization task.
6. evaluation of both the result and the course of the research.

This structured approach supports the development of a optimal solution for automating transaction-invoice mapping.

4 Mathematical Model of Optimization with Utility Function

To minimize the manual mapping of invoices with bank transactions, we propose to model the optimization problem as a multi-criteria decision-making task with a utility function. This function maximizes system efficiency while minimizing errors and processing time.

Let x represent the considered configuration and include decision variables, i.e. neural network settings and data processing algorithms.

Also let's consider the following objective functions:

1. function *F1-Score* maximizes the balance between precision and recall is given as follows:

$$f_1(x) = \frac{2 \times Precision \times Recall}{Precision + Recall}$$

2. function *Processing Time* minimizes average time per transaction and was defined as:

$$f_2(x) = \frac{1}{N} \sum_{i=1}^{N} t_i(x)$$

3. function *Error Rate* minimizes errors in mapping transactions to invoices and we assume it is represented by the following formula

$$f_3(x) = \frac{Number\ of\ Errors}{Total\ Transactions}$$

We take the following constraints to ensure the system operates within acceptable limits:

1. Minimum F1-Score for the considered configuration x:

$$g_1(x) \geq 0,90$$

2. Maximum Processing Time per Transaction:

$$g_2(x) \leq 5\,\text{s}$$

Taking the above into consideration we formulated the multi-criteria problem and transformed it into a single-objective problem using a utility function. This is given by the following formula:

$$U(x) = w_1 f_1(x) + w_2 \left(\frac{1}{f_2(x)} \right) - w_3 f_3(x)$$

Implementation steps for the above model cover:

1. Data Collection and Preparation: Gather and preprocess data on bank transactions and invoices.
2. Neural Network Design: Develop and train models for transaction classification and invoice matching.
3. Optimization Algorithm Development: Implement and test optimization algorithms.
4. System Integration: Integrate neural networks and optimization components.
5. Evaluation and Testing: Conduct testing to assess performance and refine the system.

5   Results

The application of multi-criteria optimization techniques significantly reduced manual transaction-invoice mapping time. The utility function approach balanced multiple objectives effectively, surpassing traditional single-objective optimization methods [2].

1. **Weighted Sum Method** combined multiple criteria into a single objective function, facilitating the optimization process. The utility function balanced accuracy, processing time, and errors [6];
2. **ε-Constraint Method** prioritized specific objectives by converting others into constraints, offering greater control over outcomes [10];
3. **Pareto Optimization** produced a set of optimal solutions representing trade-offs, allowing informed decision-making [19].

The combination of these techniques provided a comprehensive approach to optimizing the system, addressing efficiency and accuracy in transaction-invoice mapping.

Neural networks demonstrated high accuracy in classifying transactions and matching them to invoices. The use of CNNs and RNNs enabled handling complex financial data patterns, enhancing automation performance [13]:

1. **Accuracy** achieved an F1-score of over 0.95, indicating high precision and recall [15];
2. **Processing Time** reduced data processing time, improving efficiency compared to manual methods [9];
3. **Error Reduction** minimized error rate in transaction-invoice mapping, enhancing financial record reliability [3].

These results underscore the effectiveness of integrating neural networks with optimization techniques to enhance financial automation systems.

To illustrate the proposed multi-criteria optimization method, we present a computational example using a utility function to balance accuracy, processing time, and error rate.

Assume a dataset of 1000 bank transactions and corresponding invoices. The goal is to optimize the neural network configuration to maximize the F1-score while minimizing processing time and error rate. Decision variables x include:

1. Learning rate x_1;
2. Number of layers of the considered neural network x_2;
3. Number of neurons per layer x_3;
4. Batch size x_4.

Objective functions, constraints, and the utility function are given by formulas as defined in the previous section "Mathematical Model of Optimization with Utility Function".

Also we assume that the weights are given as follows:

$$w_1 = 0, 5$$
$$w_2 = 0, 3$$
$$w_3 = 0, 2$$

So the utility function takes following form:

$$U(x) = 0, 5f_1(x) + 0, 3\left(\frac{1}{f_2(x)}\right) - 0, 2f_3(x)$$

First step is the evaluation of the initial configuration of the prototype software. We assume the following values of the decision variables:

1. Learning rate $x_1 = 0.01$;
2. Number of layers of the considered neural network $x_2 = 3$;
3. Number of neurons per layer $x_3 = 64$;
4. Batch size $x_4 = 32$.

For the initial configuration, we also calculated values of the objective functions:

1. F1-Score:

$$f_1(x) = \frac{2 \times 0, 92 \times 0, 88}{0, 92 + 0, 88} = 0, 90$$

2. Processing Time:

$$f_2(x) = 4 seconds$$

3. Error Rate:

$$f_3(x) = \frac{50}{1000} = 0, 05$$

We computed utility function as follow:

$$U(x) = 0, 5 \times 0, 90 + 0, 3 \times \left(\frac{1}{4}\right) - 0, 2 \times 0, 05 = 0, 515$$

In the second step we adjust the configuration to:

1. Learning rate $x_1 = 0.005$;
2. Number of layers of the considered neural network $x_2 = 4$;
3. Number of neurons per layer $x_3 = 128$;
4. Batch size $x_4 = 64$.

And next we evaluate new configuration:

$$f_1(x) = \frac{2 \times 0,94 \times 0,91}{0,94 + 0,91} = 0,925$$

$$f_2(x) = 3,5 \text{ s}$$

$$f_3(x) = \frac{30}{1000} = 0,03$$

$$U(x) = 0,5 \times 0,925 + 0,3 \times \left(\frac{1}{3,5}\right) - 0,2 \times 0,03 = 0,5422$$

The new configuration provides a higher utility value indicating improved performance of the software solution.

In the next steps of proposed procedure we have to iteratively adjust decision variables to maximize the utility function. Continue optimization until the utility function converges to an optimal value or meets stopping criteria.

This example illustrates the application of the proposed multi-criteria optimization method. Using a utility function to balance accuracy, processing time, and error rate, we optimized the neural network configuration effectively. This method provides a structured approach to enhancing the performance of automated financial systems.

6 Discussion

The proposed framework for automating bank transaction-invoice mapping demonstrates significant advancements in increasing the accuracy & efficiency, as well as the error reduction through the integration of multi-criteria optimization and neural networks. However, several challenges and limitations need to be addressed to fully realize the potential of this approach.

1. **Data Quality and Variability** - one of the primary challenges is ensuring high data quality and handling variability in transaction and invoice data. Inconsistent or incomplete data can adversely affect the performance of neural network models and the optimization process. Variability in data formats, transaction descriptions, and invoice structures can introduce noise and reduce the system's effectiveness [16]. To mitigate these issues, robust data preprocessing techniques are essential. This includes standardizing transaction descriptions, normalizing data formats, and implementing methods to handle missing or incomplete data. Additionally, developing adaptive algorithms that can dynamically adjust to different data patterns will improve the system's resilience to data variability. Incorporating advanced natural language processing (NLP) techniques can enhance the ability to standardize and

interpret transaction descriptions, leading to more accurate mappings. This involves using NLP models to identify and extract relevant features from transaction and invoice descriptions, thus reducing ambiguity and improving the consistency of data inputs.

2. **Scalability and Performance** - as transaction volumes grow, the system's ability to scale while maintaining high performance becomes critical. Scalability involves not only handling large datasets efficiently but also ensuring that the optimization algorithms and neural networks can process increased data loads without significant performance degradation [11]. Enhancing scalability requires optimizing the computational resources and improving the efficiency of both the neural networks and optimization algorithms. Techniques such as distributed computing, parallel processing, and cloud-based architectures can be employed to manage large-scale data processing. Moreover, optimizing the hyperparameters of neural networks to balance computational load and performance can further enhance scalability.

3. **Computational Complexity** - the multi-criteria optimization process can be computationally intensive, especially when dealing with high-dimensional data and complex neural network configurations. This can result in increased computational demands, longer processing times, and potential difficulties in real-time application [18]. Addressing computational complexity involves using advanced optimization techniques such as metaheuristic algorithms (e.g., genetic algorithms, particle swarm optimization) and gradient-based methods for efficient search space exploration. These techniques can help navigate complex solution spaces and find optimal configurations without exhaustive searches. Metaheuristic algorithms, while powerful, often require fine-tuning and parameter adjustments to achieve optimal performance. Combining these algorithms with machine learning techniques such as reinforcement learning can provide adaptive optimization strategies that learn from past iterations and improve over time. Additionally, leveraging GPUs and specialized hardware accelerators for parallel processing can significantly reduce computational overhead.

4. **Robustness and Adaptability** - the framework must be robust enough to handle diverse and evolving financial environments. This includes adapting to changes in transaction patterns, regulatory requirements, and business processes without requiring significant reconfiguration or manual intervention. Enhancing robustness and adaptability involves developing self-learning algorithms and models that can dynamically adjust to new data patterns and operational changes. This can be achieved by incorporating continuous learning mechanisms into the neural networks and optimization models, allowing the system to evolve and improve based on ongoing data inputs. Implementing continuous learning requires designing models that can be updated incrementally with new data, avoiding the need for complete retraining. Techniques such as online learning, transfer learning, and domain adaptation can help the system adjust to new scenarios and maintain performance. Additionally, incorporating feedback loops that monitor system performance and provide corrective adjustments can enhance adaptability.

7 Future Research

The proposed framework opens several avenues for future research to further improve the automation of bank transaction-invoice mapping and extend its applicability. Here, we outline key areas for future investigation.

1. **Advanced Neural Network Architectures.** Research Focus: Exploring more sophisticated neural network architectures such as Transformers, Graph Neural Networks (GNNs), and Attention Mechanisms can significantly enhance the system's ability to understand and process complex financial data. These advanced architectures can improve the extraction of meaningful features from transaction and invoice data, leading to more accurate and context-aware mappings. Transformers, for instance, can handle long-range dependencies in sequential data, making them ideal for understanding complex transaction patterns. GNNs can model relational data structures, such as connections between transactions and invoices, providing a more comprehensive view of the data. Future research should focus on adapting these architectures to the specific needs of financial data processing, including the development of custom models and training protocols that leverage the unique characteristics of financial datasets. Additionally, integrating these architectures with existing systems and evaluating their performance in real-world scenarios will be crucial.

2. **Real-Time Data Processing.** Integrating real-time data processing capabilities to handle live transaction streams and immediate invoice matching can enhance the system's responsiveness and applicability in dynamic financial environments. Real-time processing enables immediate detection and reconciliation of transactions, reducing delays and improving the timeliness of financial reporting. This capability is particularly important for applications such as fraud detection, compliance monitoring, and cash flow management, where timely information is critical. Optimizing the neural network models for low-latency inference and integrating them with real-time data sources will be essential. Research should also explore the challenges of maintaining accuracy and performance in real-time settings, such as handling concept drift and data variability.

3. **Hybrid Optimization Techniques.** Research Focus: Investigating hybrid optimization techniques that combine deterministic and probabilistic methods can offer more robust solutions for complex financial data processing tasks. Hybrid methods can leverage the strengths of different optimization techniques, providing a more flexible and comprehensive approach to solving multi-criteria optimization problems. For example, combining gradient-based methods with metaheuristic algorithms can improve convergence rates and solution quality. Future research should develop hybrid optimization frameworks that integrate these techniques seamlessly, allowing for adaptive and efficient optimization. This includes designing algorithms that can dynamically switch between different methods based on the problem's characteristics and constraints. Evaluating these hybrid approaches in various financial contexts and comparing their performance with traditional methods will provide valuable insights.

Future research should address these challenges by exploring advanced neural network architectures and optimization techniques. Real-time data processing integration can further enhance system performance in dynamic financial environments [12]. Hybrid optimization methods combining deterministic and probabilistic approaches could offer robust solutions for complex data processing tasks [16].

References

1. Ameliańczyk, A., Grudziński, Z.: Metody optymalizacji i ich zastosowanie. Wydawnictwa Naukowo-Techniczne (1983)
2. Ameliańczyk, A., Michalowski, W.: Metody optymalizacji wielokryterialnej. Wydawnictwo Naukowo-Techniczne (2005)
3. Andrew, N.: Machine Learning Yearning. Simon & Schuster (2018)
4. Beck, K.: Test Driven Development: By Example. Addison-Wesley (2002)
5. Bertsimas, D., Tsitsiklis, J.N.: Introduction to Linear Optimization. Athena Scientific (1997)
6. Bertsekas, D.P.: Constrained optimization and lagrange multiplier methods. Maths. Operat. Res. $5(1)$, 1–25 (1980)
7. Bondarenko, A., Kovalenko, E.: Process optimization of financial institutions. J. Adv. Res. Law and Econ. $8(3)$, 831–836 (2017)
8. Boyd, S., Vandenberghe, L.: Convex Optimization. Cambridge University Press (2004)
9. Burkov, A.: Machine Learning Engineering. Packt Publishing (2020)
10. Cornuejols, G., Tütüncü, R.: Optimization Methods in Finance. Cambridge University Press (2006)
11. El-Masri, A.S.: Optimizing business processes for financial institutions. Int. J. Eng. Adv. Technol. $8(1)$, 257–262 (2018)
12. Freeman, R.E., Harrison, J.S., Wicks, A.C.: Managing for Stakeholders: Survival, Reputation, and Success. Yale University Press (2004)
13. Géron, A.: Hands-On Machine Learning with Scikit-Learn, Keras, and TensorFlow: Concepts, Tools, and Techniques to Build Intelligent Systems. O'Reilly Media (2019)
14. Goodfellow, I., Bengio, Y., Courville, A.: Deep Learning. MIT Press (2016)
15. Hope, T., Resheff, Y.S., Lieder, I.: Learning TensorFlow: A Guide to Building Deep Learning Systems. O'Reilly Media (2017)
16. Kasprzak, G.: Selected aspects of the automation and optimization of accounting processes. Prace Naukowe Uniwersytetu Ekonomicznego we Wrocławiu 454, 92–101 (2017)
17. Ng, A.: Machine Learning Yearning. Simon & Schuster (2019)
18. Vanderbei, R.J.: Linear programming: algorithms and applications. Proceedings of the IEEE $88(6)$, 902–908 (2000)
19. Vanderbei, R.J.: Linear Programming: Foundations and Extensions. Springer. Ameisen E. (2020), Building Machine Learning Powered Applications: Going from Idea to Product. (2014)

Measurements of Clothing Circumference Using Vision Methods

Piotr Kohut[1]([✉]), Lucjan Miekina[1], Michał Manka[1], Tomasz Buratowski[1],
Tomasz Klorek[2], and Bartosz Bartkowiak[2]

[1] Department of Robotics and Mechatronics, AGH University of Krakow, Krakow, Poland
{pko,miekina,mmanka,tburatow}@agh.edu.pl
[2] VISBROKER Sp. z o.o., Poznan, Poland
{tomasz.klorek,bartosz.bartkowiak}@visbroker.pl

Abstract. Vision methods allow for accelerating the measurements of critical parameters of the figure and clothing and making the results free of errors usually made during manual measurements. However, it is necessary to develop appropriate algorithms for estimating spatial parameters, such as circumferences in selected cross-sections, based on 2-dimensional images. The literature is dominated by reports on the use of an ellipse for estimating circumferences, methods involving the concatenation of two ellipses are also described, and examples of the use of a superellipse are discussed but without an in-depth analysis of the selection of its parameters and the results achieved. This article discusses these essential properties of the superellipse as a model of the figure/clothing circumference. The article presents the developed methods of image processing and analysis for measuring circumferences and selected clothing measurement parameters. The paper discusses classic circuit approximation methods using ellipse equations and the proposed superellipse (Lame) method. A vision-based algorithm was presented, which uses spatial markers to measure circumferences and selected clothing parameters. The proposed method was verified on a test stand during experiments and compared with manual measurements. The results of measurements of the circumference, length, and width of selected clothing items were obtained. Statistical estimates characterizing the developed vision measurement system were determined based on the results. The obtained findings indicate that, compared to the classical ellipse approach, in the proposed method to measure the circumference, based on Lame curves, the average absolute error does not exceed 0.55 mm. The average measurement accuracy of the developed vision system for all conducted measurements was below the assumed value of 5 mm.

Keywords: vision system · digital image processing and analysis · circumference approximation · clothing measurements · anthropometry

1 Introduction

Contactless scanning and measurement methods are widely used in the clothing and fashion industry. The demand for clothes is constantly growing, and lifestyle changes, especially those caused by external and difficult-to-avoid conditions, such as the recent

K. S. Soliman (Ed.): IBIMA-AI 2024, CCIS 2299, pp. 82–94, 2025.
https://doi.org/10.1007/978-3-031-77493-5_9

pandemic, have radically changed the customers' shopping approaches. This change is manifested by a rapid transition from traditional to online shopping. When buying devices or equipment, you can be guided by the selection of technical data, general dimensions, or tests, but buying clothes is much more subjective. When shopping in a brick-and-mortar store, the customer can try on the clothes and decide whether they like them in size and appearance. In the case of online shopping, this is much more difficult. As a result, online stores offering clothing record up to 50% returns [13], which can cause a significant decrease in the profitability of this type of business.

The following approaches are currently used in practice:

- Using the manufacturer size chart. This approach can only be successfully used if the customer knows the brand size chart. Size charts of different brands can differ significantly, resulting in incorrect purchases.
- Many online stores take 2D measurements of the main dimensions of the garment, usually placed on a flat table, and then present this data on the website. This data gives customers more information but does not provide any data on the fit of the actual customer.
- Presenting clothes on mannequins or on real models and providing customers with data on their dimensions. This approach allows you to see how the clothes look on the model but requires many models/mannequins in different sizes, which is time-consuming.

In modern methods, a virtual model of the customer is created, and then, based on the data provided, its shape is adjusted to the customer's actual posture. Due to how this data is obtained, these methods can be divided into tabular methods, in which the customer provides their dimensions, and methods using vision systems to obtain the customer's dimensions, i.e., RGB cameras or depth cameras. The fitting process itself can be carried out in both 2D and 3D. In the case of 2D fitting, only basic data such as width and length are considered when determining the fit. In the case of 2D and 3D methods, circumferences are additionally considered for a better fit. In this case, for 2D methods to determine the circumferences, it is necessary to obtain images from several views. In the area of vision-based measurement methods [2, 3], two main categories can be distinguished: markerless methods [5, 12] and marker methods [9, 10].

Since the shape of the most essential cross-sections of the human body is similar to an ellipse, it seems natural to model and estimate the perimeters using ellipses. This task requires determining only two dimensions - the lengths of both ellipse axes in a given cross-section. Both traditional vision methods [4] and methods based on artificial intelligence [7] are used for this purpose. A superellipse is a more appropriate representation of human body cross-sections, which allows for correct modeling of unusual, asymmetric cross-sections, such as hips or chest. It requires more complex calculations, including individual tuning of model coefficients in the context of the cross-section type, but the accuracy of circumference estimation is improved [6, 8]. In this paper, a comparison of the results achieved using an ellipse and a superellipse was investigated.

The paper presents a vision marker method for measuring clothing and anthropometric measurements of the human figure. The developed vision system with a built-in marker algorithm was tested on a test stand in a series of experiments and compared with manual measurements. Based on the results, the accuracy of the system measurements was estimated.

2 Methodology

2.1 Marker-Based Clothing Measurement Algorithm

The proposed method to determine characteristic tailoring dimensions from the acquired image is based on flat or spatial markers. The implemented method uses an image analysis technique based on the algorithm of area segmentation of markers and then determining their geometric centers of gravity. The obtained data allows for determining Euclidean lengths between the designated coordinates of points. An implemented program in the MATLAB environment processed the images acquired with a 5-megapixel Ximea camera. In the first stage, distortions introduced by the optical path were removed [11]. In the next step, the images were binarized using an experimentally selected threshold. In the following image processing stage, morphological opening filtration was applied to remove all small areas constituting noise. The opening operation preserves the sizes of image objects while smoothing them. The next phase included the application of a region-based image analysis algorithm, as a result of which the features of detected objects were obtained (including n-*th* order moment methods and shape coefficients). Then, markers were extracted using chosen conditions. Using the Harris detector or Hough transformation, a scale factor was determined to get tailoring measures in SI units (millimeters). After evaluating the scale factor, the Euclidean distances between the corresponding centers of gravity of detected markers were measured, and then they were expressed in SI units - millimeters. The block diagram of the developed algorithm is shown in Fig. 1.

Fig. 1. Block diagram of the developed marker-based clothing measurement algorithm

As a result of the tests carried out, four image features were implemented in the algorithm to identify spherical marker patterns (ball type): area and the following coefficients: Malinowska ($\frac{L}{2\cdot\sqrt{\pi\cdot S}} - 1$), Circularity $\frac{L}{\pi}$, and Feret $\frac{L_h}{L_v}$ (where L - circumference of the object, S - area of the object, L_h, L_v - maximum diameter of the object: horizontally, vertically). A decision tree was developed for the abovementioned features, and appropriate value ranges were experimentally selected. The centers of the markers were determined from centroids, and then the algorithm automatically combined them into appropriate pairs, defining measurement sections that represent tailoring measurements.

2.2 Spherical Markers

In the further stages of the research, spherical markers were used (Fig. 2). In the first stages, these were purchased balls with a diameter of about 15 mm, made of expanded polystyrene (styrofoam). However, due to their disadvantages, tolerance of craft and shape (lack of sphericity), and easy deformation, it was finally decided to use spherical markers designed for the needs of the research, made using additive technology, using the owned 3D printer.

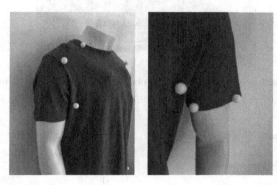

Fig. 2. Spherical markers applied to clothing made using 3D printing technology.

The experiments performed confirmed that the spherical markers designed and manufactured using 3D printing technology can be easily and correctly evenly illuminated. Regardless of the gluing method (within certain limits) on the obtained images, the markers visible as white circles could also be correctly binarized. The advantages presented proved that their selection for further tests was correct. Figure 3 shows a photo of a mannequin with clothes with spherical markers put on, which were used to measure tailoring sizes.

A series of experiments were conducted, and data were obtained based on 100 acquired photos of a male mannequin wearing a T-shirt, along with spherical markers. Measurements were taken for ten length measures specified as characteristic of this type of clothing. The collected data, mean values, and standard deviation are presented in Table 1.

The results confirm that the proposed method is characterized by high repeatability (average standard deviation value 0.022 mm). The scale factor was determined based on the circular Hough transformation.

2.3 Clothing Circumference Measurement Method

Circumference measurement has been performed through two implemented methods: a classical ellipse and superellipse (so-called Lame curve)

Fig. 3. Mannequin with spherical markers and obtained measures (scale factor was determined using the Hough method)

Table 1. Summary of vision measurement results for ten selected tailoring measures.

Name of the type of measurement	Mean [mm]	STD [mm
Shoulder width	485,65	0,02
Chest width	327,71	0,01
Waist width	298,52	0,01
Hip width	358,77	0,01
Clothing height	663,79	0,00
Left arm width	166,61	0,03
Right arm width	147,27	0,02
Inside right sleeve length	400,81	0,03
Right sleeve outer length	545,08	0,03
Right sleeve width	62,22	0,02

2.4   Approximation of Circumferences by Classical Ellipse Methods

An essential part of two-dimensional vision methods is determining the three-dimensional circumference dimension. Under the literature review, the research focused on obtaining the circumference dimension using two photos - from the front of the object and its side (frontal and lateral measurements).

First, it was decided to use the analogy of human circumferences to an ellipse. The width and depth dimensions of a human figure on a given circumference were read from the photos, and then the obtained information was treated as the lengths of the longer and shorter axes of the ellipse. It is the most common method in the literature [4] for calculating the circumference of a human using vision systems. The method also has some drawbacks, resulting from the fact that the shape of the human body is not elliptical. Despite this, it was decided to verify the generated error level using this approach. The four approximation methods of human circumferences, expressed by Eqs. (1–4), were implemented and examined.

Various approximations in the literature are adopted to simplify the calculations [1, 4, 7]

$$C \approx 2\pi \sqrt{\frac{a^2 + b^2}{2}} \tag{1}$$

$$C \approx \pi \left(\frac{3}{2}(a+b) - \sqrt{ab} \right) \tag{2}$$

$$C \approx \pi \left[3(a+b) - \sqrt{10ab + 3(a^2 + b^2)} \right] \tag{3}$$

$$C \approx \pi(a+b)\left(1 + \frac{3h}{10 + \sqrt{4 - 3h}} \right), \quad where : h = \frac{(a-b)^2}{(a+b)^2} \tag{4}$$

where: a and b are the long- and short-axis lengths of an ellipse, and C is the circumference

The results of circumference measurement by the vision system with the usage of classical ellipse approximation methods have been presented in Sect. 3.3

2.5 Approximation of Circumferences by Superellipse (Lame Curves)

To minimize the inaccuracy of the circumference approximation using an ellipse, the Lamé curve (5), also called a superellipse, was proposed to measure clothing circumference.

$$\left| \frac{x}{a} \right|^p + \left| \frac{y}{b} \right|^p = 1 \tag{5}$$

where: a and b are the semi-axes of the superellipse, and p denotes its order. For $p = 2$, an ellipse is obtained. For $p < 1$, the curve becomes concave.

Applying the Lamé curves allows for a much better (more accurate) approximation of the circumference than the standard ellipse. The parameter p, depending on the type of measured circumference, assumed values from the range of 2.5–6. The obtained results of selected circumferences of mannequins with and without clothing are discussed in Sect. 3.1.

2.6 Influence of the Lamé Curve Order on Measurement Results

The influence of the parameter p on the shape and circumference of the Lamé curve has been investigated. Lamé curves were determined based on previous measurements of the width and depth of clothing put on the mannequin (or the mannequin without clothing). Then, the influence of the parameter p (order of the Lamé curve) on the value of the calculated circumference was examined. Figure 4 shows the relationship between

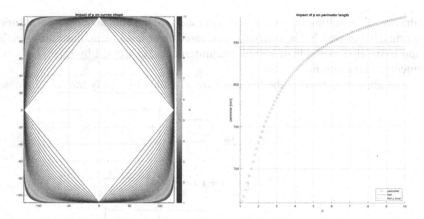

Fig. 4. Relationship between the shape of the curve (parameter p) and its length (perimeter).

the shape of the curve and its length, depending on the order of the Lame curve, for the exemplary measurement of the bust circumference of a female mannequin.

In further research, graphs of the dependencies between the error made in approximating various circumferential dimensions and the size of the Lamé curve order were plotted for each of the two types of mannequins. The graphs are presented below.

Figures 5 and 6 show the difference between circumferences measured by a tailor tape and circumferences approximated employing a given order of the Lamé curve. For instance, in the case of a female mannequin for hip, waist, and biceps circumferences, the minimum measurement difference corresponds to the range 2.7–2.9 of the parameter p, while for bust circumference for the value 5.5 of parameter p.

Similar results have been received for a male mannequin, where the minimum measurement difference between circumferences measured by a tailor tape and circumferences approximated using a given order of the Lamé curve corresponds to the range 2.8–3.5 for hip, waist, and biceps circumferences and 6.5 for bust circumference.

The required data (width and depth) to determine Lame curves were obtained using measurements made with the developed vision system described in Sect. 2 and measurements made using a tailor tape.

3   Experimental Setup

3.1   Measurements of Selected Clothing Parameters

To verify the results of the developed vision system with a built-in marker algorithm, a test stand was prepared consisting of a 5-megapixel Ximea monochrome camera, a NANLITE lighting system, female and male mannequins, spherical markers, and a selected type of clothing.

All the measurement series performed constituted four cases (scenarios) of measuring female or male mannequins without and with tight clothing. For statistical purposes, 100 photos were recorded for each case. One measurement consisted of 7 images (Figs. 7

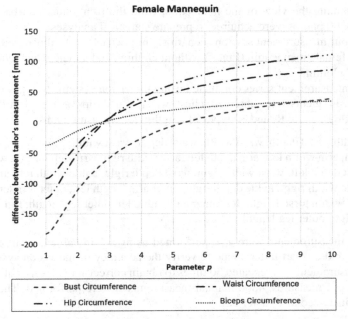

Fig. 5. Graph of the relationship between the error in approximating various circumferential dimensions and the size of the Lamé curve degree (Female)

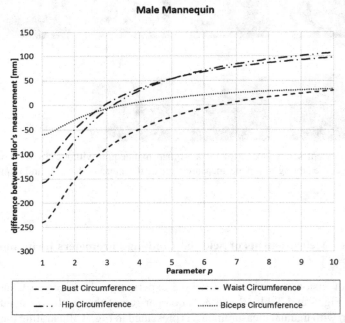

Fig. 6. Graph of the relationship between the error in approximating various circumferential dimensions and the size of the Lamé curve degree (Male).

and 8) containing the view of the mannequin from the front, side, and back. For all scenarios, 3200 photos were acquired to prepare statistical analyses.

Of the four measurement session scenarios, only two cases are illustrated in Figs. 7 and 8, for a female mannequin (Fig. 7) without clothing and a male mannequin (Fig. 8) with "tight" clothing.

For the measurement series conducted using the vision system, 10 types of circumference measurements were obtained: chest, waist, waist, hips, arm L, arm R, wrist L, wrist R, ankle L, ankle R, and 30 types of length/width measurements:

- chest width, chest depth, waist width, waist depth, waist width, waist depth, hip width, hip depth, arm width left, arm depth left, arm width right, arm depth right, wrist width left, wrist depth left, wrist width right, wrist depth right, ankle width left, ankle depth left, ankle width right, ankle depth right, outer arm length left, outer arm length right, shoulder width, torso height, left inner leg length, left outer leg length, right inner leg length, right outer leg length

Manual measurements were also performed using a 1 m caliper, a tailor's tape, a metal ruler, and a smart tailor's tape to verify the accuracy of the vision system. Each manual measurement was repeated 30 times to obtain correct statistics. For all scenarios and 40 types of measures, 4800 manual measurements were performed. The obtained results are discussed in Chapter 3.2.

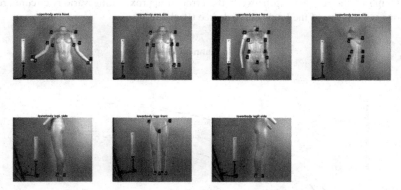

Fig. 7. Measurement series (scenario) for a woman mannequin without clothes, consisting of 7 views (images), enabling complete measurement of the measured width and depth tailoring dimensions.

3.2   Results – Measurements of Selected Clothing Parameters Including Lame Curves

The results of vision measurements for the experiments described in Chapter 3 are presented in Fig. 9 and Tables 2 and 3. A comparison of the results obtained from the vision system with manual measurements is presented in Fig. 9, illustrating the results of the absolute difference between the vision measurement and the manual measurement

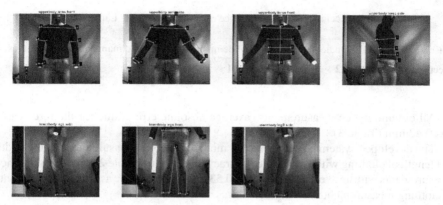

Fig. 8. Measurement series for a dressed male mannequin consisting of 7 views enabling full measurement of the measured widths and depths.

performed using a 1 m caliper. The most significant error value was 11 mm, the smallest 0.25 mm, while the average value of the absolute error was 3.25 mm.

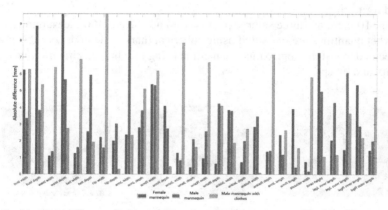

Fig. 9. Absolute difference between vision-based measurement and caliper measurement

The accuracy of the vision measurement for different measurement scenarios is presented in Table 2.

Table 2. Accuracy of dimension determination

Case	Female mannequin	Male mannequin	Male mannequinn with clothes
Accuracy [mm]	3.03	3.20	3.87

The average of the absolute error values of all measurements for the three scenarios was 3.36 mm (Table 2).

Table 3. Accuracy of circumference determination using Lamé curves

Case	Female mannequin	Male mannequin	Male mannequin with clothes
Accuracy [mm]	**0.42**	**0.31**	**0.53**

All circumference measurements' average absolute error value for the three cases was 0.42 mm (Table 3).

The developed system based on marker methods enables measurements of the width and length of clothing with an average accuracy of 3.87 mm (Table 2) and circumference measurements with an average accuracy of 0.53 mm and meets the assumed requirements of clothing measurement accuracy of 5 mm.

3.3   Results – Measurements of Selected Clothing Parameters Including Ellipses

In the next part of the research, to check whether ellipse-based approximation is sufficient to estimate selected human circumferences, a female-type mannequin without clothes to eliminate as many factors as possible that could adversely affect the measurement was prepared for testing.

In Fig. 10 there are three sample photos from a series of 100 measurements, illustrating what quantities are measured using spherical marker methods. For this purpose, it was decided to test the approximation method using four human circumferences: bust, waist, hip, and biceps.

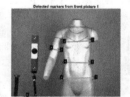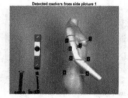

Fig. 10. Three sample photos from a series of 100 measurements

The usage of three photos results from the need to ensure the position of the scale pattern in a given measurement plane.

The collected data (estimated circumference results) from 100 measurements are presented in Table 4. The reference measurement determines the average value of 30 circumferential measurements taken with a tailor's tape measure. It can also be seen that there is no difference between the methods of approximating the ellipse with Eqs. 1–4.

As can be seen, the ellipse-based method does not sufficiently approximate the circumference dimensions. At the same time, the differences obtained are similar (percentage values) to those presented in the literature.

For the obtained measurements, the relative error ranged from several to a dozen percent (absolute error from a few to several hundred mm). Therefore, to measure the

Table 4. Comparison of the four circumferences estimation based on ellipse methods (described by Eq. 1–4) and vision measurements with the reference measurement for the case of female mannequin

	Ref. Measurement	①	Δ_1	Δ_1 %	②	Δ_2	Δ_2 %	③	Δ_3	Δ_3 %	④	Δ_4	Δ_4 %
Bust Circumference	841.4 mm	731.7 mm	-109.7 mm	-13.0%	731.0 mm	-110.4 mm	-13.1%	731.0 mm	-110.4 mm	-13.1%	731.0 mm	-110.4 mm	-13.1%
Waist Circumference	654.9 mm	626.0 mm	-28.9 mm	-4.4%	620.1 mm	-34.8 mm	-5.3%	620.1 mm	-34.8 mm	-5.3%	620.1 mm	-34.8 mm	-5.3%
Hip Circumference	862.7 mm	820.6 mm	-42.1 mm	-4.9%	813.8 mm	-48.9 mm	-5.7%	813.8 mm	-48.9 mm	-5.7%	813.8 mm	-48.9 mm	-5.7%
Biceps Circumference	248.3 mm	235.5 mm	-12.8 mm	-5.2%	235.5 mm	-12.8 mm	-5.2%	235.5 mm	-12.8 mm	-5.2%	235.5 mm	-12.8 mm	-5.2%

circumference, it is reasonable to use the proposed method based on Lame curves, for which the average absolute error does not exceed 0.5 mm.

4 Conclusion

A marker method for vision measurement was developed, and the possibility of using spherical markers for vision measurements was examined. The developed vision system based on spherical markers and employing Lame curves is characterized by high accuracy in measuring selected widths, lengths, and circumferences of clothing. The use of markers also confirmed the possibility of using a vision system to perform anthropometric measurements of the human figure.

The ellipse-based method does not sufficiently approximate the circumference dimensions, for which the relative error of circumference measurements ranged from several to a dozen percent (the absolute error ranged from a few to several hundred mm). Compared to the classical ellipse approach, after implementing the Lame curves, the average absolute error does not exceed 0.55 mm.

A series of experiments were performed to assess the accuracy of the vision system, which confirmed that the average measurement accuracy was below the assumed value of 5 mm.

The developed vision measurement methods can be used to determine the customer's optimal tailoring dimensions, which reduces the costs associated with returning clothes and makes it easier for the customer to choose the right size.

Acknowledgment. The research was carried out as part of the project entitled "MORFER-VISE2 - A universal, mechatronic clothes measurement system designed for effective sale of clothes online" (POIR.01.01.01-00-0739/21).

References

1. Aly, S., et al.: Toward Smart Internet of Things (IoT) for Apparel Retail Industry: Automatic Customer's Body Measurements and Size Recommendation System using Computer Vision

Techniques. s.l. Second International Conference on Intelligent Data Science Technologies and Applications (IDSTA) (2021)

2. Ceseracciu, E., Sawacha, Z., Cobelli, C.: Comparison of Markerless and Marker-Based Motion Capture Technologies through Simultaneous Data Collection during Gait: Proof of Concept. PLoS ONE (2014)

3. Colyer, S., Evans, M., Cosker, D.: A Review of the Evolution of Vision-Based Motion Analysis and the Integration of Advanced Computer Vision Methods Towards Developing a Markerless System, s.l.: s.n. (2018)

4. Foysal, K., Chang, H.-J., Bruess, F., Chong, J.-W.: Body Size Measurement Using a Smartphone. Electronics X(11), 1338 (2021)

5. Liu, Y., et al.: Markerless motion capture of multiple characters using multiview image segmentation. IEEE Trans Pattern Anal Mach Intell, pp. 2720–35 (2013)

6. Massiris, M., Pena-Baena, R., Oviedo-Trespalacios, O.: Hand anthropometry of Colombian Caribbean college students using software based method. s.l. Procedia Computer Science **67**, 123–131 (2015)

7. Pei, X., Wu, S., Lin, C.: An image-based measuring technique for the prediction of human body size. 2nd International Conference on Artificial Intelligence and Computer Engineering (ICAICE) (2021)

8. Rudek, M., Canciglieri Junior, O., Greboge, T.: A PSO application in skull prosthesis modelling by superellipse. Electronic Letters on Computer Vision and Image Analysis **12**(2), 1–12 (2013)

9. Uhm, T., Park, H., Park, J.I.: Fully vision-based automatic human body measurement system for apparel application. Measurement: Journal of the International Measurement Confederation, pp. 169–179 (2015)

10. Ukida, H., Kaji, S., Tanimoto, Y., Yamamoto, H.: Human motion capture system using color markers and silhouette. s.l. Conference Record - IEEE Instrumentation and Measurement Technology Conference (2006)

11. Weng, J., Cohen, P., Herniou, M.: Camera calibration with distortion models and accuracy evaluation. IEEE Transactions on Pattern Analysis and Machine Intelligence, pp. 965–980 (1992)

12. Yang, S., et al.: Markerless motion capture systems for tracking of persons in forensic biomechanics: an overview. Comput. Methods, Biomechanics, Biomed. Eng. 46–65 (2014)

13. Zalando: (2023). https://corporate.zalando.com/en/newsroom/en/news-stories/ahead-curve-returns-managementzalando. Last accessed 25 October 2023

Mechatronic Mannequin as A Way to Reduce the Number of Returns in Fashion E-Commerce

Michał Manka[1], Tomasz Buratowski[1(✉)], Piotr Kohut[1], Lucjan Miekina[1],
Konrad Jaworski[1], Dominik Dragula[2], Tomasz Klorek[2], and Bartosz Bartkowiak[2]

[1] Department of Robotics and Mechatronics, AGH University of Krakow, Krakow, Poland
{mmanka,tburatow,pko,miekina}@agh.edu.pl,
konrad.jaworski@visbroker.pl
[2] VISBROKER Sp. Z O.O., Poznan, Poland
{dominik.dragula,tomasz.klorek,bartosz.bartkowiak}@visbroker.pl

Abstract. An advanced vision algorithm that enables accurate measurements of clothes worn on a specially designed robot called Morpher has been presented in this paper. After a short introduction to the e-commerce market and its problems with the large number of returns, a new method of clothes size measurement was presented. The paper presents the new mechatronic mannequin that may change its dimensions between the 5th and 95th percentile of the human body size. This mannequin connected with the vision system may be helpful not only for online clothes sellers but also for designers, manufacturers, and clothing buyers because they provide quick and accurate information about the fit and comfort of clothing.

Keywords: Mechatronics · Vision systems · Fashion e-commerce · Morpher

1 Introduction

Recent years have dramatically changed the customer's approach to purchasing. The pandemic period, particularly, resulted in a sharp shift from traditional to online shopping. While purchasing devices or equipment can be guided in selecting technical data, general dimensions, or tests, the clothing purchase is much more subjective. In shopping at a physical store, you can try on a garment and decide whether it fits both in size and appearance. In the case of online shopping, it is much more difficult. As a result, online stores offering clothes observe up to 50% of returns [1], which may cause a significant drop in the profitability of this type of activity.

Several methods are used to determine if the clothes will fit without physically trying them:

- Based on the producer's dimension table. It can be successfully used only if the client already knows the size table of the brand. The size's tables of different brands may differ significantly, as presented in Table 1, which can lead to faulty shopping.

K. S. Soliman (Ed.): IBIMA-AI 2024, CCIS 2299, pp. 95–111, 2025.
https://doi.org/10.1007/978-3-031-77493-5_10

Table 1. Waist circumference in different producers' dimension tables.

WAIST/SIZE	XXS	XS	S	M	L	XL	2XL	3XL
ZARA	58	62	66	70	76	82	88	
H&M		72	76–80	84–88	92–96	100–104	108–112	
RESERVED		64	68	72	78	84	90	
TOMMY HILFIGER	61–65	65–68	68–72	72–76	76–81	81–86	86–92	
RALPH LAUREN	62.2	64.8–67.3	69.9–72.4	74.9–77.5	81.3–85.1	90.2–95.3	100.3–105.4	
HELLY HANSEN		68	72	76	82	90	98	102–110
EMPORIO ARMANI	56–58	61–64	66–69	71–74	76–79	81–83	86–89	91–97

- Many online shops perform 2D measurements of the clothes' main dimensions (Fig. 1), usually located on a flat table and then present this data on the webpage. Such data gives more information to the customers but does not provide any data about how it fits the actual client.

Fig. 2. An example of a description of clothes in an online store (https://mylabels.pl)

Fig. 1. Sample measurements of the jacket.

- Another approach often used by online shops is presenting clothes on mannequins or actual models and providing data about their dimensions to customers (Fig. 2). This approach allows seeing how the clothes fit on the model but requires many models/mannequins in different sizes and consumes a lot of time.

In recent years, two new groups of clothing size determination methods have begun to emerge. The first one involves using vision systems that determine the key dimensions of clothes. The second involves using a unique robotic mannequin that allows for the reproduction of a human figure to determine whether a given garment will fit. Application examples of both of these methods will be presented in this article.

2   Vision-Based Methods

In modern methods, a virtual model of the customer is created, and then, based on the provided data, its shape is adjusted to the actual clients' posture. Due to the method of obtaining this data, we can divide these methods into table methods in which the customer gives his dimensions and into methods using vision systems to obtain customer dimensions, i.e., using cameras or lidars. The fitting process itself can be done in both 2D and 3D. In the case of a 2D fit, only basic data such as widths and lengths are considered to determine the fit. In the case of 3D methods, circumferences are additionally taken into account to better fit. While the 2D / 3D methods can be automated to some extent, creating a complete virtual avatar of a client requires many hours of qualified technician work [2–4].

The garments' main parameters should also be acquired to perform the fitting process. As it was mentioned in the previous chapter, the primary sources of these data are tables provided by producers or measurements conducted on-site in the e-shop. Also, in this case, vision-based systems may be adapted to simplify the process and increase its speed and repeatability [5–8].

Among the vision-based measurement systems, we may distinguish two main methods: the marker and markerless methods.

The marker methods minimize the uncertainty of determining characteristic points on clothing; however, they require each time to be mounted on a given type, e.g., employing Velcro or adhesive tape, during each measurement session. Additionally, due to their dimensions and weight, depending on the place of installation on the clothing, they may slightly change their position or deform the arrangement of the material (e.g., installation on the sleeve of a t-shirt, Fig. 3).

A notoriously time-consuming, laborious installation task and the potential for erroneous marker placement are their main disadvantage. These drawbacks can limit the utility of marker-based vision systems within the apparel market and fashion sector and have driven the exploration of markerless solutions.

Below is an example of vision-based measurement for spherical markers placed on a T-shirt (Fig. 3).

From the user's point of view, the markerless method is more challenging to implement but also much faster; which does not require any additional physical elements attached to the mannequin or clothes.

3   Markerless Method for Measuring Selected Clothing Parameters

A dedicated method based on classical and intelligent image processing and analysis methods was developed to measure selected clothing dimensions. As the input to the algorithm, images of a dressed mannequin (dummy) obtained from a 5-megapixel camera placed at a specific distance in front of the mannequin are used. The algorithm determines the contour of the outer shell of the clothes and calculates its geometric parameters, such as length and width. The measurement results for sample garments' upper and lower body parts are shown in Fig. 5a and b.

The block diagram in Fig. 4 shows a vision algorithm for measuring clothes using computer vision methods.

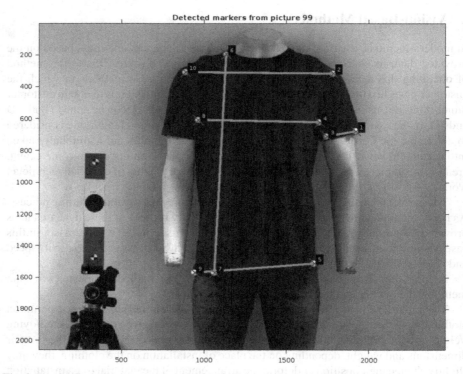

Fig. 3. An example of measuring the length and width of selected T-shirt measurements using spherical markers

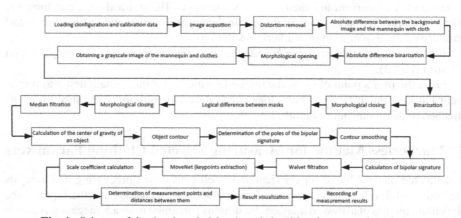

Fig. 4. Scheme of the developed vision-based algorithm for measuring clothes.

The algorithm consists of the following steps:

- In the first step, the algorithm loads a configuration file containing information on segmentation parameters, types and methods of collected measurements, etc. Calibration files containing information on the internal and external parameters of the camera are also loaded.
- The background and the image of the mannequin with clothes on are acquired using a 5-megapixel monochrome Ximea camera.
- In the next stage, optical distortions are removed from the acquired sequence of images.
- Image segmentation into background and mannequin with clothing is performed using the absolute difference between images containing the background and images containing the mannequin with clothing image.
- The resulting image is binarized and subjected to morphological filtering* to eliminate small elements and noise.
- Morphological operations are employed to smooth the resulting image, which is used as a logical mask in further stages.
- The area of interest is extracted from the image of a dressed mannequin using the mask prepared in the previous step.
- Binarization of the obtained image area and morphological closing* are further performed to extract a mask for the image of the mannequin itself.
- The difference between the mannequin mask image and the mannequin mask image with clothing is calculated to obtain a mask image containing only the segmented clothing.
- In the next stage, morphological closing and median filtration are carried out.
- The center of gravity is calculated for the extracted object (clothing).
- Then, the object's contour (clothing) is determined, and the signature poles are calculated.
- The contour is smoothed using a moving average, and a bipolar signature is calculated.
- The bipolar signature characteristic is filtered using a wavelet function.
- In the next step, the MoveNet model based on Tensorflow is applied to obtain human characteristic points – landmarks. In this case, joints, like elbows, knees, shoulders, etc. (MoveNet is a Deep Neural Network that detects 17 body landmarks)
- The scale factor is determined based on the scale markers contained in the image.
- Then, the characteristic points of the clothes worn on the mannequin are detected and located (such as the collar, shoulders, arms, cuffs, hips, body rise, etc.), and the distances between them are calculated. **This step is the primary measurement stage.**
- In the final stage, the results are displayed as graphics and charts and saved as numerical values in a file.

During the process described above two types of morphological operations were used: morphological opening and morphological closing. Morphological opening is a process of erosion followed by a dilation. Morphological closing is a dilation followed by an erosion [9].

Sample measurement results are presented in the photos (Fig. 5). The first photo shows a mannequin wearing long pants, for which the distances between various characteristic points have been determined. The measured values include waist width, hip width, body rise, thigh width, and outer and inner leg length.

The photo (Fig. 5b) shows a mannequin wearing a sweater for which the distances between selected measurement points were calculated. In this case, the following measures were determined to be of interest: the length of the garment, the width of the shoulders, the outer length of the sleeves, and the width of the garment at the bottom.

Accurate estimates of the measurement of the vision system were examined in many measurement sessions, each consisting of a sequence of 1000 images. Taking into account that for the analyzed 1000 measurement photos, on average for 50 images the correct result was not obtained, the effectiveness of the algorithm was 95%. The average repeatability value for all measurements was approximately 1 mm.

The presented algorithm was developed using a traditional shop mannequin with constant dimensions. To fully cover a wide range of clothes of various sizes requires numerous mannequins in different sizes. In order to avoid it, a dedicated mechatronic mannequin was designed, and it is presented in the following chapter.

4 Mechatronic Mannequin

From the point of view of the possibility of imaging all aspects of fitting clothing to the client's figure, the best solution seems to be the construction of a Mechatronic, robotic mannequin. Capable of changing its size following the dimensions obtained from the customer. Abels and Kruusman undertook the first work of this type from the Center for Biorobotics at Tallinn University of Technology [10, 11]. In the following years, similar solutions were also presented by Guo and co-authors [12, 13] and Alan and co-authors

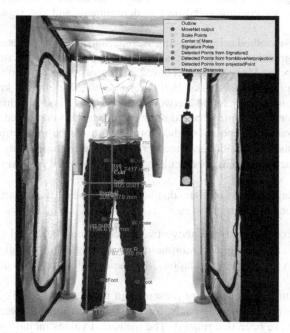

Fig. 5. a. Markerless measurements – Pants. b. Markerless measurements – Sweater

Fig. 5. (*continued*)

[14]. These works involved placing a series of drives inside the dummy's body, allowing for a change in the position of rigid panels imitating the human figure. Another solution was proposed by Li and co-authors [15]. Instead of rigid panels, their work proposed a series of belts encircling the body shaped by independent linear drives. This approach significantly improves the ability of the robotic dummy to reproduce the human figure while increasing the level of complexity of the device itself. Over time, some of these solutions have found commercial applications and are available on the market, such as I. Dummy [16], Fits.me (withdrawn from the market) [17], or Euveka [18]. Most of these projects, however, are limited to modeling changes in the torso size without considering the limbs or modeling them only as elements of constant dimensions.

The first step in designing such a mannequin is to determine the range of changes in its size and the kinematic structure of the resulting device.

In this task, the science called anthropometry will be beneficial. Anthropometry is determining the spatial dimensions of a human being. The data obtained through anthropometric measurements are used to shape the spatial conditions appropriate for specific groups of recipients, including the design of clothes. Anthropometry has defined a number of quantities whose measurements allow for a precise definition of human geometrical parameters [19]. These dimensions vary depending on their implementation period and the country where the research was conducted [20, 21]. Nevertheless, for a given population, it is possible to determine to what extent the dimensions change between the 5th and 95th percentiles and, on this basis, define the limit dimensions of such a dummy.

Based on those measurements, several dimensions were chosen to determine the size and its changes for designing purposes (Table 2).

Table 2. Dimensions of the human between the 5th and 95th percentile, based on the Ansur 2 database.

Men			Dimension	Women		
5% [mm]	95% [mm]	Delta 5–95 [mm]		Delta 5–95 [mm]	5% [mm]	95% [mm]
379	453	**74**	Calf	**68**	354	422
317	366	**49**	Thigh	**43**	312	355
264	306	**42**	High to the crotch	**43**	250	293
515	561	**46**	Chest Height	**47**	468	515
568	621	**53**	Body from crotch	**47**	530	577
384	447	**63**	shoulder width	**61**	335	396
308	387	**79**	Hips	**89**	311	400
307	365	**58**	Arm	**57**	283	340
244	295	**51**	Forearm	**50**	218	268
1648	1870	**222**	Height	**215**	1525	1740

The second critical issue for the design of the mechatronic dummy was the determination of the skeletal model that would be used as the basis of the structure. The human skeleton (Fig. 6) is a highly complex structure with tens of degrees of freedom, practically impossible to reproduce as a mechanical system.

Currently, in the literature, several approximate skeletal structures are used in robotics [22, 23] and computer animation [24, 25]. None of the available designs can be directly applied to the mechatronic mannequin (Morpher), and a new one needs to be developed (Fig. 7).

The first step in modeling the skeleton was to reduce all unnecessary elements in measuring and presenting clothing, namely feet and hands. In addition, in many cases, mannequins used in presenting clothes have a removable head and neck, a cut-out in the neckline, and removable arms and legs, as shown in Fig. 9.

Therefore, a similar solution was applied to the project. As a result, the design of the mechatronic mannequin's skeleton was created, as shown in Fig. 8. Joints were placed in the skeleton to reproduce some of the fundamental human movements on the one hand and, on the other hand, to change the dummy's size. Actual human joints have been replaced with 1-DOF rotational joints. Linear drives have been placed in the limbs, spine, hips, and shoulders to change the dummy's size between the 5th and 95th percentiles. The model and prototype of the designed Morpher are presented in Fig. 10.

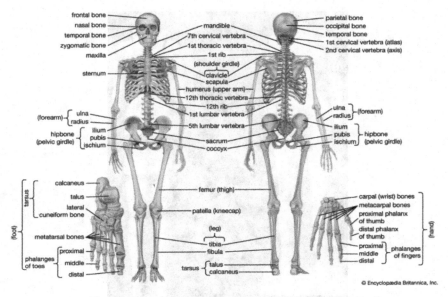

Fig. 6. Human skeleton (Encyclopaedia Britannica Inc.)

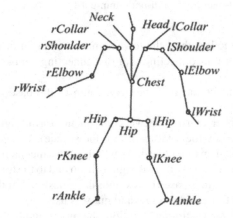

Fig. 7. Simplified human skeleton model [24]

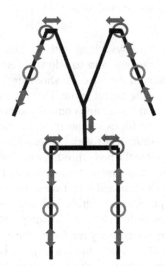

Fig. 8. Mechatronic mannequin skeleton

To simplify the procedure of putting on and taking off clothes, the Morpher has detachable limbs as well as the possibility of lower and upper mounting to the frame.

The trunk of the mannequin has been divided into four sections, allowing for independent changes of circumferences (Fig. 11); moreover, it can also change its length,

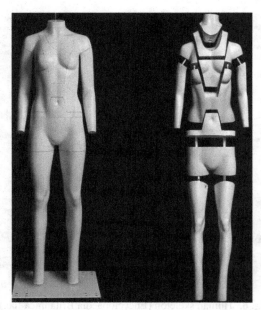

Fig. 9. Ghost-type mannequin. (https://mannequinmall.com/collections/invisible-ghost-manneq
uins/products/ultimate-female-invisible-ghost-mannequin-full-body-mm-ght-f

which allows, along with the change in the length of the lower limbs, the height of the
entire mannequin to adjust. Mechanisms for connecting and disconnecting limbs are
located in the hips and shoulders.

In the sacral spine, there are elements connecting the mannequin to the base and
external power and control sources.

The limbs of the mechatronic Morpher consist of two components (arm/thigh –
forearm/calf) of variable length connected by the rotating joint (elbow/knee). It is connected to the body through a unique mechanism (shoulder/hip), which allows mechanical
connection and the transmission of electrical and pneumatic signals from and to the torso.

The arm and forearm extension mechanism is based on a single-drive design. For this
purpose, a servo drive with an integrated trapezoidal screw and nut was used. However,
this solution gave rise to one problem. In the traditional solution, the motor and the nut
remain stationary relative to the beginning and end of the limb, respectively. At the same
time, the screw changes its position relative to the end of the arm, as shown in Fig. 12a.
To remedy this, the motor was mounted on the guides so it could move (Fig. 12b),
thus making the rotating end of the trapezoidal screw stationary without shifting. This
allowed using standard claw couplings connecting the end of the trapezoidal screw to
the elbow/knee joint. In addition, the choice of a motor with a trapezoidal screw also
meets one of the assumptions, which is the self-locking structure. The structure of the
upper limb is presented in Fig. 13, and the mechanism for the upper and lower one in
Fig. 14.

According to anthropometric data, the elongation of the arm and forearm (thigh and
calf) is not the same. Therefore, it was necessary to use screws with different pitches.

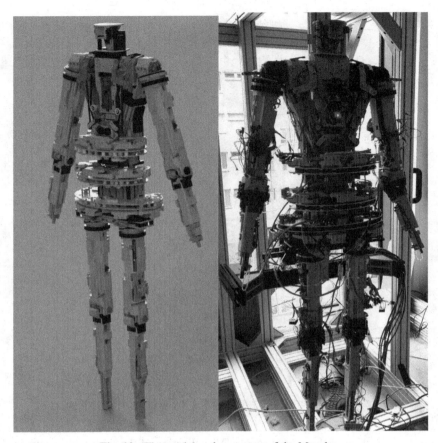

Fig. 10. The model and prototype of the Morpher.

The trapezoidal screw integrated with the Maxon motor has a dimension of tr10 × 2. The change in the length of the forearm is 50 mm, and the arm is 57 mm. To obtain such different elongation, a forearm screw M12 × 1.75 was selected. Thanks to the different pitches of the screw, which are 2 and 1.75 mm, respectively, for the arm and forearm, extending the arm by 57 mm, we obtain about 50 mm of change in the length of the forearm.

The minimum number of wires to be connected should be ensured to simplify the assembly of the limb to the torso. For this reason, it was decided to place the electronics controlling the motor and valves in the extension module. The STM32 microcontroller will control these electronics, and only the power supply and communication to the microcontroller will be needed to be transferred to the limb. The space for electronics is located in the back of the module, shown in Fig. 15.

The structure of the legs is analogous to the construction of the hands, and the only significant change was the appropriate extension of the leg and its range of motion, as

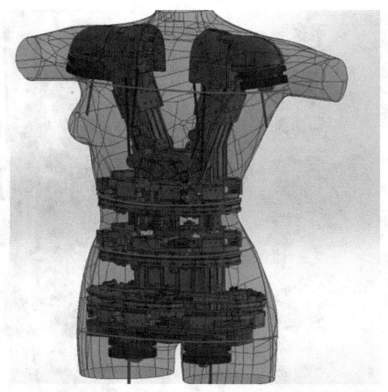

Fig. 11. Morpher's trunk with the localization of variable sections

well as the selection of the proper screws. Visualization of the limb with covers in the 5th and 95th percentile is presented in Fig. 16.

Due to requirements, the mannequin will be used both for Ghost and normal presentation photos and for measuring purposes, a V-shaped cut-out inside the mannequin torso was designed, as shown in Fig. 17. Also, in this cut-out, a cleavage mechanism is placed that ensures both the possibility of changing the circumference in the line of the shoulders and the circumference of the dummy's neck (Fig. 18).

5 Hybrid Measuring Process

Implementing the Mechatronic mannequin into the process of vision-based measurements will introduce some changes in the algorithm presented in Fig. 4.

- After the first step, where the algorithm loads a configuration for the vision system, the basic information concerning the type and the size of the clothes put on Morpher will be loaded, and based on this data, its size will be adjusted.
- Next, the operator verifies if the size is correct and will implement some manual adjustments or allow for continuing realization of the algorithm.

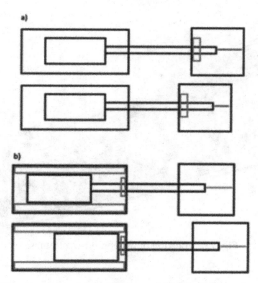

Fig. 12. a) stationary motor – a variable distance of the shaft from the end of the profile. b) movable motor on the guides – a constant distance of the shaft from the end of the profile

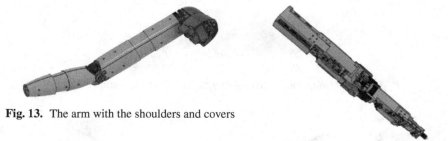

Fig. 13. The arm with the shoulders and covers

Fig. 14. The arm's mechanism

- Then, data from the internal sensors located in the mannequin will be acquired and stored with data from the vision system.
- After the final stage of the measurement process, the operator accepts the presented results, and the mannequin size will be reduced below the 5th percentile to simplify the process of undressing and dressing the mannequin.

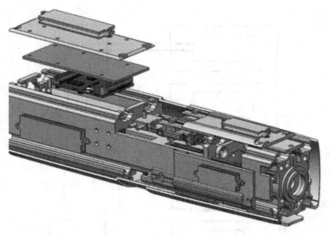

Fig. 15. Location of the control electronics.

Fig. 16. Minimal and maximal elongation of the limb with covers

Fig. 17. Torso without and with cleavage mechanism.

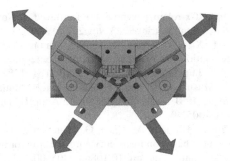

Fig. 18. Neck circumference mechanism.

6 Summary

The mechatronic mannequin presented in the article, together with the developed vision-based algorithm recognition of clothing dimensions, allows for a significant acceleration of the process of obtaining dimensions of clothing intended for online sale.

The presented mannequin effectively changes size in the range of the 5th to 95th percentile of a human in a dozen or so seconds, which allows you to reduce the number of mannequins necessary to perform measurements. In addition, internal sensors placed inside the mannequin and knowledge of its geometry allow for calculating the position of its elements and, consequently, the dimensions of the clothing worn on it.

Presented a new 2D vision algorithm that enables automatic measurements of clothing based on its shape and data entered by the user. The developed method can be used to measure both the upper and lower parts of clothing and the overall clothing, e.g., shirts, trousers, dresses, costumes, etc. The algorithm discussed employs image processing techniques and deep neural networks. To verify the effectiveness and universality of the algorithm, experiments were carried out on various data sets containing photos of male and female mannequins dressed in different types of clothing. The presented results demonstrate that the developed vision method works correctly. Experimental results prove that the algorithm achieves satisfactory accuracy and repeatability in clothing measurements, which constitutes an essential contribution to the field of image and fashion analysis.

Acknowledgment. The research was carried out as part of the project entitled "MORFER-VISE2 – an universal, mechatronic clothes measurement system designed for effective sale of clothes online" (POIR.01.01.01–00-0739/21).

References

1. https://corporate.zalando.com/en/newsroom/en/news-stories/ahead-curve-returns-manage mentzalando. Retrieved 20 Oct 2023
2. Li, J., Lu, G., Liu, Z., Liu, J., Wang, X.: Feature curve-net-based three-dimensional garment customization. Text. Res. J. **83**(5), 519–531 (2013). https://doi.org/10.1177/004051751245 0758

3. https://4f.com.pl/landing/4f-x-robert-lewandowski. Retrieved 29 Nov 2022
4. https://wearfits.com/index.html. Retrieved 23 Nov 2022
5. Li, C., Xu, Y., Feng, M., Xiao, Y., Zhang, D., Liu, H.: Automatic measurement of garment sizes using image recognition. In: ACM International Conference Proceeding Series, Part F1302, pp. 30–34 (2017). https://doi.org/10.1145/3121360.3121382
6. Shigeki, Y., Okura, F., Mitsugami, I., Yagi, Y.: Estimating 3D human shape under clothing from a single RGB image. IPSJ Trans. Comput. Vision Appl. **10**(1), 1–6 (2018). https://doi.org/10.1186/s41074-018-0052-9
7. Xie, H., Zhong, Y., Yu, Z., Hussain, A., Chen, G.: Automatic 3D human body landmarks extraction and measurement based on mean curvature skeleton for tailoring. J. Textile Instit. **113**(8), 1677–1687 (2021). https://doi.org/10.1080/00405000.2021.1944513
8. Han, X., Wu, Z., Wu, Z., Yu, R., Davis, L.S.: VITON: An image-based virtual try-on network. In: Proceedings of the IEEE Computer Society Conference on Computer Vision and Pattern Recognition, vol. 3, pp. 7543–7552 (2018). https://doi.org/10.1109/CVPR.2018.00787
9. Gonzalez, R.C., Woods, R.E.: Digital Image Processing Using MATLAB, Gatesmark Publishing (2009)
10. Abels, A., Kruusmaa, M.: Design of a shape-changing anthropomorphic mannequin for tailoring applications. In: Advanced Robotics. ICAR 2009. International Conference on IEEE, pp.1–6 (2009)
11. Abels, A., Kruusmaa, M.: Shape control of an anthropomorphic tailoring robot mannequin. Int. J. Human. Robot. **10**(02), 1350002 (2013)
12. Guo, Z., Zhang, D., Zhang, S., Liu, X., Li, J.: The design of a form-changing female fitting robot. J. Adv. Mech. Des. Syst. Manuf. **10**(8), JAMDSM0097 (2016)
13. Guo, Z., Zhang, D., Feng, S., Lin, S., Xiao, Y., Li, J.: Structural design and optimization of a panel-based fitting robot. J. Adv. Mech. Des., Syst. Manuf. **12**(4), JAMDSM0091 (2018). https://doi.org/10.1299/jamdsm.2018jamdsm0091
14. Allan, C.: A new paradigm in apparel design and fitting: an interactive robotic mannequin, I. DummyTm. J. Fashion Technol. Textile Eng **3**, 3 (2015)
15. Li, J., Weng, J., Xu, H., Zhou, C., Zhang, D., Lu, G.: Design of robotic mannequin formed by flexible belt net. Comput.-Aided Des. **110**, 1–10 (2019)
16. Kooi, C.C., Wong, G., Qian, Z.: 3D anthropometric i. Dummy for sustainable clothing design and fit. In: Digital Manufacturing Technology for Sustainable Anthropometric Apparel, pp. 117–133. Elsevier (2022). https://doi.org/10.1016/B978-0-12-823969-8.00009-5
17. Fits.me. http://www.fits.me/. Retrieved 20 Oct 2022
18. https://www.euveka.com/en/. Retrieved 20 Oct 2022
19. Gedliczka, A.: Atlas miar człowieka. Dane do projektowania i oceny ergonomicznej. CIOP, Warszawa (2001)
20. Jarosz, E.: Dane antropometryczne populacji osób dorosłych wybranych krajów Unii Europejskiej i Polski dla potrzeb projektowania, IWP, Warszawa (2003)
21. 2012 Anthropometric survey of U.S. Army personnel: methods and summary statistics, TECHNICAL REPORT NATICK/TR-15/007, Massachusetts (2014)
22. Guo, X., Xu, S., Che, W., Zhang, X.: Automatic motion generation based on path editing from motion capture data. In: Pan, Z., Cheok, A.D., Müller, W., Zhang, X., Wong, K. (eds.) Transactions on Edutainment IV, pp. 91–104. Springer Berlin Heidelberg, Berlin, Heidelberg (2010). https://doi.org/10.1007/978-3-642-14484-4_9
23. Dockstader, S.L., Murat Tekalp, A.: A Kinematic Model for Human Motion and Gait Analysis (2022)

24. Wu, X., Ma, L., Chen, Z., Gao, Y.: A 12-DOF analytic inverse kinematics solver for human motion control. J. Inform. Comput. Sci. **1**, 1–137 (2004)
25. Peng, E., Li, L.: Acquiring human skeleton proportions from monocular images without posture estimation. In: 2008 10th International Conference on Control, Automation, Robotics and Vision, pp. 2250–2255 (2008). https://doi.org/10.1109/ICARCV.2008.4795882

Ontological Modeling of the Financial Intermediation Models for Creating a System of Texts' Semantic Analysis

Olga Korableva[1] and Olga Kalimullina[2]([✉])

[1] St. Petersburg State University, Saint-Petersburg University of Management Technologies and Economics, St. Petersburg, Russia
[2] The Bonch-Bruevich Saint-Petersburg State University of Telecommunications, St. Petersburg, Russia
chemireva@mail.ru

Abstract. The study examines promising tools for evaluating financial intermediation models based on semantic text analysis technologies. Semantic web methods, such as ontologies, are used in information systems to cope with the growing need for the sharing and reuse of data and knowledge in various fields of research. There is a growing attention to the analysis of both structured and unstructured data in information systems. The relevance and scientific novelty of the research is due to the subject area, as well as the combination of tools used to solve the tasks. The originality of the study is due to the almost complete absence of similar works within the subject area under consideration. The results of the research are of great interest for the study of financial intermediation models.

Keywords: semantic analysis · ontology · models of financial intermediation

1   Introduction

The research of financial intermediation models is an important and relevant issue, since it allows us to better understand and study the movement of capital. Some agents use capital directly in production, some accumulate capital. In each case, the agents would like to lend their excess capital to other agents, who would then use it in production. In the real world, this lending takes the form of loans to individuals and businesses in order to carry out risky ventures. Capital transfer in this form is known as financial intermediation. The institutions that stand between depositors (those with excess capital) and borrowers (those with less capital, but they want to do something) are diverse, they are financial intermediation institutions. Of particular interest to study are new forms of financial intermediation, such as crowdfunding [10], ICO and others, for the study of which it is necessary to investigate a wide range of factors, such as price [4], level of trust [8], etc. In recent years, many fraudulent ICO activities have been reported, which has drawn attention to this relatively new and unregulated ICO market, which lacks disclosure requirements and, consequently, suffers from increasing problems of

K. S. Soliman (Ed.): IBIMA-AI 2024, CCIS 2299, pp. 112–120, 2025.
https://doi.org/10.1007/978-3-031-77493-5_11

information asymmetry inherent in crowdfunding [15]. Evaluation of financial intermediation models is a difficult task to analyze a significant amount of both structured and
unstructured information. Within the framework of this study, it is planned to design a
semantic search system for texts in natural language, controlled by ontologies, therefore,
the development of an ontology of the subject area is a priority task.

It is supposed to use the advantages of ontologies and their semantics to further build
a business intelligence system. Ontologies are used as an intermediate layer between
the user and the data warehouse. This helps users semantically formalize queries and
explore data, improving the capabilities of inference, knowledge extraction and interaction between data storage systems and the business intelligence system. This technology
allows you to create a "dialog interface" to support business analysis, using natural
language to translate input requests.

The aim of the study is the ontological modeling of the financial intermediation
model for the subsequent creation of a system of semantic analysis of texts and support
for managerial decision-making.

2   Theoretical Background

Work in the field of ontological engineering is actively carried out all over the world. In
the field of designing business ontologies and ontological models of enterprises, there
are two generally recognized leaders (Preprint WP7, 2011) [14]- the Canadian (TOVE
project (TOVE, 2011)) [18] and the Edinburgh School (Enterprise Project [20]) of ontological business modeling. These ontologies are classical, but not the most widespread.
Thus, the ontologies of the REA [23] family are widely used in practice, although they
are simpler than TOVE and Enterprise Project. The paper [15] explores the issue of using
knowledge portals to create ontologies, which allows for effective access to both structured and unstructured information. The paper considers the architecture of the In-Wiss
knowledge portal implemented using Semantic Web technologies based on portlets [7].

A comprehensive review of existing ontologies [1] has shown that there are very
few ontologies in the field of business and economics. So, the ontology created for the
sphere of public administration to assess the effectiveness of management is interesting
[3]. In most cases, knowledge from the requirements-filled ontology is used to create
a multidimensional model that meets the user's requirements. Ontologies are used to
capture the semantics of the data stores involved based on each user's decision-making
needs. The coordination of these ontologies makes it possible to integrate all the concepts
expressed by users into a single global ontology. Also interesting is the ontology created
for an intuitive business intelligence application called conversational business analytics [16]. Ontologies have proved useful for formalizing user requirements. Ontologies
have also proven to be very useful for supporting data mining and visualization. An
ontology-based system can guide users by helping them select and group data, giving
recommendations, and providing a way to detect semantic errors.

The developed system architecture of a data warehouse with ontologies for increasing the competencies of digital entrepreneurs is interesting [13]. Ontologies can also
be used to facilitate data interpretation and knowledge extraction, with ontologies supporting visual analysis, interactive explanation of data, and enabling collaboration and

knowledge sharing, where ontologies are used as a conceptual layer between users and data, allowing multidimensional ontology concepts to be mapped into SQL queries.

Speaking about the ontology-based data collection system, it is nessesary to mention the following recent studies. So, of particular interest is the CEO model [2], which allows you to add information from natural language texts to the ontology. The authors of the article [11] also discuss the issues of adding ontologies using natural language texts. The article [6] proposes an innovative approach based on semantic mapping, in which labels are processed by multilingual natural language processing, and then compared using language- and domain-independent knowledge acting as interlingua.

As for collecting data from unstructured sources, there is a research paper [17]- it represents the technology of extracting information from news scientific articles. The articles describe changes in the world through the events they report, the authors present an approach for creating event-oriented knowledge graphs using modern natural language processing technology and semantic web technologies. In the article [22], the authors describe a system that reads news articles in four different languages and discovers what happened, who is involved, where and when. This event-oriented information is presented as episodic situational knowledge about people in an interoperable RDF format that allows to justify the consequences of events.

The following scientific article [12] considers the localization of ontology as the task of adapting ontology to another cultural context, which is an important task in the context of a multilingual semantic network. The key task in the localization of ontologies is to translate the lexical layer of the ontology, that is, its inscriptions, into some foreign language. As part of this task, the authors of the article hypothesize that the quality of translation can be improved by adapting the machine translation system to the field of ontology. Based on the success of existing machine translation (SMT) approaches, the authors study the impact of various methods of adapting domains to the task. In particular, three methods are being investigated: (i) enriching the phrase table with subject translations obtained from existing web resources, (ii) using explicit semantic analysis as an additional technique for calculating a certain translation of a given source phrase, and (iii) adapting the language model by weighing nn-grams using scores obtained from topic modeling. The article analyzes in detail the impact of each of these three methods on the task of translating ontology labels. The authors conclude that, taken together, these methods have a positive effect on the quality of ontology translation and provide a significant improvement in its quality.

It is generally recognized that adding class separation to ontologies involves enormous difficulties. A number of approaches to this automatic generation have been proposed. However, there is no complete comparison of these approaches in the current literature. In the article [21], the authors make a comparison, presenting two fundamentally different modern approaches and assessing their relative ability to enrich a well-known, multi-purpose ontology with classes.

3 Methodology

During the research, the method of ontological modeling was used to create an expert ontology. To create algorithms at this level of research, a verbal description was used. Thus, an algorithm for automated data collection was developed.

3.1 Algorithm for Automated Data Collection from Tables in PDF, HTML and XLS Documents

Before the data collection stage, time-consuming pre-configuration is required for each type of tables contained in the sources. It consists of the following:

1. The operator provides documents in PDF, HTML or XLS formats containing tables from which data needs to be extracted.
2. The programmer creates a converter program for each type of tables, which translates tabular data into RDF triplets.

The general algorithm for data collection and preprocessing is given in Fig. 1. Preprocessing is reduced to bringing the structure of the ontology.

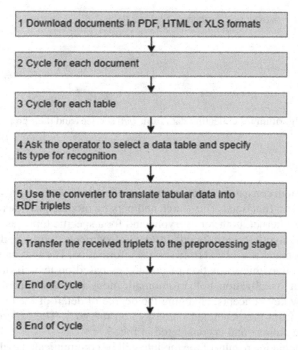

Fig. 1. General algorithm for data collection and preprocessing

Note that the pre-configuration needs to be performed only once for the source, after that data collection can be automated. Below is an algorithm for collecting data from web services or sites that provide Web API, and their preliminary processing. In this case, preprocessing is reduced to bringing to the ontology structure (Fig. 2).

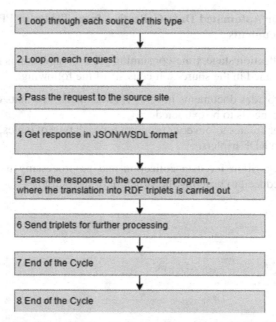

Fig. 2. Algorithm for collecting data from web services and their preprocessing

4   Results

The designed system consists of independent modules, each of which provides the implementation of certain functions. The search and parsing module provides automatic data collection on the Internet, both for everyone and for a specific topic, as well as parsing HTML pages and layout support for pdf, html, xls documents. It fills the database system with texts and separates useful text from service information. The associative-ontological module provides dynamic formation of ontologies based on texts from the generated database and their visualization, both in automatic mode and taking into account external data (adding new key concepts, changing the degree of detail of the ontology, excluding some terms from the generated ontology "on the go"). The expert ontology was developed by the authors and is considered in Fig. 3.

It is assumed that the results of the module will be communicated to the user through an interactive interface provided by the web service module. The functional scheme of the database generation module from existing sources assumes the associative formation of ontologies during the operation of the system, as well as the use of associative links formed directly on the processed texts as a conceptual graph. The results of the structural decomposition of the text are saved in JSON or XML format. Ranking according to the significance of the semantic units (terms or concepts) used and their interrelations with each other is a subject of preservation.

The algorithm for preprocessing potential instances of the "Financial Intermediation Model" or "Financial Markets" ontology classes (see the ontology diagram in Fig. 3) is given in the listing (Fig. 4).

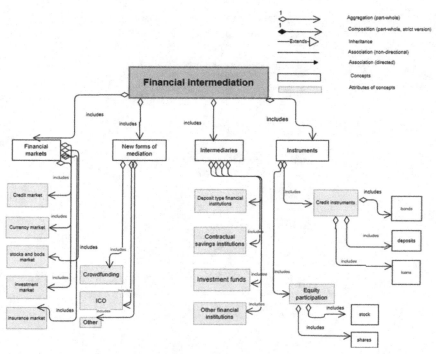

Fig. 3. Expert ontology. Note that preconfiguration only needs to be done once per source, after which data collection can be automated.

5 Discussion

Despite the fact that the data warehouse as an integrated repository is still in the focus of attention of researchers, the relationship between structured data and the semantic network is ignored. However, the growing complexity of (big) data, relationships in business domains lead to increasingly complex business analysis and the need to develop domain ontologies. Ontologies are used to eliminate heterogeneity problems, facilitate data integration, and provide requirements and data semantics. In practice, due to their semantics, rationale and interoperability, ontologies represent a new resource that traditional business intelligence systems should take into account to facilitate the integration and analysis of structured data in the new paradigm of information systems. Working with web data and other unstructured or partially structured data in a structured architecture is a problem in terms of volume, variety, speed, as well as the question of how to link and understand the meaning of different types of data. The influence of ontologies is obvious here, since they allow to formalize knowledge, which means that decisions and organizational or practical knowledge related to the system can be distributed inside or outside the organization, providing communication between business users, data sources in different information systems.

Using the ontological modeling method also helps to reduce costs and time for schema developers and data engineers, especially in cases where ontologies are used

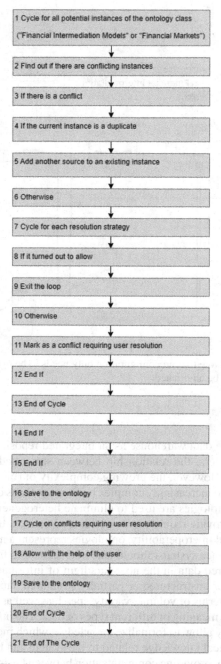

Fig. 4. Listing. Data preprocessing algorithm

to integrate different sources, since comparisons between the source and the target are easier to obtain.

BI systems can use ontologies containing knowledge about various subject areas to enrich and support the research phase, taking advantage of the interoperability of ontologies. Subsequently, BI systems can be used to measure, monitor and evaluate the effectiveness of business and strategy. Strategic information is usually not stored in the BI system. Ontologies can be a useful tool for modeling strategy and strategic information. This knowledge can then be used in a business intelligence application to manage and support information retrieval and analysis. This integration between operational data and strategy is of paramount importance to ensure proper business performance management ([9]; [19]). Moreover, business ontologies are of significant interest for creating an integrated ecosystem that allows analyzing both structured and unstructured data.

6   Conclusions

The study reviewed the use of ontologies in business intelligence systems to improve the analytical capabilities of BI systems or to simplify processes in the BI lifecycle. The paper analyzes the state of research in the field of collection/aggregation systems of weakly structured (and structured) data based on ontology, data integration systems based on ontology. With the advent of the Semantic Web, the use of ontologies has become increasingly common in information systems due to their semantic, formalization and logical qualities.

In the course of the research, the ontology of the subject area of financial intermediation was designed to create a system of semantic analysis of texts and data collection and bring them to the structure of the ontology created within the framework of the work. A prototype system for data collection is also being developed.

This study is particularly interesting because the use of ontologies to enrich data in databases is not a very common way of using ontology. Most of the papers reviewed provide methods for designing or analyze multidimensional models using ontology. Works using ontologies to enrich multidimensional models are rare. The idea here is to use the ontology as an external source to create new attributes associated with an existing business object to link domain information.

Acknowledgment. The research was carried out at the expense of a grant from the Russian Science Foundation № 23-28-00877, 2023–2024 https://rscf.ru/en/project/23-28-00877/.

References

1. Antunes, A.L., Cardoso, E., Barateiro, J.: Incorporation of ontologies in data Warehouse/Business intelligence systems – A systematic literature review. Int. J. Inform. Manag. Data Insights **2**(2), 100131 (2022). https://doi.org/10.1016/j.jjimei.2022.100131
2. Bertolazzi, P., Krusich, C., Missikoff, M.: An approach to the definition of a core enterprise ontology: CEO. In: OES-SEO Workshop, Rome, 14–15 Sep, 2001

3. Chakiri, H., El Mohajir, M., Assem, N.: A data warehouse hybrid design framework using domain ontologies for local good-governance assessment. Transform. Government: People, Process Policy **14**(2), 171–203 (2020). https://doi.org/10.1108/TG-04-2019-0025
4. Chen, Y., Liu, B.: Advertising and pricing decisions for signaling crowdfunding product's quality. Comput. Ind. Eng. **176**, 108947 (2023). https://doi.org/10.1016/j.cie.2022.108947
5. Chou, S.-C., Li, Z.-A., Wang, T., Yen, J.-C.: How the quality of initial coin offering white papers influences fundraising: Using security token offerings white papers as a benchmark. Intell. Syst. Account. Finan. Manag. (2023). https://doi.org/10.1002/isaf.1527
6. Bella, G., Giunchiglia, F., McNeill, F.: Language and domain aware lightweight ontology matching. J. Web Semantics **43**, 1–17 (2017). https://doi.org/10.1016/j.websem.2017.03.003
7. Guryanova, M.A., Efimenko, I.V., Khoroshevsky, V.F.: Mathematical methods of decision analysis in economics, business and politics. National Research University Higher School of Economics, Moscow – 2011. (2011)
8. Harrer, T., Lehner, O.M., Weber, C.: A multi-level understanding of trust development in contexts of blurred organizational boundaries: The case of crowdfunding. Scandinavian J. Manag. **39**(1), 101247 (2023). https://doi.org/10.1016/j.scaman.2022.101247
9. Kaplan, R.S., Norton, D.P.: The Execution Premium: Linking Strategy to Operations for Competitive Advantage. Harvard Business Press (2008)
10. Leone, D., Pietronudo, M.C., Gabteni, H., Carli, M.R.: Reward-based crowdfunding for building a valuable circular business model. J. Bus. Res. **157**, 113562 (2023). https://doi.org/10.1016/j.jbusres.2022.113562
11. Missikoff, M.: A tourism ontology for small and medium enterprises in European market, LEKS, FETISH Project, Deliverable D1.1, IASI-CNR, Rome, 2000] (2000)
12. McCrae, J.P., Arcan, M., Asooja, K., Gracia, J., Buitelaar, P., Cimiano, P.: Domain adaptation for ontology localization. J. Web Semantics **36**, 23–31 (2016). https://doi.org/10.1016/j.websem.2015.12.001
13. Namnual, T., Nilsook, P., Wannapiroon, P.: System architecture of data warehousing with ontologies to enhance digital entrepreneurs' competencies for higher education. Int. J. Inform. Educ. Technol. **9**(6), 414–418 (2019). https://doi.org/10.18178/ijiet.2019.9.6.1237
14. Ontological modeling of the economy of enterprises and industries in modern Russia. Part 2. World research and development: an analytical review. 87. Preprint WP7/2011/08 (part 2) Series WP7
15. Priebe, T., Pernul, G.: Towards integrative enterprise knowledge portals. In: Paper presented at the International Conference on Information and Knowledge Management, Proceedings, pp. 216–223. https://doi.org/10.1145/956863.956906 (2003)
16. Quamar, A., Özcan, F., Miller, D., Moore, R.J., Niehus, R., Kreulen, J.: Conversational BI: an ontology-driven conversation system for business intelligence applications. Proc. VLDB Endow. **13**(12), 3369–3381 (2020). https://doi.org/10.14778/3415478.3415557
17. Rospocher, M., et al.: Building event-centric knowledge graphs from news. J. Web Semantics **37–38**, 132–151 (2016). https://doi.org/10.1016/j.websem.2015.12.004
18. TOVE Ontology Project. http://www.eil.utoronto.ca/enterprise-modelling/tove/
19. Turban, E., Sharda, R., Delen, D.: Decision Support and Business Intelligence Systems (9th). Pearson Education, Inc., USA (2010)
20. Ushold, M., King, M., Moralee, S., Zorgiosm Y.: The Enterprise Ontology. Enterprise Project Deliverable: MID 3.1, Version 1.1 (1995)
21. Völker, J., Fleischhacker, D., Stuckenschmidt, H.: Automatic acquisition of class disjointness. J. Web Semantics **35**, 124–139 (2015). https://doi.org/10.1016/j.websem.2015.07.001
22. Vossen, P., et al.: NewsReader: Using knowledge resources in a cross-lingual reading machine to generate more knowledge from massive streams of news. Knowl.-Based Syst. **110**, 60–85 (2016). https://doi.org/10.1016/j.knosys.2016.07.013
23. White, J.H.: REA modeling of mining companies. J. Inform. Syst. **22**(2), 279–299 (2008)

Optimizing Delivery Routes with Spatially Distributed Orders

Tadeusz Nowicki, Paweł Pieczonka, Michał Sobolewski, and Robert Waszkowski[✉]

Faculty of Cybernetics, Military University of Technology, Kaliskiego 2 Street, 00-908 Warsaw, Poland

{tadeusz.nowicki,pawel.pieczonka,michal.sobolewski,
robert.waszkowski}@wat.edu.pl

Abstract. This paper describes an innovative approach to optimize the delivery process using genetic algorithms. The focus of the study is on the two-stage process: first, the process of allocating the salesmen to the customer in such a way that the total time required for visiting all points gets minimized; the second process is the optimization process of allocating suppliers to the customers that would minimize the shortage or overage of the product. The algorithms use balance load vertical crossover and equivalent mutation. Algorithms tested on real data include customers' locations; they include the time needed for a journey along with any number of other real-life use cases. This study explores logistics optimization possibilities, focusing on the potential of genetic algorithms to address modern supply chain optimization challenges.

Keywords: e-commerce logistics · distribution systems · logistics simulation and efficiency · genetic algorithms

1 Introduction

This paper investigates business processes [1–4] for an e-commerce company selling a specific group of products. The company employs sales representatives (salesmen) to acquire customers and assess their product needs. Final contract sizes are determined after suppliers visit customers and finalize purchases (Fig. 1).

Initial customer needs are reported online. The company has a limited number of salesmen, necessitating efficient scheduling of customer visits for order size estimation. Order sizes are categorized as small, medium, or large. Similarly, the number of suppliers is finite, requiring efficient product delivery. Delivery and unloading times increase with order size (small being the fastest, large the slowest). Assigning multiple suppliers to larger orders can significantly expedite customer fulfillment and reduce delivery times. This is a common problem in the optimization of two-stage deployment and transportation problems and is important in practical applications. Each problem of this type has its own specificity, so it is difficult to find an example in the literature that perfectly corresponds to the formulated problem. The methodology adopted in solving such a problem is to develop a mathematical model, formulate optimization problems

© The Author(s), under exclusive license to Springer Nature Switzerland AG 2025
K. S. Soliman (Ed.): IBIMA-AI 2024, CCIS 2299, pp. 121–134, 2025.
https://doi.org/10.1007/978-3-031-77493-5_12

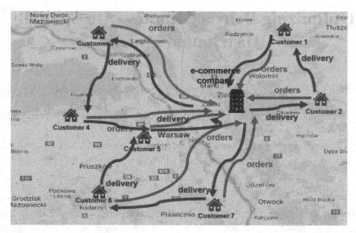

Fig. 1. The idea of the delivery process: the e-commerce company acquires geographically dispersed customers and sells goods to them.

and develop methods for solving such problems. Therefore, this research aims to develop a method for solving two problems:

- scheduling salesmen visits to customers,
- selecting supplier teams and scheduling product deliveries for each customer.

Both problems become computationally complex scheduling problem [9–12] with a large customer base. The dynamic nature of these processes necessitates frequent solution updates. Consequently, the paper explores the application of genetic algorithms for solving both problems.

The proposed approach, utilizing genetic algorithms, aims to achieve efficient product delivery while considering the spatial distribution of orders. Ensuring all stores are visited by salesmen and all ordered products are delivered presents a significant challenge. Achieving these goals is critical in the competitive e-commerce landscape, where delivery speed and rapid customer fulfillment are paramount.

The paper will detail the employed genetic algorithms, including crossover and mutation operator characteristics. It will present experimental results demonstrating the solution's effectiveness and propose future research directions to further enhance the potential and applicability of genetic algorithms for optimal decision-making in e-commerce systems.

2 Problem Description

2.1 The Problem of Assigning Salesmen to Customers

Let C be the set of customers numbers

$$C = \{1, 2, 3, ..., c, ..., C\}, \tag{1}$$

and S be a set of salesman numbers.

$$S = \{1, 2, 3, ..., s, ..., S\}. \tag{2}$$

Let's assume that α is average time of salesman meeting with customer.

Let's assume that the distances between customers are defined by elements of the matrix **D**:

$$\mathbf{D} = \left[d_{c_1 c_2}\right]_{C \times C} \tag{3}$$

where $d_{c_1 c_2}$ is the distance between customers c_1 and c_2 in the sense of time.

The matrix and vector pair $(\mathbf{X}, \mathbf{T})$ defines the strategy for scheduling meetings between salesmen and customers, where matrix **X** has the form

$$\mathbf{X} = [x_{sc}]_{S \times C} \tag{4}$$

where $x_{sc} = 1$ when it is planned that the s-th salesman visits the c-th customer and is equals 0 otherwise, while vector **T** has the form

$$\mathbf{T} = [t_1, ..., t_c, ..., t_C] \tag{5}$$

where t_c is the moment when the meeting with the c-th customer begins. Determining the pair $(\mathbf{X}, \mathbf{T})$ means that the salesmen strategy is known.

Let us assume that the constraints on the decision variables $(\mathbf{X}, \mathbf{T})$ are as follows:

- Formal requirements for decision variables:

$$x_{sc} \in \{0, 1\}, \ t_c \in R_+, \ s = 1, ..., S, \ c = 1, ..., C \tag{6}$$

- Each visit must be carried out by exactly one salesman:

$$\sum_{s=1}^{S} x_{sc} = 1, \ c = \overline{1, C} \tag{7}$$

- Each salesman must carry out at least one visit:

$$\sum_{c=1}^{C} x_{sc} \geq 1, \ s = \overline{1, S} \tag{8}$$

- Preceding visit (meeting) in terms of a time interval must be considered:

$$\left|t_{c_i} - t_{c_j}\right| \geq (\alpha + d_{c_1 c_2}) \cdot \sum_{s=1}^{S} \left(x_{sc_i} \cdot x_{sc_j}\right), \ c_i, c_j = \overline{1, C} \tag{9}$$

Let us assume that the criterion for selecting the optimal strategy:

$$F_1(X*, T*, g*) = \min_{g \in R_+} g \tag{10}$$

with additional linear constraints

$$g \geq t_c + \sum_{s=1}^{S} x_{sc} \alpha, \ c = \overline{1, C} \tag{11}$$

which means minimizing the moment when the last meeting of salesmen with customers ends.

2.2 The Problem of Selecting Supplier Teams and Scheduling Product Delivery for Each Customer

Let **B** be the set of suppliers numbers

$$B = \{1, 2, 3, ..., b, ..., B\} \tag{12}$$

where β_b is customer size (1-small, 2-average, 3-big). The unloading time of products at the customer's depends on its size and the number of suppliers, and v_c means average product unloading time at the customer c-th.

The matrix and vector pair $(\mathbf{Y}, \tau)$ defines the strategy for scheduling product deliveries by suppliers to customers, where matrix Y has the form

$$\mathbf{Y} = [y_{bc}]_{B \times C} \tag{13}$$

where $y_{bc} = 1$ when it is planned that the b-th supplier will make delivery to the c-th customer and is equals to 0 otherwise, while the vector τ has the form

$$\tau = [\tau_1, ..., \tau_c, ..., \tau_C] \tag{14}$$

where τ_c is the moment when the delivery to c-th customer begins.

Determining the pair $(\mathbf{Y}, \tau)$ means that the suppliers strategy is known. The matrix Y shows which supplier will go to a specific customer, and the vector t contains information about what time the delivery will start.

Let us assume that the constraints on the decision variables $(\mathbf{Y}, \tau)$ are as follows:

- Formal requirements for decision variables:

$$y_{bc} \in \{0, 1\}, \ \tau_c \in R_+, \ b = 1, ..., B, \ c = 1, ..., C \tag{15}$$

- Each delivery must be carried out by at least one supplier:

$$\sum_{b=1}^{B} y_{bc} \geq 1, \ c = \overline{1, C} \tag{16}$$

- Each supplier should deliver products at least to one customer:

$$\sum_{c=1}^{C} y_{bc} \geq 1, \ b = \overline{1, B} \tag{17}$$

- Preceding the visit in terms of a time interval must be considered:

$$|t_{c_i}, t_{c_j}| \geq \left(e(\tau_{c_i}, \tau_{c_j}) + d_{c_i c_j}\right) \cdot \text{sgn}\left(\sum_{s=1}^{S} (y_{bc_i} \cdot y_{bc_j})\right), \ c_i, c_j = \overline{1, C} \tag{18}$$

where $|t_{c_i}, t_{c_j}|$ is time interval between deliveries to customers, regardless of which one is earlier and $e(\tau_{c_i}, \tau_{c_j})$ is the minimum time between delivery to the customer c_i -th and c_j -th, taking into account which one precedes the other. We can take the form of a criterion:

$$F_2(Y*, \tau*, h*) = \min_{h \in R_+} h \qquad (19)$$

with additional linear constraints

$$h \geq \tau_c + \sum_{b=1}^{B} y_{bc} v_c, \ c = \overline{1, C} \qquad (20)$$

which means minimizing the moment when the last delivery to customers by suppliers ends.

3   Algorithm Description

3.1   Description of the First Genetic Algorithm: Salesmen Allocation to Customers

The first genetic algorithm is used to optimize the process of allocating salesmen to stores, aiming to understand the demand for individual products best. This algorithm utilizes input data regarding the locations of the customers and the travel costs between them. It allows for the efficient organization of salesmen visits in a way that minimizes travel time and costs while maximizing the efficiency of commercial contacts.

Population Structure - an element of the population in this algorithm consists of two main components:

- Assignment Matrix: The rows of this matrix represent salesmen, while the columns represent customers. Each cell in the matrix contains a binary value (0 or 1), where 1 indicates that the respective salesman is to visit the specified customers.
- Start Times Vector: This vector contains the start times for the presentation of offers by each salesman at the visited customers. These times are crucial to ensure that the meetings are appropriately spread out over time, enabling the effective use of the available working hours of customers.

3.2   Description of the Second Genetic Algorithm: Products Delivery to Customers by Suppliers

The second genetic algorithm is designed to optimize the process of delivering orders to customers, utilizing information obtained from the schedule created by the first algorithm. This algorithm aims to assign suppliers to customers to maximize logistical efficiency and minimize operational costs.

Population Structure - each element of the population in this algorithm consists of two main components:

- Assignment Matrix: In this matrix, the rows represent suppliers, and the columns represent orders. Each matrix cell contains a binary value (0 or 1), indicating whether the respective supplier or suppliers (depending on the order size) are to deliver packages to the specified customer.
- Arrival Times Vector: This vector specifies the times at which individual suppliers are to arrive at the customers. This is crucial for coordinating deliveries and effectively managing the suppliers' working time.

Genetic algorithms are particularly effective in solving optimization problems of high complexity and uncertainty, where traditional methods may not be effective. Genetic algorithms consist of a number of important elements which, with references to the two problems under consideration, are described below:

a) Generating the Initial Population

The process begins with the generation of an initial population of solutions, which are typically represented as sets of population elements. Each population element is a potential solution to the problem, and its quality is assessed using selection operators.

*The **First Genetic Algorithm** and the **Second Genetic Algorithm** generate the initial random population, while complying with the assumed constraints.*

b) Crossover Operators

Crossover is a process where population elements are combined to create new elements that inherit traits from their "parents." This is a key mechanism that allows for exploring new areas of the solution space.

- *The **First Genetic Algorithm** uses the vertical crossover operator. The algorithm randomly selects two population elements by pulling them out of the population building a subset. It then crosses these elements by taking the left part of one population element with the right part of the other population element. The result of this operation is a set of four population elements added to the population.*
- *The **second Genetic Algorithm** uses the vertical crossover operator. The algorithm randomly selects two population elements by pulling them out of the population building a subset. It then crosses these elements by taking the left part of one population element with the right part of the other population element. The result of this operation is a set of four population elements added to the population.*

c) Mutation Operators

Mutation involves randomly changing parts of a population element, introducing diversity and allowing for the exploration of new possible solutions, thus preventing stagnation in local minima of the solution space.

- *The **First Genetic Algorithm** uses the mutation operator, which balances the workload of the sales reps. This operator takes the placeholder assignment off the rep that has the most assignments to the rep that has the fewest assignments.*
- *The **second Genetic Algorithm** uses a mutation operator that randomizes a certain number of warehouses and then randomly assigns them to other random couriers.*

d) Improvement Operators

These operators are applied after crossover and mutation to correct any improper solutions in the newly generated population elements. They can adjust solutions so that they better meet the set criteria.

– *The First Genetic Algorithm* and *Second Genetic Algorithm* *use improvement operators that fix population elements that do not comply with the criteria. They work in an analogous way to mutation operators.*

e) Selection Operators

Selection is the process by which the best elements of the population are chosen to continue the evolutionary cycle in subsequent generations. Selection methods can vary, but they typically prefer elements with higher objective function values, increasing the chances of obtaining better solutions in the future.

– *First Genetic Algorithm* and *Second Genetic Algorithm* *use selection operators that sort all elements of the population (including new elements generated during a given cycle) from the elements with the lowest cost to the elements with the highest cost, and then select a specified number of elements starting with those with the lowest cost.*

f) Result

The evolutionary process is continued until a specific stopping condition is met, which can be defined as reaching a certain number of generations, finding a solution that meets the required criteria, or the absence of improvement in successive iterations. The best solution in the population, i.e., the element with the highest objective function value, becomes the result of the algorithm.

These steps are repeated in an evolutionary loop, where crossover, mutation, improvement, and selection (steps: from *b* to *e*) lead to the gradual improvement of solutions in each subsequent generation, until the optimal solution to the problem is achieved (Fig. 2).

3.3   The Idea of the Construction and Implementation of Two Genetic Algorithms

In solving the optimal package delivery problem using genetic algorithms, a key element is the proper modeling of input data and defining constraints that must be met during the optimization process. Below is a detailed description of the data models used in the two main genetic algorithms of our system.

3.4   The First Algorithm (SAC): Salesmen Allocation to Customers

Input Data

- Assignment Matrix: A matrix where rows represent salesmen and columns represent locations (stores). The matrix elements are binary values (0 or 1), with 1 indicating the assignment of a representative to a particular location.
- Start Times Vector: A vector containing the start time for each salesman visit to assigned locations.

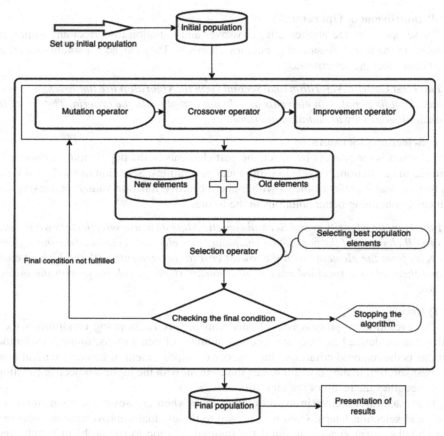

Fig. 2. Description of the main idea of genetic algorithm

- Travel Cost Matrix: A matrix representing the travel costs between locations, where the element at position (i, j) where d_{ij} indicates the travel cost from customers i to customers j.

    Constraints
- All locations must be visited.
- Each location can only be visited by one salesman.

    Stopping Condition
    The algorithm terminates after a specified number of cycles of the genetic algorithm.

3.5 The Second Algorithm (PDCS): Products Delivery to Customers by Suppliers

Input Data

- Assignment Matrix: A matrix where rows represent suppliers and columns represent warehouses. Each matrix element contains a binary value (0 or 1), indicating whether a particular supplier is to deliver packages to a specified warehouse.
- Arrival Times Vector: A vector specifying the arrival time of each supplier at the assigned warehouses.
- Customers Capacity Table: A table describing the capacities of each warehouse.
- Travel Cost Matrix: A matrix showing the travel costs between warehouses, where the element at position (i,j) - d_{ij} indicates the travel cost from customer i to customer j.

Constraints

- All warehouses must be visited.
- Each customer can be visited by no more than two suppliers.

Stopping Condition

The algorithm terminates after reaching a specified runtime.

The input data and constraints are carefully selected and designed to enable effective optimization both in terms of costs and logistics. Through the iterative application of genetic operators within the algorithm, it is possible to successively improve the quality of solutions until the optimal conditions defined by the stopping conditions are achieved.

4 Numerical Example

The experiments conducted as part of our study aimed to evaluate the effectiveness of using genetic algorithms to optimize the processes of allocating salesmen to stores and couriers to warehouses. Genetic algorithms for such problems described in Chapter 2 have already been constructed and developed and can be found in [13–15]. The research was carried out using real-world geographical data and transportation costs to best simulate actual conditions. The experiments were conducted using the defined data models and algorithms described in previous chapters.

The analyzed example illustrates the developed methods, considering the need to assess customers' need for products. The input data are the locations of orders, the number of available salesmen and suppliers:

- Number of consumers: 20;
- Number of salesmen: 4;
- Number of suppliers: 5.

We defined the order size for customers (listed below):

- Warszawa, 04-761, Zwoleńska 122/128 SMALL
- Warszawa, 02-871, Karczunkowska 139A AVERAGE
- Warszawa, 03-287, Głębocka 110 SMALL
- Warszawa, 05-077, aleja Piłsudskiego 2 SMALL
- Warszawa, 01-943, Zgrupowania AK Kampinos 15 SMALL
- Warszawa, 03-574, Radzymińska 94B SMALL
- Warszawa, 04-460, Czwartaków 26 AVERAGE

- Warszawa, 01-918, T. Nocznickiego 29, SMALL
- Warszawa, Szobera 3A SMALL
- Warszawa, 01-318, Wyki 11b, BIG
- Warszawa, 01-354, Powstańców Śląskich 9 SMALL
- Warszawa, 03-186, Modlińska 158c AVERAGE
- Warszawa, 01-903, Marii Dąbrowskiej 15 BIG
- Warszawa, 02-306, Niemcewicza 26, AVERAGE
- Warszawa, 02-118, Pruszkowska 4d SMALL

4.1 Calculations for the First Problem: Salesmen Allocation to Customers

Entry data for algorithm **SAC**:

Matrix D which defines the distances between customer is as follows:

	0	195	165	225	135	60	90	90	225	105	150	285	210	30	210	285	195	300	15	270
	195	0	15	270	105	180	120	135	15	15	255	90	240	135	300	120	45	210	90	15
	165	15	0	105	60	255	45	180	270	60	300	120	225	60	105	60	60	225	285	105
	225	270	105	0	30	195	270	285	285	225	90	300	150	90	270	240	105	255	120	45
	135	105	60	30	0	105	180	75	90	165	195	30	270	270	300	60	300	270	75	270
	60	180	255	195	105	0	285	225	135	285	210	210	105	105	150	255	60	165	180	270
	90	120	45	270	180	285	0	30	300	120	300	270	300	225	60	135	165	180	60	30
	90	135	180	285	75	225	30	0	165	30	105	285	210	30	240	285	30	75	135	240
	225	15	270	285	90	135	300	165	0	75	255	150	45	45	165	240	75	105	285	60
D =	105	15	60	225	165	285	120	30	75	0	285	150	240	90	225	165	105	285	195	150
	150	255	300	90	195	210	300	105	255	285	0	195	135	255	165	15	15	45	120	300
	285	90	120	300	30	210	270	285	150	150	195	0	45	270	180	150	105	240	285	60
	210	240	225	150	270	105	300	210	45	240	135	45	0	105	105	285	135	30	45	15
	30	135	60	90	270	105	225	30	45	90	255	270	105	0	105	15	75	225	300	240
	210	300	105	270	300	150	60	240	165	225	165	180	105	105	0	300	90	300	285	285
	285	120	60	240	60	255	135	285	240	165	15	150	285	15	300	0	225	270	180	90
	195	45	60	105	300	60	165	30	75	105	15	105	135	75	90	225	0	210	165	255
	300	210	225	255	270	165	180	75	105	285	45	240	30	225	300	270	210	0	105	45
	15	90	285	120	75	180	60	135	285	195	120	285	45	300	285	180	165	105	0	255
	270	15	105	45	270	270	30	240	60	150	300	60	15	240	285	90	255	45	255	0

Stopping condition is 10000 cycles. As a result of running the **SAC** algorithm we obtain the assignment matrix as follows.

	0	0	0	0	0	0	1	1	0	1	0	0	0	1	0	1	0	0	0	1
X =	0	0	0	0	0	0	0	0	0	0	1	0	0	0	1	0	1	0	1	0	0	0
	1	0	0	0	0	1	0	0	1	0	0	0	0	0	0	0	0	1	0	0
	0	1	1	1	1	0	0	0	0	0	0	1	1	0	0	0	0	0	1	0

and start times vector.

T =	0:00	0:00	0:00	2:24	2:24	12:00	0:00	16:48	4:48	19:12	0:00	9:36	7:12	4:48	12:00	2:24	21:36	4:48	7:12	9:36

The solution obtained suggested for example, that salesman 1 should visit customer 7 and it begins at moment 0:0 [h], and then should visit customer 8 and it begins at moment 16:48 [h] etc.

After genetic algorithm parameters modification: changing stopping condition to 80000 the results looks as follows.

0	0	0	0	1	0	0	0	0	0	1	1	0	0	0	0	0	0	1	0
1	1	0	0	0	1	1	0	0	1	0	0	0	0	0	0	1	0	0	1
0	0	0	0	0	0	0	0	0	0	0	0	0	1	0	1	0	1	0	0
0	0	1	1	0	0	0	1	1	0	0	0	1	0	1	0	0	0	0	0

$X =$ (matrix above)

and start times vector.

T =	0:00	0:24	6:48	0:00	12:48	0:48	1:12	13:36	1:12	7:36	8:00	13:12	7:36	20:24	0:00	4:00	13:12	2:24	7:36	14:00

The solution obtained suggested for second example, that salesman 2 should visit customer 1 and it begins at moment 0:0 [h], and then should visit customer 2 and it begins at moment 00:24 [h] etc.

4.2 Calculations for the Second Problem: Products Delivery to Customers by Suppliers

Entry data for algorithm **PDCS**:

Matrix D which defines the distances between customers is the same as in algorithm **SAC**. Stopping condition is 4 min. As a result of running the **PDSC** algorithm, we obtain the assignment matrix as follows:

0	0	1	0	1	0	1	1	0	1	1	1	0	0	0
0	0	0	1	0	1	0	0	0	0	0	0	1	0	0
0	1	0	0	0	0	0	0	1	0	1	0	1	0	0
1	0	0	0	0	0	0	0	0	1	0	1	1	0	0
0	0	0	1	0	0	0	1	0	1	0	1	0	1	1

$Y =$ (matrix above)

and start times vector.

τ =	21:36	12:28	13:26	0:00	17:31	11:16	18:43	6:43	20:52	6:14	3:50	14:24	0:00	13:12	16:48

The solution obtained suggested for example, that supplier 1 should visit customer 3-th and it begins at moment 13:26 [h], but in a different example three suppliers (number 1, 4, and 5) together visit customer 10 and it begins at moment 6:14 [h] etc.

After genetic algorithm parameters modification: changing stopping condition to 3 min the results looks as follows.

$$Y = \begin{array}{|c|c|c|c|c|c|c|c|c|c|c|c|c|c|c|}
\hline
0 & 1 & 0 & 0 & 0 & 0 & 0 & 0 & 1 & 0 & 1 & 0 & 1 & 0 & 0 \\
\hline
1 & 0 & 1 & 0 & 1 & 0 & 0 & 0 & 0 & 1 & 1 & 0 & 0 & 0 & 0 \\
\hline
1 & 0 & 1 & 0 & 0 & 0 & 0 & 1 & 0 & 0 & 0 & 0 & 1 & 1 & 0 \\
\hline
0 & 0 & 0 & 1 & 0 & 1 & 0 & 0 & 0 & 0 & 0 & 1 & 1 & 0 & 1 \\
\hline
0 & 0 & 0 & 0 & 1 & 1 & 1 & 1 & 0 & 0 & 1 & 0 & 0 & 0 & 0 \\
\hline
\end{array}$$

and start times vector.

$\tau =$	17:02	23:02	21:07	0:00	3:36	4:33	0:00	12:00	14:52	0:00	11:02	20:52	3:21	20:09	12:00

The solution obtained suggested for second example, that supplier 1 should visit customer 2-nd and it begins at moment 23:02 [h], but in a different example three suppliers (number 2, and 3) together visit customer 1 and it begins at moment 17:02 [h] etc.

5 Conclusions

The paper presents an innovative approach to optimizing logistics processes in the context of package delivery using genetic algorithms. The study aimed to apply these algorithms to two aspects of distribution: the allocation of salesmen to customers and the allocation of suppliers to customers. These algorithms utilized complex data models, which included assignment matrices, start-time vectors, and the costs of travel between stores to simulate real-world conditions. This solution opens new perspectives for further research on the application of genetic algorithms in distribution and supply chain management. One of these is the analysis of clustering demand for specific products, or studying the characteristics of the algorithms that can affect the running time of the algorithms or the quality of the results obtained. In summary, the use of genetic algorithms in logistics is promising and offers a solid foundation for future innovations in this field, with potential impact on improving efficiency, reducing costs, and increasing customer satisfaction in the global supply chain.

Problems of this type, including deployment and transportation problems, are defined and researched in numerous literature, for example in [17, 18]. In turn, methods for solving complex decision-making problems using evolutionary algorithms are presented in [19–21]. As a result of the conducted research, a methodology for formulating two-stage deployment and transportation problems and a method for solving it were obtained. The application of genetic algorithms made the solution of this two-stage problem effective in terms of time. It is possible to set a non-extendible time for solving this problem. Genetic algorithms will show the best solution obtained in this time period. Practically, in a relatively short time, solutions close to the optimal solution are obtained even for large-sized problems.

Acknowledgments. The work was financed by the Military University of Technology in Warsaw, Poland as part of the project No. UGB 701/2024.

References

1. Chang, J. F.: Business Process Management Systems: Strategy and implementation. Auerbach Publications. (2006)
2. Click, R.L., Duening, T.N.: Business process outsourcing: the competitive advantage. Wiley (2005)
3. Waszkowski, R., Nowicki, T., Worwa, K.: Corporate efficiency improvement with business process automation. MATEC Web Conf. **210**, 02012. https://doi.org/10.1051/matecconf/201 821002012 (2018)
4. Waszkowski, R., Nowicki, T.: Efficiency investigation and optimization of contract management business processes in a workwear rental and laundry service company. In: Procedia Manufacturing, vol. 44, pp. 551–558. Elsevier BV. https://doi.org/10.1016/j.promfg.2020. 02.256 (2020)
5. Rocke, D.M., Michalewicz, Z.: Genetic algorithms + data structures = evolution programs. J. Am. Stat. Assoc. **95**(449), 347 (2000). https://doi.org/10.2307/2669583
6. Kramer, O.: Genetic Algorithm Essentials. Springer International Publishing AG, Part of Springer Nature, Cham (2017)
7. Chong, E.K.P., Lu, W., Żak, S.H.: An Introduction to Optimization. John Wiley & Sons (2023)
8. Kramer, O.: Genetic algorithm essentials. In: Studies in Computational Intelligence. Springer International Publishing (2017). https://doi.org/10.1007/978-3-319-52156-5
9. Pinedo, M.: Scheduling: Theory, Algorithms, and Systems. Springer (2014)
10. Pochet, Y., Wolsey, L.A.: Production Planning by Mixed Integer Programming. Springer (2006)
11. Nowicki, T., Waszkowski, R.: Productivity oriented cooperative approach to scheduling IT project tasks. In: Computer Information Systems and Industrial Management, pp. 354–365. Springer International Publishing (2017). https://doi.org/10.1007/978-3-319-59105-6_30
12. Waszkowski, R., Bocewicz, G.: Visibility matrix: efficient user interface modelling for low-code development platforms. Sustainability **14**(13), 8103 (2022). https://doi.org/10.3390/su1 4138103
13. Nowicki, T., Sobolewski, M.: Genetic algorithm for determining optimal scheduling of epidemic interviews. In: 41st International Business Information Management Association Conference, Computer Science Conference Track, 27 Jun. 2023, Granada, Spain. IBIMA Publishing IBIMA Publishing. https://ibima.org/accepted-paper/genetic-algorithm-for-determining-optimal-scheduling-of-epidemic-interviews/(2023)
14. Nowicki, T., Pieczonka P.: Simulation method for determining the strategy for the anti-epidemic control of selected objects. In: 41st International Business Information Management Association Conference, Computer Science Conference Track, 27 Jun. 2023, Granada, Spain. IBIMA Publishing. https://ibima.org/accepted-paper/simulation-method-for-determining-the-strategy-for-the-anti-epidemic-control-of-selected-objects/(2023)
15. Nowicki, T., Pieczonka, P., Sobolewski, M.: Components implementation and integration for decision support in food-borne decease epidemy. In: 42nd International Business Information Management Association Conference, 23 Nov. 2023, Seville, Spain. IBIMA Publishing. https://ibima.org/accepted-paper/components-implementation-and-int egration-for-decision-support-in-food-borne-decease-epidemy/(2023)
16. Nowicki, T., Pieczonka, P., Sobolewski M.: Decision support analysis in food-borne epidemics. In: 42nd International Business Information Management Association Conference, 23 Nov. 2023, Seville, Spain. IBIMA Publishing. https://ibima.org/accepted-paper/decision-support-analysis-in-food-borne-epidemics/
17. Toth, P., Vigo, D.: The Vehicle Routing Problem. Society for Industrial and Applied Mathematics (1987)

18. Simchi-Levi, D., Chen, X., Bramel, J.: The logic of logistics: Theory, Algorithms, and Applications for Logistics and Supply Chain Management. Springer (2004)
19. Mitzenmacher, M., Upfal, E.: Probability and Computing: Randomized Algorithms and Probabilistic Analysis. Cambridge University Press (2005)
20. Zhang, X., Yan, H.: Integrated optimization of production planning and scheduling for a kind of job-shop. Int. J. Adv. Manuf. Technol. 26(7–8), 876–886 (2005). https://doi.org/10.1007/s00170-003-2042-y
21. Yu, X., Gen, M.: Introduction to Evolutionary Algorithms. Springer, London (2010). https://doi.org/10.1007/978-1-84996-129-5

Review of Artificial Intelligence Models for Constructing a Sales Forecasting Module to Enhance Decision-Making

Igor Aguilar-Alonso[1]([⊠]) and Jorge Espinoza Espinoza[2]

[1] Research Group: IT Governance and Management Platforms (IT-GOVMANPLA),
Professional School of System Engineering National Technological University of South Lima,
Villa El Salvador, Peru
iaguilar@untels.edu.pe
[2] Professional School of System Engineering, National Technological University of South
Lima, Villa El Salvador, Peru
surke@outlook.es

Abstract. In today's rapidly evolving business landscape, making informed strategic decisions is paramount for future success. Forecasting, a widely adopted practice across diverse domains, empowers us to predict uncertain future events and utilize existing data to project potential outcomes. This article aims to evaluate models that enhance decision-making, projection, and model combination. Through a concise bibliographic review of prestigious journal articles from the past five years, 97 relevant papers were identified, with 30 selected for detailed analysis. The key finding is that leveraging projections can significantly enhance decision-making by anticipating uncertain events in a company's future. Notably, the ARIMA and LSTM models emerge as standout choices for achieving this goal.

Keywords: Forecasting · Decision making · ARIMA algorithm · LSTM · Artificial Intelligence

1 Introduction

Decision-making based on multiple criteria is a constant requirement when solving complex problems. This process becomes intricate due to the presence of multiple, and sometimes conflicting, criteria, leading to the development of various multicriteria decision-making methods. Key features of these methods include accuracy, simplicity, and stability [10].

In today's competitive market, sales forecasting plays a crucial role in business planning. It helps mitigate risk in the decision-making process, enabling companies to operate efficiently. Sales forecasting is an essential function of management. Companies that market hundreds or thousands of products must be able to meet consumer demand. When a company fails to provide requested products, it negatively impacts customer service and, consequently, reduces profits, as consumers will choose companies that can fulfill their needs.

K. S. Soliman (Ed.): IBIMA-AI 2024, CCIS 2299, pp. 135–148, 2025.
https://doi.org/10.1007/978-3-031-77493-5_13

These challenges are exacerbated if company executives do not invest in Information Technology (IT) to automate business processes and perform various forecasts for better decision-making [1]. Therefore, business management must anticipate consumer demand several months in advance, considering the lead time for product delivery to suppliers. Sales forecasting is more than just an exchange; it involves effective management and control aimed at increasing market penetration, optimizing customer service, and improving overall business efficiency. Inaccurate sales forecasts can lead to increased inventory costs, rendering the investment inefficient [15].

The synergy between IT and sales forecasting allows companies to make informed decisions, reduce risks and thrive in a competitive landscape. The implementation of sales forecasting modules based on neural networks represents a strategic investment for companies seeking to improve decision-making processes.

Given that many companies, especially medium-sized enterprises, do not fully utilize the necessary IT tools for business digitization and process improvement, the implementation of a sales forecasting module using neural networks becomes essential to enhance decision-making within the company.

2 Background

2.1 Sales Forecasting in Decision Making

In today's context, decision makers have come to realize that accurate forecasting can significantly influence their work and yield meaningful outcomes. Forecasting has found widespread application across various domains, enabling us to predict uncertain future events by leveraging existing information. One specific area where forecasting plays a crucial role is sales prediction. Sales forecasting stands out as the optimal approach for anticipating a company's future requirements [5].

Sales forecasts are the essential inputs for many managerial decisions, such as pricing, store space allocation, listing/delisting, ordering, and inventory management of an item [24].

Nowadays it is common to find in companies enterprise resource planning systems which in many cases make use of the ARIMA algorithm since it is relatively simple to implement; it can interpret values in linear functions with cyclical or seasonal components. In addition, it can estimate future values by combining past values [8] which gives favorable results.

Univariate ARIMA models are considered a standard reference model in econometrics. The models compared are quite different, as are the datasets they accept as input, which makes the comparison interesting. On the one hand, the basic principles are simplicity and scalability; it is designed specifically for business forecasting problems and handles missing data very well, but if the data are not linear or trend following, the ARIMA model will be limited in terms of the estimation and precision it can give [26].

2.2 Long Short-Term Memory (LSTM) Neural Networks

Long Short-Term Memory (LSTM) neural networks are a type of recurrent neural network (RNN) designed to learn and remember long-term dependencies in data sequences.

Unlike traditional RNNs, which struggle with long-term dependencies due to issues such as the vanishing gradient problem, LSTMs are structured to retain information over extended periods.

Among the common applications of LSTM, they are widely used in sequence analysis, including classification and generation of sequences, such as DNA sequence analysis and recommendation systems. In voice recognition and natural language processing (NLP), they are applied in tasks like voice recognition, text generation, and language translation. They are also utilized in time series forecasting tasks, such as predicting future values in temporal sequences like sales, stock prices, and energy demand.

As a feature of LSTM, by introducing the concept of gates in the network structure, LSTMs can store long-term information and make effective use of historical data, which is highly suitable for time series prediction. A gate is essentially a fully connected layer with the input as a vector and the output as a real number between 0 and 1. If the value is 0, all information is discarded; if the value is 1, the cell retains all input information [16].

The LSTM architecture is designed to overcome the limitations of traditional recurrent neural networks, particularly in learning and remembering long-term dependencies in sequential data. The key to this architecture is its ability to control the flow of information through a series of gates. LSTMs use these gates to carefully manage the amount of information retained and forgotten at each step, enabling them to handle long-term dependencies and capture complex patterns in sequential data. This architecture makes LSTMs particularly useful in applications such as time series forecasting, natural language processing, and other tasks involving long data sequences.

2.3 Autoregressive Integrated Moving Average (ARIMA) Algorithm

The ARIMA algorithm is a statistical model used for time series analysis and prediction. It is widely used in econometrics and other disciplines to model data that exhibit temporal patterns, such as financial, sales, and demand data.

ARIMA is the most widely used and accurate short-term time series forecasting method for single-variable data. The algorithm holds that the values of the current time sequence are linearly related to the values of the past time sequence and to the quantity, i.e., the model contains both the auto regression element (variable of interest depends on its past observations) and moving average [16].

Arima has its advantages and limitations. The advantages of ARIMA, it is a powerful model for time series that captures linear and seasonal patterns in the data. It is relatively easy to interpret and widely used due to its robustness and reliability in various contexts. On the other hand, the limitations of ARIMA, it assumes that the time series is linear and stationary (after differentiation). It does not handle nonlinear patterns well and may be less effective when the data has a complex structure that cannot be captured by a linear combination of past values and errors.

3   Research Methodology

For this research we will use the Literature Review Methodology proposed by [21], this methodology consists of 3 phases: Planning of the review, development of the review and results of the review.

3.1   Review planning:

In this part the research questions were elaborated.
    The questions were:

- What models can be used to improve decision making?
- What models use artificial intelligence for sales projection?
- What combined models with better projection accuracy for sales forecasting?

    The main databases used were Science Direct, IEEE, Hindawi and Taylor & Francis. The following selection and exclusion criteria were used to select the literature.

    The keywords used for the search were the following: "decision-making projection", "demand forecasting", "sales forecasting machine learning".

    The criteria used to include and exclude items are detailed in the following Table 1.

Table 1. Inclusion and exclusion criteria

Inclusion criteria	Exclusion criteria
Related studies investigating the use of models to improve decision-making	Sources that are not scientific articles or conferences
Studies that seek to obtain a projection of sales/demand/prices	Research with more than 5 years old
Studies that combine different projection models Journal articles and impact conferences Articles written in English or Spanish	Languages other than English or Spanish

3.2   Carrying Out the Review

The search for articles of interest for our research was subject to the inclusion and exclusion criteria mentioned in the previous Table, as well as the search chain that was applied to each of the information sources. For the selection of the papers, a prior review of the works was necessary to then determine if their content was relevant to the research. Finally, we are left with the articles useful for our research. As can be seen in Fig. 1.

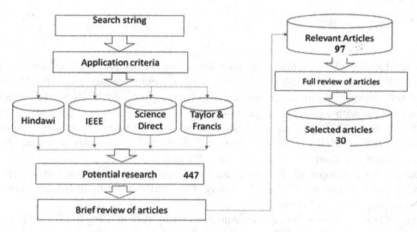

Fig. 1.   Search process of selected studies.

3.3   Review Results

The outcome of the bibliographic review process was refined following the definition of the search string, considering the established inclusion and exclusion criteria, which led to the identification of 447 potential documents. Subsequently, after reviewing the document summaries, 97 relevant documents were chosen. Finally, following a thorough review of the pertinent documents, 30 were selected. Table 2 displays the results obtained at each stage of selection.

4   Summary of the results found

4.1   Models to Improve Decision-Making

During the development of this research by [31], a decision support model that utilizes projections (ARIMA model) in conjunction with hierarchical classification is proposed. Throughout the research process, tests were conducted comparing the ARMA algorithm against the ARIMA model combined with hierarchical classification. The results clearly demonstrated that using ARIMA reduced the mean error.

In the study conducted by [23], a decision-making model was developed for a future product. This model employs a DNN (Deep Neural Network) to project future sales of

Table 2. Studies found, relevant studies and selected studies

Databases consulted	Studies Found	Relevant studies	Selected studies	Percentage
Hindawi	183	43	13	43%
IEEE	138	26	8	27%
Science Direct	88	23	8	27%
Taylor & Francis	38	5	1	3%
TOTAL	**447**	**97**	**30**	**100%**

a new product for which no historical sales data exists. A comparative analysis was also performed, including other models such as Artificial Neural Networks (ANN), Decision Trees, and Support Vector Regression. Notably, the proposed DNN model achieved superior results with a lower average error.

The study by [27], propose a decision support model using the real-time simulation model called SRDM (Simulation-based Real-time Decision Making). This model predicts orders and their variations for a laundry in real time.

During the development of this research, [33] proposed a decision-making model for the construction of the Tourism Highway. They utilized Artificial Neural Networks (ANN) to project tourism demand.

In their study, [19] developed a demand forecasting system using the DeepAR model on Amazon Web Services (AWS). The DeepAR model represents a supervised learning algorithm for forecasting scalar (one-dimensional) time series using recurrent neural networks (RNN). Unlike classical forecasting methods such as exponential smoothing (ETS) or autoregressive integrated moving average (ARIMA), which fit a single model to each individual time series, DeepAR leverages many related time series for more accurate predictions. By training an auto-regressive recurrent network model, DeepAR estimates the probability distribution of future demand based on historical data. This high-accuracy system not only enables better market strategy formulation but also contributes to reducing supply chain costs.

[32] conducted a study proposing a decision support model for optimizing production lines. They employed ARIMA, Lotka-Volterra, and Vector Auto Regression (VAR) models to calculate base plate production and generated profits. The study also includes a comparison of these models and an explanation of why they were chosen for each prediction stage.

According to the research by [2], this article introduces a variation of the Delphi method using triangular fuzzy numbers (TFNs). While maintaining the same communication with experts, the estimation procedure is modified. A numerical example illustrates the utility of this method. The study highlights that, in many cases, using the critical path method for forecasting can be more efficient due to the multiple operational steps involved. Future research may explore other forecasting approaches using various fuzzy-like structures, such as interval-valued, intuitionistic, Pythagorean, spherical, picture fuzzy sets, and neutrosophic sets, with a focus on real-world applications.

In the research by [29], a decision-making model for electrical demand was proposed. A comparison was made between three models: FAR, FARX, and AR. It was found that the FARX model achieved better results, generating a lower error. All of this was done with the aim of optimizing the supply network of a zonal electrical transformer.

In the study by [3], a model for electricity demand prediction using the LSTM neural network was developed. This model was chosen after a comparison with other models such as MLP, CNN + LSTM, and CNN, which revealed that the LSTM model best met the requirements.

In the research conducted by [6], a quality prediction module was developed for the production of customized transformers. The module utilizes the ARIMA model to predict the final product quality and, based on the results, adjust the production or output of the product.

The study by [18], developed a model for a Decision Support System using LSTM neural networks. This model demonstrated the ability to enhance financial forecasting by reducing errors in financial decision-making, thanks to the accuracy of the predicted data.

4.2 Models that Use Artificial Intelligence for Sales Projection

According to the research by [25], a projection model utilizing Bayesian networks and Machine Learning was developed to predict the sales direction of shares on the Sao Paulo stock market. The tests showed that the proposed model achieved better results compared to models such as PNN and KNN.

In the study conducted by [17], a composite model was developed using cointegration analysis and an adaptive genetic algorithm (AGA) that utilizes dense layers to store the most important variables for projection.

In the study by [9], the application of a model (ARIMA-SVNS) based on Fourier Series for projecting electricity demand variables was developed, where it was observed that it allows for better projection due to the properties of the Fourier series.

According to the research by [11], a comparative analysis of various electricity demand projection models was conducted. The models evaluated included EVTree, RF, NN, GBM, ARIMA, LM, and ENSEMBLE. The analysis revealed that each model has its own strengths and is useful depending on the specific use case.

In the research by [33], a model was proposed for decision making in the construction of the Tourism Highway, using Artificial Neural Networks (ANN) for the projection of tourism demand.

In this paper by [22], a model based on LSTM was proposed for the projection of sales at a Walmart store. A comparison of Logistic Regression, SVM, and LSTM models was made, showing that LSTM achieved more accurate results compared to the other models.

The paper by [30] analyzed three methods to forecast Amazon sales based on historical data. These models are NNAR, ARIMA, and SARIMA; the investigation aimed to determine which one best fits the sales projection in Amazon implementation.

In the paper by [35], a demand projection model called SAM is proposed. Unlike other models, SAM utilizes users' sentiment data in real-time operation. This innovative approach allows for greater accuracy in demand prediction, which is essential for resource planning and efficient management.

In the research by [14], a combined model was developed that integrates genetic algorithms and Long ShortTerm Memory (LSTM) to enhance load prediction for power systems. The combination of these techniques offers increased robustness and precision in estimating electrical load, which is crucial for ensuring system stability and reliability.

In the paper by [4], introduces an ARIMA LSTM model for macroeconomic projection. This approach combines the strengths of the traditional ARIMA model with the deep learning capabilities of LSTM. The results demonstrate that the proposed model outperforms the standard ARIMA algorithm in terms of accuracy and predictive capability.

According to [12], a backpropagation (BP) model was proposed that has extensive learning capabilities and associative memory, as well as high fault tolerance and the ability to perform non-linear data mapping. The results obtained showed that it responded well to sales forecasts for marketing studies.

4.3   Combined Models with Better Projection Accuracy for Sales Forecasting

According to the research by [25], a projection model was developed that utilizes Bayesian networks and Machine Learning (ML) to predict the sales direction of shares on the São Paulo stock market. During testing, the proposed model outperformed other models such as PNN and KNN.

In the publication by [7], a novel LSTM ensemble projection method was proposed. This approach involves multiple LSTM implementations, and the resulting weights are combined to produce a joint result. The model demonstrated superiority over other available options, with a mean square error 25% lower than competing models. It is applicable to time series data in general.

In the study conducted by [13], a decision support system (DSS) is proposed for optimizing the supply chain of fresh products. The DSS employs ARIMA, ARIMAX, and TF models to predict orders and reduce costs. Combining these models improved precision by reducing average errors.

In the research by [20], a composite prediction model was developed to enhance decision-making in supply chains. By combining multiple models (SVR, SVM, MLFANN, Time Series, Exponential Smoothing, ARIMA), better results were achieved compared to using them separately. Deep learning techniques were also applied dynamically to optimize model selection for specific cases, leading to even better results.

In [34] study, this study proposes a multilayer model using LSTM + hidden network for the prediction in Indian stock market, tests were carried out with LSTM with and without state to know which is more stable for varied data, where it was seen that using LSTM without state is achieve more stable results.

In [20], the effectiveness of time series and rule-based forecasting was analyzed. DeepAR (AWS Lambda) models demonstrated high accuracy and comparability. As data size increased, the model produced even more accurate results.

According to [16] research, a combined projection model based on the ARIMA model and short- and long-term memory (LSTM) neural networks was proposed. This model processed both linear and non-linear sales data, resulting in greater precision compared to using the components separately.

[28] proposed applying an LSTM model to improve sales projection accuracy and detect anomalies. The results confirmed the effectiveness of this approach.

In the study by [35], a composite model (CNN-LSTM) was used for sales forecasting. By analyzing customer interaction data (web) and demand, sentiment analysis was performed, leading to improved sales accuracy.

5 Analysis of the Proposals and Answers to the Research Questions

5.1 Analysis of Models to Improve Decision Making

Decision-making across diverse domains has witnessed significant enhancements due to the development and implementation of models as well as the utilization of advanced algorithms. A comprehensive review of recent research literature reveals a plethora of innovative approaches aimed at enhancing decision-making processes across various sectors, as depicted in Table 3.

In this analysis, we delve into the insights and contributions proposed by several studies, each offering unique perspectives that contribute to the advancement of this field.

Table 3. Models to improve decision making

No	References	ARMA	ARIMA	DNN	ANN	SRDM	DeepAR	Locka V	VAR	Delphi	FAR	FARX	AR	LSTM	MLP	CNN-LSTM	CNN
1	[31]	X	X														
2	[23]			X	X												
3	[27]					X											
4	[33]				X												
5	[19]						X										
6	[32]		X					X	X								
7	[2]									X							
8	[29]										X	X	X				
9	[3]													X	X	X	X
10	[6]		X														
11	[18]													X			
	Total	1	3	1	2	1	1	1	1	1	1	1	1	2	1	1	1
	Percentage	5%	15%	5%	10%	5%	5%	5%	5%	5%	5%	5%	5%	10%	5%	5%	5%

From the previous table, the models for improving decision making have been identified as ARIMA, LSTM, and ANN.

This choice is because the implementation of these models can offer specific advantages against certain types of problems. Here are the statistics corresponding to the mentioned models:

- ARIMA: Represents 15% of the utilized models. It is a linear model that can be quickly implemented and is suitable for handling time series data with linear and seasonal patterns.
- LSTM: Represents 10% of the models. It is a recurrent neural network (RNN) that excels in learning and retaining long-term dependencies in sequential data. It is especially useful for more precise time series analysis.
- ANN (Artificial Neural Network): Also represents 10% of the models. ANNs process both linear and nonlinear data, making them versatile for decision-making.

In summary, the choice between these models depends on the specific context and data characteristics. Each one offers a unique approach to enhancing decision-making.

5.2   Analysis of Models that Use Artificial Intelligence for Sales Projection

In the realm of sales and demand forecasting, a multitude of studies have developed and assessed various models leveraging advanced data analysis and machine learning techniques. As illustrated in Table 4, these approaches have consistently demonstrated their capacity to enhance prediction accuracy when compared to traditional methods.

Table 4. Models with artificial intelligence for sales projection

No	References	Bayesian networks	PNN	KNN	ARIMA	GBN	EVTree	ANN	LSTM	SVN	NNAR	SARIM	SAM	BP	SVNS	AGA
1	[25]	X	X	X												
2	[17]															X
3	[9]				X										X	
4	[11]				X	X	X									
5	[33]							X								
6	[22]								X	X						
7	[30]				X						X	X				
8	[35]												X			
9	[14]								X							
10	[4]				X				X							
11	[12]													X		
	Total	1	1	1	4	1	1	1	3	1	1	1	1	1	1	1
	Percentage	5%	5%	5%	20%	5%	5%	5%	15%	5%	5%	5%	5%	5%	5%	5%

From the previous table, which shows the different models that use artificial intelligence in their applications, we can conclude that the most used models for sales forecasting are LSTM (because it can process nonlinear data) and ARIMA (which can only process linear data). However, ARIMA is one of the simplest models to implement, contributing to its popularity in the market.

Here are the statistics corresponding to the mentioned models:

- ARIMA: Represents 20% of the utilized models. It is a linear model that can be quickly implemented and is suitable for handling time series data with linear and seasonal patterns.

- LSTM: Represents 15% of the models. It is a recurrent neural network (RNN) that excels in learning and retaining long-term dependencies in sequential data. It is especially useful for more precise time series analysis.
- Other models: Each of them represents 5%. These models can vary in complexity and applicability but are not as widely used as ARIMA and LSTM.

In summary, the choice between these models depends on the specific context and data characteristics. Each one offers a unique approach to enhancing decision-making in sales forecasting.

5.3 Analysis of Combined Models with Higher Accuracy for Sales Forecasting

In the field of sales and demand forecasting, researchers have explored various combined models to enhance prediction accuracy. As illustrated in Table 5. Among these models, the ARIMA-LSTM hybrid stands out as one of the most promising. This composite model integrates the strengths of both ARIMA and LSTM. The ARIMA model effectively handles linear and seasonal patterns, while LSTM excels at learning long-term dependencies in sequential data. Together, they offer accurate results for sales projections.

Table 5. Combined models with higher accuracy for sales forecasting and improve decision making

No	References	Bayesian networks	LSTM	ARIMA	ARIMAX	TF	SVR	SVM	MFLANN	LSTM	Hidden Layers	DeepAR	CNN
1	[25]	X											
2	[7]		X										
3	[13]			X	X	X							
4	[20]			X			X	X	X				
5	[34]									X	X		
6	[19]											X	
7	(Han, 2020)		X	X									
8	[28]		X										
9	[35]		X										X
	Total	1	4	3	1	1	1	1	1	1	1	1	1
	Percentage	6%	24%	18%	6%	6%	6%	6%	6%	6%	6%	6%	6%

From the previous table, which displays the results of different models, we can infer that the most used models for sales forecasting are LSTM (due to its capability to handle nonlinear data) and ARIMA (which can only process linear data). However, ARIMA stands out as one of the simplest models to implement, contributing to its popularity in the market. Here are the statistics corresponding to the mentioned models:

- LSTM: Represents 24% of the models.
- ARIMA: Represents 18% of the utilized models.
- Other models: Each of them represents 6%. These models may vary in complexity and applicability but are not as widely used as ARIMA and LSTM.

In summary, the choice between these models depends on the specific context and data characteristics. Each one offers a unique approach to enhancing decision-making in sales forecasting.

6 Conclusions

The most important conclusions in relation to the research carried out are indicated below:

Adaptability of Neural Networks in Decision Making: Currently, there are numerous models that use neural networks to improve decision-making due to their adaptability and continuous learning capabilities. These models have proven to be especially effective in complex and dynamic environments where relationships between variables are nonlinear.

Diversity of Sales Forecasting Models: It was observed that there is a wide variety of sales forecasting models, ranging from traditional mathematical models to those based on neural networks. Each of these models is designed to fit specific contexts and requirements, highlighting the importance of selecting the appropriate model according to the operational environment and the characteristics of the available data.

Improvement of Accuracy through Combined Models: Combined models, which integrate the advantages of different approaches, can offer new or better features, improving prediction accuracy in several cases. This synergy allows capturing both linear and nonlinear patterns, optimizing the accuracy of forecasts.

Development of New Architectures for Decision Making: Using the available data, it is possible to develop new architectures that improve decision-making in small companies. The implementation of systems based on neural networks can provide a significant competitive advantage, enabling more efficient resource management and a quicker response to market demands.

References

1. Aguilar Alonso, I., Carrillo Verdún, J., Tovar Caro, E.: Description of the structure of the IT demand management process framework. Int. J. Inf. Manag.Manag. **37**, 1461–1473 (2017). https://doi.org/10.1016/j.ijinfomgt.2016.05.004
2. Alharbi, M.G., Khalifa, H.A.E.W.: Enhanced fuzzy Delphi method in forecasting and decision-making. Adv. Fuzzy Syst. (2021). https://doi.org/10.1155/2021/2459573(2021)
3. Butt, F.M., et al. Al.: intelligence based accurate medium and long term load forecasting system. Appl. Artif. Intell. **36**(1), (2022). https://doi.org/10.1080/08839514.2022.2088452
4. Chen, S., Han, X., Shen, Y., Ye, C.: Application of Improved LSTM Algorithm in Macroeconomic Forecasting. Comput. Intell. Neurosci. (2021). https://doi.org/10.1155/2021/4471044
5. Chien-Chih, W., Chun-Hua, C., Trappey, A. J. C.: On the application of ARIMA and LSTM to predict order demand based on short lead time and on-time delivery requirements. Processes **9**(7), (2021). https://doi.org/10.3390/pr9071157
6. Chien, C.H., Chen, P.Y., Trappey, A.J.C., Trappey, C.V.: Intelligent supply chain management modules enabling advanced manufacturing for the electric-mechanical equipment industry. Complexity (2022). https://doi.org/10.1155/2022/8221706(2022)

7. Choi, J.Y., Lee, B.: Combining LSTM network ensemble via adaptive weighting for improved time series forecasting. Math. Probl. Eng. *2018*. https://doi.org/10.1155/2018/2470171
8. Coy Mondragón, G.E., Granados, Ó., Garcia-Bedoya, O.: Predicción de la serie temporal del indicador bancario de referencia (IBR) con redes neuronales. Revista Mutis **11**(1), 65–76 (2021). https://doi.org/10.21789/22561498.1748
9. Cruz, L.M., Alvarez, D.L., Rivera, S.R., Herrera, F.A.: Short-term demand forecast using Fourier series. In: 2019 IEEE Workshop on Power Electronics and Power Quality Applications (PEPQA), pp. 1–5 (2019). https://doi.org/10.1109/PEPQA.2019.8851533
10. Dahooie, J.H., et al.: An improved fuzzy MULTIMOORA approach for multi-criteria decision making based on objective weighting method (CCSD) and its application to technological forecasting method selection. Eng. Appl. Artif. Intell.Artif. Intell. **79**, 114–128 (2019). https://doi.org/10.1016/j.engappai.2018.12.008
11. Divina, F., Torres, M.G., Vela, F.A.G., Noguera, J.L.V.: A comparative study of time series forecasting methods for short term electric energy consumption prediction in smart buildings. Energies **12**(10), (2019). https://doi.org/10.3390/en12101934
12. Feng, W.: Sales forecast of marketing brand based on BP neural network model. Comput. Intell. Neurosci.. Intell. Neurosci. (2022). https://doi.org/10.1155/2022/1769424(2022)
13. Gabriella, D., Laudadio, T., Mari, R., Mastronardi, N., Carlo, M.: A reliable decision support system for fresh food supply chain management. Int. J. Prod. Res. **56**(4), 1458–1485 (2018). https://doi.org/10.1080/00207543.2017.1367106
14. Guo, X., Zhao, Q., Wang, S., Shan, D., Gong, W.: A short-term load forecasting model of LSTM neural network considering demand response. Complexity (2021). https://doi.org/10.1155/2021/5571539
15. Gustriansyah, R.: Integration of Decision-Making Method and Data-Mining Method as a Preliminary Study of Novel Sales Forecasting Method (2020). https://api.semanticscholar.org/CorpusID:225297421
16. Han, Y.: A forecasting method of pharmaceutical sales based on ARIMA-LSTM model. In: 2020 5th International Conference on Information Science, Computer Technology and Transportation (ISCTT), pp. 336–339 (2020). https://doi.org/10.1109/ISCTT51595.2020.00064
17. Huang, J., Tang, Y., Chen, S.: Energy demand forecasting: combining cointegration analysis and artificial intelligence algorithm. Math. Prob. Eng. (2018). https://doi.org/10.1155/2018/5194810
18. Jia, T., Wang, C., Tian, Z., Wang, B., Tian, F.: Design of digital and intelligent financial decision support system based on artificial intelligence. Comput. Intell. Neurosci.. Intell. Neurosci. (2022). https://doi.org/10.1155/2022/1962937(2022)
19. Khan, M.A., et al.: Effective demand forecasting model using business intelligence empowered with machine learning. IEEE Access **8**, 116013–116023 (2020). https://doi.org/10.1109/ACCESS.2020.3003790
20. Kilimci, Z.H., et al.: An improved demand forecasting model using deep learning approach and proposed decision integration strategy for supply chain. Complexity (2019). https://doi.org/10.1155/2019/9067367(2019)
21. Kitchenham, B., Charters, S.: Guidelines for performing systematic literature reviews in software engineering. Engineering **2**, 1051 (2007). https://doi.org/10.1145/1134285.1134500
22. Li, X., Du, J., Wang, Y., Cao, Y.: Automatic sales forecasting system based on LSTM network. In: 2020 International Conference on Computer Science and Management Technology (ICCSMT), pp. 393–396 (2020). https://doi.org/10.1109/ICCSMT51754.2020.00088
23. Loureiro, A.L.D., Miguéis, V.L., da Silva, L.F.M.: Exploring the use of deep neural networks for sales forecasting in fashion retail. Decision Supp. Syst. **114**, 81–93 (2018). https://doi.org/10.1016/j.dss.2018.08.010

24. Ma, S., Fildes, R.: Retail sales forecasting with meta-learning. Eur. J. Oper. Res.Oper. Res. **288**(1), 111–128 (2021). https://doi.org/10.1016/j.ejor.2020.05.038

25. Malagrino, L.S., Roman, N.T., Monteiro, A.M.: Forecasting stock market index daily direction: a Bayesian Network approach. Expert Syst. Appl. **105**, 11–22 (2018). https://doi.org/10.1016/j.eswa.2018.03.039

26. Menculini, L., et al.: Comparing prophet and deep learning to ARIMA in forecasting wholesale food prices. Forecasting **3**(3), 644–662 (2021). https://doi.org/10.3390/forecast3030040

27. Müller, M., Reggelin, T., Schmidt, S.: Operational simulation-based decision support in intralogistics using short-term forecasts. In: Kabashkin, I., Yatskiv (Jackiva), I., Prentkovskis, O. (eds.) Reliability and Statistics in Transportation and Communication, pp. 345–352. Springer International Publishing (2019)

28. Nguyen, H.D., Tran, K.P., Thomassey, S., Hamad, M.: Forecasting and anomaly detection approaches using LSTM and LSTM autoencoder techniques with the applications in supply chain management. Int. J. Inf. Manag. **57**, 0–37. https://doi.org/10.1016/j.ijinfomgt.2020.102282 (2021)

29. Shah, I., Jan, F., Ali, S.: Functional Data Approach for Short-Term Electricity Demand Forecasting. Math. Probl. Eng.Probl. Eng. (2022). https://doi.org/10.1155/2022/6709779(2022)

30. Singh, B., Kumar, P., Sharma, N., Sharma, K.P.: Sales Forecast for Amazon Sales with Time Series Modeling. In: 2020 First International Conference on Power, Control and Computing Technologies (ICPC2T), pp. 38–43 (2020). https://doi.org/10.1109/ICPC2T48082.2020.9071463

31. Villegas, M.A., Pedregal, D.J.: Supply chain decision support systems based on a novel hierarchical forecasting approach. Decis. Support. Syst.. Support. Syst. **114**, 29–36 (2018). https://doi.org/10.1016/j.dss.2018.08.003

32. Wang, C.-H., Yun, Y.: Demand planning and sales forecasting for motherboard manufacturers considering dynamic interactions of computer products. Comput. Ind. Eng.. Ind. Eng. **149**, 106788 (2020). https://doi.org/10.1016/j.cie.2020.106788

33. Wang, Y.: Traffic forecasting and decision-making of investment and construction of tourism highway under the background of artificial intelligence. In: 2020 International Conference on Smart Electronics and Communication (ICOSEC), pp. 132–135 (2020). https://doi.org/10.1109/ICOSEC49089.2020.9215286

34. Yadav, A., Jha, C.K., Sharan, A.: Optimizing LSTM for time series prediction in Indian stock market. Procedia Comput. Sci. **167**, 2091–2100 (2020). https://doi.org/10.1016/j.procs.2020.03.257

35. Zhang, M., Wang, Y., Wu, Z.: Data mining algorithm for demand forecast analysis on flash sales platform. Complexity (2021). https://doi.org/10.1155/2021/6648009(2021)

Stock Price Prediction Using Sentiment Analysis and LSTM Networks

Mohammed El Idrissi[1]([✉]), Nacir Chafik[1], and Ridouane Tachicart[2]

[1] ENSAM, Mohammed V University in Rabat, Rabat, Morocco
elidrissimohammed90@gmail.com
[2] LARGESS, Chouaib Doukkali University, El Jadida, Morocco
tachicart.r@ucd.ac.ma

Abstract. Predicting stock prices has perpetually presented a formidable challenge, primarily due to the inherent unpredictability that characterizes financial markets. In response to this challenge, our research project introduces an innovative and sophisticated hybrid approach. This approach harmoniously integrates sentiment analysis and Long Short-Term Memory (LSTM) networks, effectively enhancing the precision of stock price predictions. Our research journey encompasses a comprehensive methodology. We diligently address data preprocessing, employ advanced visualization techniques, conduct sentiment analysis through the utilization of the Valence Aware Dictionary for Sentiment Reasoning (VADER), and implement LSTM networks. This holistic approach ensures that every facet of our model is optimized for performance. To acquire the requisite data, we meticulously collected historical news headlines from Reddit WorldNews, a valuable source of real-world sentiment and events, and curated stock data from the Dow Jones Industrial Average (DJIA), a benchmark for market performance. This meticulous data collection process is vital for the accuracy and relevance of our predictions. Our experimental results underscore the robustness of our approach. When utilizing VADER for label verification, our model showcases a high level of precision, affirming the accuracy and reliability of the labels attributed to our dataset. Furthermore, our LSTM model achieves a remarkable R2 score of 97%, a testament to its capacity to forecast stock prices with an exceptional level of precision. This high R2 score signifies that our model effectively explains 97% of the variation in stock prices, reaffirming its predictive prowess.

Keywords: Stock Price Prediction · Sentiment Analysis · LSTM Networks · Financial Markets · Machine Learning

1 Introduction

Financial markets have long been a bastion of unpredictability and complexity, with the task of predicting stock prices considered an elusive pursuit. Investors and financial analysts have grappled with the challenges posed by the intrinsic uncertainty that characterizes stock market behavior. The prevailing notion, encapsulated in the random walk theory, asserts that stock prices follow a path so unpredictable that successful predictions are akin to chance [2]. However, the landscape of financial market analysis has

K. S. Soliman (Ed.): IBIMA-AI 2024, CCIS 2299, pp. 149–156, 2025.
https://doi.org/10.1007/978-3-031-77493-5_14

witnessed a transformation in recent years, propelled by advancements in artificial intelligence, machine learning, and the proliferation of data. This paradigm shift has ushered in a new era where the fusion of technology and data analytics offers a glimmer of hope for more accurate stock price predictions [5].

In this context, our research project embarks on an ambitious endeavor to bridge the gap between the enigmatic world of stock markets and the burgeoning capabilities of artificial intelligence. We propose a hybrid model that combines sentiment analysis and Long Short-Term Memory (LSTM) networks to improve the precision of stock price predictions. By integrating sentiment analysis, which extracts insights from textual data, with LSTM, a powerful sequence-based deep learning technique, we aim to leverage the strengths of both methodologies for more accurate predictions [8]. The significance of our research is underscored by the vast potential benefits it offers. Effective stock price predictions are not only of paramount interest to investors seeking to optimize their portfolios but also to financial institutions, policymakers, and the broader economy, where informed decisions can mitigate risks and drive economic stability.

Our research framework, grounded in the knowledge and expertise acquired at ENSIAS (National School of Computer Science and Systems Analysis), forms the foundation for the development of this robust model. We draw inspiration and insights from previous studies that have explored the application of deep learning and sentiment analysis in the context of financial market predictions. These studies serve as guideposts in our quest to refine and extend the boundaries of predictive modeling [4, 7].

This paper unfolds as an exploration of our research journey, encompassing data acquisition, preprocessing, sentiment analysis using Valence Aware Dictionary for Sentiment Reasoning (VADER), the implementation of LSTM networks, and rigorous experimentation to validate the effectiveness of our approach. Our ultimate goal is to enhance the accuracy of stock price predictions, offering a compelling solution in a domain historically fraught with unpredictability. The path ahead is illuminated by the potential of our hybrid model, where the marriage of sentiment analysis and LSTM networks promises to be a game-changer. As we venture into uncharted territory, we anticipate that our research will make a notable contribution to the evolving field of stock price prediction and inspire further innovation in financial market analysis.

2   Related Work

The field of predicting stock prices has witnessed a significant shift in recent years, with the advent of deep learning and sentiment analysis techniques providing new avenues for improving prediction accuracy. This section reviews the relevant studies and approaches that have paved the way for our research.

2.1   Deep Learning for Financial Market Predictions

[3] introduced the use of Long Short-Term Memory (LSTM) networks for predicting financial market movements. Their study, "Deep Learning with Long Short-Term Memory Networks for Financial Market Predictions," demonstrated the effectiveness of LSTM networks in predicting directional movements of S&P 500 constituent stocks from

1992 to 2015. This research laid the foundation for applying LSTM networks in stock price predictions and showed their outperformance compared to traditional methods.

2.2 Predicting Stock Market Movements from News Headlines

Vargas, Lima, and Evsukoff's research [9] explored the use of deep learning methods, including Convolutional Neural Networks (CNN) and Recurrent Neural Networks (RNN), in predicting stock market movements. Their work focused on using financial news headlines and technical indicators as input data. The study emphasized the strengths of CNN in capturing semantic information from textual data and RNN's ability to model complex temporal characteristics, contributing to the understanding of deep learning's applicability in financial market predictions.

2.3 Textual Analysis and Stock Market Prediction

[1] delved into textual analysis for stock market predictions. By examining financial news articles and stock quotes, they applied machine learning techniques, including Support Vector Machine (SVM) derivatives, to predict stock prices. This research highlighted the importance of combining article terms and stock prices at the time of article release for improved prediction accuracy. It provided valuable insights into leveraging textual data for stock market predictions.

2.4 Autoencoders and Stock Price Prediction

Ji's work [6] introduced the use of autoencoders in stock price prediction. The model incorporated feature selection, training text feature vectors, denoising stock price time series data using wavelet transform, and utilizing LSTM for prediction. The research emphasized the remarkable accuracy achieved through the implementation of autoencoders, offering a novel perspective on the potential of deep learning techniques in stock price forecasting.

These related studies collectively underscore the increasing interest and promising outcomes of employing deep learning, sentiment analysis, and textual data in the domain of stock market predictions. Building on the insights gained from these research efforts, our work introduces a novel hybrid model that combines sentiment analysis and LSTM networks to enhance the precision of stock price predictions.

3 Methodology

Our research methodology is meticulously designed to enhance stock price prediction accuracy through a structured fusion of sentiment analysis and Long Short-Term Memory (LSTM) networks. The methodology comprises the following key components:

3.1 Preprocessing Phase

The preprocessing phase is a crucial step in our methodology, as it involves preparing the data for analysis. It encompasses the following key tasks:

- Data Collection: Gathering historical news headlines from Reddit WorldNews and Dow Jones Industrial Average (DJIA) stock data.
- Data Cleaning: Removing any irrelevant or redundant information from the collected data.
- Data Integration: Combining the textual data with the stock price data for analysis.

3.2 Valence Aware Dictionary for Sentiment Reasoning (VADER)

VADER is an essential component of our sentiment analysis. It is a pre-built lexicon and rule-based sentiment analysis tool designed to assess the sentiment expressed in text data. This stage involves the following steps:

Sentiment Scoring: Assigning sentiment scores to each news headline, indicating the positivity or negativity of the text.

Aggregation: Summarizing the sentiment scores to capture the overall market sentiment for a given time frame.

3.3 Long Short-Term Memory (LSTM)

Our methodology leverages Long Short-Term Memory (LSTM) networks, which are a type of recurrent neural network (RNN) well-suited for sequence data. This section provides an overview of the LSTM architecture, including the following components:

3.4 Input Layer: Accepting the Preprocessed Data

LSTM Cells: These are the core units responsible for learning and retaining sequential information.

Hidden Layers: Additional layers that enhance the model's ability to capture complex patterns.

Output Layer: Generating predictions based on the learned patterns.

3.5 Stock Price Prediction

This sub-section details how LSTM is employed for stock price prediction. It includes the following steps:

- Data Sequencing: Converting the time-series data into sequences that LSTM can process.
- Model Training: Training the LSTM network on historical data, learning to predict stock price movements.
- Model Evaluation: Assessing the model's performance and accuracy using relevant metrics.

3.6 Conception of the General Model

In this stage, we construct the general model that combines sentiment analysis and LSTM for stock price prediction. This process involves:

- Integration of Sentiment Data: Combining the sentiment scores obtained from VADER with the stock price data.
- Model Fine-Tuning: Optimizing the model parameters for the best predictive performance.
- Validation and Testing: Evaluating the model on out-of-sample data to ensure its generalizability.

The methodology described above forms the foundation of our research approach to predicting stock prices by integrating sentiment analysis and LSTM networks. This structured framework enables us to navigate through the various phases, from data preprocessing to the development of a comprehensive predictive model.

4 Data Description

The dataset used in this study comprises two primary data sources:

- News Data: This dataset includes historical news headlines sourced from the Reddit WorldNews Channel (/r/worldnews). News headlines are ranked based on user votes, with only the top 25 headlines considered for each date. The dataset covers a time range from June 8, 2008, to July 1, 2016 (Fig. 1).

	Date	Label	Top1	Top2	Top3	Top4	Top5	Top6	Top7	Top8	...	Top16	Top17
0	2008-08-08	0	b"Georgia 'downs two Russian warplanes' as cou...	b'BREAKING: Musharraf to be impeached.'	b'Russia Today: Columns of troops roll into So...	b'Russian tanks are moving towards the capital...	b"Afghan children raped with 'impunity,' U.N. ...	b'150 Russian tanks have entered South Ossetia...	b"Breaking: Georgia invades South Ossetia, Rus...	b"The 'enemy combatent' trials are nothing but...	...	b'Georgia Invades South Ossetia - if Russia ge...	b'Al-Qaeda Faces Islamist Backlash'
1	2008-08-11	1	b'Why wont America and Nato help us? If they w...	b'Bush puts foot down on Georgian conflict'	b"Jewish Georgian minister: Thanks to Israeli ...	b'Georgian army flees in disarray as Russians ...	b"Olympic opening ceremony fireworks 'faked'"	b'What were the Mossad with fraudulent New Zea...	b'Russia angered by Israeli military sale to G...	b'An American citizen living in S.Ossetia blam...	...	b'Israel and the US behind the Georgian aggres...	b'"Do not believe TV, neither Russian nor Geor...
2	2008-08-12	0	b'Remember that adorable 9-year-old who sang a...	b"Russia 'ends Georgia operation'"	b'"If we had no sexual harassment we would hav...	b"Al-Qa'eda is losing support in Iraq because ...	b'Ceasefire in Georgia: Putin Outmaneuvers the...	b'Why Microsoft and Intel tried to kill the XO...	b'Stratfor: The Russo-Georgian War and the Bal...	b"I'm Trying to Get a Sense of This Whole Geor...	...	b'U.S. troops still in Georgia (did you know t...	b'Why Russias response to Georgia was right'
3	2008-08-13	0	b' U.S. refuses Israel weapons to	b"When the president ordered to	b' Israel clears troops who killed	b'Britain\'s policy of being tough	b'Body of 14 year old found in trunk; Latest	b'China has moved 10 *million*	b"Bush announces Operation	b'Russian forces sink	...	b'Elephants extinct by	b'US humanitarian missions

Fig. 1. Sample of the News data

- Stock Data: Dow Jones Industrial Average (DJIA) data is utilized as a benchmark for this research. The DJIA data spans from August 8, 2008, to July 1, 2016 (Fig. 2).

The dataset is distributed across three separate.csv files:

- RedditNews.csv: This file contains two columns – "date" and "news headlines." The news headlines are ordered by their popularity, with the top 25 headlines for each date included.

	Date	Open	High	Low	Close	Volume	Adj Close
0	2016-07-01	17924.240234	18002.380859	17916.910156	17949.369141	82160000	17949.369141
1	2016-06-30	17712.759766	17930.609375	17711.800781	17929.990234	133030000	17929.990234
2	2016-06-29	17456.019531	17704.509766	17456.019531	17694.679688	106380000	17694.679688
3	2016-06-28	17190.509766	17409.720703	17190.509766	17409.720703	112190000	17409.720703
4	2016-06-27	17355.210938	17355.210938	17063.080078	17140.240234	138740000	17140.240234

`dj.head()`

Fig. 2. Sample of the Stock data

- DJIA_table.csv: This dataset is directly obtained from Yahoo Finance, providing stock market data.
- CombinedNewsDJIA.csv: A combined dataset featuring several columns. The first column denotes "Date," the second indicates the "Label," and the subsequent columns include news headlines from "Top1" to "Top25." The "Label" represents binary values: "1" when the DJIA Adj Close value increased or remained the same, and "0" when it decreased (Fig. 3).

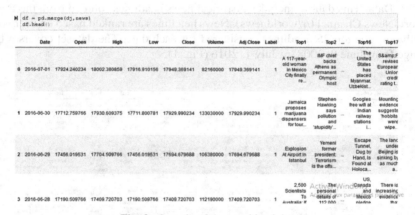

Fig. 3. Sample of the combined data

5 Experiments

In this section, we delve into the experiments conducted to evaluate the effectiveness of our approach, encompassing sentiment analysis, label verification using VADER, and the application of LSTM networks.

5.1 Label Verification Using VADER

To ensure the accuracy of the Label parameter, which represents the evolution of stock prices using daily news, we employed VADER sentiment analysis on the dataset. The goal was to validate the Label's correctness since we lacked insight into the model or method used for its determination. The results of this verification process indicated a high level of precision, affirming the accuracy of the Label parameter.

5.2 Application of LSTM

Following the successful Label verification, we proceeded to apply Long Short-Term Memory (LSTM) networks to our dataset. This dataset contains historical data and the verified Label parameter. LSTM was chosen for its suitability in regression problems, where the goal is to predict a continuous variable. Common regression metrics such as mean squared error, root mean squared error, mean absolute error, and R2 were considered. The R2 score of 97% was achieved, signifying that our LSTM model explains 97% of the target variable, demonstrating its high efficiency for this dataset (Fig. 4).

```
R2 Score:   0.9740253424487904
MAE:    81.65216290013225
```

Fig. 4. R2 Score and Mean Absolute Error of the Model

6 Conclusion

In this paper, we introduced a comprehensive methodology that combines sentiment analysis with Long Short-Term Memory (LSTM) networks to enhance stock price prediction accuracy. Our methodology underwent rigorous testing and analysis, and the results are highly promising.

The application of VADER Sentiment Analysis allowed us to verify the Label parameter representing stock price movements. This validation step was essential in ensuring the accuracy of our data and the effectiveness of our approach. Through Label verification, we confirmed that the sentiment expressed in the news headlines correlates with the actual stock price movements.

The subsequent implementation of LSTM networks proved to be highly successful. With three hidden layers, the model achieved an impressive R2 score of 97%. This score indicates that our LSTM-based model can explain 97% of the variation in stock prices, highlighting its efficiency and predictive power.

Our methodology's performance metrics, including mean squared error, root mean squared error, mean absolute error, and R2, further demonstrated the model's accuracy and precision in forecasting stock prices.

References

1. Chen, H., Schumaker, R.P.: Textual analysis of stock market prediction using breaking financial news: the azfintext system. ACM Trans. Inf. Syst. **27**(2), 12-1–12-19 (2009). https://doi.org/10.1145/1462198.1462204

2. Fama, E.F.: Efficient capital markets: a review of theory and empirical work. J. Financ. **25**(2), 383–417 (1970)
3. Fischer, T., Krauss, C.: Deep learning with long short-term memory networks for financial market predictions. Eur. J. Oper. Res. **270**(2), 654–669 (2018). https://doi.org/10.1016/j.ejor.2017.11.054
4. Gordon, J., Hernández-Lobato, J.M.: Combining deep generative and discriminative models for Bayesian semi-supervised learning. Pattern Recogn. **100**, 107156 (2020)
5. Huang, J., Chai, J., Cho, S.: Deep learning in finance and banking: a literature review and classification. Front. Bus. Res. China **14**, 13 (2020). https://doi.org/10.1186/s11782-020-00082-6
6. Ji, X., Wang, J., Yan, Z.: A stock price prediction method based on deep learning technology. Int. J. Crowd Sci. **5**(1), 55–72 (2021). https://doi.org/10.1108/IJCS-05-2020-0012
7. Makridakis, S., Spiliotis, E., Assimakopoulos, V.: Statistical and machine learning forecasting methods: concerns and ways forward. PLoS ONE **13**(3), e0194889 (2018)
8. Sonkavde, G., Dharrao, D.S., Bongale, A.M., Deokate, S.T., Doreswamy, D., Bhat, S.K.: Forecasting stock market prices using machine learning and deep learning models: a systematic review, performance analysis and discussion of implications. Int. J. Financ. Stud. **11**, 94 (2023). https://doi.org/10.3390/ijfs11030094
9. Vargas, M.R., de Lima, B.S.L.P., Evsukoff, A.G.: Deep learning for stock market prediction from financial news articles. In: 2017 IEEE International Conference on Computational Intelligence and Virtual Environments for Measurement Systems and Applications (CIVEMSA), pp. 60–65. Annecy, France (2017). https://doi.org/10.1109/CIVEMSA.2017.7995302

Unveiling Online Shopping Quality: Taxonomy-Based Multi-label Classification of Shopping App Reviews

Nada A. Hakami[✉]

Prince Sultan University, Riyadh, Kingdom of Saudi Arabia
nhakami@psu.edu.sa

Abstract. This study aims to address the growing need for effective quality assessment in e-commerce platforms, driven by the rapid evolution of online transactions globally. The absence of a structured approach to categorize and analyze shopping app reviews based on specific quality dimensions represents a significant gap in the existing literature, emphasizing the importance of this research endeavor. Methodologically, we propose a taxonomy framework designed to classify users' reviews from shopping apps into five quality-centered categories: system quality, information quality, service quality, product quality, and delivery quality. Leveraging an initial dataset of 552 instances, we employ and compare five common multi-label classification models: binary relevance, classifier chain, label powerset, multi-label k nearest neighbors, and multi-label decision tree. Our findings reveal promising outcomes in terms of classification accuracy and performance metrics. Employing binary relevance with logistic regression and BERT embedding resulted in a Hamming loss of 0.177, Macro-F1 score of 0.739, and Micro-F1 score of 0.744, Macro Recall of 0.722, and Micro-Recall of 0.728. Notably, the use of binary relevance with SVM and Glove embedding demonstrated the highest Macro-Precision and Micro-Precision at 0.944 and 0.933, respectively. Concerning the Zero-One Loss metric, the better outcome attained was 0.572 by using the Classifier Chain with Glove embeddings. These findings highlight the efficacy of our proposed taxonomy and classification methodology in effectively evaluating and categorizing shopping app reviews based on quality dimensions, thus contributing significantly to the field of e-commerce analytics and user experience enhancement.

Keywords: e-business · machine learning · multi-label classification · online shopping · apps reviews · quality of apps

1 Introduction

E-commerce platforms have undergone rapid transformations in recent years, providing businesses with the means to establish a robust online presence and extend their influence to a global audience. Reviews on shopping apps bring distinct benefits to both sellers and buyers within the constantly expanding digital marketplace. For sellers, these reviews serve as valuable feedback, offering insights into their products or services. Positive feedback serves as a potent endorsement, fostering consumer trust and enticing new customers to make purchases. Additionally, constructive criticism in reviews presents sellers with opportunities for product enhancement, enabling them to better cater to the preferences and needs of their customers. On the flip side, buyers also gain substantial advantages from app reviews. These reviews provide transparency and information that empower consumers to make well-informed decisions. They offer firsthand accounts of a product's quality, usability, and the overall customer experience, assisting buyers in evaluating whether the app aligns with their specific requirements.

Classification algorithms for app reviews provide numerous valuable benefits across various industries and applications [29]. Through accurately classifying reviews and pinpointing specific areas of concern, organizations can promptly address customer needs, rectify issues, and ultimately enhance user experiences. Moreover, app review classification algorithms empower businesses to monitor and manage their online brand image by recognizing trends and sentiments in user feedback and addressing issues mentioned. Additionally, by transforming extensive amounts of unstructured user feedback into structured data, these algorithms contribute to product development, marketing strategy, and feature prioritization.

Despite numerous research studies utilizing various classification algorithms for app reviews, limited attention has been directed towards the classification of reviews originating from shopping apps. As a result, this study endeavors to make a significant contribution to the field through five distinct avenues: 1) Introducing a new taxonomy for categorizing reviews of popular online shopping apps used in Saudi Arabia into quality-based classifications, namely: system quality, information quality, service quality, product quality, and delivery quality. 2) Developing an initial dataset comprising 552 instances by labeling reviews based on the five classes mentioned above. 3) As a review can belong to multiple categories simultaneously, we applied multi-label classification models, namely: binary relevance, classifier chain, label powerset, multi-label k nearest neighbors, and multi-label decision Tree. We compared the performance of these models using various common metrics. 4) Proposing the application of active learning in a subsequent study to enhance model performance by selecting the most valuable data points for labeling. 5) The findings from this study assist e-commerce platform owners in identifying challenges encountered by their customers, enabling them to tackle these issues and provide suitable solutions.

This research is of significant interest to various stakeholders in the e-commerce and data science domains, including app developers, marketing teams, and researchers. The insights gained from the taxonomy and classification models empower app developers to make data-driven decisions, enable marketing teams to create targeted campaigns based on user sentiments, and provide researchers with a benchmark for further advancements in multi-label text classification and sentiment analysis. By bridging theoretical knowledge with practical implications, this research fosters collaboration and innovation across industries, ultimately leading to improved app quality, customer satisfaction, and industry advancements.

2 Related Works

This section provides a review on the studies that have implemented multi-label classification [2, 3, 7, 13, 25, 27] or combination of active learning with multi-label classification [10, 20, 30] in the context of e-commerce or similar problems (Table 1).

3 Methodology

The primary objective of this study is to categorize customer reviews of shopping apps into five quality-centered classifications, namely: 1) system quality, 2) information quality, 3) service quality, 4) product quality, and 5) delivery quality. The five classifications have been adopted from a study by [1] that established quality constructs and measures for an Internet shopping mall, as depicted in Table 2. In pursuit of the research objectives, we implemented multi-label classification within an active learning framework. In this paper, we utilized the modAL framework for active learning to initialize an ActiveLearner. However, we did not include an active learning loop. Such a loop typically involves iteratively querying the learner for labels on the most informative instances and updating the model based on those labels. In a subsequent study, we plan to extend this work by incorporating an active learning loop in an interactive labeling setting. We curated a dataset comprising reviews from popular shopping apps (Amazon, Noon, and SheIn) and categorized them based on the previously mentioned five quality dimensions. We utilized multi-label classification because each review in the dataset could be associated with multiple labels concurrently. For instance, a review discussing both system quality and service quality would be assigned two labels: "1:system" and "3:service" In the experimentation of this study, Anaconda Navigator, Jupyter Notebook (version 6.4.11), scikit-learn (a freely available machine learning library), modAL (a Python library specializing in active learning), and the Python programming language were utilized. The detailed methodology adopted in this research is as follows:

3.1 Data Set

Random reviews from the previous data collection in our earlier work [12] were selected and annotated. In total we annotated 552 reviews spanning the 5 different labels set for this study. The target labels were formatted as binary (0/1) data, with [i, j1, j2, j3, j4, j5] indicating the presence (1) or absence (0) of labels j1, j2, j3, j4, and j5 in sample i. Each review has been read carefully and assigned one or more labels based on the measures provided in Table 2. This dataset will serve as the initial data for training in the active learning framework. The researcher in this study served as the sole annotator of the dataset, a decision influenced by the unavailability of multiple annotators. Also, this choice was based on a study by [33] that demonstrated that a single annotator could deliver higher quality and more consistent annotations than those provided by multiple annotators. To analyze the consistency of annotations, the researcher conducted another iteration to reannotate the reviews two months later. The results showed that, on average, 95% of the reviews were assigned the same label(s). Similar to a challenge addressed in the multi-label learning setting by [23], the remaining 5% exhibited some errors with different labels assigned. This is because each review has been articulated using diverse expressions, encompassing different emphases and perspectives, resulting in a certain level of uncertainty in labeling [23]. In total, only 27 reviews' labels were modified. Some examples of sample reviews with their annotated labels are shown in Table 3. We have published the dataset on https://github.com/Nah2024/Shopping__DS/blob/main/Shopping_DS.xlsx, encouraging further studies to utilize and enhance our dataset for e-commerce applications.

3.2 Multi-label Classification Methods

Multi-label classification models, namely Binary Relevance, Classifier Chain, Label Powerset, Multi-Label k Nearest Neighbors, and Multi-Label Decision Tree, have been used to classify the reviews in this study. Additionally, we applied six commonly known binary classifiers: Logistic Regression (LR), Support Vector Machine (SVM), Random Forest (RF), Decision Tree(DT), Stochastic Gradient Descent (SGD), and k-Nearest Neighbors (k-NN) to the multi-label classification models above.

a) **Binary Relevance:** Binary Relevance (BR) is a method that transforms the initial dataset into q datasets, where q = |B|, total number of classes (B) in a dataset, each encompassing all instances from the original dataset. Subsequently, a classifier is trained on each of these datasets. If a specific instance contains label Bj (where $1 \leq j \leq q$), it is assigned a positive label; otherwise, it receives a negative label. When classifying a new instance, BR produces the union of labels predicted positively by the q classifiers. While BR finds utility in various practical applications, it is suitable only for scenarios where there is no label dependency within the data.

b) **Classifier Chain:** Classifier chain (CC) employs Q binary classifiers similar to those in the Binary Relevance method, addressing the limitations of BR by considering the label correlation task. The classifiers are interconnected in a chain, with each classifier handling the BR problem associated with a specific label. During training, each model receives the predictions of the previous models in the chain as features. These additional features enable each chain to leverage correlations among the classes. In comparison to binary relevance method, classifier chain exhibits lower memory usage and runtime complexity [25]. We applied multiple classifiers in 10 classifier chains, including LogisticRegression, RandomForest, SVC, GradientBoosting, DecisionTree, and AdaBoost. Each chain was created with a different classifier from the list, and the classifiers were reused in a circular manner. We fit an ensemble of these classifier chains and took the average prediction.

c) **Label Powerset:** Label Powerset (LP) treats each unique combination of labels in a multi-label training dataset as an individual class in the resulting transformed dataset. For instance, if an instance is associated with the labels B1, B2, and B4, the new single-label class becomes B1,2,4. Consequently, the transformed dataset becomes a single-label classification task, allowing the application of any single-label classifier. When classifying a new instance, Label Powerset outputs the most probable class, representing a set of labels. This approach considers label dependencies and ensures that no information is lost during classification. However, its computational complexity is contingent on the number of distinct label sets present in the training set.

Table 1. Related works

Author(s)(year)[reference]	Research Purpose	Data Set	Methodology	Results
[3]	- Assessing multilabel classification and recommender systems for cross-sell purposes in the financial services sector - Multi-label classification algorithms were utilized in recommender systems to predict a set of items for each user	Belgian customer base (comprising customers and products) collected from an international financial services provider	Using the R-package to implement various multi label classification algorithms including: 1- Problem transformation methods: binary relevance and classifier chains 2-The algorithm adaptation methods: multi-label random forest and multi-label random ferns	The best-performing multi label classification algorithms were classifier chains combined with Adaboost, binary relevance combined with neural networks, and binary relevance combined with random forest, achieving F1 scores of 0.5330, 0.5269, and 0.5257, respectively
[7]	Examining customer reviews in an aspect-oriented fashion to gain deeper insights into product perceptions	- A novel dataset has been generated from the Trendyol platform (https://www.trendyol.com/) - This dataset encompasses over 50,000 reviews spanning three distinct categories, with each review being assigned multiple labels based on customer comments	Multi label learning algorithms: Binary relevance, ML-KNN, OneVsRest	Best results were obtained as follows: Micro F1 of 0.8925 using OvsR-XGB, Micro P of 0.9157 using Bert, and Micro R of 0.8837 and Hamming loss of 0.0278 using OvsR-XGB
[20]	Multi-label Classification of user reviews of mobile apps into bug reports, feature requests, user experiences and rating	Dataset of 10,982 reviews from various mobile applications developed between 2009 and 2017	- Using binary relevance with logistic regression as a base classifier for the major learner - Employing binary relevance with support vector machines as a base classifier for the auxiliary learner - Utilizing Libact, a Python library for active learning approach	- The proposed method and Random Forests outperform other classifiers, attaining an F-measure score of 0.75 - The highest F1 score reaching 0.77, was attained during the 56th and 60th iterations

(continued)

Table 1. (*continued*)

Author(s)(year)[reference]	Research Purpose	Data Set	Methodology	Results
[27]	-Expanding Aspect Based Sentiment Analysis (ABSA) methods by incorporating multi-label classification capabilities - Introducing an advanced sentiment analysis technique to categorize text into sentiment classes while taking entity aspects into account	-Restaurant reviews collected from Yelp.com -Wine Reviews scraped from winemag.com -Movie Reviews scraped from Rotten Tomatoes website	-Proposing transfer learning models in multi-label ABSA with the following improvements: improvement to the output layers' activation function, improvement to the models' loss functions, improvement to the label encodings -Applying state-of-the-art multi-label classification methods (Binary Relevance, Classifer Chains, Label Powerset, and more)	XLNet performance on restaurant and movie reviews outperforms all other models (Bert, deep learning and machine learning models), in accuracy, hamming loss, macro and micro F1s
[2]	Investigating users satisfaction by introducing aspect category detection (multi label classification) of customer's hotel reviews	Arabic SemEval-2016 dataset for the hotel reviews	- Proposing strategies for Arabic data preprocessing and tokenization - AraBERT fine-tuning for feature extraction - Proposal of a DWLF-based reweighting strategy to address the imbalanced data issue - Classification model for aspect category prediction adopting the proposed DWLF	-AraBERT-based model surpasses previous related works and achieves an F1 score improvement of over 9%
[30]	Performing an empirical investigation of active learning in the context of multi-label text classification, to assess the performance of five active learning strategies across six classification tasks	Various data sets for news and scientific documentation namely, WOS5736, WOS11967, WOS46985, AAPD, Reuters-21578, Yelp Review	-Applying active learning strategies on Bert-based models LSTM, DistilBert, and SciBert -The active learning strategies involve Least Confidence (LC), KMeans, Max Entropy, Deep Bayesian Active Learning(BALD),Monte Carlo Dropout and Coreset	-In contrast to single-label text classification, not all strategies can surpass the performance of the random baseline. For example, BALD in AAPD and Reuters underperforms compared to random base - They demonstrated the negative effect of imbalanced label distribution on the active learning performance

(*continued*)

Table 1. (*continued*)

Author(s)(year)[reference]	Research Purpose	Data Set	Methodology	Results
[10]	Predicting and diagnosing heart diseases using machine learning based models	Heart disease dataset collected from the UCI machine learning repository	-Applying multi-label classification and active learning strategies (MMC, Random, Adaptive, Quire, and AUDI) -Employing ALiPy, a module-based implementation of the active learning framework	The proposed model demonstrated an enhanced generalizability, with an accuracy and F-score of 57.4 ± 4% and 62.2 ± 3.6%, respectively
[13]	Predicting the customers recommendations in travel and tourism (the airline)	Using dataset from social media contents	-Implementing Multi label classification algorithms: K-Nearest Neighbors, Support Vector Machine, Multi-layer Perceptron, Logistic Regression, Random Forest, and Ensemble Learning - Implementing partitioning methods to partition the label space in lower spaces, aiming to transform each label set into a multi-class classification problem	The proposed model outperformed other binary classifications models in terms of accuracy
[24]	Predicting retail recommendation (most suitable retail business for the location) based on given available information	Utilizing list of sites from YellowPages, population data from Humanitarian Data Exchange (HDX) and property data sourced from brickz.my	-Creating a dataset that incorporates the features of the business area -Using deep learning technique (1D convolutional neural network (CNN) model) for multi-label classification	The accuracy of the proposed model reached 61.22%

d) **Multi-Label k Nearest Neighbors (ML-KNN):** ML-KNN extends the traditional k Nearest Neighbors algorithm for multi-label classification problems. It stores the training instances and their corresponding labels, operating as a lazy learning algorithm. The labels of the k-nearest neighbors influence the assignment of labels for a new instance. The algorithm identifies the closest instances to a test instance in the training set, counts the number of neighbors of that test instance belonging to the ith class, and employs Bayesian inference to determine the assigned labels (category vector) for a test instance.

e) **Multi-Label Decision Tree:** The Multi-Label Decision Tree (ML-DT) is an extension of the conventional Decision Tree tailored for multi-label classification. This algorithm constructs a decision tree capable of effectively forecasting the occurrence or non-occurrence of multiple labels for a given instance. Each node in the ML-DT

Table 2. Quality constructs and measurement items of internet shopping mall

Constructs	Measures	Questionnaire
System quality	Design Navigation Response time System security System availability Functionality Error free transaction Multimedia Personal travel	(The web site) has an appropriate style of design for business type (The web site) has an easy navigation to information (The web site) has fast response and transaction processing (The web site) keeps transactions secure from exposure I can use (the web site) when I want to use it (The web site) has a good functionality relevant to site type (The web site) keeps error-free transactions (The web site) provides an appropriate video-audio presentation (The web site) supports personal travel in navigation
Information quality	Contents variety Complete information Detail information Accurate information Timely information Reliable information Appropriate format Better purchase choice Comparison shopping	(The web site) has sufficient contents which I expect to find (The web site) provides complete information (The web site) provides detailed information (The web site) provides accurate information (The web site) provides timely information (The web site) provides reliable information (The web site) communicates information in an appropriate format (The web site) provides selective information for purchase choice (The web site) provides comparative information between products
Service quality	Responsiveness Reliability Confidence Empathy Follow-up service Competence	(The web site) anticipates and responds promptly to user request (The web site) can be depended on to provide whatever is promised (The web site) instills confidence in users and reduces uncertainty (The web site) understands and adapts to the user's specific needs (The web site) provides follow-up service to users (The web site) gives a professional and competence image

(*continued*)

Table 2. (*continued*)

Constructs	Measures	Questionnaire
Product quality	Product quality Product variety Product availability	(The web site) deals products with high quality (The web site) deals various products (The web site) supports high product availability
Delivery service	Reliable delivery Package safety Timely delivery Return easiness	(The web site) delivers the right product which was ordered (The web site) delivers products with safely packaged (The web site) delivers products at promised time It is easy to return the product delivered

* Note the table is reprinted from [1].

represents a decision point based on the features of the dataset. Unlike a single-label decision tree, each leaf node in ML-DT can represent a set of labels rather than a singular class. The algorithm sums all the entropies for each individual label as a solution for handling multi-label problems. Additionally, it is known for its computational efficiency [21].

3.3 Data Preprocessing and Vectorization

A data preprocessing script has been implemented to clean and process text data by removing leading/trailing whitespaces, converting text to lowercase, and removing punctuation. We compared the performance of classifiers in this research using two different vectorization methods: non-contextual embeddings (GloVe) [24] and deep contextual embeddings (BERT) [8]).The GloVe approach involves creating a global co-occurrence matrix for words in the corpus, with embedding vectors derived from the examination of word co-occurrences within a specified window. On the other hand, BERT utilizes multilayer bidirectional transformer encoders for language representations, producing contextualized embeddings for the input that are then fed into downstream tasks.

3.4 Evaluation Metrics

In our experiments, we employed metrics suited for multi-label classification problems, namely Hamming Loss (HL), Zero-One Error, Micro-Averaged Precision (MicroP), Macro-Averaged Precision (MacroP), Micro-Averaged Recall (MicroR), Macro-Averaged Recall (MacroR), Micro F1 Score (MicroF1), and Macro F1 Score (MacroF1), to evaluate and compare the performance of classifiers. Hamming loss (label-wise) calculates the fraction of labels that are incorrectly predicted while zero-one error (instance-wise) measures the fraction of instances whose most confident label is irrelevant. The F1 measure represents the harmonic mean of precision and recall, where recall indicates the percentage of relevant labels that are predicted, and precision indicates the

Table 3. Sample comments from the data set

Sample Review	Label(s)	Sample Review	Label(s)
"What happened to this app seriously it worked fine in the past but now it's completely broken I tried to buy something by using the scan credit card feature and the app will just kick me for no reason I tried to delete and install it again but nothing works and the search bar don't show you the things you wanna look for but instead stuff that's recently on sale, it's also hard to track the item and more often than not it's either 1 day or 2 days late."	1,2,5	*"Perfect and easy use app,product as described, nooneast high quality,quick and safe delivery, friendly staff"*	1,2,3,4,5
"The shopping experience on Amazon continues to deteriorate. Amazon is trying too aggressively to tell my preferences, so it just won't show all that is available. Plus the same item comes up over and over from different sellers. Additionally half of all *1"results" are sponsored ads. I am no longer shopping around in the app or on the site. It's a frustrating waste of time to find what you are looking for. Plus there are endless products that don't match images or descriptions. Amazon is dying."	1,2,3	*"It's a nice platform for online shopping. The only thing I noticed, there's a lot of missing information/details on items you want to view which are most of the times critical. Like the dimensions, weight, specifications etc."*	1,2
"Been a customer for a long time. Most products available are as promised. Some products may not be so. Me personally had no problems initially. But after being a customer for some time now, i have been logged out of my account based on suspicious activity (me trying to buy stuff) and its been a pain to verify and authenticate myself. Don't know what's happening with Amazon but you were great once upon a time. Atleast in terms of Convenience and Customer Service."	1,3,4	*"I don't want noon credits. I want the money to be returned to my credit card. Please stop this noon credit nonsense when an item is returned. Most of the time when I order electronics they all turn up to be defective or they do not work at all. And the pictures are misleading. Most of the times the products turn up to be different from what's shown in the pictures."*	2,3,4

percentage of predicted labels that are relevant. In micro-averaging, contributions from all classes are combined before computing the metric. In contrast, macro-averaging computes the metric individually for each class and then averages the results across all classes.

4   Results and Discussion

After training and testing the five models, we analyzed their performance on the initial dataset to determine the most effective classifier for categorizing the reviews. From the results shown in Tables 5 and 6, the minimum **Hamming Loss** was achieved as 0.177 with BR(LR)/BERT, followed by 0.178 when using classifier chain/BERT. On the other hand, the maximum Hamming Loss was 0.407, obtained from using LP(DT)/BERT, followed by 0.393 from LP(DT)/Glove. Regarding the **Zero-One Loss** measure, the best results were obtained using the Classifier Chain with Glove embeddings, as well as the Classifier Chain with Bert embeddings and Binary Relevance employing logistic regression and Bert embedding. The corresponding performance scores were 0.572, 0.578, and 0.584, respectively. On the other hand, Binary Relevance with decision tree and Glove, ML-DT with Glove, and Label Powerset with Bert and decision tree produced the worst Zero-One Error performance with 0.892, 0.892, and 0.886, respectively.

In the case of **Macro-F1**, BR(LR)/BERT produced the highest result of 0.739, followed by Classifier Chain/BERT with 0.712. However, the minimum scores were reported using BR(DT)/Glove, LP(LR)/Glove, and BR(SVM)/Glove with 0.508, 0.508, and 0.511, respectively. BR(LR)/BERT results in the highest **Micro-F1** score of 0.744, followed by Classifier Chain/BERT, which achieved a score of 0.720. On the contrary, the minimum scores were attained using LP(LR)/Glove, BR(DT)/Glove, and BR(SVM)/Glove, with 0.518, 0.518, and 0.538, respectively. For **Macro-Precision**, BR(SVM)/Glove achieved the highest score, followed by LP(SVM)/Glove with scores of 0.944 and 0.891, respectively. In contrast, LP(DT)/BERT and LP(DT)/Glove produced the minimum scores of 0.425 and 0.447, respectively. BR(SVM)/Glove and LP(RF)/Glove yielded the highest **Micro-Precision**, with 0.933 and 0.876, respectively. On the other hand, the minimum scores were achieved using LP(DT)/Bert and LP(DT)/Glove with 0.429 and 0.450, respectively.

With respect to **Macro-Recall**, BR(LR)/BERT and LP(SGD)/BERT produced the highest results, with scores of 0.722 and 0.714, respectively. Differently, BR(SVM)/Glove and LP(LR)/Glove result in the minimum scores with 0.362 and 0.378, respectively. BR(LR)/BERT and LP(SGD)/BERT achieved the highest **Micro-R** scores with 0.728 and 0.707, respectively. On the contrary, BR(SVM)/Glove and LP(LR)/Glove had the minimum Micro-R scores with 0.378 and 0.391, respectively. In conclusion, as a result of our experimental studies, we found that the best results were obtained with a Hamming Loss of 0.177, Macro-F1 of 0.739, Micro-F1 score of 0.744, Macro Recall of 0.722, and Micro-Recall of 0.728, using binary relevance with logistic regression and BERT embedding. Binary relevance with SVM and Glove embedding produced the best Macro-Precision and Micro-Precision of 0.944 and 0.933, respectively.

It is clear that in our experiments, Hamming Loss achieved better results compared to zero-one loss. This result is anticipated because these loss functions exhibit distinct characteristics and objectives. Unlike Hamming Lose, the Zero-One Loss is a stringent metric as it requires an exact match between the predicted and actual sets of labels, equally penalizing predictions that are nearly correct or completely incorrect. According to [11] and [6], who stated that *"minimization of the subset 0/1 loss may cause high regret for the Hamming loss and vice versa,"*. [6] added that *"one cannot expect an MLC method to perform equally well for various losses of different types."*. In addition, [32] proved that Hamming Loss can be optimized by maximizing instance-wise margin, while the Zero-One Loss can be optimized by maximizing label-wise margin.

The results in this study support the notion that Binary Relevance can achieve excellent performance in multi-label classification settings [4]. Additionally, [19] has reported that, compared to an ensemble classifier chain, Binary Relevance has demonstrated superior performance in scenarios with a complex dataset, a larger number of labels, or increased label dependency. In a similar study by [22], binary relevance showed the best performance on GenBase and medical datasets compared to other methods for multi-label classification including multilabel k-nearest neighbor, label power set, random k-label set ensemble learning, calibrated label ranking, hierarchy of multi-label classifiers and triple random ensemble multi-label classification. They proposed that various classifiers exhibit distinct performances across diverse domains. Additionally, [22] asserted that binary relevance demonstrated its efficacy in multi-label classification when evaluated on nominal datasets of relatively smaller size. On the contrary, [28] have reported that binary relevance method yielded worse performance compared to MLKNN, Random k-Label Set, and Classifier Chain.

Moreover, the experimental results in this study align with the result published by [18], which indicates transformer-based embeddings (BERT-like models) exhibit superior performance in active learning for labelling text datasets compared to vector-based representations like BOW or simple word embeddings. As is common in many multi-label datasets, class (label) imbalance poses a challenging problem that affects the performance of the classifier [23]. Class imbalance can be classified into two types: Imbalance between labels (e.g., label 1's positive class occurs more frequently than label 2's). Imbalance within labels (e.g., label 1 has ten times more positive examples than negative examples) [5]. In our dataset, the total number of instances is 552, and the number of instances belonging to labels 1, 2, 3, 4, and 5 is 218, 207, 213, 206, and 172, respectively. Accordingly, the imbalance between labels was not an issue in our dataset, as the number of instances for each label was almost very close on average. On the other hand, as shown in Table 4, our dataset shows a notable difference between positive and negative instances for each label, suggesting an imbalance within labels.

Table 4. Distribution of positive and negative instances across the five labels

Label(class)	Number of Positive Instances	Number of Negative Instances
1	218	334
2	207	345
3	213	339
4	206	346
5	172	380

Table 5. Models' evaluation using Glove embedding vectorizer

	BR(LR)	BR(SVM)	BR(RF)	BR(DT)	BR(SGD)	BR(kNN)	LP(LR)	LP (SVM)	LP (RF)	LP(DT)	LP(SGD)	LP(kNN)	CC	ML-KNN	ML-DT
HL	0.184	0.230	0.216	0.354	0.236	0.286	0.237	0.199	0.230	0.393	0.243	0.286	0.186	0.277	0.354
Zero_one_loss	0.614	0.699	0.663	0.892	0.699	0.783	0.681	0.602	0.729	0.849	0.675	0.783	0.572	0.783	0.892
MacroF1	0.695	0.511	0.607	0.508	0.672	0.612	0.520	0.639	0.544	0.463	0.638	0.612	0.695	0.608	0.508
MicroF1	0.698	0.538	0.618	0.518	0.669	0.623	0.539	0.648	0.557	0.467	0.651	0.623	0.703	0.615	0.518
MacroP	0.841	0.944	0.839	0.494	0.705	0.586	0.875	0.891	0.889	0.447	0.678	0.586	0.829	0.604	0.494
MicroP	0.831	0.933	0.829	0.5	0.664	0.585	0.865	0.869	0.876	0.450	0.662	0.585	0.813	0.605	0.5
MacroR	0.597	0.362	0.482	0.528	0.678	0.652	0.378	0.508	0.399	0.483	0.628	0.652	0.609	0.616	0.528
MicroR	0.602	0.378	0.493	0.537	0.673	0.667	0.391	0.517	0.408	0.486	0.639	0.667	0.619	0.626	0.537

Table 6. Models' evaluation using Bert embedding vectorizer

	BR(LR)	BR(SVM)	BR(RF)	BR(DT)	BR(SGD)	BR(kNN)	LP(LR)	LP(SVM)	LP(RF)	LP(DT)	LP(SGD)	LP(kNN)	CC	ML-KNN	ML-DT
HL	**0.177**	0.178	0.212	0.339	0.208	0.282	0.207	0.218	0.277	0.407	0.251	0.314	0.178	0.272	0.339
Zero_one_loss	0.584	0.596	0.663	0.855	0.627	0.729	0.602	0.627	0.717	0.886	0.681	0.765	0.578	0.723	0.855
MacroF1	**0.739**	0.681	0.605	0.545	0.697	0.625	0.690	0.668	0.518	0.433	0.664	0.540	0.712	0.625	0.545
MicroF1	**0.744**	0.700	0.622	0.552	0.704	0.629	0.693	0.674	0.553	0.440	0.667	0.552	0.720	0.625	0.552
MacroP	0.758	0.857	0.829	0.515	0.712	0.591	0.731	0.713	0.617	0.425	0.644	0.567	0.808	0.623	0.515
MicroP	0.762	0.865	0.843	0.520	0.708	0.589	0.729	0.716	0.645	0.429	0.630	0.557	0.812	0.610	0.520
MacroR	**0.722**	0.574	0.481	0.582	0.693	0.672	0.658	0.634	0.462	0.443	0.714	0.553	0.639	0.642	0.582
MicroR	**0.728**	0.588	0.493	0.588	0.701	0.673	0.660	0.636	0.483	0.452	0.707	0.548	0.646	0.639	0.588

5 Conclusion and Future Work

To summarize, this study represents primary research that explores the effectiveness of utilizing multi-label classification models to categorize reviews from shopping apps into five quality targets. The results are encouraging, with the best scores being 0.177, 0.572, 0.739, 0.744, 0.944, 0.933, 0.722, 0.728 for Hamming Loss, Zero-One Error, MicroP, MacroP, MicroR, MacroR, MicroF1, and MacroF1, respectively. The dataset used in this study comprises only 552 samples. In a subsequent work, we will apply an iterative active learning approach to increase the training dataset with informative samples, aiming to enhance the performance of the models.

Although the results attained in this work are acceptable, more room for improvement remains. This could be achieved by applying dimensionality reduction algorithms [23] to remove irrelevant and noisy data and features that do not contribute significantly to the predictive power of the model. This could enhance Zero-One Loss results, as found by [9], where optimizing Zero-One Loss yielded superior outcomes compared to Hamming loss and F measure in noise-free multi-label classification tasks. Moreover, a future study has the potential to address the imbalance within labels observed in this research, allowing for an exploration of its impact on the overall performance of the model. Furthermore, as annotations in this research were performed by only one annotator, conducting additional studies with multiple annotators would be advantageous. This approach could help assess the agreement among annotators, ensure consistency of annotations, and investigate its effect on the model's performance.

Acknowledgements. The authors would like to acknowledge the support of Prince Sultan University for covering the expenses of this publication. Also, the author would like to thank prince sultan university for their support.

References

1. Ahn, T., Ryu, S., Han, I.: The impact of the online and offline features on the user acceptance of Internet shopping malls. Electron. Commer. Res. Appl. **3**(4), 405–420 (2004)
2. Ameur, A., Hamdi, S. and Yahia, S.B.: Multi-label learning for aspect category detection of arabic hotel reviews using AraBERT. In: ICAART (2), pp. 241–250 (2023)
3. Bogaert, M., Lootens, J., Van den Poel, D., Ballings, M.: Evaluating multi-label classifiers and recommender systems in the financial service sector. Eur. J. Oper. Res. **279**(2), 620–634 (2019)
4. Chen, Z., Ju, X., Lu, G. and Chen, X.: Blocking bugs identification via binary relevance and logistic regression analysis. In: 2022 9th International Conference on Dependable Systems and Their Applications (DSA), pp. 335–345. IEEE (2022)
5. Daniels, Z., Metaxas, D.: Addressing imbalance in multi-label classification using structured hellinger forests. In: Proceedings of the AAAI Conference on Artificial Intelligence, vol. 31, no. 1 (2017)
6. Dembczyński, K., Waegeman, W., Cheng, W., Hüllermeier, E.: Regret analysis for performance metrics in multi-label classification: the case of hamming and subset zero-one loss. In: Machine Learning and Knowledge Discovery in Databases: European Conference, ECML PKDD 2010, Barcelona, Spain, September 20–24, 2010, Proceedings, Part I 21, pp. 280–295. Springer Berlin Heidelberg (2010)

7. Deniz, E., Erbay, H., Coşar, M.: Multi-label classification of e-commerce customer reviews via machine learning. Axioms **11**(9), 436 (2022)
8. Devlin, J., Chang, M.W., Lee, K., Toutanova, K.: Bert: Pre-training of Deep Bidirectional Transformers for Language Understanding (2018). arXiv preprint arXiv:1810.04805
9. Díez, J., Luaces, O., del Coz, J.J., Bahamonde, A.: Optimizing different loss functions in multilabel classifications. Prog. Artif. Intell. **3**, 107–118 (2015)
10. El-Hasnony, I.M., Elzeki, O.M., Alshehri, A., Salem, H.: Multi-label active learning-based machine learning model for heart disease prediction. Sensors **22**(3), 1184 (2022)
11. Gao, W., Zhou, Z.H.: On the consistency of multi-label learning. In: Proceedings of the 24th Annual Conference on Learning Theory, pp. 341–358. JMLR Workshop and Conference Proceedings (2011)
12. Hakami, N.A.: Identification of customers satisfaction with popular online shopping apps in Saudi Arabia using sentiment analysis and topic modelling. In: Proceedings of the 2023 7th International Conference on E-Commerce, E-Business and E-Government, pp. 1–11 (2023)
13. Jain, P.K., Pamula, R., Yekun, E.A.: A multi-label ensemble predicting model to service recommendation from social media contents. J. Supercomput., 1–18 (2022)
14. Kang, X., Shi, X., Wu, Y., Ren, F.: Active learning with complementary sampling for instructing class-biased multi-label text emotion classification. In: IEEE Transactions on Affective Computing (2020)
15. Kaur, K., Kaur, P.: MNoR-BERT: multi-label classification of non-functional requirements using BERT. In: Neural Computing and Applications, vol. 35, no. 30, pp.22487–22509 (2023)
16. Zhang, A., Li, B., Wang, W., Wan, S., Chen, W.: MII: a novel text classification model combining deep active learning with BERT. Comput. Mater. Continua **63**(3), 1499–1514 (2020)
17. Liu, S.M., Chen, J.H.: A multi-label classification based approach for sentiment classification. Expert Syst. Appl. **42**(3), 1083–1093 (2015)
18. Lu, J., MacNamee, B.: Investigating the Effectiveness of Representations Based on Pretrained Transformer-Based Language Models in Active Learning for Labelling Text Datasets (2020). arXiv preprint arXiv:2004.13138
19. Luaces, O., Díez, J., Barranquero, J., del Coz, J.J., Bahamonde, A.: Binary relevance efficacy for multilabel classification. Prog. Artif. Intell. **1**, 303–313 (2012)
20. Messaoud, M.B., Jenhani, I., Jemaa, N.B., Mkaouer, M.W.: A multi-label active learning approach for mobile app user review classification. In: Knowledge Science, Engineering and Management: 12th International Conference, KSEM 2019, Athens, Greece, August 28–30, 2019, Proceedings, Part I 12, pp. 805–816. Springer International Publishing (2019)
21. Nareshpalsingh, J.M., Modi, H.N.: Multi-label classification methods: a comparative study. Int. Res. J. Eng. Technol. (IRJET) **4**(12), 263–270 (2017)
22. Nasierding, G., Kouzani, A.Z.: Comparative evaluation of multi-label classification methods. In: 2012 9th International Conference on Fuzzy Systems and Knowledge Discovery, pp. 679–683. IEEE (2012)
23. Pant, P., Sai Sabitha, A., Choudhury, T., Dhingra, P.: Multi-label classification trending challenges and approaches. In: Emerging Trends in Expert Applications and Security: Proceedings of ICETEAS 2018, pp.433-444 (2019)
24. Pennington, J., Socher, R. and Manning, C.D.: Glove: global vectors for word representation. In: Proceedings of the 2014 Conference on Empirical Methods in Natural Language Processing (EMNLP), pp. 1532–1543 (2014)
25. Poo, Z.Y., Ting, C.Y., Loh, Y.P., Ghauth, K.I.: Multi-label classification with deep learning for retail recommendation. J. Inform. Web Eng. **2**(2), 218–232 (2023)
26. Read, J., Pfahringer, B., Holmes, G., Frank, E.: Classifier chains for multi-label classification. Mach. Learn. **85**, 333–359 (2011)

27. Tao, J., Fang, X.: Toward multi-label sentiment analysis: a transfer learning based approach. J. Big Data **7**, 1–26 (2020)
28. Tawiah, C., Sheng, V.: Empirical comparison of multi-label classification algorithms. In: Proceedings of the AAAI Conference on Artificial Intelligence, vol. 27, no. 1, pp. 1645–1646 (2013)
29. Triantafyllou, I., Drivas, I.C., Giannakopoulos, G.: How to utilize my app reviews? A novel topics extraction machine learning schema for strategic business purposes. Entropy **22**(11), 1310 (2020)
30. Türkmen, A., Bayram, B., Aydın, G.: Employee behavior analysis towards multi-label classification of customer reviews. In: Proceedings of the 16th International Conference on PErvasive Technologies Related to Assistive Environments, pp. 511–517 (2023)
31. Wang, M. and Liu, M.: May. An Empirical Study on Active Learning for Multi-label Text Classification. In The Fourth Workshop on Insights from Negative Results in NLP (pp. 94–102). (2023)
32. Wu, X.Z., Zhou, Z.H.: A unified view of multi-label performance measures. In: International Conference on Machine Learning, pp. 3780–3788. PMLR. (2017)
33. Zhou, B., Zhao, H., Puig, X., Fidler, S., Barriuso, A., Torralba, A.: Scene parsing through ade20k dataset. In: Proceedings of the IEEE Conference on Computer Vision and Pattern Recognition, pp. 633–641 (2017)

Unveiling the Dynamics in Shopping Behaviors: A Review

Nazilah Ahmad, Muhamad Ahmad Adam, and Rosmaini Tasmin[✉]

Department of Production and Operation Management, Faculty of Technology Management and Business, Universiti Tun Hussein Onn Malaysia, 86400 Parit Raja, Batu Pahat, Johor, Malaysia
{gp230001,hp220039}@student.uthm.edu.my, rosmaini@uthm.edu.my

Abstract. This study employed a robust research methodology and utilised Python programming as a comprehensive platform for analysing and visualising retail shopping trends. It addresses the pressing issue of understanding and improving shopping behaviour in dynamic retailing. Since a large portion of global consumer spending occurs in the retail industry, companies must understand the complexities of consumer behaviour to remain competitive. The research objectives are twofold: first, to examine the differences in shopping behaviour between genders, focusing on frequency, consumption amount, and product preference; second, to provide businesses and marketers with practical strategies to increase shopping participation and purchasing power. A robust research methodology was employed to achieve these goals, leveraging Python programming as a comprehensive platform for analysing and visualising retail shopping trends. The study included a large-scale survey of 4,000 respondents, with 2,652 (66%) male shoppers and 1,248 (34%) female shoppers in the United States of America (US). This extensive data set allows a detailed examination of gender-specific shopping behaviours and preferences. In addition, secondary data from annual reports and official publications supplemented the primary data collected. The research process involves various stages, including data collection, cleaning, descriptive statistics, data visualisation, statistical analysis and machine learning techniques customised to the study's specific needs. The analysis provides valuable insights into the differences in shopping behaviour between men and women and actionable recommendations for increasing shopping engagement and purchasing power. This study contributes to the existing body of knowledge on consumer behaviour in the retail industry by combining academic and industry insights in a comprehensive literature review and improving shopping behaviour by applying robust research methods and Python programming for data visualisation.

Keywords: Shopping Behavior · Phyton programming

1 Introduction

Understanding the dynamics that drive shopping behaviour is crucial to developing strategies that resonate with different consumer groups. Although shopping may seem like a simple exchange of goods and money, it contains fascinating complexities. Beyond

K. S. Soliman (Ed.): IBIMA-AI 2024, CCIS 2299, pp. 174–187, 2025.
https://doi.org/10.1007/978-3-031-77493-5_16

the surface of supermarket aisles and checkouts, a dynamic interplay of emotions, motivations, and influences shapes how we navigate the vast consumption landscape. This review explores the complex shopping behaviour web woven by gender, psychology, marketing strategies, and cultural nuances. The study began with a comprehensive survey to reveal the subtleties of shopping behaviour.

The study, Unveiling the Dynamics of Shopping Behavior: A Review, looks at the various factors that shape consumers' interactions with the retail environment. Moreover, [35] highlighted the importance of consumers' shopping orientation as a predictor of their shopping behaviours, particularly within the context of U.S. Hispanic immigrant couples and their shopping orientation toward fashion products. [17, 18] and [35] delved into the effects of big data analytics on consumers' responses in an e-commerce context, emphasising the drastic change in shopping addiction from intention to behaviour compared to group influences and privacy and security.

As consumers choose from a wide range of products and services, their shopping behaviour is influenced by various factors, including cultural differences, changing social norms, and personal preferences. This study aims to comprehensively review and analyse the large-scale survey of 4,000 respondents, with 2,652 (66%) male shoppers and 1,248 (34%) female shoppers in the United States of America (US) with the supporting of existing literature on shopping behaviour, incorporating various dimensions such as frequency, consumption patterns, preferred product categories, and underlying motivations. [31] provided a comprehensive review of the influence of store atmospherics on consumer shopping behaviour, encompassing visual, auditory, tactile, olfactory, and gustatory aspects of the store environment ([27, 31]) contributed to the understanding of augmented reality (AR) induced consumer behaviour in shopping, offering a framework for comprehending the dynamics in AR-related shopping and the factors influencing consumer adoption of this technology [27].

Understanding the differences in shopping behaviour between men and women is critical for companies looking to optimise their marketing strategies. Therefore, in this study, the analysis covers the purchased amount, frequency of purchasing, and purchased items by gender, which involves the analysis of product categories such as Clothing, Outerwear, Footwear, and accessories. The failure to address these differences, including differences in shopping frequency, consumption patterns and preferred product categories, can result in businesses being unable to target and engage with different customer segments effectively. Companies must understand that women may shop more frequently than men but spend less per trip. Resources may be allocated inefficiently, and opportunities to tailor marketing strategies and product offerings to meet the different needs and preferences of each gender are missed. Likewise, ignoring differences in preferences across product categories can result in a mismatch between supply and demand, resulting in missed sales opportunities and reduced customer satisfaction. Therefore, an in-depth study of these differences is crucial for making strategic decisions and improving overall market performance.

Additionally, implementing practical strategies to increase shopping engagement and purchasing power among men and women is necessary for companies and marketers to capitalise on market opportunities and remain competitive. Inadequate measures to increase shopping engagement, such as not using digital channels or personalised marketing methods, can reduce consumer interest and brand loyalty. Additionally, ignoring differences in purchasing power between genders may limit a company's sales potential, as failure to consider the differing affordability levels of male and female consumers may result in lost sales and decreased market share. Therefore, developing effective strategies to increase shopping engagement and purchasing power among men and women is crucial to maximise profitability and ensure long-term business success in a highly competitive market.

Examining these differences begins with the comparative dynamics between the differences in men's and women's shopping habits. The study also aims to provide valuable insights into the factors that influence consumer decision-making. Furthermore, [24] addressed the paucity of empirical evidence regarding the potential effects of the COVID-19 pandemic on consumers' online shopping behavior, mainly focusing on price sensitivity and online shopping behavior during the pandemic [24]. Specific objectives include examining changes in shopping frequency, exploring spending amounts, understanding preferred product categories, and uncovering motivations behind shopping decisions.

Furthermore, by understanding "why" half the story is only, this review reveals the "how." It analyses the strategies companies and marketers use to attract, engage and ultimately influence our purchasing decisions. It recognises the potential for improving marketing strategies to engage and empower consumers and aims to provide actionable recommendations. With a specific focus on increasing both men's and women's shopping engagement and purchasing power, the research seeks to address gaps in understanding and suggest practical strategies that businesses and marketers can implement to promote a more inclusive and effective retail environment.

1.1 Research Questions

This study aimed to address the following research questions as follows:

i. Who shops more? Men or women, according to the data set.
ii. What practical strategies do businesses and marketers implement to encourage greater shopping engagement and capacities among women?

1.2 Research Objectives

The objectives of this research are as follows:

i. Examine the differences in shopping behaviours between men and women, focusing on the frequency of shopping, spending amounts, and preferred product categories; and
ii. Propose practical strategies that companies and marketers can implement to increase shopping engagement and purchasing power.

2 Literature Review

2.1 Dynamism in Shopping Behaviors

Shopping behaviour refers to the process and activities individuals engage in when acquiring goods and services. It encompasses various aspects such as decision-making, preferences, and the factors influencing purchasing choices. Meanwhile, the dynamism in shopping behaviours refers to the ever-changing and multifaceted nature of consumer actions and decisions in various shopping contexts.

Understanding consumer behaviour is crucial for businesses to tailor their marketing strategies and offerings [20]. Emotional aspects play a significant role in consumer-brand relationships, as brands that evoke emotional connections are likelier to foster consumer commitment [13]. Additionally, the theory of planned behaviour, which includes perceived behavioural control, subjective norm, and attitude, has been found to impact online shopping behaviour [33]. Furthermore, factors such as consumer innovativeness, purchase experience, and gender influence the intention to shop for fashion products online, highlighting the multifaceted nature of shopping behaviour (Nirmala & Dewi, 2011)).

In the dynamic world of retail, studying gender differences in shopping behaviour is crucial for several reasons. First, it is essential to understand consumer preferences. Gender differences in shopping behaviour can provide insights into different preferences and needs and incorporate them into customised marketing strategies and product offerings to increase customer satisfaction and loyalty [14, 30]. Effective marketing strategies considering these differences will result in targeted campaigns that resonate with specific gender groups and increase brand awareness, loyalty, and sales [7] Additionally, understanding unique shopping behaviours can help improve customer experience. Retailers can create a more inclusive environment by adjusting store layout and services, resulting in a more satisfying shopping experience [14]. Furthermore, companies gain competitive advantages by satisfying different needs and achieving higher market share and success [30].

Furthermore, incorporating gender-specific insights into product development and store operations increases efficiency and satisfaction (Thanasi-Boçe et al., 2020). Improving employee training based on gender differences can lead to more effective customer service and performance [7]. Retailers can increase customer loyalty by satisfying diverse needs, which is crucial in today's competitive environment [30]. Studying gender differences can help companies adapt to changing trends and identify new preferences (Thanasi-Boçe et al., 2020). Finally, understanding purchasing behaviour influences informed decisions and guides growth investments [30]. This research is critical in examining the importance of gender differences in shopping behaviour. It provides valuable insights into consumer preferences and guides tailored marketing strategies and product offerings to increase customer satisfaction and loyalty. By understanding these differences, companies can gain a competitive advantage, increase market share, and ensure long-term success in a dynamic retail environment.

The influence of age, gender, and cultural differences on online shopping behaviour has been studied extensively, emphasising the need for a cross-cultural approach to understanding purchase intentions and behaviours ([1, 22]. Moreover, the rise of e-commerce and online shopping has transformed traditional retail and consumer behaviour, leading to changes in the consumption economy, retail land use, and travel behaviour ([8, 39]). Sustainable consumer behaviour has emerged as a business opportunity, with sustainability being linked to ethical consumer behaviour, indicating a shift toward more conscientious shopping habits ([5, 36]).

Moreover, the study underscores the impact of big data analytics on consumers' responses in e-commerce, suggesting a shift in shopping addiction and behaviour due to group influences and privacy concerns [17, 18]. Furthermore, the research delves into the association between online shopping behaviour and demographic characteristics, shedding light on the influence of factors such as marital status on consumer behaviour [11]. Additionally, the study emphasises the dynamic and volatile nature of consumer behaviour in the fashion industry, particularly in online shops, highlighting the need for further investigation into this evolving landscape [37].

3 Analyzing Through Python Programming for Data Visualization

Analysing data using Python involves leveraging various libraries and tools tailored to different scientific and computational domains. Python's versatility and extensive libraries make it a popular choice for data analysis in fields such as biology, chemistry, physics, and computer science ([4, 6, 12, 15, 16, 23, 25, 28, 29]).

For instance, in biology, Python is used for molecular dynamics simulations, trajectory analysis, and computational biology frameworks ([2, 16]). In chemistry, Python is gaining attention for analytical chemistry and chemometrics [21]. Furthermore, in physics, Python is utilised for biomechanics research and high-throughput (phospho) proteomics data analysis ([6, 26]). Additionally, in computer science, Python is employed for satellite data analysis, crystallographic data analysis, and electrophysiology data handling ([9, 10, 32]).

Python's data analysis capabilities are enhanced by libraries such as Pandas, xarray, and NumPy, which provide powerful tools for tabular data analysis, N-D labelled arrays, and numerical computation, respectively ([12, 25, 29]). Moreover, Python's integration with Jupyter Notebook offers an interactive computational environment for data analysis, visualisation, and sharing ([2, 15]). The language's flexibility and ease of use make it suitable for developing object-oriented scripts and libraries for specific data analysis tasks [29].

Python's suitability for data analysis is further demonstrated by its application in statistical calculations, meta-cognitive awareness in learning programming, and parallel processing for improved computational efficiency ([3, 19]). The language's support for multiple programming paradigms, including functional, procedural, reflective, imperative, and object-oriented approaches, contributes to its adaptability for diverse data analysis requirements [40]. In conclusion, Python's extensive libraries, interactive computational environment, and support for various programming paradigms make it a versatile and powerful tool for data analysis across a wide range of scientific and computational domains.

4 Research Methodology

This study adopts robust research methods and uses Phyton programming as a shopping trend analysis and visualisation platform to comprehensively analyse and simulate a retail company's data set. First, the consistency of the research objectives was established. We conducted an extensive literature review, combining academic and industrial sources, to gain insights into people's shopping behaviours and practical strategies that can be implemented to encourage them to enjoy shopping. The primary data was collected by reviewing a set of company purchasing trends using Phyton programming, which included data collection, data cleaning, descriptive statistics, data visualisation, placeholders for statistical analysis, and machine learning suitable for the study. Steps required. This involved a survey of 4,000 respondents in the United States of America (US). Secondary data from annual reports and official publications support it. The study concludes with strategic recommendations that provide actionable insights into the dynamic retail industry.

5 Results and Findings

5.1 Gender Population in Shopping Database

After analysing the data from the shopping database, it is clear that there is a notable difference in shopping habits between genders. The dataset indicates a significant shopping gap, with 2,652 (66%) male shoppers and approximately 1,248 (34%) female shoppers. This collective count represents the entire sample size under consideration. The observed difference in shopping behaviour between genders, which is contributed to the range of 52%, highlights the importance of a deeper understanding of the preferences and actions of male and female consumers. This knowledge is crucial in developing personalised marketing tactics and enhancing product selections to cater to the unique requirements of all shoppers (Fig. 1).

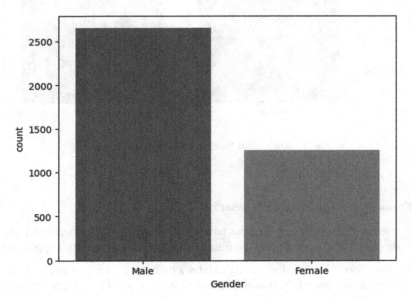

Fig. 1. A graphical analysis of gender from the shopping data set.

5.2   Analysis of Purchase Amounts by Gender

The analysis of purchase amounts unveils a substantial discrepancy between male and female shoppers. Specifically, male shoppers collectively spent $157,890, significantly 47% more than the total expenditure of female shoppers, which amounted to $75,191.

This significant variance in spending patterns could indicate various aspects.

i. Differential Purchase Behavior: Male shoppers' considerably higher total spending might imply a preference for certain high-ticket items or a higher frequency of purchases than their female counterparts.
ii. Product Preferences: Male shoppers may favour specific product categories or items, leading to higher overall expenditure in those particular areas (Fig. 2).

Fig. 2.   Analysis of Purchase Amounts by Gender.

5.3   Frequency of Purchase by Gender

The frequency analysis unveils distinct patterns in shopping habits between male and female shoppers. When comparing the intervals of purchase, it becomes apparent that:

i. Male Shoppers: They predominantly exhibit a higher frequency of purchases, spanning from approximately 370 to 400 instances, an average of 50% higher than female shoppers. These purchases occur frequently, showcasing a more active shopping behaviour. These frequent purchases are denoted by the blue colour, suggesting fortnightly intervals. Fortnightly (Blue Column) The predominant blue colour represents purchases every fortnight, suggesting a consistent and frequent shopping pattern. This could indicate regular, habitual shopping behaviour among male shoppers, possibly for routine or consumable items.

ii. Female Shoppers: On the other hand, their purchase frequency ranges from approximately 160 to 200 instances. This suggests a comparatively lower frequency of purchases, indicating a less frequent shopping pattern. The green colour denotes annual purchases (160 to 200 cases) and implies a less frequent shopping pattern among female shoppers. This might indicate larger, planned purchases for significant items or during specific occasions or sales events (Figs. 3 and 4).

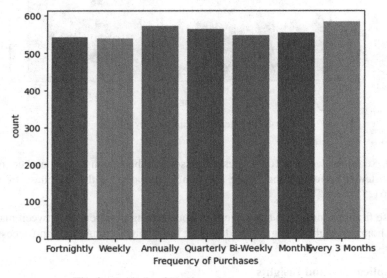

Fig. 3. Analysis of Purchase Amounts by Gender.

5.4 Analysis of Commonly Purchased Items by Both Male and Female Shoppers

The provided graph represents various clothing and accessory items and their corresponding purchase frequencies by male and female shoppers. Upon reviewing the purchase frequencies across different items, it is evident that certain products have consistently high purchase counts among both male and female shoppers:

i. Blouse, Jewelry, Pants (171): These items—blouses, jewellery, and pants—emerge as the most frequently purchased products among male and female shoppers, with a purchase frequency of 171.

ii. Shirt (169), Dress (166), Sweater (164), Jacket (163): Following closely are shirts, dresses, sweaters, and jackets, which also exhibit high purchase frequencies and are commonly sought after by both genders.

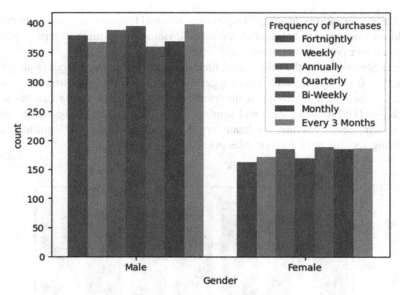

Fig. 4. Frequency of purchase by gender

iii. Belt, Sunglasses, Coat (161): These accessories—belts, sunglasses, and coats—are consistently popular among male and female shoppers, with a purchase frequency of 161.

These findings indicate a convergence in purchasing preferences between male and female shoppers, highlighting a shared interest in certain clothing items and accessories.

5.5 Implications and Insights

- Unisex Appeal: The items listed above seem unisex, appealing equally to both male and female shoppers.
- Fashion Staples: Clothing staples such as blouses, pants, shirts, and dresses appear essential for both genders, showcasing their universal significance.
- Accessory Preference: Accessories like jewellery, belts, sunglasses, and coats hold a consistent allure for male and female shoppers, transcending gender-specific fashion (Fig. 5).

6   Recommendation - Practical Strategies for Encouraging Women to Shop

This research is critical in examining the importance of gender differences in shopping behaviour. Understanding these differences can provide valuable insights into consumer preferences and guide tailored marketing strategies and product offerings to increase customer satisfaction and loyalty. To close the gap in shopping behaviour between men

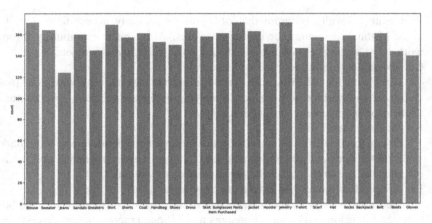

Fig. 5. Commonly Purchased Items by Both Male and Female Shoppers

and women in the United States, women must be encouraged to shop by understanding their different preferences, needs, and motivations. Practical strategies tailored to attract and empower female shoppers include:

i. Personalized shopping experience

Women value personalised recommendations and experiences. Tailoring product recommendations based on previous purchases or browsing history and offering exclusive discounts or rewards on items they frequently purchase or are interested in can improve their shopping experience.

ii. Enhanced In-Store Atmosphere

The in-store atmosphere: The design prioritises comfort and a beautiful layout, providing spacious fitting rooms, well-lit rooms, and relaxing rest areas. Combining this with interactive display or virtual try-on technology can improve the shopping experience.

iii. Curated content and reviews

Provide detailed product information, sizing guides and user reviews, including different body types and customer reviews, to build trust in purchasing decisions. Women value authenticity and seek peer opinions. Including diverse body types and customer reviews can build trust and confidence in their purchase decisions.

iv. Integrate social media

Use social media platforms to showcase products, share customer reviews, and promote user-generated content that aligns with women's lifestyles and desires. Encourage user-generated content by running contests or featuring customer stories that align with women's lifestyles and aspirations.

v. Simplify online shopping

Optimise website and app interfaces for easy navigation and mobile compatibility, implement intuitive search filters, streamline checkout, and offer multiple payment options for greater convenience.

vi. Exclusive offers and community-building

Create a loyalty program that offers members early access to new collections, birthday discounts, or exclusive events. Also, create community through workshops, styling sessions, or events that unite like-minded women.

vii. Collaborations and Influencer Partnerships

Work with female influencers or organisations that resonate with your target audience, and partner with fashion bloggers, wellness advocates, or community leaders for endorsements or collaborations.

viii. Feedback and Inclusion

Obtain feedback through surveys, focus groups or online surveys to better understand preferences and concerns and promote inclusivity in marketing and product offerings by presenting a diverse representation of women.

ix. Diverse product ranges and marketing campaigns

We offer a variety of styles, sizes and designs to suit different tastes and body types and develop marketing campaigns to celebrate empowerment, diversity and authenticity.

By recognising women's preferences for personalised experiences, community engagement and authenticity, companies can create an inclusive and empowering shopping environment that encourages active engagement and loyalty among female consumers.

7 Conclusion

The analysis of shopping behaviours between men and women in the US reveals nuanced differences across various facets of consumer activity, encompassing shopping frequency, expenditure patterns, and preferred product categories. These disparities offer insightful glimpses into the distinct approaches each gender adopts when engaging in retail activities.

Men showcase a more frequent shopping pattern, indicated by 370 to 400 instances when exploring shopping frequency. This suggests a regular, almost habitual engagement with retail spaces or online platforms. Conversely, women exhibit a lower frequency, approximately 160 to 200 cases, implying a more deliberate and less frequent shopping cadence. These differences mirror varied approaches to consumption, with men favouring routine and consistent purchases while women may opt for more measured and intentional shopping experiences.

A notable contrast emerges between male and female shoppers when considering spending amounts. The total expenditure of $157,890 by men starkly juxtaposes the $75,191 spent by women, reflecting divergent spending behaviours. This discrepancy hints at potential dissimilarities in purchasing habits, where men might engage in more frequent, albeit smaller, transactions. In contrast, women might opt for less frequent but higher-value purchases, aligning with a deliberate and selective shopping approach.

Examining the preferred product categories unveils intriguing commonalities. Both genders are interested in essential and versatile items such as blouses, jewellery, pants, shirts, dresses, and accessories like belts and sunglasses. These categories signify a unisex appeal, transcending gender-specific preferences and reflecting a mutual interest in fashion staples that resonate across diverse demographics.

These observed differences in shopping behaviours between men and women hold substantial implications for businesses. Tailoring marketing strategies to accommodate these dissimilarities is essential. For male shoppers, emphasising convenience, personalised experiences, and promoting regular, smaller purchases may enhance engagement. Conversely, focusing on creating immersive, less frequent shopping experiences and offering personalised recommendations for higher-value items might resonate better with female shoppers.

Moreover, leveraging the shared interest in specific product categories allows businesses to develop inclusive marketing campaigns and diverse product portfolios that cater to a broader audience. Incorporating these insights into inventory management, marketing strategies, and customer engagement initiatives enables businesses to align more effectively with the distinct preferences of both male and female shoppers, fostering loyalty and satisfaction within these consumer segments.

Acknowledgement. *Alhamdulillah.*

Thanks, Allah. This research has been completed with His permission and grace. My most incredible gratitude goes to my dedicated lecturer, Assoc. Prof Ts. Dr. Rosmaini Tasmin provides valuable advice and unwavering insights throughout the process. The same appreciation goes to my team, Mr. Muhamad Ahmad Adam, for his efforts and contribution in developing this study. I sincerely appreciate all Universiti Tun Hussein Onn Malaysia (UTHM) lecturers for their contributions to my academic growth.

Special thanks go to my beloved family, especially my parents, Hajah Masidah Hussain and Haji Ahmad Kasmadi; my husband, Mohd Fadzil Adenan; and all my children for your unwavering support, patience, and encouragement, especially during the most challenging stages of learning.

Finally, I would like to thank all my friends who have supported me through all the challenges. Thanks, you all, for being an integral part of this journey.

References

1. Ahmed, K.A.A., Sathish, A.S.: Unleashing the utilitarian motivations of online shopping among Indian youth. Mediterranean Journal of Social Sciences (2015). https://doi.org/10.5901/mjss.2015.v6n2p391
2. Alexander, W.M., Ficarro, S.B., Adelmant, G., Marto, J.A.: Multiplierzv2.0: a python-based ecosystem for shared access and analysis of native mass spectrometry data. Proteomics (2017). https://doi.org/10.1002/pmic.201700091
3. Aziz, Z.A., Abdulqader, D.N., Sallow, A.B., Omer, H.K.: Python parallel processing and multiprocessing: A review. Academic Journal of Nawroz University (2021). https://doi.org/10.25007/ajnu.v10n3a1145
4. Balreira, D.G., Silveira, T., Wickboldt, J.A.: Investigating the impact of adopting Python and C languages for introductory engineering programming courses. Computer Applications in Engineering Education (2022). https://doi.org/10.1002/cae.22570
5. Calderón Monge, M.E., Pastor-Sanz, I., Garcia, F.: Analysis of sustainable consumer behavior as a business opportunity. Journal of Business Research (2020). https://doi.org/10.1016/j.jbusres.2020.07.039
6. Chénier, F.: Kinetics toolkit: an open-source Python package to facilitate research in biomechanics. The Journal of Open Source Software (2021). https://doi.org/10.21105/joss.03714

7. Chukwu, A.: Unveiling gender patterns: Exploring consumer behavior in online shopping among Nigerians. Global Multidisciplinary Journal (2023). https://api.semanticscholar.org/CorpusID:268221032

8. Feng, X.: Research on the system of online shopping supply chain based on consumer behavior under the background of e-commerce. Destech Transactions on Engineering and Technology Research (2016). https://doi.org/10.12783/dtetr/ssme-ist2016/3997

9. Garcia, S., et al.: Neo: An object model for handling electrophysiology data in multiple formats. Frontiers in Neuroinformatics (2014). https://doi.org/10.3389/fninf.2014.00010

10. Greisman, J.B., Dalton, K.M., Hekstra, D.R.: Reciprocalspaceship: a python library for crystallographic data analysis (2021). https://doi.org/10.1101/2021.02.03.429617

11. Hossain, M.K., Salam, Md.A., Jawad, S.S.: Factors affecting online shopping behavior in Bangladesh: A demographic perspective. Int. J. Bus. Ecosy. Strat. **4**(3) (2022). https://doi.org/10.36096/ijbes.v4i3.351

12. Hoyer, S., Hamman, J.: Xarray: N-D labeled arrays and datasets in Python. J. Open Res. Softw. (2017). https://doi.org/10.5334/jors.148

13. Hwang, J., Kandampully, J.: The role of emotional aspects in younger consumer-brand relationships. Journal of Product & Brand Management (2012). https://doi.org/10.1108/10610421211215517. Accessed 20 May 2024

14. Iton, C.W.A.: Gender differences of perceived fresh produce retail outlet attributes in Trinidad and Tobago. Developing Country Studies, **5**, 8–15 (2015). https://api.semanticscholar.org/CorpusID:55742813. Last accessed 20 May 2024

15. Jesus Martinez, T. De, et al.: JBrowse Jupyter: A Python interface to JBrowse 2. Bioinformatics (2023). https://doi.org/10.1093/bioinformatics/btad032. Last accessed 20 May 2024

16. Kunzmann, P., Hamacher, K.: Biotite: a unifying open source computational biology framework in Python. BMC Bioinformatics (2018). https://doi.org/10.1186/s12859-018-2367-z. Last accessed 20 May 2024

17. Le, T.M., Liaw, S.: Effects of pros and cons of applying big data analytics to consumers' responses in an e-commerce context. Sustainability (2017a). https://doi.org/10.3390/su9050798. Last accessed 20 May 2024

18. Le, T.M., Liaw, S.: Effects of pros and cons of applying big data analytics to consumers' responses in an e-commerce context. Sustainability (2017b). https://doi.org/10.3390/su9050798. Last accessed 20 May 2024

19. Logroño Naranjo, S.I., Estrada Brito, N.A., Vásconez Núñez, V.A., Rosero Ordóñez, E.M.: Analysis of the use of the Python programming language for statistical calculations. Espirales Revista Multidisciplinaria De Investigación (2022). https://doi.org/10.31876/er.v6i41.813

20. Mora, P.: Understanding consumer behavior (2015). https://doi.org/10.1007/978-3-319-24481-5_2. Last accessed 20 May 2024

21. Morita, S.: Chemometrics and related fields in Python. Analytical Sciences (2019). https://doi.org/10.2116/analsci.19r006. Last accessed 20 May 2024

22. Nirmala, R., Dewi, I.J.: The effects of shopping orientations, consumer innovativeness, purchase experience, and gender on intention to shop for fashion products online. Gadjah Mada Int. J. Bus. (2011). https://doi.org/10.22146/gamaijb.5495. Last accessed 20 May 2024

23. Peña-García, N., Saura, I.G., Orejuela, A.R., Siqueira-Junior, J.R.: Purchase intention and purchase behavior online: A cross-cultural approach. Heliyon (2020). https://doi.org/10.1016/j.heliyon.2020.e04284. Last accessed 20 May 2024

24. Radusky, L.G., Serrano, L.: pyFoldX: Enabling biomolecular analysis and engineering along structural ensembles. Bioinformatics (2022). https://doi.org/10.1093/bioinformatics/btac072. Last accessed 20 May 2024

25. Rahmani, V., Kordrostami, E.: Price sensitivity and online shopping behavior during the COVID-19 pandemic. Journal of Consumer Marketing (2023). https://doi.org/10.1108/jcm-07-2021-4777. Last accessed 20 May 2024

26. Rand, K.D., Grytten, I., Pavlović, M., Kanduri, C., Sandve, G.K.: BioNumPy: Fast and easy analysis of biological data with Python (2022). https://doi.org/10.1101/2022.12.21.521373
27. Ressa, A., Fitzpatrick, M., van den Toorn, H., Heck, A.J., Altelaar, M.: PaDuA: A Python library for high-throughput (phospho)proteomics data analysis. Journal of Proteome Research (2018). https://doi.org/10.1021/acs.jproteome.8b00576
28. Riar, M., Xi, N., Korbel, J.J. Zarnekow, R., Hamari, J.: Using augmented reality for shopping: A framework for AR induced consumer behavior, literature review and future agenda. Internet Research (2022). https://doi.org/10.1108/intr-08-2021-0611
29. Ruffini, N., Müller, M.B., Schmitt, U., Gerber, S.: IntelliPy: A GUI for analyzing IntelliCage data. Bioinformatics (2021). https://doi.org/10.1093/bioinformatics/btab682
30. Sabol, J., Procházka, D., Patočka, Z.: Development of models for forest variable estimation from airborne laser scanning data using an area-based approach at a plot level. Journal of Forest Science (2016). https://doi.org/10.17221/73/2015-jfs
31. Sharma, K., Aich, S.: Consumer shopping decision making styles at departmental stores: An exploratory study of gender differences (2012). https://api.semanticscholar.org/CorpusID:539 87476
32. Spence, C., Puccinelli, N., Grewal, D., Roggeveen, A.L.: Store atmospherics: a multisensory perspective. Psychology and Marketing (2014). https://doi.org/10.1002/mar.20709
33. Stoneback, R., Burrell, A.G., Klenzing, J., Depew, M.: PYSAT: Python satellite data analysis toolkit. Journal of Geophysical Research Space Physics (2018). https://doi.org/10.1029/201 8ja025297
34. Sutisna, F., Handra, T.: Theory of planned behavior influences online shopping behavior. Aptisi Transactions on Management (Atm) (2022). https://doi.org/10.33050/atm.v6i1.1691
35. Thanasi-Boče, M., Kwiatek, P., Labadze, L.: The importance of distance and attraction in patronizing a shopping mall. Journal of Place Management and Development (2020). https://api.semanticscholar.org/CorpusID:230608000
36. Toloza, L., Cho, E., Terrell, A.: Understanding cultural adaptation of U.S. Hispanic immigrant couples and their shopping orientation toward fashion products. Family and Consumer Sciences Research Journal (2021). https://doi.org/10.1111/fcsr.12417
37. Tomşa, M.-M., Romonţi-Maniu, A.-I., Scridon, M.A.: Is sustainable consumption translated into ethical consumer behavior? Sustainability (2021). https://doi.org/10.3390/su13063466
38. Widayat, W., Nursakinah, Widjaya, R.: The relationship modelling of advertising, electronic word of mouth and brand awareness on fashion product purchasing decision. JBMP (Jurnal Bisnis Manajemen Dan Perbankan) (2022). https://doi.org/10.21070/jbmp.v8i2.1601
39. Wu, Q.: Leafmap: A Python package for interactive mapping and geospatial analysis with minimal coding in a Jupyter environment. The Journal of Open Source Software (2021). https://doi.org/10.21105/joss.03414
40. Xi, G., Zhu, F., Cao, X., Xu, F.: The interaction between e-shopping and store shopping: Empirical evidence from Nanjing, China. Transportation Letters (2018). https://doi.org/10. 1080/19427867.2018.1546797
41. Zehra, F., Javed, M., Khan, D., Pasha, M.: Comparative analysis of C++ and Python in terms of memory and time (2020). https://doi.org/10.20944/preprints202012.0516.v1

Control of Technical Parameters of Industrial Products Through Machine Vision

Vlad Gheorghita[✉]

National University of Science and Technology POLITEHNICA, Bucharest, Romania
vladgheorghita90@gmail.com

Abstract. During the production process, a lot of undesirable or faulty products are also created. Since these products cannot be used or distributed on the market, they must be discarded. Product integrity and quality inspection, which is also a result of production process efficiency and optimization, is one of the most important procedures in modern industrial applications. The quickest and most efficient way to make sure products meet the quality requirements is through an automated verification process. These systems are considered as essential by some applications because replacing them with human employees would necessitate a substantial workforce and related costs. This research provides a mechanical experimental system that will be able to verify fast and control the most important parameters of various products using the artificial intelligence approach and machine vision techniques. The cost of the designed system is low and the structure used is clear. The demonstration of the utility of the created product was carried out on a toothed wheel with many essential technical characteristics, a widely used landmark in the field of manufacturing engineering. Image processing techniques are used such as threshold function, calibration, pattern matching, measure. The experimental model designed is easy to implement and can represent a transition towards the application of modern industry 5.0 principles in different processing companies.

Keywords: artificial intelligence · machine vision · automation · metrology

1 Introduction

One of the most crucial steps in industrial production lines is object sorting. Many undesired or flawed items are also produced during the production process. These items need to be eliminated since they cannot be used or disseminated on the market. Manually classifying those improper items require a significant investment in time, resources, and accuracy. This task can be completed more quickly and cheaply with machine vision, and with more accuracy. Since the software is so efficient, there are already applications for automated examination. Only the inputs must be provided by the user to the software. However, users are free to create their own applications. One benefit of creating your own application is the cost savings, as ready-made applications require additional funding. Additionally, machine vision applications can be created to become more significant the more experienced a user is.

K. S. Soliman (Ed.): IBIMA-AI 2024, CCIS 2299, pp. 188–196, 2025.
https://doi.org/10.1007/978-3-031-77493-5_17

Three examples of machine vision systems are used in a research study by [1] to illustrate some of the key problems that metrology must address in light of new techniques. The major takeaway from this is that each business must develop its own roadmap for putting in place the appropriate procedures and methodologies in order to appropriately adapt to and align with this new generation of metrology-related systems.

[2] used inexpensive CCD cameras with infrared-pass filters that can significantly streamline image processing and pattern analysis tasks for a machine vision measurement system, according to experiments done on acquiring and processing images of hot forgings, particularly large open die forgings.

In the research by [3], machine vision and its many techniques have been explored as a means of measuring machining parameters, including tool wear, surface characteristics including surface roughness and surface flaws, and tool condition monitoring (TCM) tool wear. The manufacturing and machining sectors have created tool condition monitor as a crucial machining parameter. The advancement of non-tactile applications and computing technology has generated great interest in the development of various machine vision approaches for tool condition monitoring.

In order to measure surface roughness in a production setting, a novel technique was devised by [4]. The pattern of light scattered from the surface is examined using a microcomputer-based vision system in this technique to determine the roughness parameter. For a series of tool-steel samples that were ground to various roughness, the roughness parameters were obtained. Plotting the roughness parameters against the matching average surface roughness measurements acquired from a stylus instrument resulted in the creation of a correlation curve.

In the paper study by [7] in order to count the number of maize plants in the early stages of growth, a machine vision-based system for population sensing of maize plants was created. The total number of plant pixels and their median position were recovered as two features from each pixel row of the segmented pictures. For the purpose of final plant counts, adjacent rows from the same class were grouped together and iteratively improved.

2   Materials and Methods

The main components of the designed system for the control of some industrial products (Fig. 1) are: conveyor belt (1); area with DC motor, power source, servo motor (2); laser sensors (3); a video camera and image processing area (4); containers with the components that comply or don't comply with the condition (5' and 5″); steering arms which directs the products accordingly if they correspond (6' and 6″). The goals achieved with this experimental model are the following: development of an algorithm to recognize the shape; checking the functionality of the system; calculation of the optimal speed with which an object moves on the lane; checking the accuracy of the system and algorithm; testing and learning the algorithm with different components; realization of the control of the servomotor with the results of the image analysis. After analyzing the fulfillment of a condition, an arm will direct the product accordingly.

The control of the characteristics of a piece in the field of machine technology has a critical importance. In this paper, the purpose was sorting a group of 3D printed

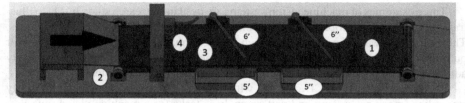

Fig. 1. Identification and control system

toothed gears through image analysis according to their characteristics (number of teeth, outer diameter, bore diameter, shape and degree of tooth damage). The system used for identification and control is created with the help of 3D printing at a low cost. The technical and dimensional characteristics are taken from the execution drawing of a toothed wheel that is part of an assembly with a pinion and a worm coupling. Several parameters can be controlled such as the dividing diameter, the step, the height above the teeth. The toothed wheel is into class 8 precision and the angle of engagement $\alpha = 20°$.

The activities that are done to analyze the characteristics of the wheel are: determination of the number of teeth "n" over which to measure the dimension W; calculate the gear module ($m = d_{ef}/(z + 2)$); the value found is rounded to the nearest standard; depending on the number of teeth "z" of the wheel, choose the number of teeth "n" and W_1 the theoretical dimension over teeth for $m = 1$ and $\alpha = 20°$; calculate the theoretical dimensions W by taking into account the "m" module and the experimental determined value W_1 is: $W = W_1 \cdot m$. The following inputs and outputs of the process can be calculated: the actual deviations of dimensions measured against the theoretical or nominal, the variation of the W dimension, the average dimension over the teeth, the average deviation over teeth.

The length over the teeth is the normal common to two antihomologous flanks over a number of "n" teeth depending on the number of teeth "z" of the wheel being checked. This common normal is tangent to the base circle. The number of teeth "n" over which the L_n dimension is measured (Fig. 2), is calculated so that the contact points of the device plates with the flanks of the teeth are as close as possible to the dividing circle, where the profile has the smallest deviations.

After determining the nominal value of the length L_n and the effective values L_{nef} for all the teeth of the wheel, the effective deviations of the length (elevation) over the teeth can be calculated by the difference $L_{nef} - L_{nnom}$. The variance of the distance over the teeth, calculated as the difference between the effective limit values or the effective limit deviations of the length over the teeth, must be compared with the prescribed tolerance.

The use of machine vision makes it possible to complete the task of control with a better level of precision in a lot less time and at a lower cost. NI Vision Assistant is a tool for prototyping and testing image processing applications. The Vision Assistant scripting functionality was used to create an algorithm for image processing. Every stage of the processing algorithm is documented through the scripting feature. After completing the algorithm, it can be tested on other images to verify his accuracy.

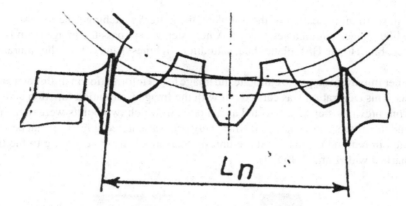

Fig. 2. The scheme for measuring the length (elevation) over the teeth

3 Image Processing

The product developed, a toothed wheel that is part of an assembly with a pinion and a worm coupling, was 3D printed. For prototyping, a versatile additive manufacturing technology was chosen, capable of using biodegradable plastics and allowing parts obtainment which are feasible to be used in a prototype, FDM technology (Fused Deposition Modeling). The algorithm starts from the product image (Fig. 3) and follows a series of functions to process the image and then the data can be exported. The images were made with the camera ESP32, a system-on-chip microcontrollers with integrated Wi-Fi. This camera is placed perpendicularly on the conveyor. The images are made in optimal conditions of brightness and contrast and then will be retrieve in NI Vision Assistant software.

Fig. 3. The product image

Finding areas in a grayscale image that match a pattern in a reference image is done using the pattern matching technique thst is unaffected by noise, blur, and varying illumination conditions. In order to employ pattern matching, the image must first be transformed to grayscale if the original image source is a color image. Regardless of the placement, rotation, or scaling of the template, the pattern matching function uses it to discover like images within a new image. A next step was to pass the image from RGB (red, green, blue) to the HSL plane (hue, saturation, lightness) and extract the saturation plane.

Another important step is to calibrate the image to get information in millimeters and not pixels. This calibration was carried out with the Image Calibration function and the image from previous step was selected as a model, in which two points were manually placed and the distance known in real world between was entered (Fig. 5). It can be seen highlighted in red, the distance and the unit of measure changed according to the two points marked with 1 and 2 (Fig. 4).

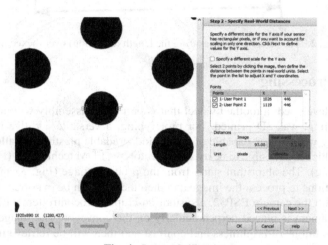

Fig. 4. Image Calibration

After finding the center of the gear wheel, the Threshold function was applied to transform the grayscale image into a binary image with values of 1 and 0, thus highlighting the objects in the image. The function Advanced Morphology was used several times to remove the noise from the image with the Remove Small Objects, Remove Large Objects and Remove Border options. Next a temporary coordinate system is set in the middle of the wheel, but because this detection is not very accurate and the center of the bore may differ from this point, an additional function was used to ensure that the center of the permanent coordinate will be exactly in the center of the bore (Fig. 5).

The gauging (measuring lengths, diameters, and angles), product inspection (finding flaws like missing pieces or components from a product), and product alignment (identifying fiducials to determine the position and orientation of a given object) can be done using the pattern matching technique. [5] mentioned that in order to match patterns, a template or reference image must be defined and kept in memory When real-world photos, such ones of items on an assembly line, are captured using a camera, the software searches for occurrences of the template images stored in memory. The product is then assessed to see if it correspond to the template image's pattern. When a rectangle box surrounds the image, pattern matching has taken place. Regions in a

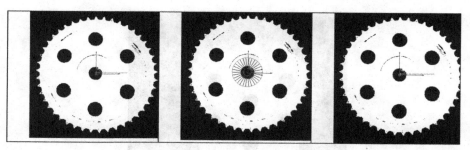

Fig. 5. Setting the temporary coordinate system, Finding the central bore, Setting the permanent coordinate system

grayscale image that match a model or template of a reference pattern can be found using geometric matching. Additionally, it is unaffected by changes in lighting, blur, noise, and geometric distortion. Similar to pattern matching, a template image is made that serves as a reference image for the acquired images to be searched. Alternatively, geometric matching describes the shape of an object based on its edges before using this description to find similar objects [6]. To effectively define object boundaries, the object and the background must be separated by contrasting regions. The advantage of geometric matching is that they can find matching objects despite motion, rotation, scale, and even occlusion (overlapping objects).

Since it is desired to count the teeth to check if the product has the 45 provided teeth, the Pattern Matching function is used. This function receives as input a standard (it can be taken from the image on which the processing is done, even from the previous step), and it is searched in the ROI (region of interest) as many times as the user specifies. In this case, the standard is enclosed in the green rectangle and is searched 45 times, this being the number of teeth in the technical specifications of the gear wheel. The modification of the following settings is considered: "Rotated" between 0 and 360°, the number of searches and the priority. Also the gear size cound be identified and compared with the tolerated dimensions on the execution drawing. The detection of the number of teeth in the program is presented below in Fig. 6.

When determining the structure of the item, edges are crucial. In an object, edges often appear where two sections are divided by a border. In order to examine the image, edges are the key alterations. The intensity of various regions in an image changes as a result of these local alterations. To locate areas in a digital image where a line of pixels' worth of brightness rapidly changes, edge detection function is utilised. Using the edge detection algorithm and a measurement function, the variance of the distance over a number of teeth, the pitch and the division diameter were also determined (Fig. 7). The variance of the distance over 3 teeth was measured at the contact points of the device plates with the flanks of the teeth as near as possible to the dividing circle, which has the fewest deviations from the ideal profile.

The script from NI Vision Assistant was exported to LabVIEW, and the block diagram and front panel are shown in Fig. 8.

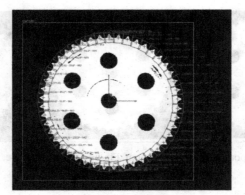

Fig. 6. Detecting the number of teeth

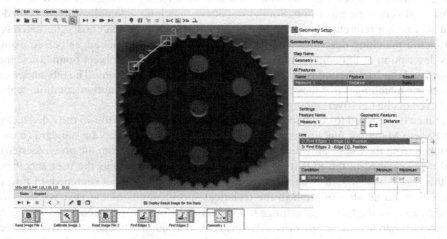

Fig. 7. Determination of the distance above the teeth

Checks were made by comparing the values such as the outer diameter, the diameter of the adjacent circles with the maximum limit, respectively the minimum limit established by the dimensional tolerances in the execution drawing and by the corresponding lighting of some LEDs on the front panel of the application. If the condition is met, the steering arm allocates the product in a container, if it does not correspond, the product will be directed to another container.

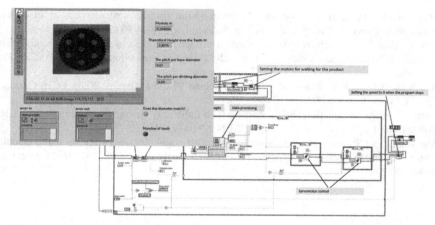

Fig. 8. The Front Panel and Block Diagram of the applications in LabVIEW software

4 Conclusion

Control of products has become a standard practice in industries. The use of machine vision in object measuring or sorting might be important since it improves accuracy and decreases product redundancy. Depending on the products and requirements to be satisfied, various visual inspection techniques can be used. By applying specific algorithms to image processing, the characteristics of some industrial products can be determined, in this case 200 3D printed toothed gears were analyzed: number of teeth, pitch diameter, base diameter and pitch, elevation over a number of teeth. Some material defects can also be analyzed, such as the degree of tooth damage. For example, for the pitch over 3 teeth that was measured on the base diameter, the errors for this batch were below 5%.

In the created application, the following parameters of the gear wheel were determined with the help of image analysis: number of teeth, outer diameter, bottom diameter, number of bores. Then other technical parameters could be calculated: the module "m", the theoretical height over the teeth "W", the pitch per base diameter and the pitch per dividing diameter. Through these procedures, classic metrological methods such as micrometers, calipers for toothed wheels or large devices specially designed for this type of products can be successfully replaced. The system designed is a more economic and fast method that can be used to automate different industrial processes in the context of industry 5.0. In the further, the reliability of the system will be tested on other types of components with different configurations and materials.

References

1. Alonso, V., Dacal-Nieto, A., Barreto, L.: Industry 4.0 implications in machine vision metrology: an overview. Procedia Manufacturing **41**(2019), 359–366 (2020)
2. Dworkin, S.B., Nye, T.J.: Image processing for machine vision measurement of hot formed parts. J. Mater. Process. Technol. **174**(1–3), 1–6 (2006)

3. Hashimi, A., Mali, H., Meena, A.: Machine vision for the measurement of machining parameters: a review. Materials Proceeding **56**(Part 4), 1939–1946 (2022)
4. Luk, F., Huynh, V., North, W.: Measurement of surface roughness by a machine vision system. Journal of Physics E: Scientific Instruments **22**(12) (1989). https://doi.org/10.1088/0022-3735/22/12/001
5. Ready, S., Kwon, K.S.: Practical Guide to Machine Vision Software. Wiley VCH, Germany (2015). ISBN: 978-3-527-33756-9
6. Relf, C.: Image Acquisition and Processing with LabVIEW (Image Processing Series). CRC Press, United States of America (2003). ISBN 9780849314803
7. Shrestha, D.S., Steward, B.L.: Automatic corn plant population measurement using machine vision. American Society of Agricultural and Biological Engineers ASAE **46**(2), Michigan, 559–565 (2003)

Automatic Coffee Roasting Process Assistance System Based on Fuzzy Logic Techniques

Paul Ciprian Patic[✉]

Automatics Department, Valahia University of Targoviste, Targoviste, Romania
patic@valahia.ro

Abstract. In this paper, one presents the method of applying fuzzy logic in the creation of a controller to be used as an intermediary between the operator and the coffee roaster. The purpose of the controller is to provide data regarding the optimal operating conditions of the coffee roaster to obtain a specific type of roast, depending on the user's preference. The concept is intended so that it can be applied with an acceptable degree of accuracy by both a domestic and an industrial roaster. Even though the roasting process has imprecisely defined steps and many variables, the controller user has the ability to define narrower or more comprehensive rule sets, depending on experience. Most professional roasters benefit from colorimeters, densimeters and other modern equipment to obtain the perfect roast, equipment that is difficult to procure being niche tools and having a very high price. The controller presented in this project is an autonomous device intended to be used before the initiation of the roasting process. Depending on the data entered at the inputs, it generates at the outputs the optimal operating parameters of the roaster, so as to obtain a specific type of roasting. The controller uses a generalized approach that does not take into account the type of equipment used for roasting, but only the reactions that take place in the coffee beans during roasting.

Keywords: Coffee roasting · Controller simulation · Density · Fuzzy logic · Frying Temperature

1 Introduction

Having in view the present paper, one will show in four chapters some data on the history of coffee, the coffee tree, the effects of coffee on the body, the economic importance of coffee and the chemistry of the coffee bean will be briefly presented. In the following, data on coffee roasting methods will be presented in more detail, including the necessary equipment, planning, rules, specific types of roasting and analysis of the price/quality ratio of home roasting compared to purchasing ready-roasted coffee from the trade. After that, is a brief presentation of fuzzy logic and how it can be implemented in the coffee roasting process. Then, the construction of the proposed fuzzy controller will be treated, the logical approach, the presentation of the mode of operation, the problems encountered in the implementation of some functions, the construction of the

K. S. Soliman (Ed.): IBIMA-AI 2024, CCIS 2299, pp. 197–217, 2025.
https://doi.org/10.1007/978-3-031-77493-5_18

rule base, their visualization and interpretation, and a simulation of the controller will be presented. Finally, possible ways to improve the presented device will be treated and a brief comparison will be made with the current software used in coffee roasting, in an attempt to argue the decision to design the fuzzy controller. The controller is designed to provide information that also depends on the degree of expertise of the coffee roaster operator. The connection to the user experience resides in the number and type of data entered at the inputs. Thus, the operator can model the controller's rule set using the knowledge accumulated during previous roasts, knowledge acquired by the "trial-failure" model.

Coffee, cultivated in tropical and subtropical regions, was originally used as food (obtained by mixing ground coffee with animal fat) and consumed by tribal warriors to have more energy in battle. Later, coffee infusion was used to mask the unpleasant taste of the poor water quality. In the 10th century, Avicenna administered coffee decoction as medicine. Starting with the 16th century, coffee spread in the Middle East but also timidly in Europe.

On the human body, coffee has beneficial effects (it protects kidney cells from cancer, through the antioxidant substances it contains, provides a series of mineral substances - iron, potassium, magnesium, manganese - and vitamins - niacin, vitamins E, C, B6, riboflavin and pantothenic acid - intensively stimulate metabolism (thanks to caffeine, which has a thermogenic effect, contributing to: weight loss through accelerated fat burning); increasing adrenaline levels, increasing blood pressure, muscle contraction capacity and stimulating breathing; improves digestion, stimulating the secretion of gastric acid and bile). Consumed in excess, it can increase the heart rate excessively, cause restlessness, tremors, insomnia, even convulsions. It can generate a slight dependence, which is manifested by the occurrence of headaches when consumption is stopped.

Being consumed in almost all countries around the globe, coffee is a very important commodity, being ranked second worldwide, after oil, in terms of economic importance.

2   General Information Regarding Coffee and the Roasting Process

Coffee roasting breaks down a multitude of soluble solid components through chemical and physical reactions. They contribute to the composition and optimization of the taste of the finished product obtained through various methods of infusion or extraction, as one present in Fig. 1.

During roasting, coffee changes a number of characteristics such as: density (which halves), color (which turns from gray-green to brownish), bean size (which almost doubles). It also causes the development of acids and oils as well as the elimination of water vapor and gases with a distinctive pop. This distinctive crackle is an important landmark in coffee roasting.

Water content is one of the most important variables in coffee roasting. Under ideal conditions this should be between 10.5% and 11.5%, thus maximizing the taste of the coffee and reducing the risk of mold.

Organic acids represent approximately 7%–10% of the mass of green coffee. Robusta coffee, being an extremely stable coffee species, contains less sugar and more organic acids and caffeine that help preserve and protect it from various diseases and predators.

Fig. 1. Coffee roasting phases

Such acids are also found in various citrus fruits such as lemon (citric acid) and lime (malic acid). Some are specific to coffee (caffeic acid, derived from quinin acid). These acids contribute to the antioxidant effect of coffee.

Gases and aromatics are the volatile compounds in coffee. After roasting, most flavors develop from these volatile substances can disappear, as [1] said.

The humidity of the coffee bean greatly affects the coffee roasting process, but also its quality and effects on the body. So:

- In the case of coffee beans with too little water content (overdried): in addition to reducing the aroma, acidity and freshness (and therefore negatively affecting the final taste) and affecting the color, over drying can cause the coffee to burn during roasts;
- In the case of coffee beans with too much water content (insufficiently dry) they mold; developing toxic fungi and the appearance of substances harmful to health, such as alpha toxins and mycotoxins, which have well-known carcinogenic effects, being able to damage the liver and kidneys in particular. Excess moisture increases the conductivity and heat capacity at the surface of the grain, but its interior may remain unaffected by temperature changes during roasting, making the process ineffective.
- It is generally considered that the optimal humidity of the coffee bean after drying is 10–12%.

2.1 Types of Coffee Roasters

Coffee roasters are specialized ovens that mix and transfer heat to coffee beans. They differ in the way they manage heat and the method of heat transfer and can usually be electric or gas fired. Electric ones represent the majority of domestic or sampling roasters, and gas-burning ones are used industrially and professionally, generally having much higher roasting capacities. The heating methods are:

• Convection
• Driving

• Radiation

As for the toasters themselves, the most common types are:

• Directly heated drum fryers (can be single drum or spaced double walls)

As one show in Fig. 2, these directly heat the drum and the air contained in it, which is then circulated among the coffee beans with a fan, once, until it is exhausted. The beans are then transferred to a cooling bin where another fan circulates air through them. During this time the operator or a mixer circulates the coffee through the basket. The advantage of such a design is that the air circulates only once through the drum, ensuring a clean roast, and the drum acts as a good medium for conserving thermal mass. The disadvantage is that overheating the drum can lead to the burning of the surface of the coffee bean.

This type of toaster is the most commonly used and heats by convection and conduction.

• Indirectly heated drum toasters

In a research study by [10], this type of toaster attempts to solve the problems of the aforementioned toasters by heating the air in a separate chamber and then circulating it through the drum. Consequently, the temperatures can be much higher without the risk of burning the coffee. The disadvantage is the low efficiency. Otherwise, it is similar to the previous type.

Fig. 2. Household drum toaster

• Fluid bed fryer

They hit the coffee with hot air keeping the beans suspended to reduce the possibility of burning the surface of the coffee. The coffee is roasted exclusively by convection. This type of toaster is very attractive due to its affordable price and small footprint. As a disadvantage, it can be difficult to operate considering that the operator must control the masses of air and gas that circulate through the coffee to avoid its degradation through too strong currents, as [6] mentioned.

• Fryer with recirculation

It circulates air from the roasting chamber to the heating chamber, then circulates it through the coffee again. These roasters are becoming increasingly popular as they are ideal for software roasting profiles. It represents the method of roasting that is closest to the ideal. The only disadvantage is that it can give the coffee a "smokey" taste.

It is noted that all these types of toasters have their advantages and disadvantages. The application proposed below is intended to be able to be used for any type of toaster. With its help, small adjustments of temperatures or frying times can be made to avoid some of the aforementioned problems.

2.2 Types of Frying

The type of roast is defined by when the coffee leaves the roasting chamber to cool. Depending on the type of roasting, various notes and aromas of the coffee can be high-lighted. In the specialized nomenclature, there is no specific standardization regarding the names of the stages in the roasting process (Fig. 3). These are named differently from one roaster to another, as follows:

- First Crack (Cinnamon): It is the first stage in which the coffee is considered to be roasted. At this stage, the coffee starts to remove water and gases from the bean and emits some sounds (pops) intense in volume, similar to those made when making popcorn; even now the sugar is starting to caramelize. The taste is still similar to the taste of the green berry, accompanied by notes of nuts, grass and some florals. The acidity is very high and the body (consistency) is weak.
- City Roast: if one takes the first crack (those "cracks" of the coffee) as a bench-mark, one can define the coffee as "City" roasted towards the end of the "first crack" or immediately after it ends. The characteristics of the drink resulting from coffee roasted in this way are: sweetness, acidity and various floral and fruity notes. This coffee is highly appreciated by specialists for the correct representation of coffee characteristics, but it is not so popular and requires a lot of skill to develop the coffee bean correctly.
- City Plus Roast: The coffee beans are processed a bit more before they are taken out of the roaster. The sugars are caramelized more, roasting this type migrates the oils more and increases the volume of the coffee bean. It is quite a popular type of roasting, widely appreciated.
- Full City Roast: It is a "closed" type of roast, bringing the development stage of the coffee beans closer to Second Crack. The taste is moderate, the notes being fruity,

with acidity and medium body. Being one of the most accessible types of coffee for beginners or simple consumers, this roasting method is very popular.

- Full City Plus Roast (Viennese): This roast is achieved when the coffee is removed moments after the Second Crack begins. The oils come to the surface of the coffee bean, the taste changes to sweet-sour, with a slight spicy sensation and smoky notes. The body is viscous.
- Dark Roast (French): The coffee begins to burn slightly, thus having a pungent taste of smoke, and the bean becomes much more fragile. The unique characters of the coffee are lost if it reaches this stage of roasting. The taste becomes sour, burnt and smoky. The body at this stage reaches its peak and then goes down, so it can be medium or viscous.
- Italian (Burnt): The smell becomes unbearable, the coffee bean becomes black in color, its surface becoming extremely oily and charred. Also, the damage at the cellular level and the burning of lipids makes the coffee bean go rancid and oxidize extremely quickly, these characters being also present in the finished product. The body is medium (Fig. 14).

Fig. 3. In order from left to right: Cinnamon, City, City+, Full City, Full City+ and burnt

2.3 Study on the Current Status of Automatic Roasting

[2] mentioned that there are two types of software used to help roast coffee. These are data acquisition software (passive) and automatic profiling software (active, being able to intervene on the device). Data acquisition software is connected to the roaster and monitors the roasting process by generating real-time analysis graphs. Automatic roasting profiling software intervenes directly, in real time, in the roasting process and aggressively modifies the operating parameters of the roaster. Their use is avoided because of the way they work. Most make too many adjustments in a very short period of time, suddenly increasing the temperature or air current in the roaster and therefore do not allow for a natural and organic profiling. They can still be used to implement the various routines required to heat and maintain the temperature in the roaster, thus making the roasting process more efficient. The lack of roasting techniques on an industrial scale that would allow obtaining some types of finished product that highlight the quality characteristics of the coffee beans (and for which it would have been necessary to take into

account all the previously mentioned parameters) led to the sale on the wide consumer market of some generic products in taste. Their quality is far from satisfying the lovers of good coffee, the beans being excessively roasted, most of them of the "dark" or "very dark" type. Starting from this finding, the idea of using fuzzy techniques in the creation of a coffee roasting optimization tool that, as a concept, can be used on an industrial scale as well as by the average user, emerged. The advantages of using fuzzy techniques for this purpose are the following, as [7] mentioned:

- They have the ability to work with a multitude of imprecise variables, meaning exactly what defines the coffee roasting process.
- Allow settings of rules that can be used in coffee roasting.
- The set rules can be improved and multiplied depending on the operator's needs and level of specialization.
- They are easy to understand and use by the operator.
- They do not need a mathematical model to describe outputs versus inputs, but can learn from various samples.

Fig. 4. Data acquisition software connected to the toaster

According with [8], currently, one has identified few studies that implement fuzzy methods in the field of coffee roasting. Most of them are intended for use on a gas roaster equipped with a thermal sensor that acquires the temperature inside the coffee beans to determine the degree of roasting. Once the temperature exceeds a certain threshold (for example: 193 °C–199 °C for an open roast, 200 °C–212 °C for a medium roast, 213 °C–220 °C for a closed roast), it stops roasting. Considering the importance of green bean characteristics, preheating, bean evacuation for cooling, flavor development and temperature vs. time graphs, and the fact that the aforementioned fuzzy models neglect these parameters, one decided to create an own model, as in Fig. 4 from above.

2.4 Coffee Roasting Cost Analysis

In the context of the existence of a limited offer of quality coffee on the wide consumer market, one found that roasting coffee at the home user level is advantageous in terms of price/quality. For this one will present the costs of roasting coffee at home compared to those of buying ready-roasted coffee from mass commerce. One factored in the cost of electricity depending on the power specifications of the roaster one was using, the price of easy to find good quality coffee that didn't vary much over time, and also the price of a kilo of coffee common in trade. For homemade roast:

The power required for the operation of the roaster is 1550 W, and it takes about 45 min to roast a kilogram of coffee (including preheating the roaster, roasting itself and cooling the coffee). It turns out that 1.08 kWh is consumed in one roasting session. The price of one kWh from the electricity supplier, after adding VAT and other distribution charges, etc. is 0.31 lei (0.06 Euro), resulting in a total cost of electricity consumed for frying of 0.35 lei (0.07 Euro). The price of a kilogram of Arabica green coffee (Columbia Supremo Huila), single origin, in Romania, is 32 lei (6.4 Euro). The total amount, without paying labor, for frying will reach 32.35 lei (6.47 Euro). Another 15% of the price is added representing the loss of mass during frying (water and volatile substances evaporate). Thus, the total price is 37.19 lei (7.44 Euro).

Comparatively, the price of one kilogram of coffee (without specifying the origin, variety, type and roasting date) from one of the brands most used by Romanians, according to an online publication, is 42.18 lei (8.44 Euro). From the same brand, a kilogram of Colombia coffee (for which the variety, type and roasting date are not specified) costs 54.18 lei per kilogram (10.84 Euro). In the world of artisan roasters, a kilogram of Colombia Huila coffee costs 92.54 lei (18.51 Euro). It is observed that home roasting presents both the advantage of price and quality.

3   Theory of Fuzzy Logic

Fuzzy logic is an extension of Boolean logic. It is a tool for using and representing imprecisely defined terms. In fuzzy logic operation, values between completely true and completely false are used, with intermediate values that express imprecise or vague information. The truth value is between 0 and 1 and includes values in between. It was initially used for: uncertainty modeling, generalization, simplification and knowledge processing. It includes fuzzy sets, defined by the fact that they do not have well-defined boundaries, their elements belonging to them only to a certain extent. Thus, they allow, through this characteristic of the membership function, the representation of those natural language concepts that are not precisely defined (Fig. 5).

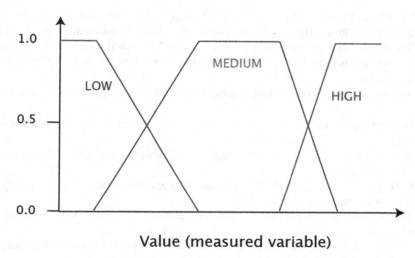

Fig. 5. The model of membership functions

3.1 Applying Fuzzy Logic to Coffee Roasting

Roasting is the most important stage in coffee processing, because it determines the aroma. In the frying process, the most common error is related to the determination of the frying time. Roasting coffee incorrectly will result in an undesirable taste. Various variables must be considered such as: temperature, density, power level (or fire size) and time. Given that each variable is fuzzy and imprecise, fuzzy logic lends itself to solving this problem. Each variable can be used in the fuzzy method and will determine the regulation system, as one observed in a research study by [9].

Fuzzy models work with fuzzy sentences. They contain words that are used as identifiers for the fuzzy set. In the presented project, examples of fuzzy words are: "Density", "Quantity", "Ventilation_stage", "Frying_type".

In a paper [5] introduced in his works on fuzzy algorithms the idea of formulating control algorithms with logic rules. These logical rules have the form:

IF (a set of conditions that must be satisfied) THEN (a set of consequences that can be inferred). The following rules were used in the project:

1. If (Density is Density(g/L)) and (Quantity is Small(g)) then (Preheating is Small) (1)
2. If (Density is Density(g/L)) and (Quantity is Optim(g)) then (Preheating is Medium) (1)
3. If (Density is Density(g/L)) and (Quantity is Big(g)) then (Preheating is Big) (1)
4. If (Density is Density_Big(g/L)) and (Quantity is Small(g)) then (Preheating is Small+) (1)

5. If (Density is Density_Big(g/L)) and (Quantity is Optim(g)) then (Preheating is Medium+) (1)
6. If (Density is Density_Big(g/L)) and (Quantity is Big(g)) then (Preheating is Big+) (1)
7. If (Quantity is Small(g)) then (Drum_speed_stage is 3)(Ventilation_step is 3) (1)
8. If (Quantity is Optim(g)) then (Drum_speed_stage is 6)(Ventilation_step is 6) (1)
9. If (Quantity is Big(g)) then (Drum_speed_stage is 12)(Ventilation_step is 12) (1)
10. If (Frying type is First_Crack_(Cinnamon)) then (Target_temperature is Cinnamon)(Approximate time is First_Crack) (1)
11. If (Frying type is City) then (Target_temperature is City)(Approximate time is City) (1)
12. If (Frying type is City+) then (Target_temperature is City+)(Approximate time is City+) (1)
13. If (Frying type is Full_City) then (Target_temperature is Full_City)(Approximate time is Full_CIty) (1)
14. If (Frying type is Full_City+) then (Target_temperature is Full_City_+)(Approximate time is Full_City_+) (1)
15. If (Frying type is Vienna) then (Target_temperature is Vienna)(Approximate time is Vienna) (1)
16. If (Density is Density_Small(g/L)) and (Quantity is Small(g)) then (Preheating is Small-) (1)
17. If (Density is Density_Small(g/L)) and (Quantity is Optim(g)) then (Preheating is Medium-) (1)
18. If (Density is Density_Small(g/L)) and (Quantity is Big(g)) then (Preheating is Big-) (1)

The process by which fuzzy logic rules are applied to fuzzy variables is called propagation.

The operation by which the input and output quantities are specified by which a fuzzy set is defined is called fuzzification. The purpose of fuzzification is to allow the definition of a rule base that includes both the knowledge related to the conducted process and those related to the methods one wants to use in this process. In the case of the controller presented here, the fuzzification allowed the definition of a rule base that includes both the knowledge acquired by the operator regarding coffee roasting and the knowledge regarding the methods they use.

The set of outputs of all rules is called an aggregation. After aggregation, a fuzzy set results for each output variable.

Defuzzification is the method by which the aggregated fuzzy sets are transformed into strict values. In the presented controller, the center of gravity (centroid) method was used.

In order to be able to use logical rules to describe the tasks of the controller, the following components are required:

- The fuzzifier: has the role of transposing the numerical expressions into fuzzy sets necessary for the activation of the rules, which in turn have corresponding fuzzy sets associated with the linguistic values.

- The inference engine: applies a transformation of the rule sets into fuzzy sets. This is where the rule handling module is implemented.
- In most applications, the mutual transformation from fuzzy sets into numerical values is necessary, a task that the defuzzifier has.

[4] mentioned that in the case, one of the most common fuzzy deduction techniques, called Mamdani, was used, a method proposed by Mamdani and Assilian to control a steam engine through a synthesis of linguistic rules obtained from experienced human operators. This method is very flexible and has good tolerances to the output data, being also extremely intuitive.

3.2 Features of Fuzzy Logic

The features of fuzzy logic are as follows:

- In fuzzy logic an exact logic is regarded as a case of approximately acceptable reasoning.
- Any data system can be represented in fuzzy logic, and this process is called fuzzification.
- The definition of a system is done as a series of elastic restrictions or an equivalence of known variables.
- The fuzzy set is represented by a characteristic function that takes values between 0 and 1 representing the degree of belonging of an element to that set.

In the presented controller, an example of fuzzy sets would be, as [3] said, citing Mamdani's research:

The set C represents the set of quantities of coffee beans in the roaster. I assigned values in the range [100–1000] so:

The quantity "Small(g)" belongs to C in percentage of 30%

The amount of "Big(g)" belongs to C in percentage of 90%".

4 Presentation of the Fuzzy Controller

The presented device is intended to be used as an intermediary between the operator and the coffee roaster. It is defined as a controller that uses fuzzy logic and is intended to provide data on the optimal setting parameters of the roaster depending on the type of roast desired. The data are represented as outputs obtained through the complex processing, based on a set of fuzzy rules, of parameters specific to the roasting process and which are entered as inputs. The controller is designed in the "Fuzzy logic designer" add-on package of the "Matlab" development environment. The simulation environment is the "Simulink" add-on package of the same development environment.

4.1 Presentation of Fuzzy Controller Inputs and Membership Functions

At the inputs, the essential parameters of the roasting process were introduced, namely, as [10] mentioned:

- The density of the coffee bean: which directly proportionally influences the preheating temperature. Measured in grams per liter (g/L), it is represented by values between [0.55–0.8] defined as "Low_Density(g/L)", "Density(g/L)" (this being the average density) and "High_Density(g/L)". The triangular appearance of the functions results from the introduction of the density values corresponding to the types of the most common coffee beans into the presented controller. The determination of the density can be done by filling a vessel whose volume is known with coffee, followed by weighing the vessel and calculating the density using its formula. The density can also be specified by the supplier or can be approximated depending on the altitude of the origin of the coffee (but imprecise) (Fig. 6).

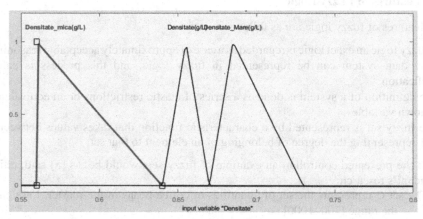

Fig. 6. The membership functions associated with the "Density" input

- The amount of beans put into the roaster, measured in grams (g). This determines the amount of thermal energy required for even frying. In the controller it has been given values between [100–1000], values representing the minimum and maximum amount of coffee roaster used in modeling this controller. The quantity can take the following values: "Small(g)", "Optimum(g) and "Large(g)". By "Optimum(g)" was defined the optimal degree of loading of the car at a charge, which is 50%–70% of its capacity. The graphical aspect of the quantity is represented by trapezoidal fuzzy numbers. The quantity is measured with a scale. Knowing the quantity, the following can be determined: the preheating temperature (also density dependent) as well as the roaster ventilation steps and the drum speed steps required to ensure the circulation of hot air masses and proper mixing. It should be noted that the speed step of the drum and the ventilation step of the roaster are different from one roaster to another. These features have been included in the controller shown for testing purposes only on the available toaster. Other devices may have these functions different from the present case or these functions may be completely absent (Fig. 7).

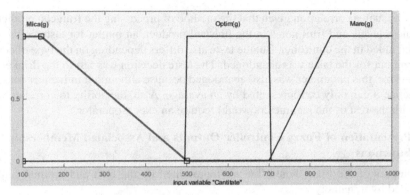

Fig. 7. The membership functions associated with the "Quantity" input

- The roasting type is only a selector for the finished product. Influences total roasting time and target temperature. In the controller it is represented by six triangular functions with values between [0–6] that correspond to the degree of roasting ("First Crack - Cinnamon", "City", "City Plus", etc.) (Fig. 8).

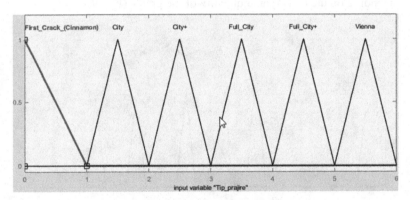

Fig. 8. The membership functions associated with the "Frying type" input

The following parameters were not included in the inputs:
- Grain moisture (which must be between 10.5% and 11.5%): was not included because the equipment required for measurement is difficult to procure and has a high price. It was decided to use green coffee for which the supplier already guaranteed optimal humidity and packaging. In the experiment carried out, the humidity before roasting was considered to be optimal;
- The processing of the coffee fruit after harvesting: it was not introduced because although it can affect the roasting curve (by affecting the humidity of the bean) the correlation between humidity and the amount of energy required for the correct development of the bean is extremely imprecise and would require a too detailed study. If

there was such a correlation given that the method of processing the fruit can predict the sweetness levels and fruit notes in the finished product, an output for taste could have been included in the controller. But the taste also differs depending on the type of coffee, so going out for the taste was abandoned. The taste decision was left to the drinker.
- Grain size: this parameter was also abandoned because although it influences roasting, in practice it can only be represented by an average. Also, the ability to correlate grain size with the rest of the parameters would require an expert operator.

4.2 Presentation of Fuzzy Controller Outputs and Associated Membership Functions

The outputs of the fuzzy controller are represented by the data and optimal settings generated by it, namely:

- Optimum preheating temperature according to the input values, to create the most suitable thermal conditions inside the roaster before inserting the beans into the machine. Preheating (measured in degrees Celsius) is represented by values between [200–315]; the lower limit is the minimum temperature required for a coffee to be considered roasted; the upper value represents the maximum temperature supported by the machine. Preheating is figured by the controller through nine triangular functions: "Small-", "Small", "Small+", "Medium-", "Medium", "Medium+", "High-", "High" and "High+"; they take values depending on the density and quantity of the grains (Fig. 9).

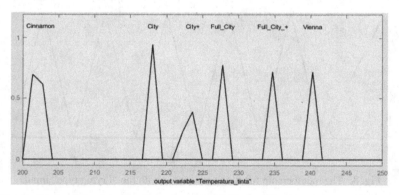

Fig. 9. The membership functions associated with the "Target_temperature" output

The total time (approximate) represents the optimal time required for the entire roasting process to reach the target temperature, for a correct development without burning the coffee bean. The approximate total time is measured in seconds and in the controller takes values belonging to the range [0–1200]. It is figured by six triangular functions (Fig. 10).

4.3 Problems Encountered in the Implementation of Some Functions

It would have been desirable for the software used in the simulation of this controller to have some functions regarding: profiling the frying curve, respectively increasing the

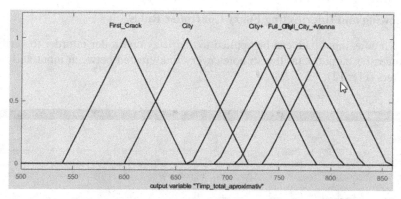

Fig. 10. The membership functions associated with the " Total approximative time" output

accuracy of prediction, but the timing solutions (timer) were missing. Likewise, some adjustments could have been made to the heating element or the ventilation stage if it had been possible to take into account the various stages of roasting the coffee beans or the time since the start of the roasting process. These adjustments would have ennobled and developed certain tastes specific to the coffee variety. One of the most promising possible solutions would be to build an assembly to count the pulses generated at a certain frequency and play an audio signal when certain values were encountered. The audio signal would have indicated the approximate stage where certain changes could be made in the roasting profile based on common phenomena. Even in the absence of profile curve monitoring software, these indications of opportune moments for adjustment could be of great help to the machine operator, according with [8].

4.4 Building the Rule Base

For the correct execution of any fuzzy controller, a set of rules is required from which the membership of each function can be determined. The following rules have been established in the presented controller (Fig. 11):

```
1. If (Densitate is Densitate(g/L)) and (Cantitate is Mica(g)) then (Preincalzire is Mic) (1)
2. If (Densitate is Densitate(g/L)) and (Cantitate is Optim(g)) then (Preincalzire is Mediu) (1)
3. If (Densitate is Densitate(g/L)) and (Cantitate is Mare(g)) then (Preincalzire is Mare) (1)
4. If (Densitate is Densitate_Mare(g/L)) and (Cantitate is Mica(g)) then (Preincalzire is Mic+) (1)
5. If (Densitate is Densitate_Mare(g/L)) and (Cantitate is Optim(g)) then (Preincalzire is Mediu+) (1)
6. If (Densitate is Densitate_Mare(g/L)) and (Cantitate is Mare(g)) then (Preincalzire is Mare+) (1)
7. If (Cantitate is Mica(g)) then (Treapta_viteza_tambur is 3)(Treapta_ventilatie is 3) (1)
8. If (Cantitate is Optim(g)) then (Treapta_viteza_tambur is 6)(Treapta_ventilatie is 6) (1)
9. If (Cantitate is Mare(g)) then (Treapta_viteza_tambur is 12)(Treapta_ventilatie is 12) (1)
10. If (Tip_prajire is First_Crack_(Cinnamon)) then (Temperatura_tinta is Cinnamon)(Timp_aproximativ is First_Crack) (1)
11. If (Tip_prajire is City) then (Temperatura_tinta is City)(Timp_aproximativ is City) (1)
12. If (Tip_prajire is City+) then (Temperatura_tinta is City+)(Timp_aproximativ is City+) (1)
13. If (Tip_prajire is Full_City) then (Temperatura_tinta is Full_City)(Timp_aproximativ is Full_City) (1)
14. If (Tip_prajire is Full_City+) then (Temperatura_tinta is Full_City_+)(Timp_aproximativ is Full_City_+) (1)
15. If (Tip_prajire is Vienna) then (Temperatura_tinta is Vienna)(Timp_aproximativ is Vienna) (1)
16. If (Densitate is Densitate_mica(g/L)) and (Cantitate is Mica(g)) then (Preincalzire is Mic-) (1)
17. If (Densitate is Densitate_mica(g/L)) and (Cantitate is Optim(g)) then (Preincalzire is Mediu-) (1)
18. If (Densitate is Densitate_mica(g/L)) and (Cantitate is Mare(g)) then (Preincalzire is Mare-) (1)
```

Fig. 11. The fuzzy rules that make up the system

4.5 Viewing and Interpreting Fuzzy Controller Rules

In this window, input data can be applied to the fuzzy controller in order to verify the post-processed output data. It also notes every link created between input and output parameters (Fig. 12).

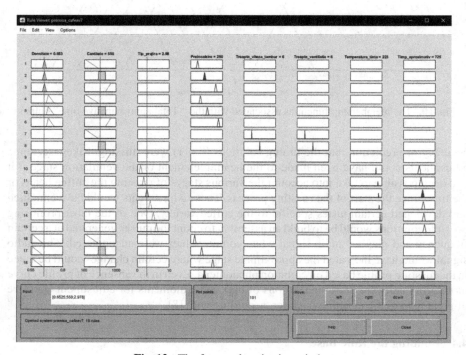

Fig. 12. The fuzzy rules viewing window

In a research study by [10], in this window you can see the membership rules between two outputs (represented on the X and Y axis) and one output (Z axis) on a 3D graph. The colors of the graph are generated in order to assist the visualization of the desired value. For example, in Fig. 13, one can see how the value of the "Preheating" output is increased in direct proportion to the values of the "Density" and "Quantity" outputs.

5 Presentation of Fuzzy Controller Simulation

In this simulation, an assembly was performed in which the fuzzy controller was applied. A multiplexer transitions the data from three blocks of numeric constants to be entered into the controller. The "Fry" block is connected to a "slider" control that dictates its value. Following the multiplexer is the fuzzy controller that processes the inputs to obtain the outputs as presented above. Next is the demultiplexer used to display the outputs on the displays related to each output (Fig. 14), as [11] mentioned.

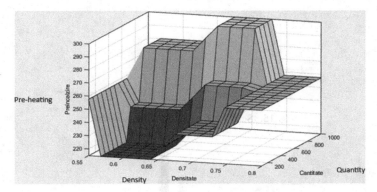

Fig. 13. 3D view of controller rules

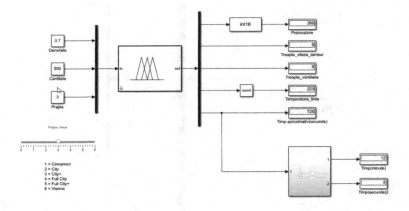

Fig. 14. Fuzzy controller simulation

Since most toasters have one-degree Celsius increments, the "Preheat" output has an int16 converter attached that converts the controller output to an integer.

A subassembly was also created to assist the operator in viewing the total roasting time. This subassembly converts the seconds to minutes and seconds as opposed to the controller output which is only expressed in seconds. The subassembly was made with two divisions by 60, the first taking out the whole part (minutes) and the second determining the rest (seconds). The resulting values are converted to integer values before being displayed by the displays attached to the subassembly (Fig. 15).

To exemplify the usefulness of the controller, a frying recipe will be generated next. It will start by entering the input data into the parameters of the "Constant" type block, then the simulation will be run. The input parameters in this case are: density of 0.65 g/Liter, quantity of 800 g of coffee and roasting type 3 (City+) (Fig. 16).

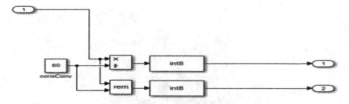

Fig. 15. Seconds Conversion Subassembly

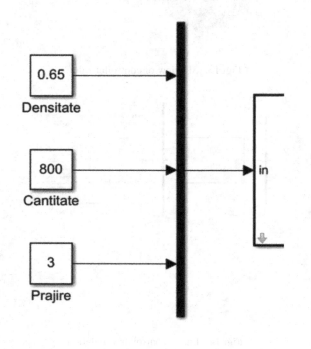

Prajire:Value

Fig. 16. Entering the input data into the fuzzy controller

The data that the user must take into account are displayed at the controller outputs. In this case, one has: the preheat is 290, the drum speed step and the fan step are both 12, the target temperature is 223 degrees Celsius, and the approximate total roasting time is 725 s (12 min and 5 s) (Fig. 17).

Comparing the results with the graph obtained after the respective frying, a percentage error of 6.19% with respect to the actual desired temperature and an error of 8.53% with respect to the approximate total time is noted. Ambient conditions at the time of roasting were not taken into account (Fig. 18).

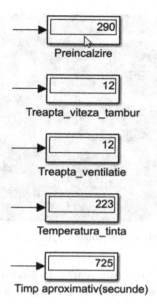

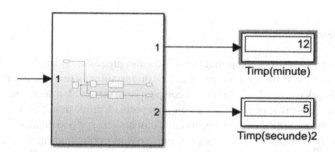

Fig. 17. The initialization parameters and the coffee recipe

5.1 Comparison with the Existing Software Offer, and Possibilities for Improvement

On the current market, there are two ways of implementing informatics in the roasting process, through data acquisition software and automatic roasting profiling software. Both types of software are used during the roasting process. The device presented in this project represents a third IT variant, intended to be used before the start of roasting. It proposes a new concept for planning the roasting process, the result of which basically consists in providing the operator with recipes for adjusting the roaster according to the specific type of roasting sought. Starting from the concept on the basis of which this controller was created, improved versions can be made that are involved both before and during the roasting process. These variants can be created with the possibility of

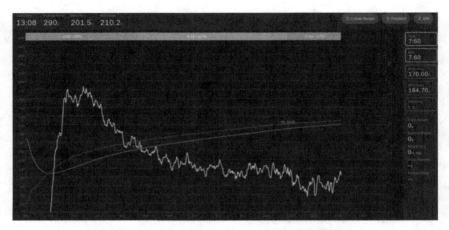

Fig. 18. The graph obtained after the simulated frying.

data acquisition during roasting and that of direct intervention in modifying roasting parameters in real time, but for their implementation another development environment than "Matlab" should be used. I believe that fuzzy logic opens up new conceptual possibilities that can be developed easily and, in many directions, the controller presented here being just a start in this sense.

6   Conclusions

Using a fuzzy controller in an application where the process and implicitly the finished product are influenced by such a large number of variables is really a reliable solution. From the feedback received from experienced people in this field, it seems to be a solution with potential. Even if this work is more conceptual, I think that it is possible that in practice, with the expertise of a professional, it can also be applied on an industrial scale, provided that the computational resources and costs in implementing such a system are justified by the benefits. As for home use, for a beginner this controller could even be the gateway to artisanal coffee roasting, resulting in increasing the quality of the daily drink at an acceptable price in the conditions where processing power these days has reached a minor price. And why not, the "utility" could even become a passion. The goal is that whatever system or approach is considered, it is practicable, simple, and has the potential to be improved or adjusted. It was not desired to automate coffee roasting, as automation would require expensive measuring or roasting devices, nor to neglect artisanal roasters who invest in such equipment, but to bring professionals and amateurs together, with the collective thought that they love coffee. A dream of all coffee lovers is, from those who roast it in the popcorn machine (one of the first experience in the field), to those who use industrial or specialized equipment, to can benefit from a little engineering hint to help them navigate through this experience. With time, for future experiences this application can be improved, using a better controller and, after that, to gain experience and enjoy a coffee that actually will have the dream taste of all coffee lovers.

References

1. Scott, R.: The Coffee Roaster's Companion (2014)
2. Harsawardana, S.B., Mahesworo, B., Suparyanto, T.: Maintaining the Quality and Aroma of Coffee with Fuzzy Logic Coffee Roasting Machine (2020)
3. Ion, I.: A Mamdani Type Fuzzy Logic Controller (2012)
4. Nurhayati, S., Pramanda, D.: The Coffee Roasting Process using Fuzzy Mamdani (2018)
5. Zadeh, L.A.: Fuzzy sets. Information and Control **8**(3) (1965). https://doi.org/10.1016/S0019-9958(65)90241-X
6. Artisan (2021)
7. Cropster (2020)
8. Takagi, T., Sugeno, M.: Fuzzy identification of systems and its application to modeling and control. IEEE Trans. Syst. Man Cybernetics **15**(1), 116–132 (1985)
9. Sugeno, M., Kang, G.T.: Structure identification of fuzzy model. Fuzzy Sets Syst. **28**(1), 15–33 (1988)
10. Ionescu, A.: System for assisting the coffee roasting process based on fuzzy logic techniques. Valahia University of Targoviste, Romania, Disertation Theme (2021, coordinated by Dragomir O.)
11. Patic, P.C., Popa, F.I., Zemouri, R.: Automatic line for sorting and identification parts in industrial manufacturing. Proceedings of the 33rd International Business Information Management Association - IBIMA 2019, 10–11 April 2019, Granada, Spain, Education Excellence and Innovation Management through Vision 2020, ISBN: 978-0-9998551-2-6, pp. 2982–2994 (2019)

References

Information Systems
and Communications Technologies

A Simulation Study on the Influence of Prioritized Multicast Connections on Traffic Effectiveness Network Nodes

Blazej Nowak[✉]

Poznan University of Technology, Poznan, Poland
blazej.nowak@put.poznan.pl

Abstract. This study delves into the ramifications of traffic prioritization methods on the efficiency of multi-service network nodes, with a specific focus on the context of multicast transmission within a Clos network. Furthermore, the paper introduces fundamental algorithms and mechanisms utilized to construct the simulation framework, tailored for analyzing the interplay between multicast traffic and prioritization within the Clos network architecture. Additionally, a comprehensive set of research findings is included, elucidating the impact of traffic prioritization mechanisms on the performance of a Clos network during multicast transmissions.

Keywords: Network traffic efficiency · network nodes optimization · simulation

1 Introduction

The continuous expansion of network services, demanding higher data rates, combined with the escalating number of connected devices in the global data transmission network, presents evolving challenges and requisites for telecommunications networks. Addressing these demands involves not only enhancing the throughput (bitrate) of telecommunications links but also accommodating differentiated service quality for diverse traffic streams within telecommunications nodes. The core component of the structure of a multi-service network node is the switching network. Hence, the contemporary challenges faced by network designers and operators are aptly reflected in studies on switching networks, encompassing works on the evolution of non-blocking network architectures [1], and research into the modeling of multi-service networks ([2–6]).

Ensuring the transmission of data, especially data requiring high bit rates that place a significant load on network links and nodes (e.g. routers), requires the use of a multiplication of connections within nodes. The traditional approach in this situation is to reserve the necessary resources inside the node for each stream separately. A newer solution, which assumes the multiplication of the use of resources only in those parts of the node where this is necessary, i.e. the partial use of individual resources by all data streams, is called multicast. Multicasting is realized in the main element of the multicast node i.e. in the switching network. Many proposals of the switching networks can be

© The Author(s), under exclusive license to Springer Nature Switzerland AG 2025
K. S. Soliman (Ed.): IBIMA-AI 2024, CCIS 2299, pp. 221–234, 2025.
https://doi.org/10.1007/978-3-031-77493-5_19

found in the literature and in practice. Still one of the highest throughput devices ([7, 8]), even for complex neural networks [9], are fields with Clos field structures.

This article focuses on characterizing the traffic attributes of switching networks with well-established structures, particularly in the context of multicast transmissions within a Clos network. Notably, Clos switching networks, including 3-stage Clos networks, have long been a fixture in network nodes with substantial capacities ([10–13]). Consequently, this study entails the development and implementation of a simulator for multi-service blocking switching networks featuring the Clos configuration, with special consideration for multicast traffic prioritization. This configuration is commonly employed in contemporary telecommunication network nodes, where prioritization stands as a fundamental traffic management mechanism. Moving forward, the devised research tool will enable the examination of the impact of multicast traffic prioritization on network traffic characteristics and, consequently, on the traffic efficiency of network nodes for various forms of multi-service traffic, among other considerations.

The article is structured into five sections. Section two delineates the network node's structure, with a specific focus on multicast traffic handling. Section three expounds on the algorithms and methodologies utilized by designers to create a simulation environment for node modeling, considering the complexities of multicast data distribution. Section four showcases the outcomes of select simulation experiments, providing insights into the implications of prioritized multicast transmissions within the Clos network. The paper culminates with a concise summary outlining the key takeaways derived from the conducted study and the implications for efficient multicast traffic management within the Clos network architecture.

2   Structure of Network Node

The core component of a network node is the switching network, and this study considers nodes built upon the Clos network framework ([10, 14]). This network can be partitioned into stages, each housing multiple switches. A single switch, the smallest element, possesses a predetermined number of inputs and outputs, establishing connections between designated inputs and outputs through a network control algorithm. The Clos network is exemplified by the investigation of a 3-stage Clos network, as illustrated in Fig. 1.

Figure 1 demonstrates the structure of the three-stage Clos network, with the following notations:

- n – the number of inputs,
- I, II, III – numbers of stages,
- r – the number of switches in stage one and three (the first and third stages),
- d - output directions
- m – the number of switches in the middle stage.

The existence of a free connection path makes the connection possible. If none of the switches of the last stage has sufficient free resources in the demanded multicast directions, the call is lost due to external blocking. If the free connection path cannot be found inside the network, then the call is lost (rejected) due to internal blocking [14]. It is crucial to understand that all resource sufficiency checks are made under rules of prioritized traffic described later in this section.

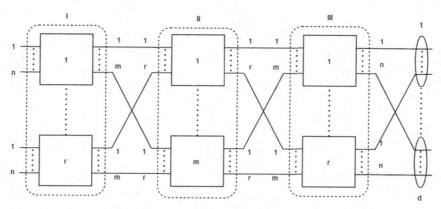

Fig. 1. Structure of three-stage Clos network.

The network control algorithm, pivotal in the selection of paths, undergoes slight modifications mentioned in [17] to incorporate the handling of priorities and the reduction of evicted connections. Building upon the classical point-to-group algorithm, the extended version endeavors to curtail the number of evicted calls [14].

Delving deeper, in the context of multicast operations within the Clos network, refers to the efficient dissemination of data to multiple recipients simultaneously. Unlike unicast, which involves point-to-point communication, multicast enables the delivery of information to multiple destinations, making it a fundamental mechanism for efficiently distributing data to numerous users within the network. In the context of prioritized multicast within the Clos network, the process becomes more intricate, necessitating careful management to ensure that critical data is delivered to the intended recipients while maintaining optimal resource utilization. Prioritizing multicast traffic becomes essential to ensure that vital information reaches its destination promptly, even in scenarios with high traffic intensity. This balancing act between efficient data distribution and resource optimization underscores the significance of well-crafted algorithms and strategies, as explored in the article. By considering the priorities associated with different multicast streams, the algorithm dynamically adjusts the routing and allocation of resources, ensuring that higher-priority multicast data is efficiently delivered to the intended recipients while optimizing resource utilization across the network. This approach enhances the overall efficiency of the network, allowing for the seamless transmission of critical data to multiple nodes simultaneously. Figure 2 depicts a multicast connection which is split into two directions (1 and d) in the third stage.

Within the simulation environment described in this article, the principles governing the handling of multicast traffic within the Clos network encompass the efficient allocation of resources based on the priorities assigned to different multicast streams. Prioritized traffic follows three rules:

– All call classes possess assigned priorities.
– Service of low-priority calls does not impact the blocking probability of high-priority calls.

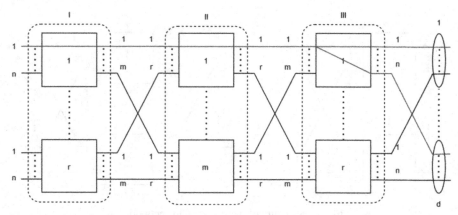

Fig. 2. Three stage Clos network servicing a multicast connection with a split in third stage.

– Absence of free resources prompts the termination of service for lower-priority calls upon the arrival of a higher-priority call.

By dynamically adjusting the routing paths and resource allocation mechanisms, the network ensures that the multicast data is delivered to the intended recipients in a timely and efficient manner, thereby enhancing the overall performance and reliability of the network in supporting multicast operations.

3 Simulation Environment

The C# programming language was employed to implement the simulator for the three-stage Clos network accommodating multicast, multi-service traffic, featuring prioritization and the reduction of the rejected or evicted set of calls. The simulation methodology adopted the event-viewing approach, organized via a chronological list of events [15]. The path-finding algorithm was a customized rendition of the point-to-group algorithm. This adapted algorithm was subsequently extended to encompass the handling of call priorities and the algorithm for minimizing the set of calls to be evicted from the service. Consequently, the algorithm explores all available paths, rather than terminating at the first accessible path [17] The resultant simulator facilitates the exploration of a diverse mix of multi-class traffic with varying demands, multicast destination directions and associated priorities. Within this simulation environment, diverse traffic types, including Erlang, Engset, and Pascal traffic, commonly referred to as BPP traffic (Bernoulli, Poisson, Pascal), are subject to investigation.

The input data for the simulator is as follows:

– the parameters of the three-stage Clos network (Fig. 1):

  – m – the number of switches of the middle stage,
  – n – the number of input links in the switch of the first stage and output links in the switch of the last stage,

- r – the number of switches of the first and last stages;

- f - capacity of a single link;
- list of traffic classes with defined traffic type (Erlang, Engset, Pascal) and, where necessary, the number of traffic classes n - $C_{i,\{er,en_n,pa_n\}}$;
- list of resources demanded by each of the classes - t_i;
- priority for each of the classes - p_i;
- D - a static set of output directions required by multicast connection;
- a – average intensity per allocation unit.

As a result of employing the event-viewing methodology, two primary events were identified within the simulation framework, specifically:

- connection request,
- end of connection.

Upon the occurrence of the connection request event, the network assesses the availability of resources, taking into account the selected algorithm for path selection. If the necessary resources for servicing the incoming data are insufficient, the simulator incorporates the prioritization of this data. This involves assessing whether data with lower priority, currently in service, can be potentially displaced. These identified connections are then marked for potential termination. If the cumulative resource consumption of the identified connections is equal to or greater than the resources required for the new incoming connection, the identified instances are terminated, enabling the network to prioritize the new connection with higher precedence. In cases where the network still lacks the necessary resources to accommodate the incoming data, the new data is lost. Regardless of whether the data has been successfully admitted for service or not, the system schedules the next subsequent event.

Conversely, if the subsequent event is the end of connection, the switching network resources are released, signifying the completion of the connection. The comprehensive algorithm for the simulation process is depicted in Fig. 3, elucidating the intricate dynamics involved in managing prioritized multicast data within the Clos network.

When confronted with the necessity of evicting calls from the connection path, the challenge arises in determining the specific calls that should be terminated. The solution described in [17] which minimizes the push out losses is used.

In regards to multicast traffic it is crucial to understand that in a given stage of the Clos network connection is split to reach multiple destinations (multicast directions) as shown in Fig. 2. Every step depicted in Fig. 3 that checks for sufficient resources for incoming connection is tested against every multicast direction the connection demands. This can result in a compulsory requirement which can wipe out a lot of existing connections that are currently being handled if the incoming connection has high enough priority and the split occurs in the early stages of the Clos network.

Post-simulation, the results are archived in three distinct text files. These files encapsulate the outcomes for internal, external, and overall losses. Internal losses arise from the failure to establish a connection path necessary for servicing a particular call within the network, whereas external losses stem from the unavailability of free resources within

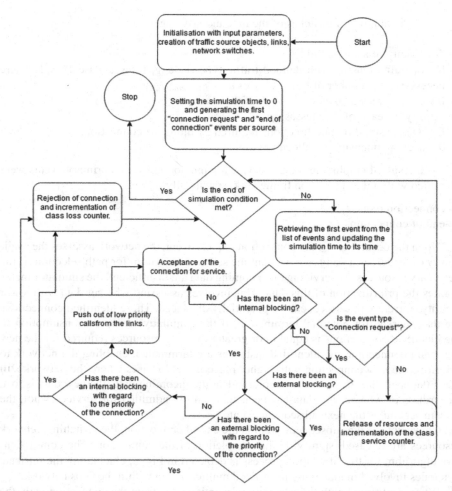

Fig. 3. General algorithm for the simulation of the switching network with prioritized and multicast traffic classes.

the designated output links of the network. Total losses encompass both the aforementioned types of losses plus the losses coming from lower priority connection terminations, providing a comprehensive overview of the impact on calls within the network.

4 The Results of Sample Simulation Experiments

The simulation analysis was conducted on a three-stage Clos network. The implemented simulator accommodates numerous traffic classes, priorities, demand scales, traffic types, various traffic distribution ratios, and all relevant parameters associated with a three-stage Clos network. The multicast split happens in the third section of the network. Each class has assigned a set of output directions (multicast directions).

The study postulated a network configuration comprising four switches within each stage ($m = r = 4$) with 4 inputs and outputs ($n = 4$), while the capacity of each of the input/output was 50 allocation units ($f = 50$). Another assumption was that the setting up of connections in the network was controlled by the modified point-to-group selection algorithm as described in [17].

The simulation study was divided into 4 scenarios. In each, the network with the same structure was offered different set of 3 Erlang classes with a different priorities and multicast directions for individual call classes.

The network was offered the following sets of 3 call classes:

- Erlang class designated by C_0, demanding 2 allocation units ($t_0 = 2$),
- Pascal class designated by C_1, demanding 5 allocation units ($t_1 = 5$),
- Engset class designated by C_2, demanding 10 allocation units ($t_2 = 10$),

The ratio of offered traffic for individual classes was always the same: $a_0 \cdot t_0 = a_1 \cdot t_1 = a_2 \cdot t_2$.

The following dependencies between the priorities and multicast directions of traffic classes were assumed in individual scenarios:

- scenario 1: $p_0 = p_1 = p_2, dir_0 = [1, 3], dir_1 = [2], dir_2 = [4]$
- scenario 2: $p_0 > p_1 > p_2, dir_0 = [1, 3], dir_1 = [2], dir_2 = [4]$
- scenario 3: $p_0 = p_1 = p_2, dir_0 = [1, 3], dir_1 = [2, 3], dir_2 = [4]$
- scenario 4: $p_0 > p_1 > p_2, dir_0 = [1, 3], dir_1 = [2, 3], dir_2 = [4]$

where p_i is the priority of calls of class i and dir_i are the required multicast directions. Multicast happens in the last (third) section.

Each simulation trial underwent 7 repetitions, resulting in a 95% confidence interval for 7 sets of simulations, calculated using Formula [18]:

$$\left(X - t_\alpha \sqrt{\frac{\sigma^2}{d}} ; X + t_\alpha \sqrt{\frac{\sigma^2}{d}} \right),$$

where X represents the mean value computed from d repeats of the simulation, t_α is the quantile value for the t-Student distribution for d-1 degrees of freedom, whereas σ^2 is the variance of the distribution. A singular simulation extended over 100,000 time units, with the initial series spanning 200 time units. The entire experimental process, encompassing 7 series for one scenario, was included within the interval of 18 - 22 min on a computer, using the Windows 10 operating system and with the AMD Ryzen 7 5800 H 3.20 GHz processor and memory of RAM 32 GB.

The results of each of the simulations are presented in the form graphs as the dependence of the loss probabilities on the intensity per one allocation unit in the system (a) expressed by the following formula:

$$a = \sum_{i=0}^{2} \frac{a_i \cdot t_i}{n \cdot m \cdot f},$$

where i is the index of class, a_i, t_i are the intensity and number of demanded resources, respectively, while n, m, f is the number of the inputs of the switch of the first stage, the number of switches of the first stage and the capacity of a single link, respectively.

The eviction calls to prioritize higher-priority occurs concurrently with the internal and external losses within the network, contributing to the overall (total) tally of losses. Consequently, these losses can be deduced by subtracting the losses arising from internal and external blocking from the total losses.

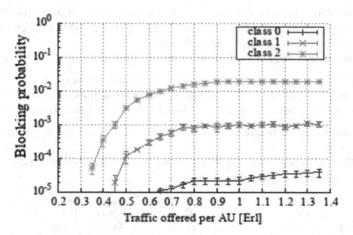

Fig. 4. Internal blocking probability for scenario 1.

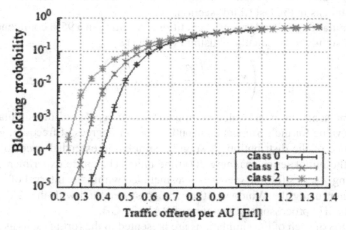

Fig. 5. External blocking probability for scenario 1.

Figures 4, 5 and 6 show internal, external and total blocking probabilities for scenario 1 where priorities between classes are equal. Required multicast directions by each class do not collide - none of the directions is required by more than one class. Results present rather standard behavior - classes demanding more resources have higher blocking probability. For high intensities the gap between each class shortens. What is crucial in understanding these results is the fact that each class has it's own multicast direction.

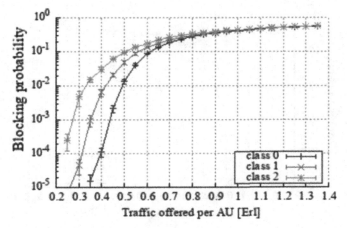

Fig. 6. Total blocking probability for scenario 1.

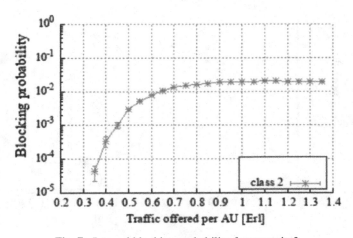

Fig. 7. Internal blocking probability for scenario 2.

The second scenario's results, shown in Figs. 7, 8 and 9, presents internal, external and total blocking probabilities when every class has separate required directions but priorities are different. Class 0 has the highest priority while class 2 has the lowest. The first thing to notice is that the internal blocking is non-existent in Fig. 7 for class 0 and 1. We can assume it is due to the fact that classes with higher priority in case of internal blocking can just push out a class with lower priority. It is important to notice that added priorities in this scenario only affect cases when a request of a given class would meet internal blocking. Priorities in this scenario will not affect external blocking due to the fact of each class having different required directions.

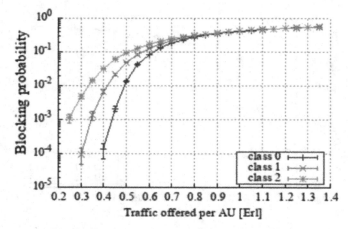

Fig. 8. External blocking probability for scenario 2.

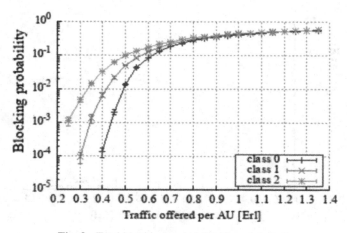

Fig. 9. Total blocking probability for scenario 2.

The third scenario results are presented on Figs. 10 and 11. Internal blocking graph was omitted due to very insignificant occurrence probability. In this scenario all classes have the same priority and class 0 and 1 have common required multicast direction - direction number 3. When analyzing the charts we can notice that class 0 and 1, despite having lower allocation unit demand, have higher blocking probability than class 3. It is due to class 0 and 1 having common required direction which greatly affects their blocking probability. In previous scenarios classes did not share common directions and now some of them do which essentially doubles the third direction exposition to traffic.

Fourth scenario is shown in Figs. 12 and 13. Again internal blocking was omitted due to it's insignificance. In this scenario every class has different priority with class 0 having the highest and class 2 having the lowest. Class 0 and 1 share common direction - third direction. In this scenario the effect of priorities is extremely prominent, the difference

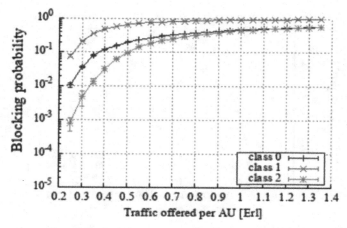

Fig. 10. External blocking probability for scenario 3.

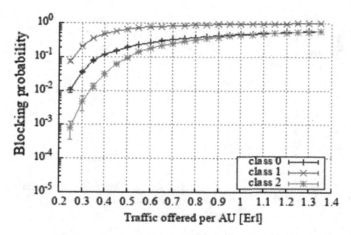

Fig. 11. Total blocking probability for scenario 3.

between class 0 and class 1 blocking probabilities is significant. Class 1 which has higher priority than class 2 has higher blocking probability despite having higher priority, it is due to sharing common direction with class 0 which has even higher priority. Comparing Figs. 9, 10, 11, 12 and 13 from the second scenario shows the impact of different priorities among classes that share the same direction.

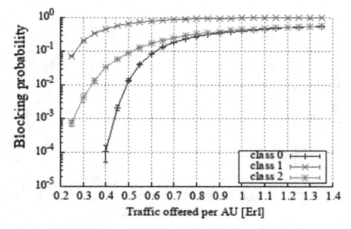

Fig. 12. External blocking probability for scenario 4.

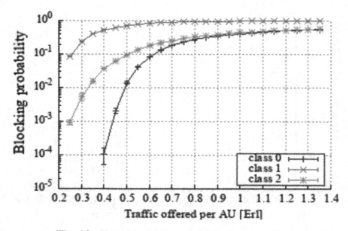

Fig. 13. Total blocking probability for scenario 4.

5 Conclusions

This article introduces a way to simulate systems that handle multicast connections which on top of that have assigned priorities. The proposed simulation holds promise as a base for more complex systems that handle multicast traffic.

Analysis of the experiment results has been carried out in section four. It has been concluded that multicast connections with priorities on top of them can drastically change the shape and values of blocking probabilities. It seems that common multicast directions among traffic classes have even greater impact than priorities. Further research on multicast connections with priorities should be carried out to confirm this thesis. Further research should include:

– multicast splits in earlier sections

– dynamic direction requirements for classes, for example randomly chosen two directions out of three

The core objective behind developing the simulator, was to address and propose a resolution to the lack of tools that allow to simulate Clos networks handling prioritized multicast traffic. To the author's knowledge it is the first simulator of Clos switching network that handles prioritized multicast connections.

Acknowledgements. The research was funded by the Ministry of Education and Science (project no. 0313/SBAD/1310).

References

1. Kabaciński, W.: Nonblocking Electronic and Photonic Switching Fabrics. Springer (2005)
2. Sobieraj, M., Zwierzykowski, P., Leitgeb, E.: Simulation studies of elastic optical networks nodes with multicast connections. Human-centric Comp. Info. Sci. **12**, 05-1–05-13 (2022)
3. Stasiak, M., Sobieraj, M., Zwierzykowski, P.: Modeling of multi-service switching networks with multicast connections. IEEE Access **10**, 5359–5377 (2022)
4. Sobieraj, M., Zwierzykowski, P., Leitgeb, E.: Determination of traffic characteristics of elastic optical networks nodes with reservation mechanisms. Electronics **10**(15), 1853-1–1853-18 (2021)
5. Sobieraj, M., Zwierzykowski, P., Leitgeb, E.: Modelling and optimization of multi-service optical switching networks with threshold management mechanisms. Electronics **10**(13), 1515-1–1515-20 (2021)
6. Głąbowski, M., Ivanov, H., Leitgeb, E., Sobieraj, M., Stasiak, M.: Simulation studies of elastic optical networks based on 3-stage Clos switching fabric. Optical Switching and Networking **36** (2020). https://doi.org/10.1016/j.osn.2020.100555
7. Yang, S., Xin, S., Zhao, Z., Wu, B.: Minimizing packet delay via load balancing in clos switching networks for datacenters. International Conference on Networking and Network Applications (NaNA), pp. 23–28. Hakodate, Japan (2016). https://doi.org/10.1109/NaNA.2016.14
8. Sehery, W., Clancy, C.: Flow optimization in data centers with clos networks in support of cloud applications. In: IEEE Trans. Netw. Ser. Manage. **14**(4), 847–859 (2017). https://doi.org/10.1109/TNSM.2017.2761321
9. Hojabr, R., Modarressi, M., Daneshtalab, M., Yasoubi, A., Khonsari, A.: Customizing clos network-on-chip for neural networks. In: IEEE Transactions on Computers **66**(11), 1865–1877 (2017). https://doi.org/10.1109/TC.2017.2715158
10. Clos, C.: A study of non-blocking switching networks. Bell Labs Tech. J. **32**(2), 406–424 (1953)
11. Benes, V.E.: A thermodynamic theory of traffic in connecting networks. Bell Labs Tech. J. **42**(3), 567–607 (1963)
12. Dorren, H.J.S., Calabretta, N., Raz, O.: A 3-stage CLOS architecture for high-throughput optical packet switching. Proceedings of Asia Communications and Photonics Conference and Exhibition, pp. 1–6. Shanghai, China (2009)
13. Aakanksha, M., Shailendra, G.: Tarun: routing in all-optical three stage-clos interconnection networks. Int. J. Comp. Sci. Eng. **2**(1), 19–22 (2012)
14. Sobieraj, M.: Modelowanie pól komutacyjnych z mechanizmami progowymi i wielousługowymi źródłami ruchu, PhD dissertation. Poznań University of Technology (2014)

15. Tyszer, J.: Object-Oriented Computer Simulation of Discrete-Event Systems. Springer (1999). ISBN: 0792385063
16. Nowak, P.Z.: Simulation studies of the impact of traffic prioritization mechanisms on the traffic efficiency of multi-service network nodes. Proceedings of the 39th International Business Information Management Association (IBIMA), part 3, pp. 434–449
17. Nowak: A Simulation Study on The Influence of The Call Push-Out Scenarios on Traffic Effectiveness of Multi-Service Network Nodes. Proceedings of the 40th International Business Information Management Association (IBIMA). Seville, Spain (2022). ISBN: 979-8-9867719-1-5, ISSN: 2767-9640
18. Durka, P.: Wstęp do współczesnej statystyki. Adamantan (2003). ISBN 83-85655-82-4

Advantages of Introducing the DVB-T2 Standard in Terrestrial Television

Bogdan Uljasz[(✉)]

Faculty of Electronics - Military, University of Technology, Warsaw, Poland
bogdan.uljasz@wat.edu.pl

Abstract. The article draws attention to the delays in introducing the DVB-T2 standard in some European countries. The article is intended to show the advantages of the new DVB-T2 standard over the old DVB-T. The standards were compared with the literature. The article provides qualitative measures for comparison. The research model was presented and used in the measurement comparison. At the end, the research results and a summary are presented. The summary mentioned the narrowing of the available spectrum for terrestrial television. It was mentioned that the new standard will provide the same or greater programming offer in changing spectral conditions.

Keywords: terrestrial communications · digital television · measures of the quality of information transmission

1 Introduction

Despite the first tests of the DVB-T2 standard, many countries have not completed the implementation of this technique. The article presents measurement results showing the advantages of using the new standard. The new standard allows you to expand the programming offer, improve the quality of the transmitted image, and increases resistance to channel interference. The new standard requires the purchase of a new TV set or external decoder. Today, a set-top box is now relatively cheap. The change in the standard means an improvement in the program offer, with little inconvenience of the required purchase.

Since 2008, after the first tests of the second-generation DVB-T2 digital terrestrial television, Europe has been changing the broadcasting standard. The change in the broadcasting standard also means new H.264 or H-265 (HEVC) codecs. H.264 ensures broadcast quality in the HD standard [4]. H.265 ensures broadcast quality in the UHD (4 k) standard [17]. The leaders of this change are Austria and Germany, which completed this process in 2019. Some countries still broadcast in the old DVB-T standard, in SD quality. An example is Poland (https://www.emitel.pl/strefa-klienta/odb ior-rtv/sprawdz-parametry-emisji/ 30/09/2023: MUX 3, MUX 8), Italy or Spain (the Spanish government wanted 2023, all channels on digital terrestrial television were broadcast in HD quality. In the summer, the end date was moved to February 14, 2024: https://www.wirtualnemedia.pl/artykul/jak-odbierac-kanaly-hd-sd-dvb-t2-cnmc-

© The Author(s), under exclusive license to Springer Nature Switzerland AG 2025
K. S. Soliman (Ed.): IBIMA-AI 2024, CCIS 2299, pp. 235–245, 2025.
https://doi.org/10.1007/978-3-031-77493-5_20

terrestrial-digital-TV-high-definition-Spain 30/09/2023). Some countries have not yet determined the end of migration to the DVB-T2 standard for all broadcast multiplexes.

To increase the programming capabilities and quality of broadcast channels, many broadcasters decide to use a more powerful HEVC codec with DVB-T2.

The delay in introducing the new standard is usually due to economic reasons for recipients. A change in the standard requires the purchase of a new TV set or a set-top box for your existing TV. The article presents a comparison of both generations of standards. The DVB-T2 standard is more efficient.

2 Comparison of Standards

The DVB-T and DVB-T2 standards use the OFDM technique. The standards partially support different options for bandwidth, FEC modulation/correction factors, carrier numbers, multiple guard times, etc. As shown in Table 1 below, DVB-T2 supports more options compared to DVB-T [1–3, 5, 10–12, 14–16].

Table 1. Comparison of DVB-T and DVB-T2 technology parameters

Characteristics	DVB-T	DVB-T2
Coding FEC	Convolutional coding + RS: 1/2, 2/3, 3/4, 5/6, 7/8	LDPC + BCH: 1/2, 3/5, 2/3, 3/4, 4/5, 5/6
Modulation	QPSK, 16QAM, 64QAM	QPSK, 16QAM, 64QAM, 256QAM
Guard interval	1/4, 1/8, 1/16, 1/32	1/32 1/4, 19/128, 1/8, 19/256, 1/16, 1/32, 1/128
Size FFT	2 K, 8 K	1 K, 2 K, 4 K, 8 K, 16 K, 32 K
Scatter pilot	8% from the total number	1%, 2%, 4%, 8% from the total number
Continual pilot	2,0% from the total number	0,4%-2,4%
Bandwidth	5, 6, 7, 8 MHz	1,7, 5, 6, 7, 8, 10 MHz
Typical data transfer rate	24 Mbps	40 Mbps
Maximum data transfer rate	31,7 Mbps	50 Mbps

Compared to DVB-T, the DVB-T2 standard has greater possibilities in selecting the values of given parameters as well as system configuration. Configuration options increase the options for setting transmission modes. Additional options ensure better matching of the transmission channel.

3 Measures Used to Assess the Quality of a Television Signal

3.1 MER (Modulation Error Ratio)

MER is a measure of the quality of a digital signal, especially used in DVB-T2 digital television broadcasting. MER is the ratio of modulation errors, i.e. deviations of points on the constellation diagram from their theoretical position, to the RMS value of the signal amplitude. MER is expressed in dB and is used to quantify signal quality, with a higher MER value indicating better signal quality.

The formula for MER can be written as [10]:

$$MER = 10 \cdot \log_{10}\left(\frac{A^2}{E^2}\right) \qquad (1)$$

where:

A - signal amplitude

E - magnitude of the error vector

MER values typically range from a few dB to approximately 35 dB for terrestrial DVB-T2 transmissions. A good DVB-T2 broadcast station usually has a MER of around 35 dB. The maximum MER value for a decoded signal depends on the modulation order, coding rate and receiver quality. With a code rate of 1/2 and a modulation order of 256QAM or 64QAM, it decodes the signal at approximately 15.5 dB or 11 dB MER. For DVB-T, higher MWR values are required for proper reception.

When receiving DVB-T2 signals using a roof antenna, a MER ranging from 18 dB to 30 dB at the antenna point is expected. For portable receivers with an indoor antenna, MER values can range from 12 dB to 20 dB.

It is worth noting that DVB-T2 distinguishes between MER for the basic signal and MER for individual Physical Layer Pipes (PLP), i.e. individual data streams. When the signal quality is good, the MER values for L1 and PLP should be similar. However, in case of a weak signal, a better approach may be to use the MER for L1 as a basis to avoid frequent violations of MER limits on individual PLPs.

3.2 CBER (Correctable Bit Error Ratio)

CBER is a measure used in digital data communication systems to determine the number of correctable errors per unit of transmitted data.

In the case of the DVB-T2 standard, CBER is expressed as the ratio of the number of corrected bits to the total number of transmitted bits in the transmission frame. This is an indicator of transmission quality that informs about the effectiveness of error correction techniques in the DVB-T2 system.

The formula for calculating CBER in the DVB-T2 standard is as follows [10]:

$$CBER = \frac{\text{number of corrected bits}}{\text{The total number of bits transferred in the frame}} \qquad (2)$$

A lower CBER value means better broadcast quality because fewer errors are corrected, indicating less interference or better performance of error correction techniques in a DVB-T2 system. CBER is one of many transmission quality indicators analysed in the DVB-T2 standard, alongside other measures such as BER (Bit Error Ratio), LBER (Limited Bit Error Ratio) or FER (Frame Error Ratio), which allow for the assessment of the transmission quality in the system. DVB-T2. DVB-T additionally uses the VBER (Viterbi Bit Error Ratio) measure.

3.3 QEF (Quasi Error-Free)

An important value occurring in the case of VBER and LBER is QEF, called the error-free reception limit. QEF is a coefficient that determines the maximum BER value at which the image quality on the TV screen is satisfactory. For DVB-T and DVB-T2 the values are different. This is due to the use of different image compression methods. The quality of the video signal is good when only one unrecoverable error is generated per hour of transmission. The QEF limit is equal to one level after error correlation and has a constant value of $1*10^{-4}$ (for VBER in DVB-T) and $1*10^{-5}$ (for LBER in DVB-T2).

4 Test Stand for Comparison of Standards

The laboratory station for testing the transmission capabilities of the DVB-T2 system consisted of a computer, DekTec StreamXpress software, the RANGER NEO Lite signal analyser and the DTU-315 GOLD modulator card.

DekTec StreamXpress software was used to control the transmission process of DVB-T and DVB-T2 signals, enabling the generation, analysis and transmission of DVB data streams on the modulator card. The software has a built-in 30-track radio channel simulator module. The software was installed on a PC with Windows 11. The DTU-315 modulator requires a USB 3.0 interface for control. The PC must be equipped with this interface.

The test file "Transport Stream 16385" was used as the signal source for the modulator. The use of this source made it possible to precisely adapt the source to the set data rate in the radio channel (Fig. 1).

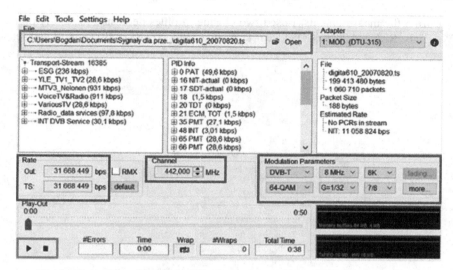

Fig. 1. Example settings of modulator parameters for the DVB-T waveform [8]

The DVB-T2 standard offers greater variety and number of operating modes. Waveform requires specifying additional configuration parameters (Fig. 2).

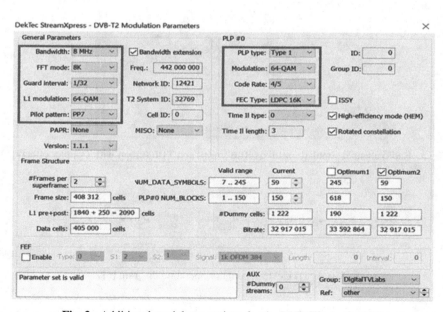

Fig. 2. Additional modulator settings for the DVB-T2 standard [8]

During the measurements, I used two channel profiles dedicated to testing digital TV signals: RL6 and TU6 (COST 207-TU6 and COST 207 RL6) [9] (Figs. 3 and 4).

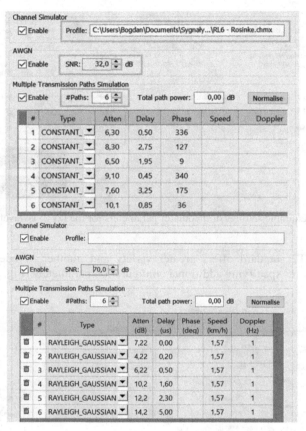

Fig. 3. Radio channel simulator settings RL6 (rural) and TU6 (urban with Doppler effect) [8]

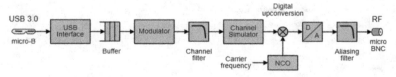

Fig. 4. DTU-315 modulator operation diagram [6]

The DTU-315 GOLD modulator is used to generate signals in all DVB standards at radio frequencies. The DTU-315 modulator is a typical modulator used by television broadcasters.

The RANGER NEO Lite signal analyser is a multifunctional device that allows you to monitor, analyse and measure various parameters of radio signals, including DVB-T2 signals (Figs. 5 and 6).

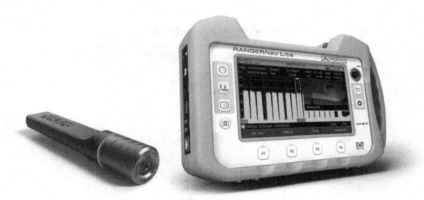

Fig. 5. View of the DekTec DTU-315-GOLD [6] modulator and multifunctional signal analyser DVB Promax Ranger NEO LITE [7]

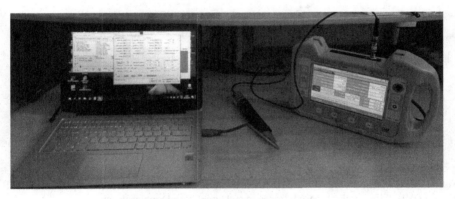

Fig. 6. View of the measurement system

The use of a radio channel simulator provided the opportunity to compare both standards in identical channel conditions.

5 Measurement Results with Analysis

The standards were compared during simulations with the TU6 channel, where the Doppler effect occurs.

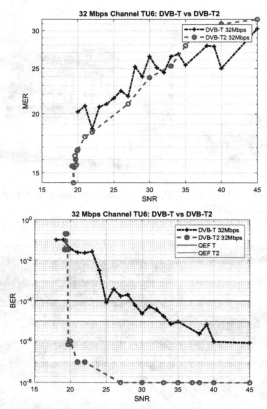

Fig. 7. MER = f(SNR) and BER (CBER/LBER) = f(SNR) characteristics: comparison of DVB-T2 and DVB-T for similar binary bit rates in a channel with Doppler decay

Figure 7 shows a comparison of both standards at the maximum bit rate achieved by the older DVB-T standard. In DVB-T2, at the input of the H.265 decoder, the required QEF value is achieved with a lower SNR value by approximately 7 dB. We know that there is a significant lack of artifacts in the image for BER values $> 1*10^{-7}$. This was not possible for the received signal in the DVB-T standard (Fig. 8).

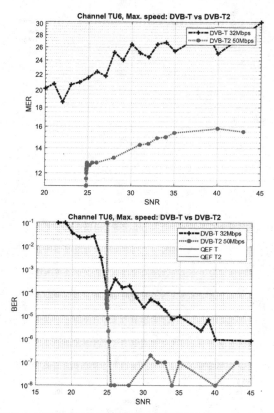

Fig. 8. MER = f(SNR) and BER (CBER/LBER) = f(SNR) characteristics: comparison of DVB-T2 for maximum and comparable binary bit rates for DVB-T in a channel with Doppler dropouts

The signal quality was the same for both standards at their maximum bit rates (for SNR = 25 dB). However, with higher SNR values, fewer artifacts will be noticeable in the image transmitted in the newer DVB-T2 standard (Fig. 9).

Based on the MER and BER charts, it can be concluded that the redundant coding used in the DVB-T2 standard is much more efficient. In DVB-T2, lower BER values are obtained with a worse MER value.

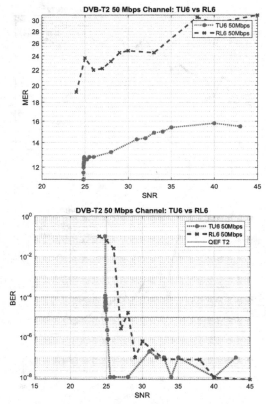

Fig. 9. MER = f(SNR) and BER (CBER/LBER) = f(SNR) characteristics: comparison of DVB-T2 with the maximum bit rate in the channel without Doppler dropouts and with Doppler dropouts

6 Conclusions

The introduction of the new DVB-T2 standard ensures channel throughput at the level of 150% of the previous DVB-T with the same quality of the transmission channel. The additional use of the HEVC codec allows you to increase the throughput to 200% of the previous DVB-T standards with H.264 or even 300% for DVB-T with H.262. The introduction of the DVB-T2 standard with HEVC allows for the transmission of the same number of TV programs in higher quality.

Reducing the spectrum available in the European Union from 470–790 MHz by almost 100 MHz to 470–694 MHz will force the use of a new standard due to smaller spectral resources. The freed band is intended for 5 G.

But in the future, will DVB-I [13] together with 5 G replace DVB-T2 transmitters.

Acknowledgment. This work was financed by the Military University of Technology under Research Project no. UGB/22-863/2023/WAT on "Modern technologies of wireless communication and emitter localization in various system applications".

References

1. Batool, S., Din, I.U., Raza, Z., Shahid, A.: Performance evaluation of DVB-T2 in comparison with DVB-T for terrestrial broadcasting in Pakistan. Wirel. Commun. Mob. Comput. **2018**, 1–10 (2018)
2. Hertel, J.: DVB-T2—the second generation terrestrial digital video broadcasting standard. IEEE Trans. Broadcast. **60**(2), 339–347 (2014)
3. Kim, J.H., Park, K.M., Lee, J.H.: The effect of CFO on performance of DVB-T2 system in mobile channel environment. Wireless Pers. Commun. **94**(2), 769–789 (2017)
4. Swiderski, A., Pawłowski, M.: DVB-T2 as the terrestrial DTV system for Poland. Int. J. Electro. Telecomm. **62**(4), 393–398 (2016)
5. Wong, K.L., Loo, K.H.: DVB-T2: the next generation digital terrestrial television broadcasting standard. IEEE Trans. Broadcast. **59**(4), 803–814 (2013)
6. DTU-315 [Online] [Date of access: 30.09.2023]. https://www.dektec.com/products/USB/DTU-315/
7. Promax [Online] [Date of access: 30.09.2023]. https://www.promaxelectronics.com/ing/products/tv-cable-satellite-signal-and-spectrum-analyzers/ranger-neo-lite/multifunction-tv-signal-and-spectrum-analyzer/
8. StreamXpress [Online] [Date of access: 30.09.2023]. https://www.dektec.com/products/applications/StreamXpress/Books
9. Failli, M.: COST 207 Digital land mobile radio communications, EUR 12160 EN. Office for Official Publications of the European Communities, Luxemburg (1989)
10. Fischer, W.: Digital Video and Audio Broadcasting Technology. Springer, Monachium (2008)
11. 2nd Generation Terrestrial. The World's Most Advanced Digital Terrestrial TV System, DVB Fact Sheet, August 2013 Standards and recommendations
12. ETSI: Digital Video Broadcasting (DVB); Frame structure channel coding and modulation for a second generation digital terrestrial television broadcasting system (DVB-T2). ETSI EN 302 755 V1.3.1 (2012-04) (2012)
13. ETSI EN: DVB-I service delivery over 5G Systems; Deployment Guideline's ETSI TR 103 972 V1.1.1. (2023)
14. ETSI TR: Digital Video Broadcasting (DVB); Frame structure channel coding and modulation for a second generation digital terrestrial television broadcasting system (DVB-T2). ETSI TS 102 755 V1.1.1 (2023-02) Conference Paper (2023)
15. Kim, J.H., Lee, S.J.: DVB-T2 based low power broadcasting system for urban area. Asia-Pacific Signal and Information Processing Association Annual Summit and Conference (APSIPA), pp. 1018–1022. IEEE (2015)
16. Li, L., Lin, Y., Li, Z.: Performance analysis of DVB-T2 physical layer for high altitude platform communication system. 12th International Symposium on Communication Systems, Networks & Digital Signal Processing (CSNDSP), pp. 1–5. IEEE (2017)
17. Vlachos, G., Koumaras, H.: DVB-T2 physical layer and performance analysis for 4K/UHD broadcasting. International Conference on Telecommunications and Multimedia (TEMU), pp. 177–181. IEEE (2016)

Consensus Mechanisms in Blockchain Networks

Malgorzata Michniewicz[✉]

Military University of Technology, Warsaw, Poland
malgorzata.michniewicz@wat.edu.pl

Abstract. Presenting the evolution of consensus mechanisms in blockchain technology. This article aims not only to provide a historical context of these mechanisms but also to analyze their characteristics and their impact on the development of the blockchain ecosystem. By understanding where these mechanisms came from and where they may be headed, readers will be better prepared to assess current and future blockchain projects and to comprehend key aspects of the technology that is revolutionizing various industries worldwide.

Keywords: consensus mechanism · blockchain · evolution

1 Introduction (A Brief Definition and Significance of Consensus Mechanisms)

A consensus mechanism consists of rules and procedures that enable reaching a consensus. Consensus is an agreement between nodes in the network, containing a set of verified transactions recorded in a block.

Consensus mechanisms drive the entire blockchain ecosystem, and their development signifies the strength of improving and advancing trust-based technology in the network, as well as establishing new standards for indisputable proof of transactions in the network.

Currently, there are over 60 types of consensus mechanisms [4]. The research identifying the applied consensus mechanisms was conducted on November 17, 2020, based on data from the www.coinpaprika.com website.

Among nearly 1359 tokens operating for over 2 years on the market, 60 different types of consensus were identified, with the most popular being Proof of Work, Proof of Work & Proof of Stake, Proof of Stake, Delegated Proof of Stake, Byzantine Fault Tolerance, Proof of Authority, and Proof Importance.

2 History and Evolution of Consensus Mechanisms

In 1982, David Chaum proposed in his dissertation, Computer Systems Established, Maintained, and Trusted by Mutually Suspicious Groups [1] an outline of a distributed blockchain ledger, marking the beginnings of everything when the Internet was taking shape.

K. S. Soliman (Ed.): IBIMA-AI 2024, CCIS 2299, pp. 246–251, 2025.
https://doi.org/10.1007/978-3-031-77493-5_21

Then, in 1991, Stuart Haber and W. Scott Stornetta came up with the idea to timestamp records related to network transactions so that people could be sure that the data contained in those records was credible and had not been tampered with. They wanted to use timestamps for securing digital records. However, they needed a third party to confirm this state, but they could conspire with this third party, so a fourth party was needed to confirm it, and the problem compounded exponentially. Therefore, they concluded that they couldn't achieve this. Scott Stornetta realized that if there were enough people involved in the agreement, it no longer qualified as a conspiracy but became a consensus. The concept of witness consensus emerged from their earlier work, and from that point on, the idea of recording entries in a block and timestamping the block using cryptography to link it to the next block, with copies of the ledger stored in nodes, was born.

The term "Blockchain" was not used to describe this technology. The first patent for a cryptographic block sequence was written in the 1990s by Scott Stornetta and Stuart Haber. They tried to find a way to secure digital records and develop a system that wouldn't require a trusted third party. The concept they adopted was that when a sufficient number of involved parties are in agreement, it's not a concept but a consensus.

On October 31, 2008, Satoshi Nakamoto (an anonymous person) published the so-called "Bitcoin Whitepaper" [3], in which he described the idea of creating the Bitcoin network and the operation of the first consensus mechanism based on Proof of Work. The first block, known as the "genesis block," was mined on January 3, 2009, and the distributed ledger appeared in the form of a successfully functioning implementation called Bitcoin.

The exchange of data is facilitated through the internet, which provides connectivity between nodes in a system based on the principle of peer-to-peer equality among participants.

Blockchain technology is a transaction ledger, a kind of ledger in which transactions and their details (date, location, amount, anonymous participants, and their encrypted signatures) are recorded and verified using consensus algorithms. This document operates on equal terms among all participants in a given system, whether individuals, businesses, countries, or institutions, and is not subject to central supervision or control.

Each block contains an agreed-upon set of transaction information within a fixed unit of time, e.g., 10 min, and is cryptographically linked to the previous block, creating a chain of blocks. Each completed transaction is encrypted, participants are identified by a string of characters, and after a certain time, the transaction becomes part of a block. A block is a group of transactions linked to the previous block, hence the name "blockchain". It is then distributed to all parties connected to this network.

Once a transaction is recorded on the blockchain, it cannot be changed or canceled, making this technology both accurate and secure from an audit perspective, providing a credible audit trail where the authenticity and validity of transactions can be verified.

When a block meets the requirements of the Proof-of-Work algorithm, it cannot be easily altered. Any attempt to change this block would require re-computation not only of that block but also of all subsequent blocks. The Proof-of-Work algorithm also helps determine which blockchain is the "real" one. Instead of relying on the number of IP addresses, it relies on computational power: one processor equals one vote. The longest blockchain with the most computational work is considered the correct one. If the majority of this computational power comes from honest users, their blockchain will be the longest. Therefore, to change a previous block, a malicious actor would need to recalculate that block and all the blocks that follow it, and then work faster than all the honest users combined.

3   Evolution of Other Consensus Mechanisms

The World Economic Forum in its document, "Building Block(chain)s for a Better Planet", discusses the potential of blockchain technology to address environmental issues such as climate change, biodiversity loss, and water scarcity. At the same time, it emphasizes that consensus mechanisms in blockchain are crucial for ensuring the security, reliability, and transparency of transactions and data on decentralized networks. The document also highlights challenges and limitations associated with consensus mechanisms, such as energy costs, scalability, the risk of attacks, and the lack of standardization and regulation.

The evolution of consensus mechanisms in blockchain technology has over time encompassed various variants and optimizations to minimize energy consumption, increase transaction speed, scalability, and network security. Each consensus mechanism was designed to meet the challenges related to scalability, security, and decentralization in blockchain, which, in turn, influenced the overall development of the blockchain ecosystem.

Currently, there are many different consensus mechanisms – more than 60, such as Proof of Work (PoW), Proof of Stake (PoS), Delegated Proof of Stake (DPoS), Proof of Authority, Proof of Importance, etc. This diversity allows blockchain to be tailored to different applications and needs. The future of blockchain will likely involve further development and optimization of these existing mechanisms, as well as the introduction of new ones.

Consensus mechanisms will continue to evolve to meet the growing challenges and needs of blockchain technology. As this technology advances, we can expect to witness more advanced, sustainable, and interdisciplinary solutions that will impact many aspects of our lives.

4   Major Consensus Mechanisms - Description of Characteristics and Applications

4.1   Proof of Stake

Proof of Stake (PoS): PoS depends on the number of tokens held by a user to determine who can add a new block to the chain.

Key Features of Proof of Stake:

Stake: Stake refers to the number of tokens a user has locked in their wallet for a specific period. Owners of a larger stake have a better chance of adding a new block to the chain.

Security: In PoS, an attacker would need to possess 51% of all tokens, which is significantly more costly and less likely than acquiring 51% of computational power, as in PoW.

Energy efficiency: PoS consumes significantly less energy than PoW since it does not require intensive computations. Instead, block creation is determined by the number of tokens held.

Examples of Proof of Stake Usage:

Ethereum 2.0: Ethereum transitioned from PoW to PoS as part of the Ethereum 2.0 upgrade, aiming to improve scalability and network efficiency.

Cardano: Cardano is a smart contract platform that has been using PoS in its Ouroboros protocol from the beginning.

Polkadot: Polkadot, a multi-chain platform, uses PoS to secure its main network.

Tezos: Tezos is a blockchain platform that employs a variant of PoS called Liquid Proof of Stake, allowing token holders to delegate their voting rights without transferring ownership.

4.2 Delegated Proof of Stake

A type of extended PoS mechanism is **Delegated Proof of Stake (dPoS)**: In dPoS, cryptocurrency holders vote for delegates who represent their interests and make decisions regarding the network. These decisions may include changes to the network protocol or the selection of new delegates.

Advantages of DPoS include lower energy consumption compared to Proof of Work and greater scalability. However, a downside is that cryptocurrency holders must trust the delegates and their decisions.

Examples of DPoS-based blockchains include BitShares, EOS, and Steem.

4.3 Byzantine Fault Tolerance

Byzantine Fault Tolerance (BFT): BFT is a property of a system that allows it to function correctly, even when part of the system behaves incorrectly or maliciously.

The name comes from the Byzantine Generals problem, which describes a situation in which there must be agreement between different units despite the presence of dishonest or inefficient units.

In the context of distributed systems like blockchain, BFT refers to the system's ability to achieve consensus even in the presence of nodes acting contrary to expectations (e.g., due to failures, errors, or malicious intent).

There are several types of BFT algorithms, including:

Practical Byzantine Fault Tolerance (pBFT): pBFT is an algorithm that allows distributed systems to achieve consensus in the presence of Byzantine nodes. It is often used in blockchain networks that require consensus to be reached quickly.

Federated Byzantine Agreement (FBA): FBA is another type of BFT algorithm that is used in blockchain networks such as Stellar. It allows you to achieve consensus in a network in which each node decides which other nodes it trusts.

Delegated Proof of Stake (dPoS): dPoS is a consensus mechanism that connects PoS elements and BFT. In dPoS networks, token holders vote for delegates who have the right to create blocks and confirm transactions. dPoS is known for being efficient and scalable, but may lead to centralization of power among a small number of delegates.

5 Comparisons of Consensus Mechanisms - Key Features: Energy Efficiency, Scalability, Security, Interoperability

Energy and Ecology: The PoW mechanism used by Bitcoin is known for its high energy consumption. The future of blockchain will need to address this issue by transitioning to more energy-efficient consensus mechanisms like PoS. Achieving more environmentally sustainable solutions will become a priority.

Scalability: Current consensus mechanisms have limitations regarding scalability, meaning some blockchains may struggle to process a high volume of transactions simultaneously. Developing and improving these mechanisms will be crucial for widespread blockchain adoption in various sectors, such as finance, logistics, healthcare, and education.

Security and Decentralization: Consensus mechanisms directly impact the level of blockchain security and decentralization. The future of blockchain will need to strike a balance between network security and maintaining its decentralized nature. This might require more sophisticated solutions and innovative approaches.

Interoperability: The ability for different blockchains to work together is becoming increasingly important. Consensus mechanisms will need to evolve to allow interoperability between different blockchain networks, enabling smoother data and value flow between them.

The blockchain community plays a significant role in shaping consensus mechanisms. Decisions regarding changes in mechanisms are often made based on community consultations, so it's essential to consider the diversity of perspectives and user needs.

6 Conclusions

The beginnings of blockchain and the integration of PoW in Bitcoin have revolutionized how we perceive and conduct financial transactions. This innovation has opened the doors to many new possibilities that continue to shape the world of cryptocurrencies and blockchain technology.

Choosing the right consensus mechanism is crucial for the success of a blockchain-based project, taking into account features like energy consumption, performance, scalability, and decentralization.

Consensus mechanisms in blockchain technology have contributed to significant advancements in the field of innovation and technology globally. With their ability to provide transparency, security, and decentralization, these mechanisms have laid the foundation for many modern solutions across financial, logistical, healthcare, and educational sectors. As blockchain technology continues to develop further, we can anticipate it playing an even more crucial role in shaping the global I&T landscape, leading to even greater integration, interoperability, and innovation across various sectors.

References

1. Chaum, D.: Computer Systems Established, Maintained and Trusted by Mutually Suspicious Groups, pp. 11–15 (1982)

2. Lantz, L.: Blockchain. A Guide to Blockchain Technology. Cryptocurrencies, Smart Contracts, and Decentralized Applications, Helion (2022)
3. Nakamoto, S.: Bitcoin Whitepaper 3 (2008). https://bitcoin.org/bitcoin.pdf
4. Michniewicz, M.: Security Audit of Blockchain-Based Systems – "The Technological Dimension of Personal Data Protection" – FNCE, 148–149 (2021)
5. Mougayar, W.: Blockchain in Business. Opportunities and Applications of the Blockchain. Helion (2019)
6. Shetty, S.S., Kamhoua, C.A., Laurent, L.N.: Blockchain and the Security of Distributed Systems (2020)
7. World Economic Forum: Building Block(chain)s for a Better Planet, pp. 9–34 (2018). https://www3.weforum.org/docs/WEF_Building-Blockchains.pdf

Evolution and Deployment Options of Enterprise Systems: The Case of SAP S/4HANA Enterprise Application Suite

Przemysław Lech[1]([✉]), Dariusz Samól[2], and Mariya Shygun[3]

[1] Faculty of Management, University of Gdańsk, Sopot, Poland
przemyslaw.lech@ug.edu.pl
[2] Westernacher Poland, Sopot, Poland
dariusz.samol@westernacher.com
[3] Kyiv National Economic University, Kyiv, Ukraine
shygun@ukr.net

Abstract. This research aimed to examine the architecture of a modern Enterprise System based on the case of SAP S/4HANA, present a refined definition of Enterprise Systems, and identify the possible deployment options and their implications for the clients. The motivation for this study is twofold. Firstly, many authors tend to equate Enterprise Systems with Enterprise Resource Planning and consider the topic mature and well-researched. The evolution of Enterprise Systems, resulting in the change of the scope of possible solutions within enterprises, the complexity of implementation projects and the impact on the operations of the companies which use such systems are not represented in the literature. Secondly, the change in the deployment options of Enterprise Systems, including the invention of the cloud, is also not well represented. We applied the analysis of the source documentation as a research method. We found that Enterprise Systems have evolved from Enterprise Resource Planning to organisation-wide, multi-component systems, covering major business processes and management functions of an enterprise and including both transactional (Enterprise Resource Planning, Supply Chain Management) and analytical sub-systems. We also identified three main deployment options for Enterprise Systems: public cloud, private cloud, and on-premise. We discussed the major consequences of choosing each option, which involve a trade-off between the ease of implementation offered by a cloud solution and the scalability provided by the private cloud and on-premise solutions. The paper concludes with suggestions for further research directions.

Keywords: ERP · Cloud · SAP · Enterprise System Architecture

1 Introduction

Enterprise Systems (ES) have existed in Information Systems theory and practice for at least thirty years. For many researchers and practitioners, an Enterprise System is a synonym for Enterprise Resource Planning (ERP), a part of legacy systems in most organisations worldwide. As such, they seem to be on a declining interest trend in the mainstream Information Systems research agenda.

K. S. Soliman (Ed.): IBIMA-AI 2024, CCIS 2299, pp. 252–266, 2025.
https://doi.org/10.1007/978-3-031-77493-5_22

This paper aims to systematise and refresh the perspective on Enterprise Systems and draw possible future research directions. In particular, this paper aims to answer the following research questions:

- RQ1: What is the architecture of the contemporary Enterprise System?
- RQ2: What is the up-to-date definition of an Enterprise System?
- RQ3: What deployment options for Enterprise Systems do modern enterprises have?
- RQ4: What implications are related to each of the ES deployment options?
- RQ5: What are possible future directions of research regarding Enterprise Systems?

The study was based on the SAP S/4HANA system. SAP S/4HANA is the newest representation of the SAP Enterprise Systems product family, the successor of SAP R/3, mySAP.com, SAP ECC and SAP Business Suite. The differences between the previous incarnations of the SAP Enterprise System (starting from SAP R/3 and ending with SAP Business Suite) were mostly evolutionary. Additional functionality was added incrementally, and the user interface was slightly altered from version to version. However, the core functionality and basics of the user interface remained unchanged. SAP S/4HANA is different as the system was rebuilt due to the database change from any database to the in-memory platform based on a columnar database - SAP HANA. Also, an entirely new (albeit in most versions of SAP S/4HANA – optional) user interface was released – SAP FIORI. What is most important: SAP S/4HANA provides functionality far exceeding the traditional scope of ERP suites. Also, SAP as a company is a leader in the ERP market share (Top 10 ERP Vendors, Market Size and Market Forecast 2021–2026; 2022) [23] and is among the top three companies regarding the market share of all Enterprise Application Software, including office applications, e-mail, and CRM (Market Share: Enterprise Application Software, Worldwide, 2020; 2021) [13]. The facts mentioned above make SAP S/4HANA a reasonable proxy to examine a modern Enterprise System and how this family of systems will evolve in the coming years.

The primary research method used in this study was the analysis of documentation, including:

- SAP S/4HANA Cloud 2208 Feature Scope Description (2022) [16]
- SAP S/4HANA 2022 Feature Scope Description (2022)
- Getting Started With SAP S/4HANA (2022) [7]
- SAP S/4HANA Cloud and On-Premise Deployment Options I SAP Blogs (2019)
- Difference between SAP S/4HANA: Public Vs Private edition: RISE with SAP I SAP Blogs (2022)
- SAP Transformation Navigator (2023) [15].

The findings from the analysis of documentation were confronted with the practical knowledge of the two authors of this paper as:

- one of the authors has more than twenty years of experience as an SAP solution architect;
- one of the authors has more than twenty years of experience as an SAP project manager.

Based on the practical experiences, the authors critically reviewed the documentation regarding the implications of the SAP S/4HANA deployment options and directions of future research regarding Enterprise Systems.

The remainder of the paper is structured as follows. First, we present the definitions of the Enterprise System in the research literature. Then, we proceed with the analysis of the architecture of the SAP S/4HANA system to determine the directions in which contemporary Enterprise Systems evolve. As a conclusion of this analysis, we present a refined definition of an Enterprise System. In the next step, we identify the possible deployment options for the Enterprise System and discuss the implications of choosing each option. Finally, we conclude with the proposals of directions for future research.

2 Enterprise System – A Review of the Current Literature

To determine the up-to-date perception of Enterprise Systems, a literature search was done in Google Scholar, Science Direct and Web of Science using the terms "Enterprise System" and "Enterprise Systems". The time range was set to 2013 - 2023 so that only relatively new publications were included. Papers by the authors of this study were deliberately excluded. The list of papers which contained direct definitions, descriptions or exemplifications of Enterprise Systems, together with the respective quotes, is presented in Table 1.

The above papers explicitly included Enterprise Systems (ES) in their titles. The literature search also returned multiple Enterprise Resource Planning (ERP) Systems papers. This fact and the analysis of the definitions in Table 1 lead to the conclusion that many authors equate Enterprise Systems with ERP. [2], as well as [8], use the terms ES and ERP interchangeably, while [14, 20] and [25] present ERP as the only example of ES.

At the other end of the spectrum, there are (too) broad definitions, such as the ones of [4] and [1], which, if taken literally, consider any software application used in an organisation as an ES. However, the latter authors provide a more specific characteristic of ES in their discussion: "In the literature, the term "ES" refers broadly to business information systems that integrate information flow across the entire organisation". The remaining authors also highlight the fact that an Enterprise System is organisation-wide or cross-functional ([3, 19, 22]). Another characteristic of Enterprise Systems is that an Enterprise System must be integrated with regards to the process and information flow, which, on the technical level, means that the system is using one database ([2]; Humlund and Haddara, 2019; [19, 22, 25]). Finally, four definitions ([2, 3, 22, 24]) highlight explicitly that an Enterprise System is a packaged (i.e. standard/commercial off-the-shelf - COTS) software. Therefore, we submit that Enterprise Systems are a subgroup of enterprise application software, which meets the following criteria jointly:

- are organisation-wide – i.e. support major business processes and management functions of an enterprise;
- standard – i.e. are delivered as packaged software;
- integrated – i.e. include mechanisms of automatic propagation of information within the system (e.g. through the common database).

In other words – the Enterprise System is the central system in a company and a primary source of information. We suggest a label enterprise application software (or enterprise applications) to cover a broader category of "any software system that

Table 1. Definitions and descriptions of an Enterprise System

Reference	Definition of an Enterprise System
[1]	An enterprise system (ES) is any software system that allows an organisation to operate its business and manage its data to achieve specific goals
[2]	Enterprise systems are software packages that are generally based on relational databases, which impact and facilitate business events such as order capturing, to accounting, and to warehouse management. Enterprise Resource Planning (ERP) systems are organisation-wide and integrated information systems that are capable of managing and coordinating all the resources, information, and functions of a business from shared data stores
[3]	Enterprise Systems are complex, customisable software packages that support business processes, information flows, reporting and executive decisions in large organisations. ES are complex off-the-shelf information technology (IT) solutions that promise to meet the information needs of organisations. The term 'ES' refers to systems that coordinate organisation-wide activities, such as enterprise resources planning (ERP) and supply chain management (SCM)
[4]	Enterprise systems (ESs) are used to support data acquisition, communication, and all decision-making activities
[8]	A new enterprise system adoption, by its very nature, enforces its own logic on a company's strategy, organisation, and culture. In addition, Enterprise Resource Planning (ERP) systems aim to integrate the business operations through a [business] processes perspective
[9]	Each project in the implementation considers an individual ES module which is interdependent with the other projects and modules; e.g. an Enterprise Resource Planning (ERP) module, a Supply Chain Management (SCM) module, a Business Intelligence (BI) module, and/or a Customer Relationship Management (CRM) module
[12]	Enterprise Systems are integrated solutions that support key business processes within and between organisations. Such systems include Finance, Human Resources, Supply Chain, Sales and Marketing, Management Reporting and Metrics, Planning and Analysis, Performance Management, Product Development, and Customer Relationship Management
[14]	The agile approach is found helpful for the implementation of large-scale enterprise systems (ES), such as enterprise resource planning (ERP) systems
[19]	Large IS or enterprise systems (ES) are referred to as highly integrative and complex real-time business applications sharing a common database and streamlining business processes across various functional departments. Examples of ES include enterprise resource planning (ERP) systems, supply chain management (SCM) systems, customer relationship management (CRM) systems, business-to-business (B2B) systems, inter-organisational systems (IOS) and e-commerce systems

(continued)

Table 1. (*continued*)

Reference	Definition of an Enterprise System
[20]	[...] more and more firms have implemented Enterprise Systems (ES), such as ERP (Enterprise Resource Planning), to improve business efficiency and support business strategy
[21]	Enterprise systems integrate a company's core business processes. They are designed to automate the flow of information, materials, and financial resources within a company and across a supply chain or network. [...] Enterprise systems, the most well-known examples of which are enterprise resource planning (ERP) systems, aim to integrate information flows across the organisation to increase the organisation's competitiveness
[22]	ES are complex application software packages that support the management of the whole company, integrating all areas of its functioning. Initially known as Enterprise Resource Planning (ERP) systems, ES emerged from manufacturing resource planning systems and were developed as support technology for a variety of transaction-based back-office functions. Since then, ES have evolved to include support for front-office and even interorganizational activities, including supply chain management (SCM), customer resource management (CRM), and sales force automation
[24]	Enterprise Systems are commercial software packages that enable the integration of transaction-oriented data and business processes throughout an organisation
[25]	[...] advanced enterprise system such as enterprise resource planning (ERP) system. ERP is a management process business software that comprehensively integrate the applications of organisational management and functions, such as product planning, development, manufacturing, sales and marketing, while automating office functions associated with technology, services and human resources

allows an organisation to operate its business and manage its data to achieve specific goals" [1]. That is in line with the Gartner Information Technology Glossary (2023) [6], which states that "Enterprise application software includes content, communication, and collaboration software; CRM software; digital and content creation software, ERP software; office suites; project and portfolio management; and SCM software"– any software used in a company.

Only one of the above definitions [3] highlights an essential feature of an Enterprise System, which is adaptability to a company's specific requirements. Enterprise Systems may be adjusted to the specific requirements via configuration, i.e. "setting the system parameters to determine the way the system operates by choosing from the existing options" and/or customisation, i.e. developing a new code to alter or extend the functionality of the system [11]. Enterprise Systems vary from simple systems that provide limited configuration but work "out-of-the-box" to complex systems, providing plenty of configuration options but requiring an implementation project during which configuration is done so that a system becomes operational in a given company.

Not without reason, many authors equated Enterprise Systems with ERP, as ERP systems were the first commercial of-the-shelf software packages which supported the firm's core processes in an integrated way. As [22] state: "ES emerged from manufacturing resource planning systems and were developed as a support technology for a variety of transaction-based back-office functions". However, Enterprise Systems have evolved since the introduction of ERP in the 1990s, and equating ES and ERP is no longer valid. In the following section, we attempt to define a contemporary Enterprise System based on the analysis of the architecture of SAP S/4HANA.

3 Contemporary Architecture and Refined Definition of an Enterprise System Based on SAP S/4HANA

To determine the state-of-the-art architecture of an Enterprise System, we analysed the functionality of two versions of the SAP S/4HANA system: SAP S/4HANA Cloud, which is the cloud solution provided by SAP in a public cloud, and SAP S/HANA on-premise system. The following pieces of documentation were the primary sources of information:

- SAP S/4HANA Cloud 2208 Feature Scope Description (2022) [16]
- SAP S/4HANA 2022 Feature Scope Description (2022) [17]
- Getting Started With SAP S/4HANA (2022) [7]
- SAP S/4HANA Cloud and On-Premise Deployment Options I SAP Blogs (2019) [18]
- Difference between SAP S/4HANA: Public Vs Private edition: RISE with SAP I SAP Blogs (2022) [5]
- SAP Transformation Navigator (2023) [15].

SAP S/4HANA on-premise (SAP S/4HANA 2022) was the leading system to be analysed, providing broader functionality than the public cloud edition. The Feature Scope Description document shows the functionality of SAP S/4HANA via a process lens. Although this is a valuable view from the perspective of an enterprise aiming at covering its processes with an Information System, for this study, it is more interesting to decompose SAP S/4HANA into sub-systems which constitute its primary building blocks:

1. **Enterprise Management** is a sub-system providing the basic set of functions typical for the scope of ERP. Enterprise Management is considered the successor of SAP R/3 and SAP ECC. Its functions are grouped into structures reminding the former SAP R/3 "modules", clearly visible in the traditional graphic interface (SAP GUI) user menu. These main grouping structures are currently called "Business Areas" and have their specific names: Sales & Marketing, Finance, Manufacturing (former Production in SAP ECC), Supply Chain (former Logistic Execution), Service, Asset Management, Research and Development with Engineering (former Project Portfolio Management), Sourcing and Procurement, and Human Resources. As for SAP R/3/SAP ECC, Enterprise Management's functionality is wide and covers all typical enterprise's primary processes/business functions.

2. Nevertheless, even on this basic level, the system has been extended by new functions. The most significant change is replacing the traditional General Ledger with Universal Journal in Finance. This made a substantial impact on unifying Financial Accounting and Management Accounting by avoiding the need for double posting and generating multiple transactional documents. The other significant change is represented by new algorithms for Material Requirements Planning: MRP Live and Demand Driven Replenishment. The first algorithm enables user interactions during the planning run (which was impossible in the SAP ECC MRP transaction). The second one is based on the concept of Demand Driven MRP, the planning method which recently gained worldwide recognition due to its lower sensitivity to forecast volatility. Demand-driven replenishment involves multi-echelon inventory planning, execution, and optimisation. It protects and promotes smooth demand and supply flow within the organisation by strategically placing inventory buffers. SAP S/4HANA has also gained the ability to perform simulations previously exclusively possessed by Advanced Planning and Scheduling class systems. Predictive Material and Resource Planning simulates production by using a predictive MRP algorithm. It enables evaluation capacity, production, and purchasing requirements together with the internal material flow on detailed levels. Finally, the significant re-design replacement concerns the group of functions for creating and dispatching shipments. A new component has been added here, named Transportation Management Basic Shipping.

3. **SAP S/4HANA Extended Warehouse Management** formerly existed only as a separate system. Now, it is deployed as a sub-system of SAP S/4HANA in the so-called "embedded" version. SAP S/4HANA Extended Warehouse Management's scope comprises automating warehouse operations, including inbound processing, crossdocking, outbound processing, warehouse storage, and physical inventory management. In addition, it supports workforce management, slotting and advanced inventory optimisation, delivery billing, transit warehousing for logistics service providers, and connectivity to warehouse automation equipment. These capabilities allow warehouse users to plan and process inbound and outbound deliveries directly transferred from the Enterprise Management part of SAP S/4HANA. These deliveries are automatically decomposed into warehouse tasks and transparently executed at the appropriate time, with relevant resource consumption. Furthermore, embedding the warehousing system into SAP S/4HANA created a new opportunity for integrating it with the Manufacturing Business Area, where material staging is performed according to the production process needs. In future releases of SAP S/4HANA, inventory-oriented Warehouse Management (mentioned in the Enterprise Management section above) will be entirely replaced by SAP EWM.

4. **SAP S/4HANA Transportation Management**, like a warehousing solution, existed only as a separate system, as the operation logic of a transportation system is far beyond the standard set of ERP functions. Traditional ERP-like thinking focuses on transactions which impact the organisation and its resources. Standard ERP solutions are built around processes involving materials, semi-finished goods and products purchased, stored, moved, transformed, sold and shipped by the company. In contrast, the transportation system focuses on cargo regardless of who owns it. This cargo is moved beyond organisational boundaries, where various organisations play various supply chain roles. They can be identified as shippers, logistics providers or transportation

companies having a profile of airline, marine operator, railways or land vehicle operator. Transportation operations are performed as domestic or international (export) and can be multimodal where different means of transport are combined. The functions supporting these different transportation types are available in SAP Transportation Management, now embedded in SAP S/4HANA. In order to provide more transparent management and licensing, it is split into two parts: Basic and Advanced Shipping. The main difference between these parts is that the first one contains functions relevant to a shipper (an organisation which uses transportation as an execution component of its own supply chain, preferably with its own products).

5. In contrast, Advanced Shipping fits the broader scope of functions, typical for an organisation which plays more roles in the supply chain. Hence, the following functions in Basic Shipping are in use: freight agreements, inbound/outbound freight orders, booking (in marine transport) management, freight settlement, tendering, subcontracting and charge management. Basic transportation planning and execution are possible here. In contrast, Advanced Shipping provides functions including strategic freight management, service product catalogue, service order management, driver management and integration to SAP Extended Warehouse Management. Overall, the entire transportation planning with resource and route optimisation is possible in Advanced Shipping. This scope of functions allows transportation planners to manage entire transportation planning and execution from one unified planning cockpit.

6. **SAP S/4HANA Extended Production Planning and Scheduling** was formerly delivered by SAP separately, and it was known as Production Planning and Detailed Scheduling or PPDS. This solution enables the planning of production orders and the creation of detailed schedules of their operations on a very high-resolution time axis (days, shifts, hours and minutes). In contrast, by its design, MRP can calculate production quantities in daily buckets only. In PPDS, both heuristic and optimisation algorithms can be used for modelling practically continuous materials flow and manufacturing activities in time. Calculating the expected capacity load on the resources is possible, while some can be defined as bottlenecks. Thanks to that, finite scheduling with automatic selection of production resources is possible. Now, the whole solution is natively embedded with SAP S/4HANA. There is also a new function of Extended Production Planning, which was not known before, called Production Planning Optimizer. It integrates purchasing, manufacturing, and distribution. As a result, tactical planning and sourcing decisions can be simulated and implemented based on a single, global, consistent model. Production Planning Optimiser can work cooperatively with MRP or replace MRP completely, depending on the user's needs.

7. **Augmented Business Intelligence** in SAP S/4HANA is a sub-system that provides analytical support for the organisation. Although SAP S/4HANA is not an analytical system, it creates an opportunity for using analytical data on the user interface level. Combining online transaction processing (OLTP) and online analytical processing (OLAP) drives analytics as part of the transactional processes, called "Embedded Analytics". The system provides tools for creating Key Performance Indicators (KPI), reports, visualisations and initial data analysis. In particular, it enables reporting of business data from virtual data models and helps create analytical queries.

The above list of functionalities answers the **RQ1:** What is the architecture of the contemporary Enterprise System? A contemporary Enterprise System consists of the following sub-systems:

- Enterprise Resource Planning sub-system (ERP) covering the following business areas:

  o Sourcing and Procurement
  o Production planning and execution, including Material Resource Planning (MRP) and Demand Driven Replenishment,
  o Sales & Marketing,
  o Finance,
  o Supply Chain,
  o Service,
  o Asset Management,
  o Research and Development with Engineering (former Project Portfolio Management),
  o and Human Resources;

- Warehouse Management sub-system (WMS), allowing for advanced management of warehouse processes - including inbound processing, cross-docking, outbound processing, warehouse storage, and physical inventory management;
- Transportation Management sub-system (TMS) – allowing for advanced management of logistics outside of the company's premises - including freight agreements, inbound/outbound freight orders, booking management, freight settlement, tendering, subcontracting and charge management;
- Advanced production planning and scheduling system - providing heuristic and optimisation algorithms for scheduling of continuous materials flow and manufacturing activities in time;
- Analytical sub-system – providing the tools for creating Key Performance Indicators (KPI), reports, visualisations and data analysis.

As can be seen from the evidence presented above, an Enterprise System's architecture, based on the example of SAP S/4HANA, goes far beyond traditional Enterprise Resource Planning (ERP). ERP still constitutes the system's core but is supplemented by the Supply Chain Management systems (WMS and TMS) and planning and analytics sub-systems. Therefore, we submit that Enterprise Systems are a subgroup of enterprise application software, which meets the following criteria jointly:

- are organisation-wide – i.e. support major business processes and management functions of an enterprise;
- are standard – i.e. are delivered as a packaged software which may be configured and/or customised to the specific needs of an organisation;
- are integrated – i.e. include mechanisms of automatic propagation of information within the system (e.g. through the common database).

In other words – the Enterprise System is the central system in a company and a primary source of information. We suggest a label enterprise application software (or enterprise applications) to cover a broader category of "any software system that allows an organisation to operate its business and manage its data to achieve specific goals" [1].

Based on the above discussion, we provide the refined definition of an Enterprise System as the answer to the **RQ2: What is the up-to-date definition of an Enterprise System?** - *Enterprise System (ES) is a standard, integrated, configurable, and customisable, organisation-wide, multi-component Information System covering major business processes and management functions of an enterprise. It constitutes a primary and predominant source of information for the organisation and consists of transactional and analytical applications, including Enterprise Resource Planning (ERP), Supply Chain Management (SCM), Business Intelligence/Business Analytics and others.*

In addition, SAP provides complementary enterprise software applications which may be integrated with SAP S/4HANA to constitute an Enterprise Applications Suite. Other complementary enterprise software applications provided by SAP include:

- SAP Ariba – building a network of suppliers with a broad scope of processing transactional and non-transactional data of sourcing and procurement processes;
- SAP SuccessFactors – creating a solid alternative for standalone HR solutions delivered from the cloud;
- SAP Fieldglass – supporting external services procurement and managing workforce beyond the organisational boundaries;
- SAP Concur – providing self-service for employees by managing business trips. Concur services start from travel planning, purchasing required services, and document scanning and end with the final settlement of all related travel costs;
- SAP Digital Manufacturing Cloud – performing the role of a modern Manufacturing Execution System. It provides short-term production planning and scheduling functions, shop floor management, quality management, and manufacturing analytics. It integrates with other standalone MES solutions, production lines and IoT devices. Its typical activity comprises identifying bottlenecks and optimising user workflows by reading sensors and machines on the shop floor.

Together, those systems form the Enterprise Application Suite. Although the systems mentioned above include integration tools and scenarios with SAP S/4HANA, one can imagine an architecture where the Enterprise System and the other supplementary enterprise software applications come from different sources on a best-of-breed basis, as the integration between the systems has to be established.

4   Deployment Options for an Enterprise System

In this section, we aim to answer the following research questions:

- RQ3: What deployment options for Enterprise Systems do modern enterprises have?
- RQ4: What implications are related to each of the ES deployment options?

The answer to RQ3, regarding the SAP S/4HANA system, can be derived from the documents describing SAP's current offering (Difference between SAP S/4HANA: Public Vs Private edition, 2023; [10]; SAP S/4HANA Cloud and On-Premise Deployment Options I SAP Blogs, 2019). According to SAP, the SAP S/4HANA system is available via the following deployment options:

- SAP S/4HANA Cloud, public edition/essential edition – is a Software as a Service (SaaS), subscription-based offering on multi-tenant cloud infrastructure, delivered and managed by SAP. The functionality is limited to the so-called core ERP, which is pre-configured. The extensions or alterations of the existing code are not permitted.
- SAP S/4HANA Cloud, private edition – is a subscription-based, SAP-managed, single-tenant cloud solution based on a dedicated landscape of a cloud infrastructure operated by SAP and running at a Hyperscaler, e.g. Microsoft Azure, AWS, Google Cloud. It offers full SAP S/HANA functionality, as well as complete configuration and customisation options;
- SAP S/4HANA on-premise or on-premise in the cloud – is a perpetual license solution in which the responsibility for the management and maintenance of the whole infrastructure is on the client or may be subcontracted to the independent cloud provider, like Microsoft Azure, AWS or Google Cloud. It provides full SAP S/4HANA functionality. It leaves the clients full responsibility but gives them full authority to configure and customise the system.

Setting aside a business/legal dimension, i.e. whom the client pays to, one can extract the following criteria for differentiating between the above options:

- functionality/scope;
- configuration options – i.e. the possibility to adopt the system to the company's needs via setting configuration parameters;
- customisation options – i.e. the possibility to adopt the system to the company's needs via adding the programming code or altering the existing code;
- responsibility for the system maintenance on the functional level;
- responsibility for the system maintenance on the technical level;
- responsibility for the infrastructure.

The classification of SAP S/4HANA deployment options according to the criteria mentioned above is presented in Table 2.

Table 2. Classification of SAP S/4HANA deployment options

Deployment option	Scope	Configuration	Customisation	Functional maintenance	Technical maintenance	Infrastructure
Cloud, public edition	Limited	Limited	Limited	Provider	Provider	Provider
Cloud, private edition; on-premise in the cloud	Full	Full	Full	Client	Provider/ client	Provider
On-premise	Full	Full	Full	Client	Client	Client

Summing up, there are the following deployment options:

- Public cloud – multi-tenant standard solution delivered on a Software-as-a-service basis. It offers limited functionality and restricted configuration options. No customisation via programming is possible as, on the technical level, the system is shared by multiple clients. The system is pre-configured and requires limited configuration to be ready to use.

- Private cloud/on-premise in the cloud – single-tenant cloud solution delivered on an Infrastructure as a Service (IaaS) or Platform as a Service (PaaS) basis. The client rents either a piece of infrastructure (IaaS) or a piece of infrastructure together with a vanilla system (PaaS) from the cloud supplier. The system is dedicated to one client, and the client is responsible for configuring and customising the system to its needs (usually with a third-party ES consultancy) and maintaining it on the functional level. A cloud provider is responsible for maintaining the infrastructure and (in some options) for maintaining the system on a technical level (e.g. patching the system or performing technical upgrades).
- On-premise – the system is installed, configured, customised and maintained in the data centre owned by the client. The client is responsible for all the elements of the hardware and software.

The information in the table also allows us to answer the RQ4: What implications are related to each ES deployment option?

Implication 1. Cloud-based, SaaS Enterprise Systems (here SAP S/4HANA Cloud, public addition and SAP S4HANA Cloud, extended edition) offer limited adjustment options. Although this conclusion is intuitive, it does not seem to gain enough traction in the literature. If the system is offered in the cloud to multiple clients, it cannot be adjusted precisely to the needs of any of those clients. Such a system offers ready-to-use functionality on a take-it-or-leave-it basis, with limited configuration options and no customisation options. A company choosing a SaaS cloud-based Enterprise System faces a trade-off: it gains access to a system at a relatively low cost, with relatively low employee engagement, but the system cannot be adjusted to fit the enterprise's processes. Therefore, cloud-based SaaS solutions are fit as entry-level for small or simple businesses. Whether they can serve medium or big enterprises is a matter of doubt and should be subject to careful research.

Implication 2. Infrastructure as a Service (IaaS) or Platform as a Service (PaaS) cloud offering (here SAP S/4HANA Cloud, private edition and On-premise in the cloud) provides the client with elasticity regarding functional adjustments of the system to the company's needs. It also releases the client from the technical, repetitive, non-value-adding tasks related to infrastructure maintenance. This option is viable for medium-sized and big enterprises which do not have the scale to employ their IT department. Another factor is whether functional adjustments and further functional maintenance are done in-house or subcontracted to external consultancy.

As Enterprise Systems cover the core processes of an enterprise, including the value-adding processes which diversify an enterprise from its competitors, it is implausible that it would be viable to change those processes so that they fit a ready-to-use, off-the-shelf, public cloud system. A private cloud seems a more viable option for mid-sized and big enterprises, as it outsources the technical, repetitive, non-value-adding tasks and leaves the company free to shape the system according to its functional needs. While researching "cloud adoption", a common theme in the literature, it is necessary to clearly define what "cloud" means and what services are moved to it.

5 Research Directions in the Area of Enterprise Systems

Based on the current trends in Enterprise Systems architecture and deployment options, we suggest the following research directions for the future.

Architecture - as Enterprise Systems provide a scope which is both very broad and deep, a question arises of how a target architecture looks like in companies. What are the determinants shaping this architecture? When and why do companies implement a monolithic Enterprise System, and when do they opt for a best-of-breed approach?

Implementation - the implementation process of an ERP component of an Enterprise System is a complex, timely, and resource-consuming endeavour. The system needs to be tailored to the company's needs through configuration and (in most cases) customisation. The implementation of the whole scope of an Enterprise System in one big bang is even more complex and risky. Therefore, the question arises: how do companies approach the implementation of an ES? How do they phase the projects?

Cloud - as was stated in the above sections – offering an Enterprise System in a public cloud drastically reduces the possibilities of configuring and customising the system. Much research must be done to precisely diagnose what cloud Enterprise Systems offer, who uses them, and what trade-offs those users face.

6 Conclusions

The first aim of this paper was to analyse the up-to-date architecture of an Enterprise System based on SAP S/4HANA and present a refined definition of this class of systems. As a result, the following definition of an Enterprise System was presented: Enterprise System (ES) is a standard, integrated, configurable, customisable, organisation-wide, multi-component Information System covering major business processes and management functions of an enterprise. It constitutes a primary and predominant source of information for the organisation and consists of transactional and analytical applications, including Enterprise Resource Planning (ERP), Supply Chain Management (SCM), Business Intelligence/Business Analytics and others.

Current Enterprise Systems offer functionality far beyond the traditional scope of an Enterprise Resource Planning (ERP) system. They integrate ERP and Supply Chain Management and offer forecasting, planning and analytics functionality. Such a variety of options offers new opportunities for process re-design and harmonisation for the companies which implement and use modern Enterprise Systems. However, new challenges related to an even more complex implementation process also arise.

The second aim of the paper was to examine the possible deployment options for modern Enterprise Systems and evaluate the implications of these options. Although the current trend of moving information systems into the cloud is also present in Enterprise Systems, one has to keep in mind that multi-tenant offering in a public cloud is related to high readiness to use but also to limited possibilities of adjusting the system to the needs of a client company. The possible clients of cloud ES should be aware of this trade-off. Moving the infrastructure into the cloud on an IaaS or PaaS basis, with the system under the client's control, is a different, promising direction. Therefore, while discussing or researching the cloud, it is necessary to precisely define what infrastructure, systems and/or services are being analysed.

Finally, we outlined the possible future directions regarding Enterprise Systems. As Enterprise Systems have evolved significantly, the research questions regarding the target architecture, deployment variants and implementation process in enterprises worldwide need to be re-addressed.

References

1. Almutairi, A., Naeem, M.A., Weber, G.: Understanding enterprise systems adaptability: An exploratory survey. Procedia Computer Science **197**, 743–750 (2021)
2. Appelbaum, D., Kogan, A., Vasarhelyi, M., Yan, Z.: Impact of business analytics and enterprise systems on managerial accounting. Int. J. Account. Inf. Syst. **25**(March), 29–44 (2017)
3. Arasanmi, C.N., Wang, W.Y.C., Singh, H.: Examining the motivators of training transfer in an enterprise systems context. Enterprise Information Systems **11**(8), 1154–1172 (2017)
4. Bi, Z., Xu, L.D., Wang, C.: Internet of things for enterprise systems of modern manufacturing. IEEE Trans. Industr. Inf. **10**(2), 1537–1546 (2014)
5. Difference between SAP S/4HANA: Public Vs Private edition: RISE with SAP | SAP Blogs. Retrieved 10 February 2023. https://blogs.sap.com/2022/04/04/difference-between-sap-s-4hana-public-vs-private-edition-rise-with-sap/
6. Gartner Information Technology Glossary. Retrieved 15 February 2023. https://www.gartner.com/en/information-technology/glossary/enterprise-application-software
7. Getting Started With SAP S/4HANA. Retrieved 20 February 2023. https://help.sap.com/doc/819cdef021e44d7aad27b31c8bb1ebfc/2022/en-US/START_OP2022.pdf
8. Humlung, O., Haddara, M.: The hero's journey to innovation: gamification in enterprise systems. Procedia Comp. Sci. **164**, 86–95 (2019)
9. Jiang, J.J., Klein, G., Chang, J.Y.T.: Teamwork behaviors in implementing enterprise systems with multiple projects: results from chinese firms. J. Syst. Softw. **157**, 110392 (2019)
10. Kofalt, J.: A buyers guide to S/4HANA cloud extended edition (EX). Retrieved 04 March 2023. https://www.techtarget.com/searchsap/feature/S-4HANA-Cloud-extended-edition-EX-Buying-team-overview
11. Lech, P.: Tailoring the enterprise system to the organisational needs - the case of SAP implementation, European, Mediterranean & Middle Eastern Conference on Information Systems, pp. 224–231 (2016)
12. Leonard, J., Higson, H.: A strategic activity model of enterprise system implementation and use: scaffolding fluidity. J. Strat. Inf. Syst. **23**(1), 62–86 (2014)
13. Market Share: Enterprise Application Software, Worldwide, 2020 (2021). Retrieved 12 February 2023. https://www.gartner.com/en/documents/4001203
14. Nakayama, M., Hustad, E., Sutcliffe, N.: Agility and system documentation in large-scale enterprise system projects: A knowledge management perspective. Procedia Comp. Sci. **181**, 386–393 (2021)
15. SAP Transformation Navigator. Retrieved 10 March, 2023. https://support.sap.com/en/tools/upgrade-transformation-tools/transformation-navigator.html
16. SAP S/4HANA Cloud 2208 Feature Scope Description (2022). Retrieved 13 February 2023. https://help.sap.com/s4hanacloud
17. SAP S/4HANA 2022 Feature Scope Description (2022). Retrieved 12 February 2023. https://help.sap.com/s4hana_op_2022
18. SAP S/4HANA Cloud and On-Premise Deployment Options | SAP Blogs (2019). Retrieved 10 December 2022. https://blogs.sap.com/2019/08/22/sap-s4hana-cloud-and-on-premise-deployment-options/

19. See, B.P., Yap, C.S., Ahmad, R.: Antecedents of continued use and extended use of enterprise systems. Behav. Info. Technol. **38**(4), 384–400 (2019)
20. Shao, Z.: Interaction effect of strategic leadership behaviors and organisational culture on IS-business strategic alignment and enterprise systems assimilation. Int. J. Inf. Manage. **44**(13), 96–108 (2019)
21. Smolander, K., Rossi, M., Pekkola, S.: Heroes, contracts, cooperation, and processes: changes in collaboration in a large enterprise systems project. Inf. Manage. **58**(2), 103407 (2021)
22. Soja, P., Paliwoda-Pekosz, G.: Comparing benefits from enterprise system adoption in transition and developed economies: an ontology-based approach. Inf. Syst. Manag. **30**(3), 198–217 (2013)
23. Top 10 ERP Vendors, Market Size and Market Forecast 2021–2026 (2022). Retrieved 12 February 2023. https://www.appsruntheworld.com/top-10-erp-software-vendors-and-market-forecast/
24. Vos, J.F.J., Boonstra, A.: The influence of cultural values on enterprise system adoption, towards a culture – enterprise system alignment theory. Int. J. Inf. Manage. **63**, 102453 (2022)
25. Zainol, Z., Fernandez, D., Ahmad, H.: Public sector accountants' opinion on impact of a new enterprise system. Procedia Computer Science **124**, 247–254 (2017)

Quality of Experience Studies in TV Systems: Insights and Lessons Learned

Pawel Andruloniw[1]($\boxtimes$), Piotr Zwierzykowski[1], and Karol Kowalik[2]

[1] Institute of Communication and Computer Networks, Faculty of Computing and Telecommunications, Poznań University of Technology, Fiberhost S.A., Poznan, Poland
pawel.andruloniw@doctorate.put.poznan.pl,
piotr.zwierzykowski@put.poznan.pl
[2] Fiberhost S.A., Poznań, Poland
karol.kowalik@fiberhost.com

Abstract. The evaluation of video quality in over-the-top (OTT) services is crucial to customer satisfaction, which ultimately determines customer loyalty and profitability. This evaluation may take place objectively based on signal-related metrics or subjectively by considering the customer's subjective feelings when consuming content. This short paper presents a subjective quality survey in the DSCQS formula implemented in a production television system using adaptive streaming. The survey is implemented in the form of two video sequences. TV users were asked to rate their perception of video quality on a scale of 1 to 100. Additional information was collected regarding age, viewing level, and vision correction. When designing a survey of this type, it is important to remember that you may get results that are not related to the actual perceived video quality of the test sequence. It could be feedback after a crash or degradation of the TV service or even other Internet related services. The study was developed as part of the QoE rating estimation system for live TV services.

Keywords: over-the-top · subjective assessment · adaptive streaming · dscqs

1 Introduction

The Quality of Experience (QoE) assessment in video systems considers aspects that reflect the user's subjective feelings towards the content in question. The implementation of a suitable method to achieve such an assessment might be challenging depending on the video system. Profits from video streaming-based applications are predicted to increase by 82% for Eastern European countries by 2029 compared to 2023 (Digital TV Research, 2024). Similar increases are predicted for many other regions. This indicates that people are becoming more willing to consume video content. Given the high level of competition, it is important to investigate whether the delivered quality of video streams is satisfactory to customers. An objective video assessment can take into account various metrics related to Quality of Service (QoS), such as availability, latency or jitter. QoE algorithms that objectively assess video quality can analyze video frames and measure

K. S. Soliman (Ed.): IBIMA-AI 2024, CCIS 2299, pp. 267–273, 2025.
https://doi.org/10.1007/978-3-031-77493-5_23

their quality level based on no-reference methods, which do not require comparison to the original video [8]. Subjective methods provide a slightly different assessment of video quality compared to objective methods. The assessment can vary each time, even when we are talking about images of the same quality and the same assessor. The final value depends on the assessor's current feelings, perception and even mood. It takes into account both technical aspects of the signal and non-technical aspects related to the user's perception, i.e. actually assessing the video quality of a given OTT service. The use of subjective assessment in a ready-made system can often require adjustments that are not feasible. Different surveys have been performed in different ways. For example, a common approach is to perform the survey on personal computers and a small screen. Unfortunately, in this way the results may not be representative of services viewed on TV. Many surveys are performed on TVs or larger displays by plugging the screen into a computer, or using a dedicated web application. This approach yields a score that reflects the perception of quality on a large screen. In the case of TV services provided via a set-top box (STB) device, there is another difference related to the adaptation algorithm on the device. A web or PC application may adapt the stream differently than a set-top box with closed software. To address this difference and perform the test in the same environment in which the customer watches the TV service, it was decided to use the VOD catalog of the TV service. By placing the test sequences in the on-demand movie catalog, we ensure that the set-top box user will perform the test on the same set-top box, TV, and even on the same network. This article presents an example implementation of the method for collecting user ratings in a production TV system based on adaptive streaming technology. The second section describes subjective quality in video services. In the third section, we present the implementation of the chosen method on a production TV system. The fourth section presents a summary, conclusions, and outlines future work.

2   Assessment Outline

The International Telecommunications Union has issued recommendations BT.500–15 on the study of subjective perception of video quality [5]. The recommendation includes single and double stimulation methods, as well as methods based on analysis by a single observer and a group of evaluators. Additionally, various rating scales in discrete and continuous approaches that can address quality and distortion are indicated. The methods described in BT.500–15 have been applied in many different studies. It has been verified that a rating of 3.0 is the lower limit of video quality for mass systems. Below this rating, video quality is more likely to be perceived negatively. An average rating of 3.5 may be an acceptable limit of distortion for the average observer [10]. The EVP expert method and the hidden reference method were compared to see if the ratings of average observers and experts were different. It was found that the assessors used the available rating scale ranges at about the same level [9]. The DSCQS method was used to check what bitrate level for the H.264 codec and 4 K resolution guarantees good quality. A value of 23 Mbps resulted in a good score, while 40 Mbps was a quality that was difficult to distinguish from the original [11]. Similarly, the codecs were tested using the DSIS method. In the case of H.264, VP9 and H.265, a score of 4.5 was estimated at bitrates of 4 Mbps in H.264 and VP9 and 3 Mbps in H.265 [1]. The double-stimulus continuous quality scale (DSCQS) method was applied to analyze quality within a production TV system. In this method, videos are displayed in pairs. One of the videos can be selected as a reference for the other. The advantage of this method is the use of a continuous quality level scale (Fig. 1). Rating can be done on a scale of 1 to 100. The score is then divided into five equal parts yielding a floating point Mean Opinion Score (MOS) on the Absolute Category Rating (ACR) scale also proposed by the ITU. By collecting scores on this scale and then dividing to obtain an ACR score, there is less chance of neglecting or underestimating small distortions. With a typical ACR scale of 1 to 5, small distortions may be diminished while greater distortions are exaggerated.

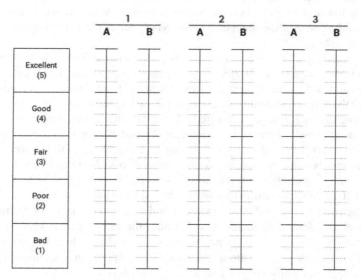

Fig. 1. Continuous-quality scale with ACR division

Another advantage of this method is that it allows for two variants. The first variant is for a single evaluator, who can switch flexibly between films A and B and make an evaluation when he becomes assured. The second variant is a sequence of A and B films, which are displayed according to a predetermined order and number. This option is prepared for multiple evaluators simultaneously. The advantage of the second option is that it allows for more results to be obtained in a shorter time with respect to the first variant. The evaluation is conducted after the evaluator has viewed both videos in the pair. Sessions should not exceed 30 min to prevent evaluator fatigue.

3 Implementation on Production TV System

The DSCQS assessment has been implemented in a production television system, where video is provided using HTTP adaptive streaming technology. The streams are delivered using the MPEG-DASH protocol [4]. The channels, associated recordings, and other on-demand content are available in streams of several bit rates. The decoder will play the stream that is optimal for the lack of interruptions in the presentation of content, depending on the condition of the network and the current state of the infrastructure. When the state of the system and network is unaffected, the decoder will download the stream with the highest available bit rate, ensuring the best available quality for the selected channel. Typically, bit rates can range from a few hundred kilobits per second to a few or a dozen megabits per second. The bit rate level is related to the resolution of the video, the number of frames per second, and the compression algorithm used. Assuming a consistent compression level for each video stream, it can be concluded that higher video quality will result in a higher bit rate. Adaptive streaming also includes synchronized audio streams. When assessing quality, audio streams are often deprioritized due to their significantly lower bit rate compared to video content. However, it is crucial to consider that when audio issues arise, such as lack of synchronization, the expected rating may be negatively affected.

The typical single channel consists of 3–4 video streams, which are compressed using the H.264 codec [6] or H.265 codec [7] and contains one or two audio streams. Recordings and additional content associated with a channel inherit its configuration. To estimate the subjective quality assessment for such content, two test sequences were prepared. The first was compressed with H.264, while the second was compressed with H.265. Each sequence contains 15 video pairs A and B. For H.264-encoded videos, seven streams were prepared with bitrates ranging from 800 kbps to 10 mbps, while for H.265 there are five streams ranging from 1 mbps to over 6 mbps. In total, a database of 180 test videos with different bit rates was prepared. A total of 30 H.264-encoded videos and 30 H.265-encoded videos were selected from the entire video database. The images were paired with a reference image A and a second image B. In each sequence, a pair was placed for which image A and B have the same quality. This method tests the evaluators' vigilance. The sequence begins with a welcome board with instructions, then a QR code is displayed with a link to a mobile app where ratings can be made. Next, a test sequence consisting of four videos is displayed.

The videos provide an overview of the test method, duration, and available quality. Once the test sequence is complete, the actual sequence is displayed, consisting of 15 pairs of A and B videos. Each video lasts 30 s. The assessor watches the pair of videos, followed by a brief board requesting a rating. At this point, the user makes the evaluation. In the DSCQS method, it is permissible to make an evaluation while watching the second video of the pair. Figure 2 illustrates the structure of the study sequence. The entire study takes under 24 min.

Furthermore, the evaluation form includes an additional page with four questions about the age of the evaluator, visual defects, the correction used during the test, and the size of the screen on which the test was performed (Table 1). The additional information is being collected to determine if factors such as age or visual impairment can affect the level of assessment. With further use of such data, it would be possible to vary the level of estimated assessment according to age or the vision correction used.

The assessments are collected via a form accessible via the mobile app. The user scans a QR code displayed throughout the survey to gain access to the corresponding form. The rating scale is designed as a continuous scale, therefore the response fields

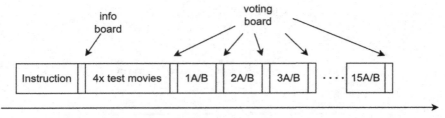

Fig. 2. DSCQS sequence structure

Table 1. Available extension questions and answers after assessment

No.	Question	Available answers
1	How old are you?	under 18/18–25/26–39/40–59/60 and over
2	Do you have a visual impairment?	yes/no
3	Do you currently have glasses or contact lenses that help you to see properly?	yes/no
4	What is the size of the TV screen on which the survey is being conducted?	under 30 inches/31–42 inches/43–55 inches/56 and over

had to be implemented as sliders with 1 point accuracy. On a single page two sliders are displayed. Above the sliders, a division into five equal parts according to the ACR scale is displayed (Fig. 3a). Once the survey is completed, the scores are sent to a system that aggregates the data.

The test sequences have been placed in the VOD catalog, allowing them to be accessed by any user. Alternatively, the test can be performed in organized groups in a prepared laboratory. The evaluation form was also prepared in paper form for those who do not have a phone capable of scanning QR codes. The use of the QR code has eliminated the problem associated with data collection for individual evaluations at users' homes.

4   Lessons Learned and Conclusions

The preparation and implementation of the survey presented several challenges. For subjective evaluation of TV systems based on set-top boxes, it was essential that the survey could be carried out by making the content available through set-top boxes and displaying it on the TV. To illustrate, a video encoded at 6 Mbps would be displayed differently on a TV set and in a video sharing app, such as YouTube, due to the additional compression. Another aspect to consider is data collection. The DSCQS survey requires a continuous scale, so the assessment form must be implemented to cover this requirement. Evaluations collected on a sheet of paper have a reading error related to the size of the printed scale and the care taken by the evaluator to mark it. Preparing a form that is

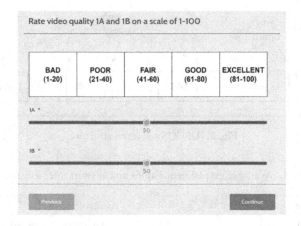

(a)

(b)

Fig. 3. Single page from the evaluation form – (a). Evaluation sequences in the VOD catalogue available on the STB – (b).

accessible via QR code as a mobile app significantly solves the problem of making it available to a wider population. Ultimately, the collected assessments must be analyzed for their reliability. Default values on the sliders are 50. It may happen that a user, out of curiosity, fills out a form in a few minutes giving a default answer. In addition, there is the possibility of getting negative ratings alone due to the user's bad mood, which was aroused by a malfunctioning service. Operators often provide bundled services providing Internet and TV as one. Problems with the Internet that do not affect the quality of the video, but make the customer unable to use this service can provoke such a person to send negative ratings alone. It is important to keep in mind the possibility of such ratings and filter them out accordingly. Further research will be related to analyzing the obtained ratings and using them to create machine learning-based models to estimate user ratings. Such estimation can be used for proactive monitoring of services in the TV system.

Acknowledgments. The authors thank the Polish Ministry of Education and Science for financial support (Applied Doctorate Program, No. DWD/4/24/2020).

This research was funded in part by the Polish Ministry of Science and Higher Education (No. 0313/SBAD/1311).

References

1. Brachmański, S., Klink, J.: Subjective assessment of the quality of video sequences by the young viewers. 2022 International Conference on Software. Telecommunications and Computer Networks (SoftCOM) (2022)
2. Digital TV Research: digitaltvresearch.com (2024). https://digitaltvresearch.com/product/eastern-europe-ott-tv-and-video-forecasts/. Accessed 11 June 2024
3. ISO/IEC: ISO/IEC 23009, Information technology — Dynamic adaptive streaming over HTTP (DASH) (2022)
4. ITU-R,. BT.500-15 Methodologies for the subjective assessment of the quality of television images. Geneva: ITU-R (2023)
5. ITU-T: Recommendation H.264 (08/21) (2021)
6. ITU-T: Recommendation H.265 (08/21) (2021)
7. Kowalik, K., Andruloniw, P., Partyka, B., Zwierzykowski, P.: Telecom operator's approach to QoE. J. Telecomm. Info. Technol. **30**(06), 26–34 (2022)
8. Pastor, A., et al.: "Discriminability-Experimental Cost" tradeoff in subjective video quality assessment of codec: DCR with EVP rating scale versus ACR-HR. 2024 Picture Coding Symposium (PCS) (2024)
9. Sugito, Y., Bertalmio, M.: Non-experts or experts? statistical analyses of MOS using DSIS method. ICASSP 2020 - 2020 IEEE International Conference on Acoustics, Speech and Signal Processing (ICASSP) (2020)
10. Xu, J., Jiang, X.: Assessment of subjective video quality on 4K ultra high definition videos. 2015 8th International Congress on Image and Signal Processing (CISP) (2015)

Self-optimizing SD-WAN

Dariusz Gasior[✉]

Faculty of Information and Communication Technology, Wroclaw University of Technology,
Wroclaw, Poland
dariusz.gasior@pwr.edu.pl

Abstract. The paper concerns resource management in the Software-Defined Wide Area Networks (SD-WANs). In the context of SD-WAN, SDN principles are extended to manage and optimize traffic across geographically dispersed networks, crucial for large enterprises and service providers. The paper highlights the Virtual Network Embedding (VNE) problem, which involves mapping virtual network nodes and links to physical network resources, ensuring efficient resource allocation, and meeting Quality of Service (QoS) requirements. The proposed solution framework, the Automatic Resource Managing System (ARMS), leverages machine learning for problem classification and algorithm selection, enhancing resource management automation in SDNs. The paper also explores the application of Vertical Federated Learning (VFL) in multi-domain SD-WANs, allowing collaborative yet privacy-preserving resource management across different network domains. Initial experimental results demonstrate the feasibility of the proposed approach, showing promising accuracy, precision, and recall metrics for algorithm selection in VNE problems.

Keywords: resource allocation · resource management · sdn · networking

1 Introduction

Software-Defined Networking (SDN) has emerged as one of the most critical and transformative topics in the field of networking, as highlighted by numerous industry publications e.g., by [7] and [2]. The traditional network architecture, characterized by its rigidity and complexity, often struggles to meet the dynamic demands of modern network environments. SDN addresses these challenges by decoupling the control plane from the data plane, thereby providing centralized network management and programmable network configurations. This paradigm shift enables more flexible, efficient, and scalable network operations.

Particularly noteworthy is the application of SDN in wide-area networks (WANs), where the benefits of centralized control and programmability can be maximized. The ability to manage and optimize traffic flows across vast and geographically dispersed networks is essential for service providers and large enterprises alike. SDN facilitates the dynamic allocation of resources, improves fault tolerance, and enhances overall network performance and security. As such, SDN in the context of WANs is not only

K. S. Soliman (Ed.): IBIMA-AI 2024, CCIS 2299, pp. 274–289, 2025.
https://doi.org/10.1007/978-3-031-77493-5_24

a technical advancement but also a strategic imperative for organizations aiming to maintain competitive advantage in a rapidly evolving digital landscape.

Some concepts of possible SD-WAN architecture have been already developed and presented e.g., by [20] and [21]. However, researchers indicate that there are still very few results concerning methods and algorithms concerning resource management for SD-WAN (see publications by [21] and [19]. We believe our result is a step towards filling this gap.

2 Resource Management in Software-Defined Networks

2.1 SDN Basis

Software-Defined Networking (SDN) represents a revolutionary approach to designing, building, and managing networks (for more details see book by [9]. The fundamental principle behind SDN is the decoupling of the network control plane from the data plane, allowing for more flexible and efficient network management. In traditional networking, the control and data planes are tightly integrated within network devices like routers and switches. This integration often leads to complex and static network configurations that are difficult to manage and scale. SDN, however, abstracts the control plane to a centralized controller, enabling a more dynamic and programmable network infrastructure.

One of the primary features of SDN is that its control mechanism is either centralized or at least act as centralized as it is described by [6]. The SDN controller, which acts as the brain of the network, has a comprehensive view of the entire network, and can make intelligent decisions based on global network information. This centralization allows for more efficient traffic management, improved network utilization, and easier implementation of complex policies. Network administrators can program the network behavior using software applications that communicate with the SDN controller via standardized interfaces like OpenFlow as it is described in book by [1]. This programmability enables rapid deployment of new services, real-time network adjustments, and fine-grained control over network traffic.

Another significant aspect of SDN is its ability to support network virtualization. SDN can create multiple virtual networks on top of a single physical infrastructure, each with its own set of policies and controls. This capability is particularly beneficial for data centers and cloud environments, where it is essential to isolate and manage diverse workloads efficiently. Network virtualization allows for greater flexibility, resource optimization, and enhanced security by segregating traffic between different tenants or applications.

2.2 Virtual Networks as an Effective Way to Manage Resources in SDN

In the context of Software-Defined Networking (SDN), virtual networks play a crucial role by enabling more efficient and flexible management of network resources (for more details concerning SDNs see publications [4, 5]. Virtual networks leverage this capability to abstract physical network resources, creating multiple isolated virtual networks on a shared physical infrastructure. It must be determined where should be located each node of the virtual network and what path in the physical network should be used to serve as the virtual link. This process is called the Virtual Network Embedding (VNE) problem and its idea is shown in Fig. 1. This abstraction is achieved using technologies like virtual LANs (VLANs) as it is described by Lehocine et al. (2017), virtual private networks (VPNs), and overlay networks, which encapsulate data packets to maintain separation and proper routing.

Resource management in SDN with virtual networks involves dynamically allocating and reallocating physical network resources to meet the specific needs of each virtual network (for further details see publication by [10]. This process, known as resource reservation, ensures that each virtual network receives the necessary bandwidth, latency, and reliability. Resource reservation starts with defining service level agreements (SLAs) or policies that outline the required performance characteristics for different types of network traffic. For instance, critical applications may need guaranteed bandwidth and low latency, while other services might be more flexible.

SDN controllers play a key role in this process by automating the configuration of network devices such as switches and routers. These devices are programmed to prioritize and allocate resources according to the needs of each virtual network. Advanced SDN tools can dynamically adjust these allocations based on real-time network conditions and traffic patterns, using algorithms and artificial intelligence to optimize resource usage.

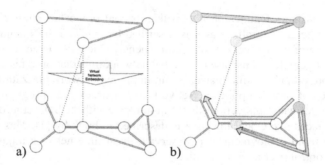

Fig. 1. Illustration of virtual network embedding process.

In Software Defined Networks (SDNs), it is assumed that a network application generates a request outlining the requirements for all data transmissions to be served. Practically, this is a virtual network request. This request is sent to the SDN controller via the northbound interface. The SDN controller must then determine if there are sufficient resources to set up the required virtual network, a process known as admission control. If the request is accepted, the next step is to map the virtual nodes to the physical nodes. The application's requirements may specify strict relationships between these nodes, or there might be multiple possible mappings for some virtual nodes. During the mapping process, the computing resources of the physical nodes need to be reserved. Usually, the required resources are specified as a minimum value, but reserving more can improve user experience and potential future revenue. Once node mapping is complete, virtual links must be established. If the two physical nodes hosting adjacent virtual nodes are not directly connected, the virtual link must be routed through the physical network. Finally, the necessary resources on the physical links must be reserved.

To illustrate this, consider a telemedical application with a patient needing urgent medical consultation. A high-quality video conference between the patient and their doctor is required. Additionally, the doctor needs access to the patient's medical records, which are stored on two different servers. Data transmission must occur between the doctor's node and one of these storage servers. If the SDN controller finds sufficient resources, the mapping procedures begin, as shown in Fig. 1a. The mappings between the virtual nodes for the doctor and patient are predetermined. The SDN controller decides which physical node will host the virtual node related to the storage server. Once this decision is made, the necessary computing resources on these nodes are reserved. Then, the routes between the chosen physical nodes are determined to serve as virtual links, as depicted in Fig. 1b.

Assuming a fluid flow network model, we may try to give a general formulation of the Virtual Network Embedding problem which is a crucial task related to resource management for virtual network environments. Let us introduce the following notation:

N_s – a set of physical network vertices.

E_s – a set of physical network links (edges).

d_{uv}^{ji} – a binary indicator if the physical link between nodes u and v may be used by ith virtual link in jth virtual network,

z_v^{ji} – a binary indicator if the physical node v may be used by ith virtual link in jth virtual network,

C_{uv} – the amount of available capacity on the physical link between nodes u and v,

R_v – the amount of available computing resources in the vth physical node.

J – a set of virtual networks; j – virtual network's index.

I_j – a set of virtual links in jth virtual network; i – virtual link's index.

$b_{min}^{ji} \geq 0$ – a minimal required amount of the link's capacity that may be allocated for ith virtual link in jth virtual network (QoS requirement);

b_{max}^{ji} – a maximal possible amount of the link's capacity that may be allocated for ith virtual link in jth virtual network (operator's constraint);

$r_{m,min}^{j} \geq 0$ – a minimal required amount of the computing resources for virtual node m in jth virtual network (QoS requirement);

$r_{m,max}^{j}$ – a maximal possible amount of the computing resources for virtual node m in jth virtual network that may be allocated (operator's constraint);

$\overline{x}_{mv}^{j}$ – binary indicator if it is possible to map (locate) virtual node m in jth virtual network to physical node v.

Let optimization variables be defined as follows (see Fig. 2):

b^{ji} – ith virtual link's capacity (in jth virtual network).

x_{mv}^{j} – a variable indicating mapping a virtual node m (in jth virtual network) to a physical node v.

f_{uv}^{ji} – the total amount of flow (virtual link mapping) between physical nodes u and v establishing part of ith virtual link in jth virtual network,

r_m^{j} – the amount of computing resources allocated to the virtual node m in jth virtual network.

p^j – variable indicating if jth virtual network is accepted (admission control)

$$\mathbf{b} = \left[b^{ji} \right], \mathbf{x} = [x_{mv}^j], \mathbf{f} = \left[f_{uv}^{ji} \right], \mathbf{r} = [r_m^j], \mathbf{p} = \left[p^j \right]$$

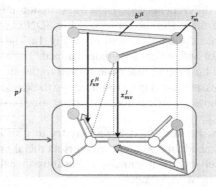

Fig. 2. Optimization variables for Virtual Network Embedding problem.

For the VNE problem, we should consider the following constraints:

- communication resources' constraints:

$$\forall_{u,v \in N_S \cup N_{S'}} \sum_j \sum_i p^j (f_{uv}^{ji} + f_{vu}^{ji}) \leq C_{uv}$$

- computing resources' constraints:

$$\forall_{m \in N_{S'}} \forall_{v \in N_S} \sum_j \sum_m p^j x_{mv}^{ji} r_m^j \leq R_v$$

- flow preservation constraints:

$$\forall_j \forall_i \forall_{u \in N_S} \sum_{v \in N_S} f_{uv}^{ji} - \sum_{v \in N_S} f_{vu}^{ji} = 0$$

$$\forall_j \forall_i \sum_{v \in N_S} x_{s_{ji}v}^{ij} f_{s_{ji}v}^{ji} - \sum_{v \in N_S} x_{s_{ji}v}^{ij} f_{vs_{ji}}^{ji} = p^j b^{ji}$$

$$\forall_j \forall_i \sum_{v \in N_S} x_{t_{ji}v}^{ij} f_{vt_{ji}}^{ji} - \sum_{v \in N_S} x_{t_{ji}v}^{ij} f_{vt_{ji}}^{ji} = p^j b^{ji}$$

- routing constraints:

$$\left(f_{uv}^{ji} + f_{vu}^{ji} \right) \leq M a_{uv}^{ji}$$

$$\sum_u \left(f_{uv}^{ji} + f_{vu}^{ji} \right) \leq M z_v^{ji}$$

where M is a big number.

 – a virtual node may be mapped only to the one of indicated physical nodes:

$$\forall_j \forall_i \forall_{m \in N_{S'}} \forall_{v \in N_S} x_{mv}^{ji} \le \bar{x}_{mv}^{ji}$$

 – a virtual node must be placed (mapped) somewhere if the corresponding virtual network is accepted and it may be placed only on one physical node:

$$\forall_{m \in N_{S'}} \sum_{v \in N_S} x_{mv}^{ji} = p^j$$

 – minimal link's capacity constraints:

$$\forall_j \forall_i b^{ji} \ge p^j b_{min}^{ji}$$

 – minimal computing resources for nodes:

$$\forall_j \forall_m r_m^j \ge p^j r_{m,min}^j$$

 – maximal link's capacity constraints:

$$\forall_j \forall_i b^{ji} \le p^j b_{max}^{ji}$$

 – maximal computing resources for nodes:

$$\forall_j \forall_m r_m^j \le p^j r_{m,max}^j$$

 – domain constraints:

$$\forall_j \forall_i b^{ji} \ge 0$$

$$\forall_j \forall_m \forall_v x_{mv}^j \in \{0, 1\}$$

$$\forall_j \forall_i \forall_u \forall_v f_{uv}^{ji} \ge 0$$

$$\forall_j \forall_m r_m^j \ge 0$$

$$\forall_j p^j \in \{0, 1\}$$

Many objectives may be considered. Each of them reflects different network administrator's expectations. Some of the possibilities are as follows:

• total QoE (quality of experience):

$$Q(\mathbf{f}, \mathbf{x}, \mathbf{r}, \mathbf{b}, \mathbf{p}) = \sum_j \sum_i w^{ji} \varphi\left(b^{ji}\right)$$

where $\varphi(b^{ji})$ is the iso-elastic utility function as it was proposed by [16] (which may represent QoE as suggested by [11].

– load balancing:

$$Q(\mathbf{f}, \mathbf{x}, \mathbf{r}, \mathbf{b}, \mathbf{p}) = \sum_u \sum_v \left(\frac{\alpha_{uv}}{C_{uv} + \delta} \left(\sum_j p^j \sum_i f_{uv}^{ji} \right) \right) + \sum_v \left(\frac{\beta_v}{R_v + \delta} \left(\sum_j p^j \sum_i x_{mv}^{ji} r_m \right) \right)$$

where δ is a small positive number.

Formally, we may state VNE as the following optimization problem:
Given:

$$N_s, E_S, J, I_j, a_{uv}^{ji}, C_{uv}, R_v, b_{min}^{ji}, b_{max}^{ji}, r_{m,min}^j, r_{m,max}^j, \bar{x}_{mv}^j, Q$$

Find:

$$\mathbf{f}^*, \mathbf{x}^*, \mathbf{r}^*, \mathbf{b}^*, \mathbf{p}^* \rightarrow \max Q(\mathbf{f}, \mathbf{x}, \mathbf{r}, \mathbf{b}, \mathbf{p}) \tag{1}$$

such that given constraints are fulfilled.

In general, it is a mixed non-linear programming problem (MINLP). However, some special cases are considered for practical scenarios. For example, we may consider online VNE problem for fixed $\mathbf{b}, \mathbf{r}, \mathbf{p}$ and $|J| = 1$ as it was presented by [3], online VNE problem for fixed $\mathbf{b}, \mathbf{x}, \mathbf{f}, \mathbf{r}$ and $|J| \geq 1$ as it was suggested by [14], and online VNE problem for fixed $\mathbf{x}, \mathbf{r}, \mathbf{p}$ with given routing and no QoS requirements as proposed by [8].

2.3 Resource Management Automation

Self-organizing networks (SONs) are a transformative concept in the realm of computer networking, characterized by their ability to autonomously configure, manage, optimize, and heal themselves without requiring human intervention as it is described in book by [17]. In the context of Software-Defined Networking (SDN), SONs leverage the decoupled architecture of SDN to automate the management of network resources and dynamically adapt to changes in the network environment. This automation significantly enhances the efficiency, reliability, and scalability of networks, making them more resilient and easier to manage.

A critical aspect of self-organizing networks is their capacity for self-optimization. Self-optimization refers to the network's ability to continuously monitor its performance and dynamically adjust resources to enhance efficiency and performance (Fig. 3). In SDN, this process is facilitated by the centralized SDN controller, which collects real-time data on network traffic, congestion, and performance metrics from various network devices. This data forms the basis for informed decision-making, allowing the SDN controller to reallocate resources, adjust routing paths, and modify network configurations to maintain optimal performance.

Once potential issues are identified, the SDN controller can proactively adjust network configurations to mitigate them. For instance, if the controller detects that a particular link is experiencing high traffic volumes that could lead to congestion, it can dynamically reroute traffic through less congested paths. This rerouting is achieved through

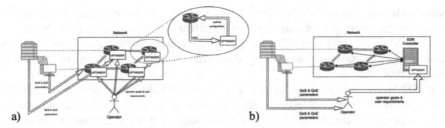

Fig. 3. Idea of self-optimization in a) classic networks b) SDNs.

the programmability of SDN, where the controller sends updated routing instructions to the relevant network devices. By doing so, the network can balance the load more effectively, ensuring that no single path becomes a bottleneck and that traffic flows smoothly across the entire network.

Another key element of self-optimization in SDN is bandwidth management. The SDN controller can allocate bandwidth dynamically based on the current needs and priorities of different types of traffic. For example, during peak usage periods, the controller might prioritize bandwidth for critical applications such as video conferencing or real-time data analytics, while deprioritizing less critical traffic like software updates or non-essential file transfers. This prioritization ensures that essential services maintain high performance and that the overall network remains efficient and responsive.

Quality of Service (QoS) policies play a crucial role in this context. QoS policies define the priority levels and resource allocation rules for different types of network traffic. The SDN controller enforces these policies by configuring network devices accordingly. For example, it can set higher priority levels for voice and video traffic, ensuring low latency and minimal jitter, which are crucial for maintaining call and video quality. By contrast, bulk data transfers can be assigned lower priority, ensuring they do not interfere with more time-sensitive traffic.

Moreover, self-optimization contributes to better resource utilization and cost efficiency. By ensuring that network resources are used effectively, organizations can avoid over-provisioning and reduce unnecessary expenditures. The dynamic allocation of resources also allows for more scalable and flexible network operations, enabling organizations to respond quickly to changing demands and market conditions.

2.4 SD-WAN

Software Defined Wide Area Networks (SD-WAN) can be seen as a multi-domain extension of SDN, essentially functioning as a network of networks. While SDN focuses on managing and optimizing network operations within a single domain, such as a data center or Local Area Network (LAN), SD-WAN expands this concept to cover Wide-Area Networks (WANs).

In SD-WAN, the principles of SDN are applied across multiple network domains, connecting geographically dispersed sites like branch offices, data centers, and cloud services. This integration allows SD-WAN to dynamically route traffic across various connections (such as MPLS, broadband, and LTE) based on real-time conditions and application requirements, optimizing overall network performance and reliability.

Thus, SD-WAN builds on SDN's centralized management and programmability but extends its capabilities to create a cohesive and efficient wide area network by interlinking multiple networks.

In SD-WAN, each network comprising the SD-WAN architecture can be administered and managed by a different entity. The business objectives of these entities may vary, but they must collaborate to serve certain requests. This collaboration ensures that diverse business goals align to achieve shared objectives within the SD-WAN ecosystem.

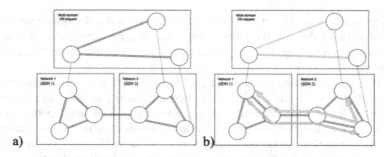

Fig. 4. Virtual Network Embedding in SD-WAN.

The VNE problem may be considered also for SD-WAN as it is shown in Fig. 4 (see Fig. 4a and Fig. 4b correspond to Fig. 1a and Fig. 1b, respectively). However, in this case, to serve the virtual network request two SDN networks must perform appropriate mapping and resource reservation. The result depends on the decisions of both networks' (domains') administrators.

In trying to formulate the VNE problem for SD-WAN we must introduce additional notation:

D – set of domains,

N_S^d – a set of vertices managed in dth domain,

E_S^d – a set of links (edges) managed in dth domain,

J^d – a set of virtual networks that need to use resources in domain d,

b^{jid} – ith virtual link's capacity (in jth virtual network) determined by domain d,

p^{jd} – variable indicating if jth virtual network is accepted (admission control) by domain d,

$$p^j = \min_d \ p^{jd},$$

$$b^{ji} = \min_d \ b^{jid}.$$

Now we may give the problem statement from dth domain perspective:
Given:

$$N_s, E_S, J_d, I_j, d_{u_d v_d}^{jdi}, C_{u_d v_d}, R_{v_d}, b_{min}^{jdi}, b_{max}^{jdi}, r_{m,min}^{jd}, r_{m,max}^{jd}, \overline{x}_{mv}^{jd}$$

Find:

$$\mathbf{f}_d^*, \mathbf{x}_d^*, \mathbf{r}_d^*, \mathbf{b}_d^*, \mathbf{p}_d^* \rightarrow \max Q(\mathbf{f}, \mathbf{x}, \mathbf{r}, \mathbf{b}, \mathbf{p})$$

such that given constraints are fulfilled.

We use an index with subscript d to indicate that this index belongs to a set of indices related to dth domain. Furthermore, we use subscript with optimization variables to indicate that in different domains they may be different since some input data is not known. It means values of:

$$J_q, a_{u_q v_q}^{ji}, C_{u_q v_q}, R_{v_q} (\mathrm{q} \neq d)$$

may not be known.

If domains exchange given data or they send it to some central coordinator (e.g., global SDN controller) the problem is the same as for single–domain networks.

Usually, domains do not want to exchange all the information about network state, local requests, etc. But they accept to exchange some information (H) that:

is based on the local data,
is necessary to solve the problem,
cannot be used to restore the original data (H^{-1} does not exist).

In distributed cases, it may be required to exchange information about the algorithms that are used to solve the problem (if the optimal solutions may not be found in reasonable time and some heuristics need to be used).

3 Proposed SD-WAN Automatic Resource Managing System

In this paper, we propose a framework that enables automatic resource management for SD-WANs. Our proposal is based on the following assumptions:

- usually, the VNE problem does not have to be considered in its general form (1), but the special case given in the literature (e.g., by [3, 8, 14] is to be solved,
- which special case should be considered may be determined based on the current state of the network, the administrator's goals, and requests' descriptions,
- there is a set of possible solution algorithms dedicated to each special case,
- the quality and the performance of the algorithm may depend on the input data (given values of the parameters),
- we may automatically determine the special case of the problem we are dealing with and which of the dedicated algorithms should be used.

However, first, let us introduce the SDN Automatic Resource Managing System which is suitable for centrally managed networks (single domain). The architecture of our SDN Automatic Resource Managing System (ARMS) is depicted in Fig. 5. It consists of two main layers:

- Problem Classification layer,
- Optimization Module layer.

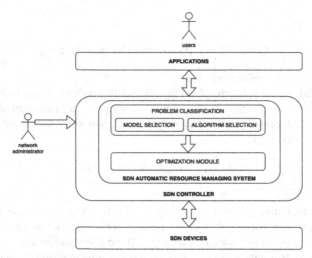

Fig. 5. Architecture of SDN Automatic Resource Managing System (ARMS)

3.1 Problem Classification Layer

The Problem Classification layer is responsible for determining the precise problem version (case) we deal with. It chooses an appropriate model selection. We may try to explain this task as some optimization process.

Model selection. It is quite clear, that for given input data we may use many problem formulations (many mathematical models). We assume that one model is better than the other if the algorithms related to the first model may achieve better performance or quality than the ones related to the other one. The precise objective may be arbitrarily determined and given in terms of function Q.

More formally, we may introduce this problem as follows.

Let I_S be an input data.

Given: I_S

$$M^* \rightarrow \max_{M \in D(I_S)} Q(M, I_S)$$

where:

Q – objective function which evaluates the model M when the input data is I_S.

$D(I_S)$– set of the feasible models for input data I_S.

Algorithm selection. Once we have the problem and related mathematical model determined, we may choose the algorithm that suits best for current task. The algorithm may be evaluated in terms of the execution time or the obtained objective function value.

Given: I_S, M

$$A^* \rightarrow \max_{A \in \Delta(M, I_S)} \Phi(A, I_S, M)$$

where:

Φ – algorithm evaluation function,

M – mathematical model used for a problem with given input data I_S,

$\Delta(M, I_S)$ – set of feasible algorithms that solve problems with input data I_S and mathematical model M.

Both problems may be seen as the classification tasks. Thus, we propose to consider applying some machine learning methods to solve them. In our experiments, we proposed to use neural network (NN) classifiers as it is described e.g., by [15].

3.2 Optimization Module Layer

Optimization Module Layer may be seen as a kind of optimization solver. The solution of the Model Selection problem together with input data generates a problem instance which is further used with the algorithm chosen by solving the Algorithm Selection problem as it is presented in Fig. 6.

The algorithm is run in the SDN controller, and the obtained solution is transformed into the network devices' configurations.

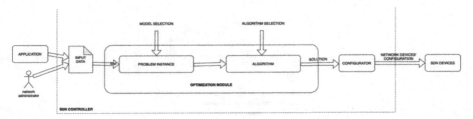

Fig. 6. Architecture of the optimization module.

3.3 Automatic Resource Managing System for Multidomain SDN (SD-WAN)

Now, we may introduce the automatic resource managing system, which is based on the introduced one but is more suitable for multidomain SDNs. Such a system consists of a central SD-WAN coordinator and a set of local auxiliary SDN controllers – one for each domain. So, the architecture is compatible with the one proposed e.g., by Wang et al. (2013) and it is depicted in Fig. 7. Since the proposed Problem Classification layer in SDN Controller consists of two neural network classifiers, we propose to apply Vertical Federated Learning (VFL) approach in a way given by [13]. When applying VFL, we expect that there are many data sources. Every source has partial data concerning the same example. Some computations are to be performed locally on devices next to data sources. Such devices are called parties. There are many parties, but it is assumed that one knows the real output, while others – do not. The ML (machine learning) model is divided into modules. The active party's module takes the outputs of all the passive parties' modules as its input. Modules are partial models. The output of the active party's module is the final output (of the model).

This approach fits perfectly since:

– Each SDN domain knows only its part of the user's requirements.

- Each SDN domain knows its state (and usually does not want to share this information).
- The network state must be reflected in ML features.
- The SD-WAN coordinator knows all the users' requirements.
- Decisions concerning multi-domain traffic (requests) may be made by the coordinator.

This means that each SDN domain has partial data. Since it does not want to share with other domains, some computations must be done locally, but the final decision may be made centrally. Thus, the SD-WAN coordinator may act as an active party and local SDN controllers act as passive parties. The main idea of this approach is given in Fig. 8.

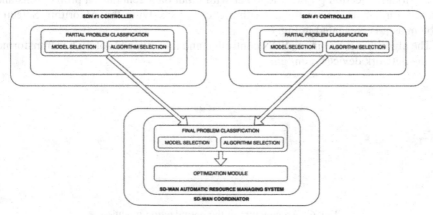

Fig. 7. The architecture of the SD-WAN ARMS

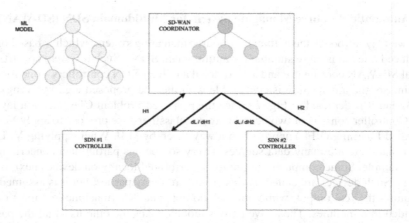

Fig. 8. The concept of the application of the VFL to resource management in SD-WANs.

4   Simulation

We have performed some initial experiments as a Proof-of-Concept for our approach. We assumed that there is only one problem solved in SDN, i.e. only one special case of (1) is solved, namely the one given in [16] (online VNE for fixed **b**, **x**, **f**,**r** and $|J| \geq 1$). So, it is only to decide which algorithm should be used for given data. We assumed that the execution time is crucial, so it was the function Φ.

There were two classes, i.e., {Algorithm 1, Algorithm 2}. Algorithm 1 was the greedy one, while Algorithm 2 was the exact one (the lpsolve55 was used). The classifier was NN.

The training set's element is as follows: {[[1st physical network features], [2nd physical network features], [virtual networks features], [class]]) - physical network features were available resources for each link, virtual network resources were: a maximal requested resource for a virtual link, a minimal requested resource for a virtual link, and average requested resources for a virtual link, the class was determined by comparing solving time of both algorithms.

There are 3 parties:

1st passive party (SDN #1 Controller) - features: [1st physical network features].

2nd passive party (SDN #2 Controller) - features: [2nd physical network features].

active party (SD-WAN Coordinator) – features: [virtual network features], label: class.

The training set was balanced, and the model was trained with 3000 samples and tested with 1000 samples. The simulation environment was implemented in Python and the Tensor Flow with Flower framework (https://flower.ai) were used in our experiment.

For algorithm evaluation, the accuracy, precision, and recall metrics were used. The results are given in Table 1.

Table 1. The results of the initial experiment

metric	value
Accuracy	0.73
Precision for Algorithm 1	0.69
Precision for Algorithm 2	0.78
Recall for Algorithm 1	0.82
Recall for Algorithm 2	0.64

The obtained results seem very promising, but further research should be carried out.

5   Final Remarks

In this article, we have shown that most of the resource management problems solved in the literature are only special cases of the generalized problem (1). However, each of them has a set of dedicated algorithms that suits him perfectly and cannot be applied to the other problems. We introduced the system which may determine which problem should be considered in the particular case and it chooses an adequate algorithm to solve it. Then we extended our approach to the environment of SD-WAN by applying the VFL approach.

References

1. Azodolmolky, S.: Software defined networking with OpenFlow. Packt Publishing (2013)
2. Bhardwaj, R.: Top 10 Networking technology trends for 2024 (2023). https://networkinter view.com/top-10-networking-technology-trends/. Retrieved 15 February 2024
3. Blenk, A., Kalmbach, P., Van Der Smagt, P., Kellerer, W.: Boost online virtual network embedding: Using neural networks for admission control. Proceedings of 12th International Conference on Network and Service Management (CNSM), 2016 (2016)
4. Chowdhury, N.M., Kabir, M., Boutaba, R.: Network virtualization: state of the art and research challenges. IEEE Commun. Mag. **47**(7), 20–26 (2009)
5. Chowdhury, N.M., Kabir, M., Boutaba, R.: A survey of network virtualization. Comput. Netw. **54**(5), 862–876 (2010)
6. Das, T., Gurusamy, M.: Resilient controller placement in hybrid SDN/legacy networks. Proceedings of 2018 IEEE Global Communications Conference (GLOBECOM). IEEE (2018)
7. Deamer, C.: Discover the Latest Trends in WAN and LAN Technologies with Colin Deamer (2023). https://medium.com/@colindeamer27/discover-the-latest-trends-in-wan-and-lan-tec hnologies-with-colin-deamer-5257082f76a2. Retrieved 15 February 2024
8. Drwal, M., Gasior, D.: Utility-based rate control and capacity allocation in virtual networks. Proceedings of the 1st European Teletraffic Seminar (2011)
9. Gasior, D.: 2020. Springer, Resource Allocation for Software Defined Networks (2011)
10. Haider, A., Potter, R., Nakao, A.: Challenges in resource allocation in network virtualization. Proceedings of 20th ITC specialist seminar (2009)
11. Khan, MA, Toseef, U.: User utility function as quality of experience (qoe). Proceedings of the ICN (2011)
12. Lehocine, M.B., Batouche, M.: Flexibility of managing VLAN filtering and segmentation in SDN networks. Proceedings 2017 International Symposium on Networks, Computers and Communications (ISNCC). IEEE (2017)
13. Liu, Y., et al.: Vertical Federated Learning: Concepts, Advances, and Challenges. IEEE Transactions on Knowledge and Data Engineering (2024)
14. Mirahsan, M., Senarath, G., Farmanbar, H., Dao, N.D., Yanikomeroglu, H.: Admission control of wireless virtual networks in HetHetNets. IEEE Trans. Veh. Technol. **67**(5), 4565–4576 (2018)
15. Ozyildirim, B.M., Avci, M.: Generalized classifier neural network. Neural Networks **39**, 18–26 (2013)
16. Palomar, D.P., Chiang, M.: A tutorial on decomposition methods for network utility maximization. IEEE Journal on Selected Areas in Communications **24**(8), 1439–1451 (2006)
17. Ramiro, J., Hamied, K.: Self-organizing networks: self-planning, self-optimization and self-healing for GSM, UMTS and LTE. John Wiley & Sons (2011)
18. Segeč, P., Moravčik, M., Uratmová, J., Papán, J., Yeremenko, O.: SD-WAN-architecture, functions and benefits. Proceedings of 2020 18th International Conference on Emerging eLearning Technologies and Applications (ICETA), pp. 593–599 (2020)
19. Troia, S., Sapienza, F., Varé, L., Maier, G.: On deep reinforcement learning for traffic engineering in SD-WAN. IEEE J. Sel. Areas Commun. **39**(7), 2198–2212 (2020)

20. Wang, J., Shou, G., Hu, Y., Guo, Z.: A multi-domain SDN scalability architecture implementation based on the coordinate controller. Proceedings of 2016 International Conference on Cyber-Enabled Distributed Computing and Knowledge Discovery (CyberC) (2016)
21. Yang, Z., Cui, Y., Li, B., Liu, Y., Xu, Y.: Software-defined wide area network (SD-WAN): Architecture, advances and opportunities. Proceedings of 28th International Conference on Computer Communication and Networks (ICCCN) (2019)

Concept and Phases of the Rogue Access Point Attack

Piotr Augustyniak[✉], Olgierd Rogowicz, and Piotr Zwierzykowski

Faculty of Computing and Telecommunications, Institute of Communication and Computer
Networks, Poznań University of Technology, Poznan, Poland
piotr.augustyniak@doctorate.put.poznan.pl,
piotr.zwierzykowski@put.poznan.pl

Abstract. This paper provides an analysis of an attack on wireless networks
referred to as Rogue Access Point The concept and phases of a RAP attack are
presented. Different variants of the attack were presented. Difficulties and typical
network security measures that an attacker may encounter are discussed. The
article also contains a brief description of methods and techniques that can be
used to secure a network against such an attack. The article is the result of a
literature review and experiments carried out.

Keywords: Rogue Access Point · wireless LAN · MITM (Man in the Middle) ·
WLAN Security

1 Introduction

Rogue Acces Point is an attack that operates in two different domains of physical signal
transmission. At the same time, with its operation it tries to penetrate wired networks
and exploit wireless networks. This distinguishes this type of attack from the Evil Twin
attack, which is focused entirely on operating in wireless networks. [1]. The Rouge
Access Point (RAP) concept is well presented in the descriptions of the world's leading
manufacturers of computer network equipment, including wireless networks, i.e. Cisco
Systems or Juniper Networks.

Juniper Networks defines RAP as follows: *"A rogue access point is a device not
sanctioned by an administrator, but is operating on the network anyway. This could be
an access point set up by either an employee or by an intruder. The access point could
also belong to a nearby company."*[1]

A similar definition can also be found in the Cisco Systems materials: *"A Rogue AP is
an access point that has been installed on a secure network without explicit authorization
from a system administrator. Rogue access points pose a security threat because anyone*

---

[1] https://www.juniper.net/documentation/en_US/junos-space-apps/network-director4.0/topics/
concept/wireless-rogue-ap.html.

K. S. Soliman (Ed.): IBIMA-AI 2024, CCIS 2299, pp. 290–302, 2025.
https://doi.org/10.1007/978-3-031-77493-5_25

with access to the premises can ignorantly or maliciously install an inexpensive wireless AP that can potentially allow unauthorized parties to access the network. "[2]

Through the maintenance of the structure of successive standards in conjunction with the layered structure of the OSI/ISO model, and by considering the assumptions and operation of the Rogue Access Point, in an attacked network, it is irrelevant what type of Ethernet potential criminals may be dealing with. This is due to the nature of the vulnerability being exploited, which is associated with all the versions that are created in succession.

The purpose of the article is to show how relatively uncomplicated the execution of the attack is, which as a result may lead to frequent use of this method, especially by people who do not necessarily have expert knowledge of technologies and protocols used in wireless networks. The article consists of five sections: introduction, description of the concept of the attack, and analysis of the various phases of the attack, followed by a discussion of the logic of the attack. The article ends with a summary.

2   Rogue Access Point Attack

The Rogue Access Point attack, abbreviated RAP or Rogue AP, is an attack involving the unauthorized physical connection of an Access Point device to an attacked network without the knowledge and consent of the network administration. The attached device can then interfere with the network environment in various ways, allowing the attacker to control it through the established wireless connection beyond the physical network area (Fig. 1) [2, 3].

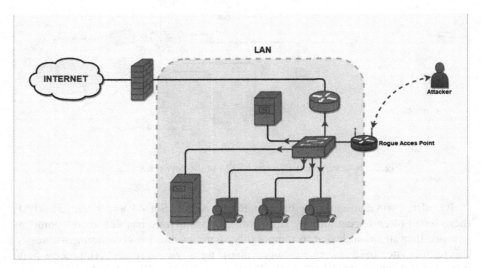

Fig. 1. Diagram of how a Rogue Access Point works in a network under attack

---

[2] https://www.cisco.com/assets/sol/sb/AP541N_Emulators/AP541N_Emulator_v1.9.2/help_R ogue_AP_Detection.htm.

The aim of the RAP attack is to gain wireless access to the internal network by bypassing the security measures that stand in the way in the connection envisaged by the network infrastructure developers. Remote access to the Rogue AP additionally provides the ability to be outside the area where the network is physically located, allowing the attacker to establish a connection to the device from a safe distance.

The form that the final attack will take is a matter for the main targets of the attackers, for whom the long-term operation of the Rogue AP and its successful cloaking does not necessarily matter. This means that there is potentially a good chance of the attack succeeding without prior preparation and gathering the information needed to mask its presence. The direct connection of a Rogue AP, which focuses only on the correct provisioning of the Wi-Fi network managing it by the attackers, will most often have the potential for deep network intrusion, as the safeguards against this type of incident are still low. However, the most complete and developed form of Rogue AP is to transform it from a model of a kind of leech or poisoner connected to the infiltrated network to a man-in-the-middle model. If the first model of operation requires only physical connection to the network, the second requires only connecting and rewiring a device already operating on the network, as presented in Fig. 2.

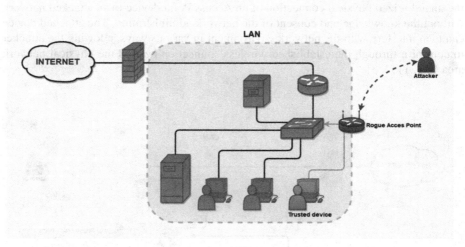

Fig. 2. Rogue Access Point as MiTM in the network under attack

It is also worth distinguishing between Rogue AP and SoftAP and unauthorized AP. These terms often appear side by side. SoftAP, or 'software enabled access point', is software that allows a device to temporarily share an internet connection wirelessly. This term is often used interchangeably with the term 'virtual router'. The access point created in this way is used to share the internet connection with other devices, such as smartphones, tablets or laptops. It is often the case that employees, in order to increase their convenience and facilitate their work on the company network, connect their own wireless devices to the network and create a SoftAP using them. An unauthorized AP, on the other hand, is not only an illegal SoftAP in the workplace, but also directly connected private access point devices without authorization, which propagate new WLANs through it, configured at the discretion of the connecting party. These incidents are a serious threat to those setting up WLANs and to the organization as a whole. Similar incidents certainly violate the basic rules and policies for the use of internal networks of most companies. There is a reckless bypassing of security measures to protect the internal network altogether, which may be cumbersome and slow from an employee's point of view, but exist for a very specific purpose. If the default security is left in place or an open access point is created, there is a significant risk of such a network being used by third parties with different intentions and security knowledge than reckless employees. The exploitation of such an opportunity could be identical in effect to a planned Rogue AP attack. These threats are just as dangerous and the responses and measures used by security teams to combat it should be just as swift and prioritised [4].

3 Phases of the Attack

An attack, by its definition, is complete when two main objectives are achieved. The first is to physically tap into the network under attack with the ability to communicate at a basic level with other devices on the network. The second is to provide remote access by establishing a separate WLAN. It is an optional matter for attackers not to leave any trace of their actions and to move around the network in such a way as to be treated as a negligible threat event or as a low-ranking anomaly. Discretion is not always a priority during an attack, in some cases it is more important to focus on executing the main objectives of the attack and, as soon as this is achieved, to leave the scene and sever all links with the action carried out. Once the Rogue AP is fully nested within the network under attack, attackers have a number of options for further interference.

3.1 External Reconnaissance of the Network

In order to carry out a successful attack, a certain basic level of knowledge about the infrastructure of the network under attack, as well as possible security features within it, is necessary. This is important in order to understand which information is crucial and which criminals care most about during the attack itself. Only by obtaining specific information can the intruders begin to prepare and attempt to undermine more advanced security mechanisms such as port security on network devices. For network administrators, knowledge of the most vulnerable points allows them to focus on techniques to protect against this type of attack, so they can eliminate the weakest links, or improve their monitoring and surveillance methods.

It would be impossible to list all the options criminals have when gathering information used in an attack. Reconnaissance can be effectively carried out by an outsider, taking the role of a customer, visitor or service technician with a ladder, for example. The possibility of a low standard of network area security in terms of monitoring and prevention against physical intrusion by uninvited guests should be accepted in advance. Physical security issues are often independent of the entity that owns the network, and responsibility in this area lies with the owner of the building in which the organization operates. This area is sometimes not given sufficient attention and those appointed to perform security duties do not meet basic requirements. Unfortunately, even with the best selection of security personnel, routine and oversights can creep in. Intrusion by an outsider is a very real matter, and access to parts of the premises that should not be open to the public is as likely as possible. The situation is even more serious when the more common and dangerous situation of criminals interacting with individuals associated with the target under attack is considered in the risk assessment. The actions of a third-party, whose room for manoeuvre is much wider and of less interest, is in most cases significantly more dangerous in its consequences. By allowing them to have a greater range of access, as well as the lack of strict surveillance due to the top-down exclusion of associates from the suspect pool, there are opportunities to be in the right place at the right time, wanting to gather sensitive information without attracting attention. Nevertheless, this is not the most dangerous form of collaboration between criminals and insiders. The person who can start cooperating with the criminals is also often a direct employee of the organization under attack. The chance of co-operation from an employee with the authority to move freely on the network infrastructure as well as on the network itself, even a trainee with a set of basic rights, highlights the need to leave nothing to fate in terms of securing every possible entry into the administered network even from a trusted area.

A significant problem for attackers is to select and recognize the logical location of the point from which they will launch their attack. During the attack, there is a physical attachment to the network under attack. For this reason, one of the most important issues is to select the correct port from the pool of available ports. Port restrictions that are encountered may be established flow control policies. Gaining access to a port not covered by special security measures is invaluable to attackers. Attackers will also seek to find network entry in an area without an adequate firewall between them and sensitive information [4]. When thinking about corporate networks, the most common choice when testing how much a port allows will be common and poorly protected network sockets and devices such as switches, APs and wired connections to printers, scanners, TVs, projectors or VoIP phones. All similar devices mostly operate on the basis of frequent interaction with employees. For example, a floor-wide shared printer will usually be connected in some way to the stations of employees whose duties include printing and scanning documents. In such a case, it is highly likely that this type of device will also be connected to the company's main network. Thus, it can be assumed that terminal devices communicate with the network and have access to network resources when they operate on certain inputs. These types of devices are usually exposed to the public due to continuous operation in order to improve their operation, so it is not a problem to access them. While this is a likely scenario, there are also more cautious approaches to building corporate networks. Administrators often choose to isolate a group of such devices from the main network, even at a physical level, in order to increase security, thus preventing the attack from spreading to further areas of the company. An executed attack that ends with the installation of a Rogue AP in such an isolated network for attackers is usually ineffective, although confidential and valuable data can also be intercepted in such a network. In addition to the typical network entrances mentioned, any physical port within reach can be exploited. Attackers are really reliant on the fantasies of those responsible for the architecture of the network under attack.

Frequently, simply connecting an unknown device to a network showing a low level of professionalism may be enough. Where attackers believe that the network they are dealing with may have a certain level of security, they will try to legitimize the presence of their device on the network. Otherwise, mechanisms that simplistically categorize the anomalies encountered and take the next action based on this can quickly block the attack and put a stop to the practice before it starts for good. If generally available solutions and good practices are used, attackers are still able to successfully complete the entire action relatively easily, Criminals, in order not to be detected and identified as an undesirable and dangerous element by basic defense systems and other network monitoring systems, in most cases need two addresses. The first, Media Access Control, a globally unique 48-bit network card hardware address. One of the most critical elements in the entire attack. Divided into a 24-bit manufacturer part and a 24-bit unique part, the address is the main identifier of the device on the local network. Based on this physical address, recognition at the data link layer of the ISO/OSI model takes place. One of the simplest methods of obtaining this address is to read it from the device housing. Most manufacturers of devices with a network card place the card's MAC address on the back of the housing. Most manufacturers of devices with a network card place the card's MAC address on the back of the card. There is usually nothing to prevent attackers from reading the address and using it in an attack if there is physical access to the device. If this information has not been placed on the device or has been removed from it, it is possible for an attacker to disconnect the device and connect it to a specially configured small device such as a microcomputer. Once connected, the crafted device will run a scan or intercept the transmitted frames and read the necessary information from them. The ways to get this data are many and not limited to the very general examples mentioned above. Rewiring a device to a Rogue AP under our control and extracting information from it in this way gives the opportunity to get an IP address by the way. This 32-bit numerical identifier of network elements in the network layer of the reference model is another important element, the acquisition of which enables a more effective attack. The acquired address must correlate with the MAC address that we plan to use when impersonating while connecting the Rogue AP. There may be many elements in the network that record the association of a device's IP address with its MAC address. In this case, it is advisable to know the specific IP address of the device associated with the specific MAC address.

Port Security is the simplest and most basic method of countering unwanted devices on the network, which involves checking that the MAC address of a connected device is trusted based on the switch's previous configuration. The name comes from Cisco's device ecosystem, other network device vendors may call this mechanism differently, but the principle will be similar. The exact check is based on verifying that the MAC address appears on a unique list of authorized MAC addresses associated with a specific port. If the verification is positive, the device is allowed through the specific port, otherwise the port with the connected intruder is blocked. With this protection, individual ports can detect, prevent and record attempts by unauthorized devices to communicate through the switch [4]. A similar protection is a technique that functions under the name of MAC Lockdown, also known as Static Addressing. By assigning a MAC address to a designated port, it prevents it from changing them. MAC Lockdown also binds the device to a specific VLAN. MAC Lockdown allows you to lock down a specific MAC address, so that the switch blocks all traffic to or from the specified address. One of the simplest options to nullify these protections is to use the previously acquired MAC address of a trusted device allowed to traffic and connect the Rogue AP to the port where the device with the used MAC address is connected [6].

A popular security feature appearing on the network is DHCP Snooping. This is a range of techniques whose use enhances the security of the network infrastructure. DHCP snooping can be configured on switches to exclude rogue DHCP servers that have been connected to the network and that attempt to spoof addresses within the network. In addition, information about hosts that have successfully completed a DHCP transaction is collected in an association database, which can then be used by other systems, for example to ensure IP integrity in a switched domain at the data link layer. This protection does not directly protect against Rogue APs, only in the event of an optional Rogue AP attempting to impersonate a DHCP server. However, the most important element of this technique in the case of the attack in question is the collection of information about the address bindings of devices already operating in the network. This is vital information for the attacker, who needs to create a trustworthy identity for the Rogue AP that is consistent with the information held by network security [7].

DAI, or Dynamic ARP Inspection, is another second-layer protection used that involves the switch checking all ARP requests and responses. Each intercepted packet is checked to ensure that the MAC address is correctly associated with an IP address before the local ARP cache is updated or the packet is forwarded to the correct destination. The association information is retrieved from the DHCP Snooping database. In addition, DAI can also validate ARP packets against user-configured ARP ACLs, in order to support hosts using a statically configured IP address. Invalid ARP packets will be discarded by the DAI [8, 9]. In order to bypass this protection, the acquisition of an associated IP address and MAC address pair is required.

IP Source Guard is another method often included in basic security along with the previous three. It is based on examining every packet sent from a host connected to an untrusted access interface on the switch. The IP address, MAC address, VLAN and interface associated with the host is checked against entries stored in the DHCP snooping database. If the packet header does not match a valid entry in the database, the frame is discarded and is blocked from further transmission. The operation of IP Source Guard is similar to DAI with the difference that in this case the entire traffic is examined, not just the ARP-related traffic [10].

One of the more advanced access control solutions is the IEEE 802.1X standard. It provides a mechanism whereby network switches and access points can delegate authentication responsibilities to a specialized server, such as a RADIUS server, so that the authentication of devices on the network can be managed and updated centrally. In addition, it uses encryption and authentication mechanisms in this solution that make it very difficult for attackers to intercept and read any communication during the authentication process [11]. This is an example of a security feature that will effectively discourage most criminals from attempting an attack, due to the complexity and the need to commit significant resources and time to simply attempt to circumvent it. As intended in the paper, a study of such a case was omitted.

3.2 Preparation of Software and Hardware

Before starting operations, attackers need to properly prepare the equipment they will use to launch their attack. The best choice seems to be a microcomputer equipped with a Wi-Fi card, which additionally has a small size and passive cooling for quiet operation. A computer intended for use as a RAP should be equipped with a single free ethernet port or have the possibility to complete the configuration by adding appropriate adapters. However, opting to develop a RAP into a MiTM requires the provision of two free ports.

The network architecture and security features encountered may force attackers into this solution. From the attacker's point of view, the MiTM solution offers many advantages. The greatest advantage of the MiTM variant is that it becomes an unobtrusive part of the network, merely flipping intact frames from one interface to another with the ability to view them. The MiTM variant does not have to worry about, basic security or acquiring an IP-MAC pair, as it does not generate traffic by default, but only forwards it. Another advantage of this model is the ability to maintain full uninterrupted functionality of the network under attack. This reduces the risk of alerts about malfunctioning of the end device, either by monitoring systems or by employees using the device. Another reason may be the desire to preserve the original communication of the end device with the rest of the network. This allows the device to mask its presence by transmitting content broadcast by a trusted device. Furthermore, this traffic can be passively interfered with in order to read useful information. During the configuration of the device, the port connected to the trusted device and the port connected to the attacked network must be set up, if only by means of a network bridge emulation. Left to its own devices, it still needs to set up, in the correct way, a WLAN network, which will become remote access to the network under attack. The problem with this form of remote management is its visibility by security systems located within the monitored infrastructure. For example, one technique to defend against Rogue APs is to listen and collect Beacon frames visible by the company's APs and categorize the BSSIDs collected through this into 'Rogue AP' and other categories. Where an AP will be categorized in some solutions is determined by comparing its broadcast BSSID MAC with the MAC addresses of APs wired into the network. If these addresses show a high similarity, it can be concluded that the device is transmitting a WLAN connected to the network infrastructure. On this basis, a particular BSSID is qualified as a 'Rogue AP' threat. Therefore, the connected device should adopt a random BSSID when establishing a wireless network [4].

3.3 Connection to LAN and Creation of WLAN

These stages involve joining the Rogue AP network under attack. Getting to the selected location can be achieved by the same means as for the reconnaissance, also using the same insiders. The plan to install a Rogue AP in a pre-selected location will attempt to take as little time as possible, and the entire operation will most often be on a plug-and-play basis. The semi-autonomous Rogue AP, when plugged in, initializes a WLAN whose signal extends beyond the physical area of the network and is easily picked up by an attacker. As soon as the attacker connects seamlessly to the Rogue AP, the attack is considered successful. At this point, the attacker can further adjust any parameters of the device, proceed with internal reconnaissance and infiltration of the network, or mute WLAN broadcasting for a strictly defined period of time so that the Rogue AP does not induce unnecessary activity when it is not needed.

3.4 Internal Reconnaissance and Network Infiltration

A successful attack is allowed to use more elaborate techniques that can focus on intercepted traffic or injecting their own traffic. The attackers' possibilities are limited only to how careful they want to be when affecting the network. Achieving such an effect and therefore circumventing all the difficulties along the way does not mean total freedom. There may still be safeguards in place on the network to analyse and react to suspicious traffic within. This means that, despite the Rogue AP attack ending successfully, subsequent actions taken on the target under attack may not have the intended effect. At this point, a separate section begins which involves re-collecting data, setting priorities and assumptions and deciding on next steps. An attack completed successfully by the attackers should be seen as them gaining a better tactical position in obtaining larger targets. The range of possible decisions that can be made at this stage is very wide, from moving from Rogue AP to Evil Twin attack, MAC or IP Spoofing, transmission of copies of traffic via WLAN to a remote attacker to DoS of network devices. Ultimately, attackers can leave the device as a dormant agent to launch another attack at a later date.

4 RAP Attack Analysis

Performing a Rogue Access Point attack is a difficult undertaking due to the need to be physically present on the infrastructure under attack. On the other hand, the logic of this attack itself is not complicated and is based on the basic principles of network operation. Several variants of this attack are presented in this paper. The first case is a variant that can be carried out in the most basic way, connecting the Rogue AP directly to the network with no expectation of any security, and then further action depending on the information gathered from the traffic inside the network. A more developed form of this variant involves acquiring the IP address and MAC address of a trusted device that is on the network, then creating a Rogue AP with a configured interface according to the acquired addresses. In this case, the Rogue AP, once connected to the network, appears in the network as a terminal device, from the category of trusted devices. The last variant discussed is when the Rogue AP is installed in a place between a trusted device and the rest of the network and operates on a MiTM basis.

In the case of the first two variants, projecting the attack onto the 7-layer ISO/OSI reference model, the entire process takes place at the network layer and the data link layer. The relationship that occurs between the layers and how the two layers work together is the essence of the attack logic. The first step is to connect to the infrastructure under attack. The Rogue AP will from now on be connected to a network device, most likely a switch or router, which has the task of segregating traffic in this part of the network. The protocol that will become active here will be the ARP protocol. This is used to map network layer addresses to the physical addresses of devices that are on the network. The main task of the ARP protocol is to find the MAC address of the device to which an attempt is made to send data, based on a known IP address. This allows data to be directly routed to the appropriate device on the local network. Each network device operating on IP addresses has its own ARP table in which it stores the acquired IP-MAC relationship information. If the request does not relate to the device in question, it will take no further action. A Rogue AP that receives such a frame may use the IP address provided and then reply with its MAC address, thus intercepting traffic that will be directed to the original owner of the intercepted IP address. Attackers have plenty of options for how they can intercept network traffic. If the Rogue AP is connected to a Layer 2 switch, they can apply an attack on CAM tables, for example by CAM flooding. The CAM table, unlike the ARP table, stores port associations with MAC addresses. Learning and replenishing the table is done by analyzing the traffic passing through the switch. The CAM flooding. Attack involves sending large numbers of false frames with different MAC addresses to the network switch in order to populate the CAM table, which is constantly learning and mapping more new MAC addresses, leading to overloading the switch and impeding or disrupting the normal flow of network traffic. Switch may begin to behave like a hub, forwarding each frame to all devices, giving the opportunity to eavesdrop on network traffic. In the advanced version, where the attackers will use the previously acquired IP and MAC address pair, if the ARP tables of the devices in the network have not been reset, the frames will be sent directly to the Rogue AP, which pretends to be an existing device in the network. If this is not the case, an ARP query will be sent again. The enhanced version has the advantage of using a trusted address pair in the network, thus bypassing most of the security measures outlined in Sect. 3.1.

The second variant is a simplified version of this attack, as it does not require knowledge of the addressing used on the network under attack from the outset. It is sufficient to connect the Rogue AP to the network and switch the trusted device to the Rogue AP, and prior to the attack itself, perform bridging of the two interfaces used. In addition, the attackers must configure the Rogue AP so that it establishes a wireless network through which the attackers can manage it. The mechanics of this variant are clear and no further analysis is required. The only point that can be elaborated on is the bridging itself. A bridge in this context is a piece of software used to connect two or more network segments. A bridge behaves like a virtual network switch, operating transparently and therefore, so to speak, invisibly to other devices on the network. Any real and virtual devices can be connected to it. In GNU/Linux, brctl software, which is part of the system kernel, is used to create network bridge emulations. Once a bridge is created, ports are assigned to it. Each bridge can have any number of ports, while one port can belong to only one bridge. The bridge will forward frames from one port to another, without interfering with their headers, just sending them on their way. This Rogue AP will be unnoticeable to other network devices. Traffic that will pass through both ports can then be copied and sent to the attacker via a pre-set Wi-Fi network (Fig. 3).

4.1 Passive Defense

Concerning the configuration of networks for the security of layer two of the ISO/OSI model, in which the described attacks operate, most network equipment vendors offer a

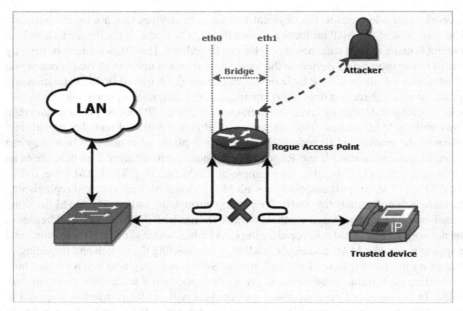

Fig. 3. A diagram illustrating the operation of a Rogue AP established between a network and a trusted device

certain default set of tools, which with some operate under different terms or with slight variations. Using Cisco's terminology and offerings, such a basic package would include Port Security, DHCP Snooping, Dynamic ARP Inspection and IP Source Guard. The implementation of such a complete and layered set is a good starting point in building a secure network. Port Security prevents attacks on the CAM table and DHCP server such as the Starvation attack. It allows administrators to determine which MAC addresses are allowed on a specific network port, helping to prevent unauthorized access to the network by Rogue APs. DHCP snooping prevents attacks on DHCP. Through the monitoring of DHCP traffic on the network. This will allow the detection of an amnion caused by a new device connecting to the network and the blocking of untrusted DHCP servers. Dynamic ARP Inspection prevents attacks using the ARP protocol. It verifies the correctness of ARP packets and their association with IP and MAC addresses. IP Source Guard, on the other hand, checks the source of IP packets and blocks traffic from untrusted sources by verifying IP and MAC address matches. Additionally, the network should be segmented using VLANs and vulnerable areas should be isolated at the physical level from the rest of the network [11].

Such a security architecture may prove intimidating against a more determined attacker. The standard that should appear in such a network is an AAA server, which provides end-to-end authorisation, authentication and control of user access to the network, as well as tracking and reporting information on user activity. The AAA server receives an authentication request from the user, who provides, for example, a login and password for this purpose. The server verifies the user and sends information about possible access to the network device, which decides on the user's access to network traffic. All user activity is tracked and monitored. This server can be used in both LAN and WLAN networks, effectively making it difficult for attackers to gain access to the network. Popular open source solutions are FreeRADIUS [11] and TACACS+ from Shrubbery Network [13].

The most important thing when it comes to WLANs is the absolute use of AES-based encryption, a method of securing the network by choosing WPA2 CCMP, or even establishing a new standard in the company by introducing devices using WPA3. Only Wi-Fi networks secured in this way, working with an AAA server, guarantee security when used.

Methods of controlling network access have been outlined so far. However, it appears that the above security features may not stop an attack if the Rogue AP is used as a MiTM that will operate transparently on the LAN. In such a case, traffic encryption would need to be incorporated into all of the aforementioned security components. This can be provided by MACsec, which uses cryptographic algorithms to encrypt and authenticate Ethernet frames. Unfortunately, not all devices support this protocol. Newer and much more expensive devices providing encryption between network devices can represent a significant, and therefore often unacceptable, expense for small and medium-sized companies.

4.2 Active Defense

Besides introducing safeguards in the configuration and by introducing additional modules to provide a higher level of security, it is also important to respond to threats in real time by monitoring and analyzing network traffic. To this end, it is worthwhile to use tools that enable the detection and response to attacks, implement solutions for rapid incident response and carry out actions such as IP address blocking or device isolation. All this is not possible without the use of specialized tools, which may exceed the budget of the companies from whose perspective we are looking at the problem. The network under administration should equip itself with some type of system such as IDS, i.e. an intrusion detection system, IPS an intrusion prevention system, or WIPS, i.e. a system to prevent intruders in wireless networks. At the level of sophistication and network needs of such enterprises, popular and respected open source projects built and developed for this purpose may prove to be a solution to complement the network defense layer [14].

5 Summary

The purpose of this article is to present the concepts and phases of an attack on a Rouge AP wireless network. The ubiquity and affordability of mobile devices potentially encourages company employees to extend company networks in undesirable ways. In this case, there is no need to wait for the actions of an external aggressor, as often the presence and unreflective actions of company employees can open up a protected network to a potential attacker(s). It is worth noting that the use of WAP (Wireless Access Point) devices, allows the aggressor to penetrate the company network from a safe distance. It can therefore be concluded that this type of attack is particularly dangerous because it does not require the aggressor to overcome firm security. It is sufficient to exploit a vulnerability created intentionally or unintentionally by its employee.

Acknowledgments. The authors thank the Polish Ministry of Education and Science for financial support (Applied Doctorate Program, No. DWD/6/0058/2022). This research was funded in part by the Polish Ministry of Science and Higher Education (No. 0313/SBAD/1310).

References

1. Augustyniak, P., Rogowicz, O., Zwierzykowski, P.L.: Theoretical and practical aspects of the evil twin attack. The attacker's perspective and defense methodology. In: Soliman, K.S. (eds.) Artificial Intelligence and Machine Learning. IBIMA-AI 2023. CCIS, vol. 2101, pp. 224–236. Springer, Cham (2024). https://doi.org/10.1007/978-3-031-62843-6_23. https://sin.put.poznan.pl/publications/details/i57960
2. Juniper Networks: Understanding Rogue Access Points (2018). https://www.juniper.net/documentation/en_US/junos-space-apps/network-director4.0/topics/concept/wireless-rogue-ap.html. Accessed 10 Apr 2023
3. Harrison, S.: Rogue Access Point, Cisco Meraki (2017). https://meraki.cisco.com/blog/2017/09/rogue-access-point. Accessed 10 Apr 2023
4. SolarWinds Success Center: What are rogue Access Points (AP) (2022). https://support.solarwinds.com/SuccessCenter/s/article/What-are-rogue-Access-Points-AP?language=en_US. Accessed 10 Apr 2023
5. Cisco: Configuring Port Security (2007). https://www.cisco.com/c/en/us/td/docs/switches/lan/catalyst4000/8-2glx/configuration/guide/sec_port.html. Accessed 10 Apr 2023
6. Aruba: Port security, Hewlett Packard Enterprise Development (2021). https://www.arubanetworks.com/techdocs/AOS-CX/10.07/HTML/5200-7885/Content/Chp_Port_sec/por-sec-fl-10.htm. Accessed 10 Apr 2023
7. Cisco: Catalyst 3750-X and Catalyst 3560-X Switch Software Configuration Guide, Cisco IOS Release 15.0(2)SE and Later. Chapter: Configuring DHCP Features and IP Source Guard (2018). https://www.cisco.com/c/en/us/td/docs/switches/lan/catalyst3750x_3560x/software/release/15-0_2_se/configuration/guide/3750x_cg/swdhcp82.html#24258. Accessed 10 Apr 2023
8. study-ccna.com: Dynamic ARP Inspection (DAI) Explanation & Configuration (2023). https://study-ccna.com/dynamic-arp-inspection-dai. Accessed 10 Apr 2023
9. Cisco: Catalyst 4500 Series Switch Cisco IOS Software Configuration Guide, 12.2(25)EW. Chapter: Understanding and Configuring Dynamic ARP Inspection (2020). https://www.cisco.com/c/en/us/td/docs/switches/lan/catalyst4500/12-2/25ew/configuration/guide/conf/dynarp.html. Accessed 10 Apr 2023
10. Juniper Networks: Security Services Administration Guide: Understanding IP Source Guard for Port Security on Switches (2021)
11. Bromirski, Ł.: Bezpieczeństwo sieci (a raczej zaledwie parę przykładów) (2007). https://lukasz.bromirski.net/docs/prezos/securecon2007/bezpieczenstwo_sieci.pdf. Accessed 10 Apr 2023
12. The FreeRADIUS Server Project. https://freeradius.org/. Accessed 10 Apr 2023
13. Shrubbery Networks: TACACS+ daemon. https://www.shrubbery.net/tac_plus/. Accessed 10 Apr 2023
14. Augustyniak, P., Skóra, J., Zwierzykowski, P.L.: Review and criteria for selecting open-source tools for managing wireless local networks. In: Soliman, K.S. (eds.) Artificial Intelligence and Machine Learning. IBIMA-AI 2023. CCIS, vol. 2101, pp. 195–209. Springer, Cham (2024). https://doi.org/10.1007/978-3-031-62843-6_21. https://sin.put.poznan.pl/publications/details/i57958

Studies and Assessments on the Optimization of Bandwidth in Wireless Networks Using Genetic Algorithms

Vlad–Sebastian Angheluță[1] and Claudia Cârstea[2]([⊠])

[1] Technical University of Cluj Napoca, Cluj, Romania
[2] "Henri Coandă" Air Force Academy of Brasov, Brașov, Romania
`claudia.carstea@afahc.ro`

Abstract. Time Sensitive Networking (TSN) is a process that encompasses a set of standards designed to increase the determinism of packet transmission in converged networks. The main purpose of this method is to provide mechanisms to ensure low and predictable transmission latency and high availability for demanding applications such as real-time audio/video streaming, automotive and industrial control. To provide the necessary guarantees, engineers came up with a formula called "Periodic Transmission Ethernet". Achieving the required quality of service (QoS) levels requires the appropriate selection and configuration of modeling mechanisms, but this is difficult due to the diverse requirements for coexisting flows in the presence of potential end-system-induced fluctuations. Thus, a method for transmitting Ethernet messages is described in a real-time distributed system that implements a periodic control algorithm, where many network nodes and at least one switch meet, connected to each other through a communication channel. However, the TTE static segment scheduling problem is considered to be an NP-complete problem due to its constraints, complex topology, and large scale uncertainty (i.e., large volume of packets). To improve the TT traffic scheduling performance, this paper aims to present a method that integrates genetic algorithms (GA) to optimize bandwidth under quality of service (QoS) constraints and minimize total energy consumption.

Keywords: Time Sensitive Networking (TSN) · Quality of Service (QoS) · Periodic Transmission Ethernet · Genetic Algorithms (GA)

1 Introduction

Administration of non-deterministic IT systems is one of the main problems that need to be solved within the contemporary management theory. At the present time, humanity is faced with managing complex systems with inefficient structures and functionality. For this reason, their study is more than necessary in the field covered by this paper. Unlike deterministic systems, non-deterministic systems exhibit unpredictable behavior influenced by both external random factors and internal dynamics. We find similar behaviors in crowds, the organization of factories, the way computer networks work,

K. S. Soliman (Ed.): IBIMA-AI 2024, CCIS 2299, pp. 303–307, 2025.
https://doi.org/10.1007/978-3-031-77493-5_26

etc. In this context, the objective of this article is to present the current disturbances that complicate the work of network engineers in order to manage computer systems - in this case networks with periodic transmission - and to propose a concrete configuration that integrates a genetic algorithm (GA) into a network systems management device, or a Network Controller (NC). This method is intended to optimize the bandwidth and minimize the total energy consumption under quality of service (QoS) constraints in wireless networks with periodic transmission to configure and run the GA according to the specified requirements.

1.1 Wireless Networks

It was said that the advancement of wireless technology has given rise to many complicated security policies and protocols. With this evolution, data processing by algorithms started to be slower and slower, and this slowness increases in proportion to the amount of data processed. Scalable and reliable communication networks are required to support various aspects of applications, services and transmissions. Some of the recent improvements to help improve the efficiency of wireless communication and data delivery include sensor networks, machine-to-machine communications, the Internet of Things, millimeter wave techniques, multi-input and multi-output technology, and more [2]. As a result, the QoS norms have imposed the development of models that have the network user at the center.

The study of nature is a rich source of inspiration for researchers working in the field of artificial intelligence and machine learning. In particular, the human brain and the biological process of evolution have helped to develop and guide research in the neural network and evolutionary algorithm communities [5]. A genetic algorithm (GA) is a metaheuristic computational method, inspired by biological evolution, that aims to mimic the robust procedures used by various biological organisms to adapt as part of their natural evolution [5].

The main reasons why this algorithm was chosen are the following:

1. Generality and versatility: GA is applied in a wide variety of settings and can be easily adapted to many problems as it is a very general technique. Furthermore, it can work even when the actual objective is not precisely known.
2. The ability to find good solutions: By working with a population of candidate solutions, genetic algorithms can exploit the diversity of solutions which are substrings of chromosomes that denote performing elements of a solution ensemble. This algorithm "evolves" in ways similar to natural selection and can solve complex problems even if a problem is not fully understood [3].
3. Easy to implement: GAs are computationally simpler compared to other complementary AI techniques, such as neural networks, because they only require changing and moving genes in chromosomes (as opposed to neural networks that require additive for multiple its hidden layers). GAs are easy to implement and can be quickly prototyped in digital signal processors (DSPs) or field programmable gate arrays (FPGAs) - making their integration into cloud systems easy [5].

1.2   Artificial Intelligence

A substantial amount of recent studies have looked at the use of wireless caching as a promising solution for 5G. Among these studies, investigations have been made on cache encoding and how it allows network devices to create multicasting opportunities for specific content through encoded multicast transmissions, so as to significantly improve bandwidth efficiency [1]. Consideration has been given to improving caching efficiency that can be achieved by dynamically learning content popularity and updating cached content at the edge of the network. Despite considerable interest, such studies focus on the problem of data placement in isolation, assuming the use of unicast or multicasting during transmission, and thus ignoring the potential benefits of joint placement and transmission code design [6]. The most recent work has provided a very large data platform that allows the use of learning algorithms to determine how much content will be accessed. The most common global optimization method for training neural networks is through the use of genetic algorithms, especially in non-deterministic networks. Other global optimization algorithms can be used to search for a good difficulty set, such as Simualted Annealing [1]. Deep learning networks have been introduced and perfected by Microsoft over the last 10 years, they produce a lower training error (and test error) than their counterparts by re-feeding the output data from the less used layers of the network. Therefore, unlike traditional functions that are defined as $y = f(x)$, these functions are defined as $y = f(x) + x$. [4].

1.3   Working Method

In this study, the premises used for bandwidth optimization are inspired by "Bandwidth Optimization of Wireless Networks Using Artificial Intelligence Technique" by Tamuno-Omie Joyce Alalibo, Sunny Orike and Promise Elechi. Using the generalized bandwidth reservation scheme in 2003 by Jau-Yang Chang and Hsing-Lung Chen, Real Time Users (UTR) and Fictitious Users (UF) are assumed to share the total bandwidth A. A consists of 3 parts: free bandwidth, real-time traffic bandwidth, and dummy-time traffic bandwidth. Another assumption is that UTRs have a higher bandwidth demand because they generate a huge amount of traffic. When the initially allocated bandwidths are not sufficient, UTRs are allowed to request additional bandwidth, which is allocated to them from unused bandwidth reserved for UF or from free unreserved bandwidth. UTRs are denied additional bandwidth when UF bandwidth and unreserved free bandwidth are exhausted. Bandwidth allocation is done so that free bandwidth for future users joining the network is always available. Since bandwidth is a limited resource for UTR, the GA method is proposed to optimize bandwidth allocation.

Incorporating genetic algorithm (GA) into the bandwidth allocation process in a wireless network environment, where the bandwidth is shared between UTR and UF, presents a sophisticated approach to resource management under the constraints of limited availability. For this, it is desired to minimize the discrepancies between all users (both UTR and UF), while ensuring that a section of the bandwidth, A, is always available to a possible user. Discrepancy between users can be defined as failure to provide sufficient bandwidth.

Variables

- A - Total bandwidth;
- A $_{UTR}$ - UTR Allocated Bandwidth;
- A $_{UF}$ - Allocated Bandwidth UF;
- A $_{DISP}$ - Spare bandwidth.

  Constraints:

- A $_{UTR}$ + A $_{UF}$ + A $_{DISP}$ = A;
- UTR have priority over UF;
- A $_{DISP}$ must be continuously maintained above a threshold.

1.4 Mathematical Representation

A chromosome represents a potential strategy for allocating bandwidth to a user.

1. *Representation of Chromosomes*

   Let any chromosome C be a vector of real numbers, where each element C $_i$ corresponds to the lane allocation for a specific user: $C = [C_1, C_2, C_3, ..., C_n]$, where n is the total number of users.

2. *Initial Population*

   Let the initial population P of size m : $P = \{C_1, C_2, C_3, ..., C_m\}$.

3. *Evaluation Function*

   Let f(C) be the evaluation function, which is defined as the element that determines the quality of a chromosome (bandwidth allocation strategy). The given example will incorporate factors such as meeting minimum requirements and QoS constraints.

   $$f_{(c)} = \alpha \sum_{i=1}^{n} S(c_i, d_i) - \beta \sum_{i=1}^{n} L(c_i; d_i), \text{ where:}$$

   - $S(c_i, d_i)$ - measures the fulfillment of the minimum requirements of the bandwidth allocated c_i to d_i, for user I;
   - $L(c_i; d_i)$ - calculates the decrease in service quality;
   - şiβ - are dynamic factors that allow the algorithm to prioritize between user prioritization (α) or a stricter quality of service (β).

4. *Selection Function*

Using probabilistic selection, any chromosome passed through the evaluation function, relative to all chromosomes in the initial population, results in the following formula:

$$P_s(C) = \frac{f(C)}{\sum_{j=1}^{m} f(C_j)}, \text{ where:}$$

- $P_s(c)$ - is the probability that some chromosome C will be selected for reproduction in the next generation;
- $\sum_{j=1}^{m} f(C_j)$ - is the sum of the evaluation function of all chromosomes; m represents the total number of chromosomes;

5. *Hybridization and Mutation Function*

For a uniform hybridization, each gene i is determined by randomly choosing between two parents C_a and C_b, with equal probabilities, to create Descendants O_1 and O_2.

$$\begin{cases} c_{a_i} \\ c_{b_i} \end{cases} \text{ each with probability 0.5. Whether } \begin{cases} c_{b_i} \\ c_{ai} \end{cases} \text{if} \begin{cases} O_{1i} = c_{ai} \\ O_{1i} = c_{bi} \end{cases}.$$

Finally, for a successful mutation in a binary code, let C_j be the gene at position j of chromosome C: $C'_j = 1 - C_j$. Thus, if C_j had the value 0, it will now become 1, and vice versa.

6. *Evolution*

The process of evolution from generation to generation can be represented as a general iteration to which the function of mutation, hybridization and selection is applied in this order: $P_{g+1} = $ Mutation (Hybridization(Selection(P_g))). The ultimate goal is to improve the output of the evaluation function with each run/each new generation.

2 General Conclusions and Contributions

By developing a complex mathematical framework, a chromosome representation for bandwidth allocation strategies is proposed, where each chromosome is a vector of real numbers that corresponds to the bandwidth allocation for a specific user. Thus, an evolutionary mechanism is described that allows the transition from one generation of chromosomes to another, continuously optimizing the performance of the bandwidth allocation system.

The central conclusion is that the use of genetic algorithms can significantly improve bandwidth planning and allocation in wireless networks. By modeling resource allocation problems as NP-complete problems, it is reviewed how genetic algorithms are effective in optimizing these processes, providing solutions that not only respect quality of service (QoS) constraints but also minimize energy consumption.

References

1. Chen, M., et al.: Artificial neural networks-based machine learning for wireless networks: a tutorial. IEEE Commun. Surv. Tutor. **21**(4), 3039–3071 (2019). https://doi.org/10.1109/COMST.2019.2926625
2. Jiang, C., et al.: Machine learning paradigms for next-generation wireless networks. IEEE Wirel. Commun. **24**(2), 98–105 (2017). https://doi.org/10.1109/MWC.2016.1500356WC
3. Holland, J.H.: Genetic algorithms computer programs that 'evolve' in ways that resemble natural selection can solve complex problems even their creators do not fully understand. Sci. Am. Mag. **267**(1), 66–72 (1992)
4. He, K., et al.: Deep residual learning for image recognition. In: 2016 IEEE Conference on Computer Vision and Pattern Recognition (CVPR), Las Vegas, NV, USA, pp. 770–778. IEEE (2016). https://doi.org/10.1109/CVPR.2016.90
5. Mehboob, U., et al.: Genetic algorithms in wireless networking: techniques, applications, and issues. Soft Comput. **20**(6), 2467–2501 (2016). https://doi.org/10.1007/s00500-016-2070-9
6. Fadlallah, Y., et al.: Coding for caching in 5G networks. IEEE Commun. Mag. **55**(2), 106–113 (2017). https://doi.org/10.1109/MCOM.2017.1600449CM

The Usage of the *Postthreadmessage* Mechanism for Non-standard Interprocess Communication in the Windows Operating System

Kacper Kukuła and Michał Glet[✉]

Faculty of Cybernetics, Military University of Technology, Warsaw, Poland
KacperKukula@proton.me, michal.glet@wat.edu.pl

Abstract. Our work explores a novel approach to exploit Windows API functions beyond their original purposes and use them for inter-process communication (IPC). The methodology used includes an analysis of the functionality of Windows API functions and the development of custom solutions for establishing inter-process connections. We show how to use a mechanism designed to handle a thread's message queue as an intermediate medium to detect other processes capable of communicating in this way, and then dynamically establish a connection between them. Motivated by the need to extend the capabilities of IPC in Windows operating systems, this research shows how unconventional uses of these mechanisms can improve inter-process communication.

Keywords: Windows · IPC · *PostThreadMessage* · inter-process communication

1 Introduction

Inter-process communication (IPC) plays a very important role in operating systems, facilitating data exchange and computation synchronization among different processes (application components). In the Windows operating environment, standard IPC mechanisms include the clipboard, mailslots, named and anonymous pipelines, shared memory, RPC (Remote Procedure Call), Windows sockets and more [1]. However, leveraging Windows API flexibility allows to use of more advanced communications techniques. One of the methods involves the use of the thread's message queue handling mechanism as an intermediary for inter-process communication. While message queues are generally used for transferring messages between threads within the same process, they can also be used in an inter-process context, although this is not their typical use case. Moreover, the use of the *PostThreadMessage* [4] function allows for anonymous transmission of the messages and achieves awareness of the presence of other processes that understand the implemented communication protocol.

2   The *PostThreadMessage* Summary

The *PostThreadMessage* is a Microsoft Windows API function designed for inter-thread communication. Its main purpose it to allow communication within the same process. It allows a thread to add a message to the message queue of another thread. This function is particularly useful e.g. where direct communication between threads is required without resorting to shared data or other mechanisms that may involve more complex synchronization. It is also very often being used to post messages from background threads to the UI thread in GUI applications, to update the user interface. The C++ function signature looks like this:

$$BOOL\ PostThreadMessage($$
$$DWORD\ idThread,$$
$$UINT\ Msg,$$
$$WPARAM\ wParam,$$
$$LPARAM\ lParam)$$
$$;$$

The *idThread* is an identifier of the thread to which the message is to be posted. The *Msg* is a message to be posted. The *wParam* and *lParam* are an additional message-specific information.

To receive messages sent by the *PostThreadMessage*, the target thread must have a message loop that retrieves messages from its message queue. This is typically done using the *GetMessage* [4] or *PeekMessage* [4] functions.

3   The Concept of Collective Consciousness

A described custom IPC mechanism utilizing *PostThreadMessage* can be used to implement the collective consciousness conception. To initialize a connection establishment, one or more-character strings must be generated. These strings are transformed into message identifiers and a constant, serving as a connection key. It's crucial that the connection key and at least one of the message identifiers must be identical across all instances at launch time.

The *wParam* and *lParam* parameters in the *PostThreadMessage* call can carry data with a total size of up to 128 bits (64 bits on ×86 systems). These parameters will be used for transferring the connection key and the identifier of the thread that sent the message. An exception is made for using the *WM_COPYDATA* message type, which allows sending data of any size - however, this is a standard Windows message type.

The initiating process broadcasts a message with a predefined identifier to all processes present in the system by alerting their threads. Message contains the connection key and the thread identifier. It then awaits replies. Upon receiving responses, the process checks if the connection key value is equal to the expected one. If yes it sends the value of the intended communication method to the respondent (e.g. the name of the ALPC server, encoded in the *wParam* and *lParam* fields) (Fig. 1).

The communication algorithm can be easily expanded to produce logical structures capable of supporting communication of a larger number of processes than two. In a

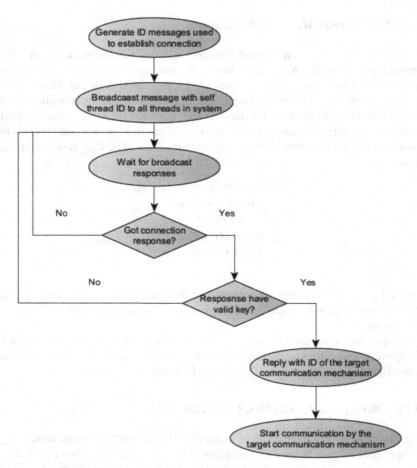

Fig. 1. Flowchart of process identification protocol for establishing communication

such case, the processes can act as a logical circle. To achieve it, an organizational layer must be included. It will be responsible for determining the neighbors for each of the communicated processes. In this context, the thread identifier can be used as the client identifier since this value on Windows family operating systems is distinct for every running thread (Figs. 2, 3 and 4).

The communication protocol can be easily enhanced with an extra layer of security by implementing a mechanism of cyclic updates of the connection key value or detecting connection attempts that utilize incorrect message identifiers and/or connection keys.

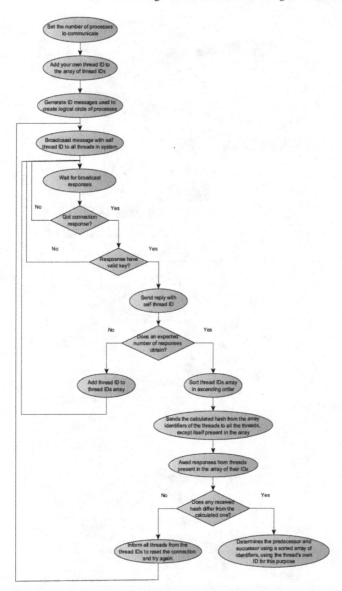

Fig. 2. An example of extending *PostThreadMessage* communication to get a logical circle from processes that support the implemented protocol

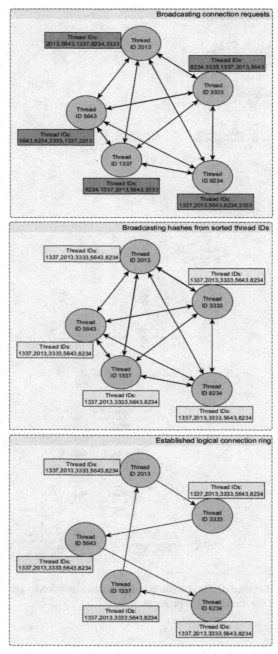

Fig. 3. An illustration of the most important states during connection establishment in a logical circle

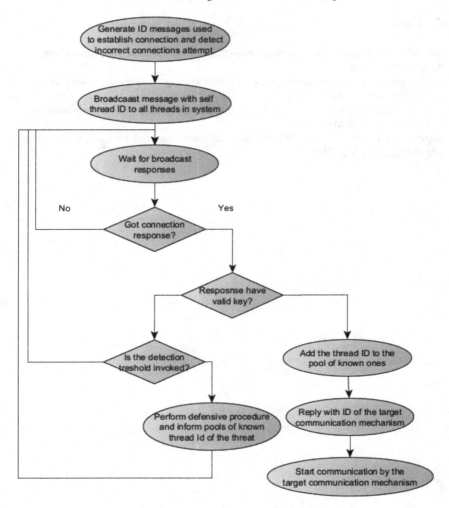

Fig. 4. An example of detection invalid connection attempts

4   Conclusions

Based on the results of the above study, it was possible to describe the conception of communicating two independent processes using a Microsoft Windows API function not originally intended for this purpose. The use of this method is similar to the mechanism of signals present on systems of the UNIX family. The proposed concept of the protocol for establishing communication allows discovering other instances of processes that have the ability to interpret the exchanged messages and handle the transmitted parameters. The protocol can be extended in an straightforward manner due to the low complexity of the presented idea.

References

1. https://learn.microsoft.com/en-us/windows/win32/ipc/interprocess-communications. Accessed Mar 2024
2. https://learn.microsoft.com/en-us/windows/win32/winmsg/using-messages-and-messagequeues. Accessed Mar 2024
3. https://learn.microsoft.com/en-us/windows/win32/api/winuser/nf-winuserregisterwindowmessagea. Accessed Mar 2024
4. https://learn.microsoft.com/en-us/windows/win32/api/winuser/nf-winuser-postthreadmessagea. Accessed Mar 2024

Two-Way Free-Space Laser Communication Earth-UAV Without UAV Emission Revealing Its Presence

Krzysztof Szajewski[1]([✉]) and Anna Szajewska[2]

[1] Military University of Technology, gen. Sylwestra Kaliskiego 2 Street, Warsaw, Poland
`krzysztof.szajewski@wat.edu.pl`
[2] Fire University, 52/54 Słowackiego Street, Warsaw, Poland
`aszajewska@apoz.edu.pl`

Abstract. This paper presents a prototype two-way FSO (Free Space Optical) communication system using a single light source. The concept involves selectively reflecting modulated laser light. Communication occurs in both directions simultaneously. Digital data in the form of modulated laser light reaching the UAV is reflected in a corner cube retroreflector through a modulator. The modulator imposes data from the UAV onto the return beam to the ground station. This system is dedicated to communication with UAVs where difficult radio propagation conditions prevent the use of standard RF communication. The system practically has no radio signature and is difficult to eavesdrop on. The described system sends data only when it is illuminated by an external light source from the ground station. Return digital information is sent in the same direction from which the UAV was illuminated.

Keywords: free space optical · modulating retroreflector · corner cube retroreflector

1 Introduction

The ongoing conflict in Ukraine has revealed new vulnerabilities in modern observation and reconnaissance systems mounted on UAVs. Before the outbreak of the war in Ukraine, UAVs represented an expensive and sophisticated technology used at the tactical level. Currently, on the modern battlefield, the use of UAVs has taken on the character of company equipment and often personal equipment. The large quantity of UAV equipment used has prompted a response from the opponent, resulting in the development of various electronic warfare systems, most of which are radio jamming systems. The shortening of UAV lifespan was already observed in the first year of the conflict, where the operating time of expensive and initially effective UAVs like the Bayraktar was drastically reduced to 1 h of flight. Currently, there are four main causes of UAV detection and two direct causes of UAV loss. Detection methods include: thermal signature, acoustic signature, radar reflection, and radio signature. Detecting a radio signature is currently the most commonly used technique because UAVs, usually equipped with a pilot camera,

K. S. Soliman (Ed.): IBIMA-AI 2024, CCIS 2299, pp. 315–322, 2025.
https://doi.org/10.1007/978-3-031-77493-5_28

emit electromagnetic waves to transmit the image to the operator. The source of electromagnetic waves can be easily detected with radio receivers. The accuracy of localization increases inversely proportional to the wavelength of the electromagnetic wave, and the detection efficiency increases with the power of emission. For this reason, it is harder to detect signal sources where power is spread at the expense of transmission bandwidth. To neutralize UAVs, direct means or electronic warfare means are used. Currently, radio propagation conditions on the battlefield are extremely unfavorable. In the case of a strong jamming signal, ground RF transmission becomes possible only by increasing the transmitter's power, which in turn increases the radio signature and simultaneously increases the risk of detection, even with spread spectrum radio. It can be concluded that the main factors affecting UAV lifespan are emission and resistance in the radio wave range. Therefore, there is a strong need to search for alternative ways of transmitting digital data (video stream and telemetry data). High hopes are pinned on wireless optical transmission OWC (Optical Wireless Communications), of which directed communication FSO (Free Space Optics) is a variant. FSO work was and is conducted in solving other communication problems such as high-speed train communication [2], vehicle location systems [9–11], and underwater communication at wavelengths least absorbed by water (450 nm–550 nm) [12]. There is also work on mixed FSO-RF systems [13] and the use of FSO in space where atmospheric turbulence and optical aberration problems do not occur. In addition to inter-satellite links for mega-constellations, work is underway on satellite up-down links [4]. Theoretical work on FSO for one-way communication has been conducted by [3]. In the described solution, the application of a modulating retroreflector (MRR) matrix was considered, which modulated the return light beam. It should also be noted that FSO systems, compared to RF communication, offer great potential due to the lack of electromagnetic interference. FSO systems do not require a license, making them an attractive alternative. FSO systems, often called "last mile communication," offer high bandwidth [5]. For military applications, communication on stabilized platforms such as ship-to-ship or ship-to-land has been developed. However, these links are limited by the horizon [6] because the communication is conducted in the line of sight (VLOS). Weather and atmospheric quality also affect connection quality. Atmospheric turbulence is a significant drawback affecting light scattering, especially in FSO over long distances.

2 Concept of Earth-UAV FSO Communication

The concept of a two-way data link in a point-to-point topology is shown in Fig. 1. The system uses a corner cube retroreflector (CCR), which is often used in various optical measurements. A spectacular application of corner-cube prisms was the project carried out in 1969 by the Apollo 11 crew, during which a reflector consisting of a prism matrix was left on the moon by sending laser pulses from Earth to the reflector, one can determine the round-trip light travel time and thus, the distance. These measurements have been continuously conducted since 1969, allowing precise distance determination between Earth and the Moon [1].

In the described solution, the communication idea is based on two different module constructions: stationary and mobile. The stationary device sends a frequency-modulated

FSK laser light beam towards the mobile device. Frequency modulation is done by switching between two generators. The stationary device requires constant positioning to aim the laser light beam at the modulator. In a clear atmosphere where particles are smaller than the laser wavelength, the scattered light intensity can be determined based on the general formula for Rayleigh scattering (formula 1):

$$I(\theta, r) = I_0\left(\frac{1 + cos^2(\theta)}{r^2}\right) \qquad (1)$$

where:

I(θ, r) - scattered light intensity at a distance r from the source and at an angle θ relative to the primary beam direction,

I_0 - incident light intensity,

θ - scattering angle,

r - distance from the light source.

Beyond theoretical Rayleigh scattering caused mainly by the divergence of the laser diode beam, light is refracted when passing through a medium of different density, such as heated air or encountering obstacles (dust, fog, etc.), and is absorbed or scattered. Theoretical analysis of these factors is often more challenging than empirical measurements, which provide reliable results. On the mobile device side, part of the scattered laser light hits the active area of a PIN photodiode, where the signal is amplified, filtered, and then decoded. The remaining light falls on a liquid crystal modulator and is used to power the return channel, as proposed in [7]. The modulator blocks the laser beam between the source and the prism. The modulator is keyed by the control system in the rhythm of the digital sequences transmitted in the return channel. After passing through the modulator, the light is reflected in a corner-cube prism and directed back towards the ground station in the same direction, but with the opposite orientation. The return beam may be slightly shifted in the prism system. The shift depends on the prism size. On the way back, the light passes through the modulator a second time. In the return channel, amplitude modulation is superimposed on the frequency modulation from the stationary module. The reflected and modulated light reaches the detector system of the stationary module, where it is amplified, filtered, and decoded. In the described concept of the mobile module, the light is exclusively modulated or absorbed, so the mobile module does not emit but only selectively reflects light when illuminated from an external source. The power consumed by the liquid crystal modulator is negligible compared to RF systems and the light returns exclusively the same way it arrived.

By using corner-cube prisms in the mobile part, there is no need for precise positioning of the receiving system in the UAV. The modulator's alignment with the stationary module should only be rough, within $\pm30°$. Thus, the device does not need to have complex and heavy stabilization and positioning mechanisms. Positioning and stabilization can be applied only on the stationary module side, where small weight and size are not mandatory.

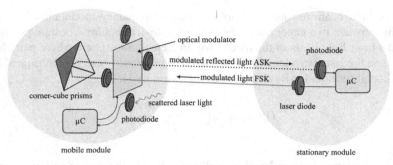

Fig. 1. Concept of FSO using reflected light modulator (own elaboration).

3   Implementation – Modulator and Receiver Construction

On the stationary side, a laser diode with a wavelength of 550 nm and a power of 5mW was used as the light source. The wavelength was dictated by the properties of the liquid crystal modulator, which has a built-in filter for this wavelength. An adjustable collimator was used to regulate the laser beam convergence. The laser diode was keyed using an IRF510 transistor. The modulating signal for the laser diode, with a frequency of 200 kHz and 250 kHz, was provided by an arbitrary generator. To detect the green laser light, a BPW21-O PIN photodiode, which generates current under wavelengths in the 350–820 nm range, was used. The photodiode was connected to a transimpedance amplifier built on the TL074 chip. The photodiode has a dark current of 2 nA and an active area of 7.45 mm^2. The same detection system was used in the second communication module (on the UAV side). The MRR system was built using a geodetic glass prism with a working field diameter of 24.1 mm and a reflected beam displacement range of 0–30 mm. Figure 2 shows the view of the MRR.

A liquid crystal shutter with dimensions of 96 × 35 mm was placed in front of the prism. The modulator was powered by a function generator with a variable sinusoidal signal with an amplitude of 1.9 Vpp. The amplitude was experimentally determined to achieve the highest signal amplitude in the PIN photodiode reception path. Both modules (stationary and mobile) were set up for testing at a distance of 100 m in a closed room with constant lighting. In reality, the devices were placed next to each other, and a mirror doubling the distance was placed 50 m away from them. No optical lens systems were used to enhance the signals reaching the detector during the experiment.

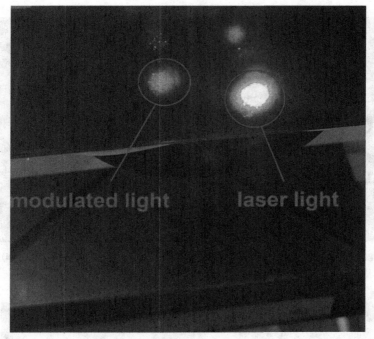

Fig. 2. View of the prototype MRR built from a geodetic prism and a liquid crystal shutter (own elaboration). (Color figure online)

4 Results

From the perspective of potential application, the most interesting observations concern the reflected and modulated laser light beam. Experimentally, the maximum limit frequency of the liquid crystal modulator was established at just 300 Hz. Further increasing the frequency led to the signal amplitude vanishing in the transimpedance amplifier of the photodiode detector. The low frequency resulted from the high inertia of the liquid crystal shutter. Figure 3 shows the voltage level after the first operational amplifier stage. In Fig. 3a, the signal was modulated at 100 Hz. The amplitude is approximately 6 mV. Increasing the frequency to 300 Hz (Fig. 3b) resulted in a signal amplitude reduction to 2 mV.

In Fig. 4, access to the laser view and the return beam illuminating the photodiode shift the return light spot from the deflection of the laser beam at the angle of the prism sensor. The displacement between the laser beam and the return light spot is twice the deviation between the prism and the incident laser beam. In this case, this deviation is located at a distance of 10 mm from the photodiode, located at a distance of 20 mm from the laser beam. This dependence forces you to aim at the modulator with a 10 mm offset.

An alternative solution is to set the laser collimator in such a way that the beam is separated. In Fig. 5, access to the vertical view.

Uneven illumination from the return beam results from imperfections of the modulator and collimator.

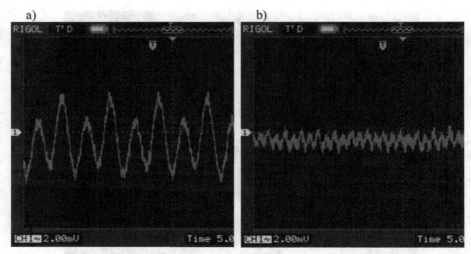

Fig. 3. Signals obtained from the reflected light modulated by a liquid crystal shutter a) 100 Hz, b) 300 Hz (own elaboration).

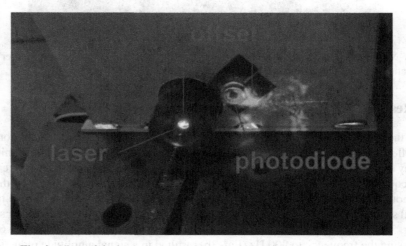

Fig. 4. View of the laser diode and detection photodiode (own elaboration).

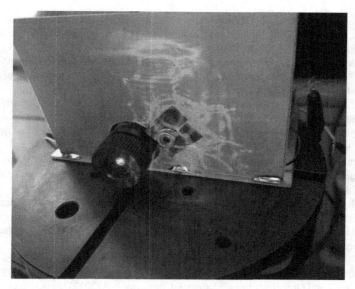

Fig. 5. View of a blurred spot of modulated light (own elaboration).

5 Conclusion

The article presents a comprehensive approach to the issue of optical communications, including key technological aspects and experimental research results. The presented results indicate the great potential of FSO, especially in the context of application in UAVs. Experiments have shown that the use of a liquid crystal modulator, despite its frequency limitations, enables effective reflection and modulation of the laser beam, which is crucial for the development of feedback communication systems. Further research should focus on minimizing the inertia of modulators and improving the precision and stability of optical systems, which will allow increasing the modulation frequency and thus improving signal quality. Moreover, it is necessary to develop methods to compensate for the impact of weather conditions, such as fog or dust, which may significantly affect the quality of optical transmission. From a practical application perspective, optical communication systems have the potential to be integrated with existing RF systems. Further research in this direction will focus on eliminating the liquid crystal shutter and replacing it with a piezoacoustic modulator or using other solutions described in [8].

Acknowledgment. This work was financed/co-financed by Military University of Technology under research project: UGB WAT 531-5000-22-702-47207.

References

1. Bender, P.L., et al.: The lunar laser ranging experiment. Science **182**(4109), 229–238 (1973). https://doi.org/10.1126/science.182.4109.229

2. Chen, X., Ding, J., Lai, H.: 5G oriented optical communications in highspeed trains. In: Wireless and Optical Communications Conference (WOCC), Beijing, China, pp. 1–5 (2019). https://doi.org/10.1109/WOCC.2019.8770560

3. Dabiri, M.T., Hasna, M.: Performance analysis of modulating retroreflector array for UAV-based FSO links. IEEE Commun. Lett. **27**(12), 3280–3284 (2023). https://doi.org/10.1109/LCOMM.2023.3328452.(2023)

4. Fuchs, C., Moll, F., Poliak, J., Reeves, A., Schmidt, C.: Optical satellite links for telecommunications and time-transfer. In: 2023 IEEE International Conference on Space Optical Systems and Applications (ICSOS), Vancouver, BC, Canada, pp. 168–174 (2023). https://doi.org/10.1109/ICSOS59710.2023.10491220

5. Ghassemlooy, Z., Popoola, W., Rajbhandari S.: Optical Wireless Communications, System and Channel Modelling with MATLAB®, 2nd edn. CRC Press (2019). https://doi.org/10.1201/9781315151724

6. Haan, H., Gerken, M. Tausendfreund, M.: Long-range laser communication terminals: technically interesting, commercially incalculable. In: 8th International Symposium on Communication Systems, Networks & Digital Signal Processing (CSNDSP), Poznan, Poland, pp. 1–4 (2012). https://doi.org/10.1109/CSNDSP.2012.6292696

7. He, J., Tao, Z., Yu, X., Wen, G., Mu, Y.: Discuss performance of corner-cube prism for modulating retro-reflector terminal in free-space laser communication. In: 2012 Symposium on Photonics and Optoelectronics, Shanghai, China, pp. 1–3 (2012). https://doi.org/10.1109/SOPO.2012.6271057

8. Lai, K.Y., Chen, W.T., Wu, Y.H., Chen, Y.F., Tsai, J.C.: 3D-printed and PDLC-tuned corner cube retroreflector for sunlight communication. In: 2019 International Conference on Optical MEMS and Nanophotonics (OMN), Daejeon, Korea (South), pp. 164–165 (2019). https://doi.org/10.1109/OMN.2019.8925163

9. Tsumura, T.: Improving positioning, guidance, system and communication technology of AVCS by optics. In: Proceedings of Conference on Intelligent Transportation Systems, Boston, MA, USA, pp. 765–768 (1997). https://doi.org/10.1109/ITSC.1997.660570

10. Tsumura, T., Fujiwara, N., Hashimoto, M.: A new method of position and heading measurement of ground vehicle by use of laser and corner cubes. In: 34th IEEE Vehicular Technology Conference, Pittsburgh, PA, USA, pp. 271–276 (1984). https://doi.org/10.1109/VTC.1984.1623275

11. Tsumura, T., Okubo, H., Komatsu, N., Aoki, N.: Optical two-way communication system for vehicles using lasers and corner cubes. In: Pacific Rim TransTech Conference. Vehicle Navigation and Information Systems Conference Proceedings. 6th International VNIS. A Ride into the Future, Seattle, WA, USA, 1995, pp. 535–538 (1995). https://doi.org/10.1109/VNIS.1995.518889

12. Uysal, M., Nouri, H.: Optical wireless communications—an emerging technology. In: 16th International Conference on Transparent Optical Networks (ICTON), Graz, Austria, pp. 1–7 (2014). https://doi.org/10.1109/ICTON.2014.6876267

13. Zhang, J., Liu, H.: Performance analysis of a mixed FSO-RF communication system with energy harvesting. In: 5th International Conference on Frontiers Technology of Information and Computer (ICFTIC), Qingdao, China, pp. 30–34 (2023). https://doi.org/10.1109/ICFTIC59930.2023.10455784

Author Index

Printed in the United States
by Baker & Taylor Publisher Services